Holy People,
Holy Land

Holy People, Holy Land

A Theological Introduction to the Bible

Michael Dauphinais
and Matthew Levering

Brazos Press
Grand Rapids, Michigan

Published by Brazos Press
a division of Baker Publishing Group
P.O. Box 6287, Grand Rapids, MI 49516-6287
www.brazospress.com

Printed in the United States of America

Library of Congress Cataloging-in-Publication Data
Dauphinais, Michael, 1973-
    Holy people, holy land / Michael Dauphinais and Matthew Levering.
        p.   cm.
    Includes bibliographical references and index.
    ISBN 1-58743-123-8 (pbk.)
    1. Bible—Criticism, interpretation, etc. 2. Covenant theology. I. Levering, Matthew Webb, 1971- II. Title.
    BS511.3.D37 2005
    230'.041—dc22   2005015584

Contents

Acknowledgments   7
Introduction: In the Footsteps of St. Augustine   9

1. The Lost Eden   23
2. Abraham: Descendants and Land   41
3. Moses: Law and Tabernacle   57
4. David: King and Temple   81
5. Psalms and Prophets: New King, New Temple, New
   Covenant   111
6. Gospel of Matthew: The King and His Kingdom   137
7. Gospel of John: The Temple of the Trinity   167
8. Romans: The Righteousness of God and the Body of Christ   193
9. Hebrews: The Priest-King of the New Covenant   213
10. Revelation: The Lamb as King and Temple   231

Conclusion: Transformation and Holiness   249
Index   257

5

Acknowledgments

Since our reading of scripture flows from our Catholic faith, one might ask in what ways our reading of scripture will be useful for non-Catholics as well. First, ecumenical dialogue at times flounders when presented with the particular biblical texts whose interpretation has in the past divided Christian communities. Our approach to the Bible in terms of the holiness of "people" and "land" offers a way of exploring the Old and New Covenants through a lens that can be shared by all Christians, since these terms do not belong to the history of ecclesial division.

Second, non-Catholic readers will find that while our approach displays our Catholic commitment, Protestant biblical exegetes have exercised a deep influence upon our interpretations. We are indebted for many of the book's ideas to the scholarship of leading Protestant thinkers, such as Stephen Fowl, Stanley Hauerwas, Richard B. Hays, Christopher Seitz, Ben Witherington III, N. T. Wright, and David S. Yeago, to name only a few. Our indebtedness to Jewish thinkers such as Jon D. Levenson and Michael Fishbane is significant as well. Such debts build communion, insofar as we as Catholic theologians find ourselves profoundly grateful for the insights of scholars whose rich understanding of the Bible exposes a shared love of and devotion to God's Word. Just as we have benefited from the insights of those who do not share our Catholic commitment, so also, we hope, non-Catholic readers will find enrichment through our insights.

In addition to those mentioned above, we wish to acknowledge our profound gratitude for the crucial encouragement and support of Rodney Clapp and Brazos Press. Rodney read through the entire manuscript and offered helpful comments throughout; while he is not responsible for the weaknesses of the book, he is responsible for many of its strengths. Rebecca Cooper, managing editor of Brazos Press, deserves similar thanks for her care and attention during the process of bringing the manuscript to press.

During our years at Ave Maria, we have been privileged to teach the scriptures to a number of superb students; their interest and collaboration greatly stimulated our work on this book. Gregory Vall, now our colleague at Ave Maria University, read the manuscript critically and assisted us in drawing upon contemporary biblical scholarship. His friendship has been a boon throughout the preparation of the work. Another esteemed colleague, Fr. Bevil Bramwell, O.M.I., gave the book a test-run in an undergraduate course on scripture, for which we are grateful. Without the helpful criticisms of Rodrigo Morales, who also read the entire manuscript during its preparation, the book would be much poorer. Fr. Matthew Lamb has been a mainstay to our work, especially as regards the projects of the Aquinas Center for Theological Renewal; without him, it is difficult to imagine this book coming to be. The same could be said for Timothy Gray, a penetrating thinker and lasting friend from our Duke Divinity School years who at Duke encouraged us to study the Bible. For the supportive and prayerful climate in which theology is done at Ave Maria University, we wish to thank also Fr. Joseph Fessio, Sr. Gertrude Gillette, Marc Guerra, Bill Murphy, and Bill Riordan. Fr. Fessio and Bill Riordan have graciously supported and mentored Michael in his work as associate dean. Lastly, Charles Colson and Fr. Richard John Neuhaus kindly invited Matthew to participate in the Evangelicals and Catholics Together meetings that they host in New York City; the delight of getting to know wonderfully biblically literate evangelical colleagues provided further impetus for this book.

Throughout the years of our friendship and work together, we have been sustained by, and have been blessed to share our lives with, our beloved wives Nancy Dauphinais and Joy Levering. Our children, too, have made these years joyous in so many ways that we could not have known or expected when we first met as graduate students at Duke Divinity School.

The book is dedicated to those who, God be praised, gave us the gift of life and so many other ongoing gifts: our parents Michael and Joyce Dauphinais and Ralph and Patty Levering. Words could not express our debts to them. May God bless them now and forever; may they be "filled with all the fullness of God" (Eph. 3:19).

Introduction

In the Footsteps of St. Augustine

Holy People, Holy Land

Inspired by the need for theological teaching of the Bible as the basis of instruction in Christian doctrine, the present book explores the theological meaning of the Bible from Genesis to Revelation. The Bible begins with Genesis's account of God's creation of all things. The original man and woman live in spiritual harmony in a well-ordered garden and enjoy God's presence. Adam and Eve experience a holy intimacy with God that is mirrored by the depiction of the original holy land of Eden. Adam and Eve's sin of pride, however, brings an end to their status as *holy people*, and as a result they are expelled from the *holy land*.

After God has manifested his intention to have mercy upon human-kind in the covenant with Noah, whose sign is the rainbow, God's mercy comes next to Abraham. The covenantal promises that God makes to Abraham involve two aspects: a *renewed people* and a *renewed land* in which the people will dwell with God. These two aspects are extended and deepened by the two covenants that follow upon, and partially fulfill, the covenant with Abraham. In the covenant with Moses at Sinai, God provides the people with a Law that teaches the people the paths of the promised holiness, and God instructs Moses regarding the construction of the tabernacle where God will dwell with his chosen people. Similarly, in the covenant with David, God promises an eternal kingship and a temple. The task of a true king is to establish his people in justice, and the purpose of a temple is to establish permanently God's presence dwelling liturgically in and with his people.

Law and kingship have to do with becoming just (*holy people*), and tabernacle and temple have to do with God's indwelling by which we share in God's holiness (*holy land*). As this covenantal history moves toward its climax, Israel's historical books reveal that the holiness promised by the law has not come about. Due to their lack of justice, the people are exiled from the land and the Davidic kingship and temple come to an end. From the prophets, however, we learn that God himself is going to come to Israel as king and definitively establish his people in holiness by dwelling perfectly with them. According to the prophets, all the nations will share in this restoration and fulfillment of holy people dwelling with God in a holy land.[1]

The New Testament recounts the accomplishment of this promise in Christ Jesus and in his mystical Body, the Church. Christ himself is the true embodiment of *holy people* and *holy land*, thereby uniting in his Body the two aspects of holiness. Christ is both the eternal Davidic king, establishing his people in holy justice, and the true temple, offering the perfect worship to God. The longed-for fulfillment is already truly present in Christ Jesus and his Church, and yet "according to his promise we wait for new heavens and a new earth in which righteousness dwells" (2 Peter 3:13). Eternal life is the ultimate fulfillment of holy people and holy land to which the entire Bible directs us.[2]

---

1. Influenced by the work of N. T. Wright, the biblical scholar Gary Anderson has summarized the Old Testament in the following manner:

> The narrative of the Torah, in its final canonical form, has two principle foci: entering the land of Israel and keeping the commandments given by God at Mt. Sinai. The former theme becomes, over time, strongly eschatological, or future-oriented, in tone. Throughout the Second Temple period—after the return of Ezra, Nehemiah, and many of those banished to Babylon—many Jews continued to pray for an end to the exile. When Israel is finally gathered into the Promised Land, the Messiah will arrive, the Temple will be properly rebuilt, and the nations of the earth will stream to Zion to give honor to God for what he has done. The commandments, on the other hand, remain the focus of daily life, albeit with a future orientation. Many of them can only be fulfilled when Israel is in full possession of her land. (Gary A. Anderson, *The Genesis of Perfection: Adam and Eve in Jewish and Christian Imagination* [Louisville: Westminster John Knox, 2001], 177.)

These "two principle foci"—the promised land and the holy people—appear in different and increasingly profound modes throughout the biblical narrative. Under the rubric of holiness, therefore, these two "foci" of land and people guide our account of the meaning of the Bible.

2. This understanding of the entire Bible as ordered to Christ and his mystical Body assumes that history, and the biblical revelation, is governed by divine Providence. While anti-historicist, this assumption is not anti-historical. Historicism requires a philosophy of history that rules out, without historical justification, divine Providence. Furthermore, identifying in the Bible a christological (or eschatological) ordering does not indicate that we deny the diversity in the Bible, but rather means that we read the Bible from an

In offering this theological and catechetical survey of the scriptures, we take our starting point from St. Peter. He instructs believers, "Always be prepared to make a defense to any one who calls you to account for the hope that is in you, yet do it with gentleness and reverence" (1 Peter 3:15).[3] The Christian faith makes claims about Jesus Christ that presuppose the narrative of the Old Testament. Peter thus boldly adapts texts from the Old Testament to describe to his audience the story into which they have been called: "Come to him, to that living stone, rejected by men but in God's sight chosen and precious; and like living stones be yourselves built into a spiritual house, to be a holy priesthood, to offer spiritual sacrifices acceptable to God through Jesus Christ. . . . But you are a chosen race, a royal priesthood, a holy nation, God's own people, that you may declare the wonderful deeds of him who called you out of darkness into his marvelous light" (1 Peter 2:4–5, 9).

For St. Peter, as for us, the key to the whole story is new creation in holiness. After discussing the prophets, Peter proclaims that the grace of God they prophesied has now been given in Christ. Therefore, Peter urges, "do not be conformed to the passions of your former ignorance, but as he who called you is holy, be holy yourselves in all your conduct; since it is written, 'You shall be holy, for I am holy'" (1 Peter 1:14–16). In light of the gift of holiness to believers in Christ Jesus, Peter enthusiastically proclaims, "You have been born anew" (1 Peter 1:23).[4] Holiness is revealed most fully, through its consummation in Christ, as being separated from sin and coming to share in the life of love.

---

ecclesial perspective in which divine Providence is christological. Christopher R. Seitz has eloquently explored the problem of historicism in his collection of essays *Figured Out: Typology and Providence in Christian Scripture* (Louisville: Westminster John Knox, 2001), especially 3–10. On the difficulties for reading scripture that occur once the doctrine of Providence has become unintelligible, see Hans W. Frei, *The Eclipse of Biblical Narrative: A Study in Eighteenth and Nineteenth Century Hermeneutics* (New Haven, CT: Yale University Press, 1974), 66–85.

3. In quoting biblical passages, we have employed the Revised Standard Version, Catholic edition, originally published in 1966 and recently reprinted by Ignatius Press. It seems clear that the inclusive language translations, done hurriedly, have not yet sufficiently guarded against the loss in translation of crucial theological meaning within the Bible. See Gregory Vall, "Inclusive Language and the Equal Dignity of Women and Men in Christ," *The Thomist* 67 (2003): 579–606.

4. For the biblical understanding of holiness, including a chapter exploring 1 Peter, see Jo Bailey Wells, *God's Holy People: A Theme in Biblical Theology* (Sheffield: Sheffield Academic Press, 2000). Holiness is often associated with "separation" in the Old Testament, a theme taken up by Augustine in working out his distinction between the two cities separated by their loves, the City of God and the City of Man. Wells, discussing Leviticus, shows that God separates his chosen people not on the basis of any deserving, but by freely drawing them in love away from sin and into his justice, ultimately his justice in Christ (see Wells, *God's Holy People*, 81).

Following Augustine

If St. Peter provides the inspiration for our reading of the Bible, St. Augustine acts as our guide.[5] Around sixteen hundred years ago—three and a half centuries after the death of St. Peter—a deacon of Carthage named Deogratias asked the great theologian Augustine, then forty-six years old and bishop of Hippo, to give an account of his hope, for the purposes of aiding in the catechesis or instruction of persons in the doctrines of the Christian faith. Despite the pressing weight of other pastoral duties and the central importance of his task of writing scholarly books defending and explicating Catholic doctrine, Augustine accepted the invitation to write a short treatise for a broad audience. Augustine justifies neglecting his other tasks by explaining that "I feel constrained not only by that love and service which is due from me to you on the terms of familiar friendship, but also by that which I owe universally to my mother the Church, by no means to refuse the task, but rather to take it up with a prompt and devoted willingness. For the more extensively I desire to see the treasure of the Lord distributed, the more does it become my duty, if I ascertain that the stewards, who are my fellow-servants, find any difficulty in laying it out, to do all that lies in my power to the end that they may

5. Here in accord with the seventh thesis presented by *The Scripture Project*, composed of fifteen scholars and pastors led by Ellen F. Davis and Richard B. Hays. Their important collaborative effort to renew theological exegesis produced nine theses, which undergird our work as well:

1. Scripture truthfully tells the story of God's action in creating, judging, and saving the world; 2. Scripture is rightly understood in light of the church's rule of faith as a coherent dramatic narrative; 3. Faithful interpretation of Scripture requires an engagement with the entire narrative: the New Testament cannot be rightly understood apart from the Old, nor can the Old be rightly understood apart from the New; 4. Texts of Scripture do not have a single meaning limited to the intent of the original author. In accord with Jewish and Christian traditions, we affirm that Scripture has multiple complex senses given by God, the author of the whole drama; 5. The four canonical Gospels narrate the truth about Jesus; 6. Faithful interpretation of Scripture invites and presupposes participation in the community brought into being by God's redemptive action—the church; 7. The saints of the church provide guidance in how to interpret and perform Scripture; 8. Christians need to read the Bible in dialogue with diverse others outside the church; 9. We live in the tension between the "already" and the "not yet" of the kingdom of God; consequently, Scripture calls the church to ongoing discernment, to continually fresh rereadings of the text in light of the Holy Spirit's ongoing work in the world.

See Ellen F. Davis and Richard B. Hays, eds., "Nine Theses on the Interpretation of Scripture," *The Art of Reading Scripture* (Grand Rapids: Eerdmans, 2003), 1–5.

be able to accomplish easily and expeditiously what they sedulously and earnestly aim at."[6]

In his treatise, Augustine summarizes the reasons that led Deogratias to seek his aid. Although Deogratias was well known in the Carthage of his day for being skilled at teaching Christian doctrine in an informed and interesting manner, nonetheless Deogratias worries that he does not know exactly where he should begin or end his discussion of Christian doctrine. Deogratias has also frequently found that, in Augustine's words, "in the course of a lengthened and languid address you have become profitless and distasteful even to yourself, not to speak of the learner whom you have been endeavoring to instruct by your utterance."[7] Augustine first consoles Deogratias by assuring him that he, Augustine, has likewise to himself often seemed boring and inadequate in discourse, since his discourse often fails to reproduce, in his view, the apprehension that he possesses intellectually. Yet Augustine then adds, one hopes not to Deogratias's chagrin, that despite Augustine's own sense of inadequacy, his auditors respond with "earnestness" in their desire for him to say more, and show "delight" in what he has said.[8]

What is it, then, that Augustine would say to these auditors? He tells Deogratias that one ought to begin with a full narration of the Christian faith. He explains, "The narration is full when each person is catechized in the first instance from what is written in the text, 'In the beginning God created the heaven and the earth,' on to the present times of the Church."[9] No doubt Deogratias's heart sunk at this moment. But Augustine presses on quickly to assure Deogratias that this does not mean "that we ought to repeat by memory the entire Pentateuch, and the entire book of Judges, and Kings, and Esdras, and the entire Gospel and Acts of the Apostles, if we have learned all these word for word."[10] Nor, continues Augustine, need Deogratias paraphrase everything that is found in these books.

What then is necessary? Augustine states, "But what we ought to do is to give a comprehensive statement of all things, summarily and generally, so that certain of the more wonderful facts may be selected which are listened to with superior gratification, and which have been ranked so remarkably among the exact turning points (of the history);

6. St. Augustine, "The Catechising of the Uninstructed," trans. S. D. F. Salmond, in *Augustine: On the Holy Trinity, Doctrinal Treatises, Moral Treatises*, Vol. 3 of Nicene and Post-Nice Fathers, First Series, ed. Philip Schaff (Peabody, MA: Hendrickson, 1994 [1887]), 283 (ch. 1, no. 2).
7. Ibid., 283, ch. 1, no. 1.
8. Ibid., 284, ch. 2, no. 4.
9. Ibid., 285, ch. 3, no. 5.
10. Ibid.

that, instead of exhibiting them to view only in their wrappings, if we may so speak, and then instantly snatching them from our sight, we ought to dwell on them for a certain space, and thus, as it were, unfold them and open them out to vision, and present them to the minds of the hearers as things to be examined and admired."[11] The other details, then, need only cursory attention for the purposes of introduction; they "should be passed over rapidly, and thus far introduced and woven into the narrative."[12] The purpose of this method, Augustine says, is to ensure two things: that the key points attain the prominence they deserve, and that the hearer is not so surfeited with facts that he or she will be either uninterested or unable to remember the key points.

Yet, is this not to make a biblical "canon within the canon"? In other words, since the *entire* Bible is the inspired word of God, should we focus on some books more than others? Augustine's answer is twofold. First, he notes, the key to the whole Bible is holiness, that is, charity or love: our eye must "be kept fixed upon the end of the commandment, which is 'charity, out of a pure heart, and a good conscience, and faith unfeigned,' to which we should make all that we utter refer."[13] Augustine makes this same point in his *On Christian Doctrine* and elsewhere, with regard to what is obscure or of lesser importance in the scriptures.[14] It follows that an introduction to the scriptural narrative should keep attention focused upon charity, by which God "separates" from fallen humanity a people united by their love for God. Second, Augustine points out that charity is fully revealed in Christ Jesus, and therefore "for no other reason were all those things which we read in the Holy Scriptures written, previous to the Lord's advent, but for this,—namely, that His advent might be pressed upon the attention, and that the Church which was to be, should be intimated beforehand, that is to say, the people of God throughout all nations; which Church is His body, wherewith also are united and numbered all the saints who lived in this world, even before His advent, and who believed then in His future coming, just as we believe in His past coming."[15]

Since love is the fulfillment of the Law (Rom. 13:10), and Christ's laying down his life for us is the supreme manifestation of love (John 3:16, 15:13), the entire scriptures point to Christ as the fulfillment of God's plan to reunite us to himself in love. To be holy means to love in

---

11. Ibid.
12. Ibid.
13. Ibid., ch. 3, no. 6.
14. Augustine, *On Christian Doctrine*, trans. D. W. Robertson Jr. (New York: Macmillan, 1958), Book II, ch. 5.
15. Augustine, "The Catechising of the Uninstructed," 285–286, ch. 3, no. 6.

truth. As St. John says, "Beloved, let us love one another; for love is of God, and he who loves is born of God and knows God. He who does not love does not know God; for God is love. In this the love of God was made manifest among us, that God sent his only Son into the world, so that we might live through him. In this is love, not that we loved God but that he loved us and sent his Son to be the expiation for our sins. Beloved, if God so loved us, we also ought to love one another" (1 John 4:7–11). God is love, and he wills to unite us to himself in love.

Theological Reading of Scripture

As Stephen Fowl has argued, "Christians, by virtue of their identity, are required to read Scripture theologically."[16] St. Augustine, a master of such reading, thereby provides the blueprints for our book.[17] Like Deogratias, we hope to follow St. Augustine's insights into the method by which Christian teachers, obeying St. Peter's admonishment, may render an account of their faith in Christ (cf. 1 Peter 3:15).

First, by focusing our reading of the Bible around the theme of holiness, we adopt Augustine's fundamental insight that the entire Bible is about charity. The "land" that God intends to lead his people to is the state of union with God in holiness (love), a union that will have a bodily dimension since we are bodily creatures, but will be fundamentally a spiritual union since "God is spirit" (John 4:24). The locus of this union is the body of Israel's Messiah, Jesus of Nazareth, whose mystical Body remains visibly and sacramentally present in the Church. As the incarnate Son of God, Jesus, in his humanity, is filled with the divine Spirit and is therefore the perfect embodiment of "holy land" and the Head of the "holy people."

16. Stephen E. Fowl, *Engaging Scripture: A Model for Theological Interpretation* (Oxford: Blackwell, 1998), 30; see also his short essay on "biblical theology," "The Conceptual Structure of New Testament Theology," in *Biblical Theology: Retrospect and Prospect*, ed. Scott J. Hafemann (Downers Grove, IL: InterVarsity Press, 2002), 225–236. See also *La révélation divine* (*Dei Verbum*), *Constitution dogmatique de Vatican II*, with an introduction by Henri de Lubac, S.J. (Lyon: Editions 'La Bonté,' 1966).

17. St. Augustine's model of reading grounds medieval interpretation as well. Thomas Aquinas's inaugural sermons as a Master of *Sacra Pagina* at the University of Paris both demonstrate the influence of Augustine's *On Christian Doctrine*, and provide inspiration for the present book. See his "Commendation of and Division of Sacred Scripture" and "On the Commendation of Sacred Scripture" in Ralph McInerny, ed. and trans., *Thomas Aquinas: Selected Writings* (New York: Penguin, 1998), 5–17. See also Francis Martin, "*Sacra Doctrina* and the Authority of Its *Sacra Scriptura* According to St. Thomas Aquinas," *Pro Ecclesia* 10 (2001): 84–102.

Second, the fact that the entire Bible points to Christ justifies the decision to highlight certain aspects of the biblical narrative. As St. Augustine exemplifies, biblical catechesis (itself an eminently theological task) requires a reading of the Bible that does not go into every detail, but that instead focuses on illumining central points. Catechesis, given limits on its time and scope, cannot hope to address all details. Similarly, believers require catechesis about the meaning of the Bible in order to be able to articulate the unity, as God's revelation, of the wide variety of biblical books, genres, and stories.

Can and should divine revelation be interpreted by those who are trained, as we are, primarily in the theological tradition of the Church, rather than in historical-critical exegetical scholarship? The Church's ability to teach depends upon an affirmative answer to this question. It would be disastrous to imagine that only since the nineteenth century, with the advent of historical criticism, has the Church been able to interpret faithfully her scriptures.[18] Is not the Bible, however, about history? It would seem that theological claims about the meaning or the unity of the Bible might depend strictly upon the outcome of historical research. If so, should not the task of studying and writing about the Bible be left to those who have learned the relevant original languages, historical hypotheses, and archeological findings?

We should first observe that historical-critical research assists theological and catechetical reading of scripture by offering insights into the diverse contexts in which the books of the Bible were written and edited, and by stimulating more informed analysis of the meaning of the words of scripture. Yet, the Methodist theologian Stanley Hauerwas has rightly warned against "thinking that we must rely on the latest biblical study if we are to proclaim the gospel."[19] Historical-critical research cannot

18. See the *Catechism of the Catholic Church*, nos. 128–130. See also Richard John Neuhaus, ed., *Biblical Interpretation in Crisis: The Ratzinger Conference on Bible and Church* (Grand Rapids: Eerdmans, 1989); Jon D. Levenson, *The Hebrew Bible, the Old Testament, and Historical Criticism: Jews and Christians in Biblical Studies* (Louisville: Westminster John Knox Press, 1993). Luke Timothy Johnson and William S. Kurz, S.J., make this point in *The Future of Catholic Biblical Scholarship: A Constructive Conversation* (Grand Rapids: Eerdmans, 2002).

19. Stanley Hauerwas, *Unleashing the Scriptures: Freeing the Bible from Captivity to America* (Nashville: Abingdon, 1993), 7. Francis Watson has rightly bemoaned the fact that "[t]he line of demarcation between 'biblical studies' and 'systematic theology' has normative force and does not represent a mere division of labour" (Watson, *Text and Truth: Redefining Biblical Theology* [Grand Rapids: Eerdmans, 1997], 3). He goes on to remark,

This attempt to exclude theology from the field of biblical interpretation has had a marked effect on the practice of theology itself. Theologians can hardly abandon all concern with the Bible, yet their relation to it has become indirect and second-hand. The field assigned to them is now post-biblical, and consists in the history

possess the primary place in the Church's reading of her scripture, but instead must minister to theological reading. Why so? Briefly put, the primary *historical* locus of scripture, and of the reading of scripture, is the faithful community formed by God's words and deeds. The existence of a community formed by these words and deeds is a historical reality. A Christian could not read scripture "historically" without reading scripture in the historical community of faith formed by God's words and deeds and thus with eyes illumined by faith.[20] As the *Catechism of the Catholic Church* teaches, "Sacred Scripture is written principally in the Church's heart rather than in documents and records, for the Church carries in her Tradition the living memorial of God's Word, and it is the Holy Spirit who gives her the spiritual interpretation of Scripture."[21]

It follows that the history of the scriptures, including the complex history *within* the scriptures, cannot be separated from the historical witness of the community.[22] Historical-critical research helps the Church reflect upon the origins and complexity of the texts in scripture, and thereby deepens the Church's awareness that divine revelation occurs in human history and through human (even if divinely inspired) writing. If the meaning of the biblical canon could not be explicated, however, without adverting continually to parallel hypothetical accounts that seek both to identify the process by which various parts of the story came to be written and to adjudicate their authenticity, then it would be impossible to preach the gospel. If we believe in faith that scripture is revelation, then going "behind the text" to reconstruct the hidden,

of Christian doctrine from the Apologists to the present, understood in the light of and for the purpose of contemporary theological construction. Since this history is a history of dialogue with the biblical texts, a relation to biblical interpretation is retained; and direct appeal to biblical material is still practised. Yet the pervasive effect of the line of demarcation is seen in the theologian's characteristic assumption that, in drawing upon material from the Old or New Testament, he or she has entered someone else's professional domain. At home with Irenaeus, Schleiermacher and Barth, one is in danger of trespassing if one engages too freely in the interpretation of Isaiah, Paul or John. The biblical writings are no longer the intellectual property of the theologian. Where theologians accept biblical scholars' property-rights in this area, the fact that for Christian faith truth is textually mediated will be systematically distorted (4).

20. On the inevitably "circular" character of all enquiry, dependent as it is upon traditions, see Alasdair MacIntyre, *After Virtue*, 2nd ed. (Notre Dame, IN: University of Notre Dame Press, 1984); idem, *Whose Justice? Which Rationality* (Notre Dame, IN: University of Notre Dame Press, 1988); idem, *Three Rival Versions of Moral Enquiry* (Notre Dame, IN: University of Notre Dame Press, 1990).

21. *Catechism of the Catholic Church*, no. 113.

22. Cf. the valuable essays in Charles Colson and Richard John Neuhaus, eds., *Your Word Is Truth: A Project of Evangelicals and Catholics Together* (Grand Rapids: Eerdmans, 2002).

esoteric history cannot substitute for or predominate over the word that the Holy Spirit has willed, in history, to be revealed.[23]

It is necessary instead to begin by apprehending the form of God's saving Word to which faith responds and which unites the community of faith. Once one has seen this form, one is able to appreciate historical-critical research in its proper context. As Jesus teaches, "I thank thee, Father, Lord of heaven and earth, that thou hast hidden these things from the wise and understanding and revealed them to babes; yea, Father, for such was thy gracious will" (Matt. 11:25–26). The meaning of the Bible is witnessed to by the saints whose lives have been formed in the pattern of Christ. For Christians the canonical scriptures not only reveal but also *participate in* the ongoing working out in history of God's saving plan, since through the biblical word God invites believers to participate in the divine realities of salvation that the Church itself teaches and performs.

But does this theological/catechetical reading of the Bible, which sets to the side textual and historical-critical issues, "flatten" the history of the Bible by ignoring the rough-hewn history of the making of the biblical narratives?[24] As the history of doctrinal exposition and development makes clear, divine revelation hardly excludes the "living conversation" about its meaning; indeed, such conversation belongs to the doctrinal development of our understanding of what God has revealed.[25] Nonetheless, if God has inspired the biblical texts, then within the diversity there will be a central thread of *unified* meaning.[26]

To illumine this unity, guided ecclesially by teachers such as St. Augustine, is our task. In speaking of a "theological" reading of the Bible, therefore, we mean an interpretation that (flowing from faith) seeks to illumine the divinely inspired, salvific meaning of the Bible, guided by the doctrinal and spiritual insights of the theological tradition and focused upon the canonical Bible rather upon questions regarding the origin and authenticity of the Bible's narratives. As Hans Frei has shown,

---

23. See Hans Urs von Balthasar, *Theo-Drama*, Vol. 4, *The Action*, trans. Graham Harrison (San Francisco: Ignatius Press, 1994), 459–462. Balthasar warns against a rationalism that would function as a new gnosticism or hidden knowledge, blind to the form of God's revelation in Christ.

24. Cf. the view to this effect of Baruch Halpern, *The First Historians: The Hebrew Bible and History* (University Park: Pennsylvania State University Press, 1996 [1988]).

25. Cf. John Henry Cardinal Newman, *An Essay on the Development of Christian Doctrine* 6th ed. (Notre Dame, IN: University of Notre Dame Press, 1989 [1878]).

26. Francesca Murphy has pointed out, "If we downplay the thread of *integration* in the Bible, we lose the *space* in which the drama unfolds." See Francesca Aran Murphy, *The Comedy of Revelation: Paradise Lost and Regained in Biblical Narrative* (Edinburgh: T. & T. Clark, 2000), 31. Cf. *Catechism of the Catholic Church*, nos. 113–114.

the rise of historical criticism, governed at its outset by Enlightenment epistemological presuppositions, resulted in the division of biblical scholarship—supposedly undertaken from a standpoint of neutrality—from prayerful reading.[27] Without renouncing historical-critical research, many theologians and exegetes now realize that this separation was a mistake. As Frei points out, at stake was and is whether the Bible "is a coherent world of discourse in its own right, whose depictions and teachings had a reality of their own . . . [namely] the reality into which all men had to fit, and in one way or another did fit."[28]

The Unity of the Bible's Salvific Meaning

This book, in sum, seeks to renew an Augustinian mode of reading and teaching the Bible, for the purposes of offering an introduction to the Bible's theological meaning. Informed by historical-critical research and governed by theological presuppositions and priorities, the book identifies the themes of "holy people" and "holy land" as a covenantal thread—certainly not the only possible thematic pattern, but a valuable one—by which to follow the meaning of God's plan for human history as revealed in the Bible.[29] As the biblical scholar Henry Wansbrough has remarked, "The promises of a holy People of God are fulfilled to a new intensity by the divine presence of Christ in his community of the new

27. See Hans W. Frei, *The Eclipse of Biblical Narrative: A Study in Eighteenth and Nineteenth Century Hermeneutics.*

28. Ibid., 90.

29. Cf. the works written by theologians in the 1950s and early 1960s, which have now been largely forgotten: e.g., Louis Bouyer, *The Meaning of Sacred Scripture*, trans. Mary Perkins Ryan (Notre Dame, IN: University of Notre Dame Press, 1958); Dominique Barthélemy, O.P., *God and His Image: An Outline of Biblical Theology*, trans. Dom Aldhelm Dean, O.S.B. (New York: Sheed and Ward, 1966); John Bright, *The Kingdom of God: The Biblical Concept and Its Meaning for the Church* (New York: Abingdon, 1953). For a contemporary overview of the approaches of "biblical theology," see Scott J. Hafemann, ed., *Biblical Theology: Retrospect and Prospect* (Downers Grove, IL: InterVarsity Press, 2002). In an essay in Hafemann's volume titled "Biblical Theology and the Wholeness of Scripture: Steps Toward a Program for the Future," Paul R. House has summarized various foci identified within biblical theology: "Many of the best OT and NT theologies of the past have utilized central or centering themes to carry out their program. One thinks of Walther Eichrodt's stressing of covenant, George Eldon Ladd's emphasis on the kingdom, Geerhardus Vos's commitment to revelation, G. B. Caird's tracing of salvation, Samuel Terrien's focus on the presence of God, Peter Stuhlmacher's highlighting of revelation and righteousness, and the list could be extended" (275). Our approach integrates all of these themes. Yet, it is worth mentioning that our book is intended as a theological and catechetical reading of the Bible rather than as a contribution to "biblical theology" as opposed to "systematic theology."

covenant."[30] It is this fulfillment that we hope to illumine by focusing upon the holiness that befits an adopted son (John 1:12) or a bride (Rev. 19:8) of God. We become holy people when God, restoring and perfecting our fallen minds and hearts, dwells within us (holy land) by grace.

In accord with Augustine's catechetical model, the chapters of this book explore the story of the Bible from the first chapter of Genesis to the final chapter of the book of Revelation. Commenting upon the description of the son of man in Daniel 7, Ben Witherington III and Laura Ice have remarked, "This after all was the messianic hope of various early Jews—a royal figure would come on earth and rule in such a way that the Holy Land and the holy people would be re-established."[31] Not surprisingly, at each stage in the biblical story, we find the prominence of the themes of holy people and holy land.[32]

To recapitulate what we have outlined above, the biblical story reveals that human beings were created to dwell harmoniously with God. The story of Eden depicts holy people living in a holy land—a harmony that is ruptured by sin. The rest of the Bible shows how God seeks, through a progression of covenants, to restore his created images to holiness.[33] God calls Abraham and promises him land and descendants, a holy land and holy people. The covenant with Moses centers on the law to instill righteousness in the people and the tabernacle that is God's dwelling in the midst of the people during their journey. The covenant of David establishes his throne of kingship as the instrument for instilling righ-

30. Henry Wansbrough, "The Jewish People and Its Holy Scripture in the Christian Bible," *Irish Theological Quarterly* 67 (2002): 272.

31. Ben Witherington III and Laura M. Ice, *The Shadow of the Almighty: Father, Son, and Spirit in Biblical Perspective* (Grand Rapids: Eerdmans, 2002), 79.

32. Our debt to the work of Jon D. Levenson, *Sinai and Zion: An Entry into the Jewish Bible* (San Francisco: Harper & Row, 1985) will be evident. Levenson finds in the covenant at Sinai the theme we identify as "holy people," and in the covenant at Zion (the Davidic covenant) the theme we identify as "holy land." Levenson would, of course, take issue with our Christian view that these covenants are fulfilled, though not revoked, by Jesus. Levenson holds that "the canon of the Christian Bible, like any canon, flattens historical differences. In Levenson's view, the Christian claim that Christ fulfills the covenants of Israel is mistaken on historical-critical grounds and inevitably leads to supersessionism: "After 'the end was reached,' why consider the Jews?" (Levenson, *The Hebrew Bible, the Old Testament and Historical Criticism*, 23). But it would be impossible to consider the Messiah of the Jews without considering the Jews. Christopher J. H. Wright has approached the twin themes of people and land from a sociological perspective in *God's People in God's Land: Family, Land, and Property in the Old Testament* (Grand Rapids: Eerdmans, 1990).

33. On the theological significance of the covenantal history, see, e.g., Levenson, *Sinai and Zion*; Delbert R. Hillers, *Covenant: The History of a Biblical Idea* (Baltimore: Johns Hopkins University Press, 1969); Ernest W. Nicholson, *God and His People: Covenant and Theology in the Old Testament* (Oxford: Clarendon Press, 1986). See also the *Catechism of the Catholic Church*, nos. 51–67.

teousness among the people and for building the temple in which God would make his name dwell. The people of Israel, nonetheless, lose the throne of David and enter a period of exile. Even when they enter back into the physical holy land, there is no more Davidic king and the glory cloud never descends upon the reconstructed temple. The prophets not only foresee and explain the destruction of the kingdom of David, but they also promise a time when God will restore his blessings of holiness upon his chosen people.

This long-awaited restoration becomes a reality with the coming of Jesus Christ, the holy one of God. Matthew depicts Jesus as the Davidic king who establishes an eternal holy kingdom. John shows that Jesus is the eucharistic temple of God's permanent dwelling with man. Paul in his Letter to the Romans emphasizes the new creation of a holy people through the justification available to both Jews and Gentiles who enter the mystical Body of Christ. The Letter to the Hebrews shows how Jesus is the new high priest and king who has accomplished the new exodus into the promised land of heaven. Revelation concludes the entire story, the story of God's wondrous mercy, by unveiling that the Lamb that was slain has now become the king and the temple. In the Lamb, the people of God are again restored in justice and dwell before the throne of God—God has given back a hundredfold what human beings rejected in sin.[34] This book thus traces the theme of holiness from the covenant of creation to the new and eternal covenant of Jesus Christ. We find that, as St. Augustine put it, "the New Testament lies hidden in the Old and the Old Testament is unveiled in the New."[35] Our book is an introduction to the Bible's inexhaustible riches; our framework, one among other possible frameworks. The theological and catechetical reading offered here thus complements other studies of the Bible that comment in detail on particular books or that hold up other architectonic themes.

34. Similarly, N. T. Wright's *Following Jesus: Biblical Reflections on Discipleship* (Grand Rapids: Eerdmans, 1995) contains short chapters about Jesus titled "The Final Sacrifice: Hebrews," "The Kingdom of the Son of Man: Matthew," "The Glory of God: John," and "A World Reborn: Revelation."

35. Quoted in the *Catechism of the Catholic Church*, no. 129; cf. *Dei Verbum* no. 16. We agree with Richard Bauckham's cautionary remark:

Those who try to map the broad outlines of the biblical narrative, discerning the purposes of God portrayed in it, are often tempted to override the untidy complexity of the actual narrative and non-narrative contents of Scripture. . . . The Bible does, in some sense, tell an overall story that encompasses all its other contents, but this story is not a sort of straitjacket that reduces all else to a narrowly defined uniformity. (*Bible and Mission: Christian Witness in a Postmodern World* [Grand Rapids: Baker Academic, 2003], 93)

The Senses of Scripture and Catholic Reading

Before proceeding, we should note that in interpreting particular biblical passages, we depend largely upon the "literal sense" of the Bible—the meaning intended by the biblical authors and by God in the Bible's various genres, such as history, poetry, and parable.[36] Since God is the primary author of the Bible, however, meanings are present even in the literal sense that might not have been consciously known by the original author of a particular passage, but that become apparent when the Bible is read canonically.[37] Catholic exegesis traditionally also upholds the "spiritual" sense of scripture, in which the Holy Spirit illumines for readers applications to their own lives (the moral sense), possible connections between images and events in the Old Testament and those in the New (the allegorical sense), and hints of the glory of eternal life (the anagogical sense).

It is our hope and prayer, in short, that by discovering the harmonic thread of holiness or charity that underlies God's revelation in scripture, readers of all different religious backgrounds will be prepared to uncover and understand the intricate details of the whole symphony of revelation.

36. See *Catechism of the Catholic Church*, no. 109.

37. On the relationship of the literal and spiritual senses, see St. Thomas Aquinas, *Summa Theologiae* I, q. 1, a. 10; and *Commentary on Saint Paul's Epistle to the Galatians*, trans. Fabian Larcher, O.P. (Albany, NY: Magi Books, 1966), ch. 4, lecture 7. For further discussion of the senses of scripture, see the *Catechism of the Catholic Church*, nos. 115–118; Henri de Lubac, S.J., *Medieval Exegesis*, Vols. 1 and 2, *The Four Senses of Scripture*, trans. respectively by Marc Sebanc and E. M. Macierowski (Grand Rapids: Eerdmans, 1998 and 2000).

1

The Lost Eden

"In the beginning God created the heavens and the earth" (Gen. 1:1). This announcement sets up the entire scriptures, which recount the relationship between the infinite Creator and his finite creatures. This relationship, as we will see, continually displays the inexpressible love and mercy of God. Caught up in pride, human beings often do not recognize the love of God; we often focus only upon what we can see, and think in terms of power rather than in terms of wisdom and love. The Puritan poet John Milton captures our blindness well in his depiction of the fallen angel Satan. Since the Bible reveals the incredible profundity, even to death on a cross, of God's love for us, it may be good to begin our journey through the Bible with Milton's poetic description of what we become when we fail to see God for who he really is. In Milton's *Paradise Lost*, Satan, having fallen from heavenly communion with God, tries to justify his exchange of "that celestial light" for "this mournful gloom":

"Be it so, since he [God]/ who is now sovereign can dispose and bid/ What shall be right: furthest from him is best/ whom reason hath equalled, force hath made supreme/ above his equals. Farewell happy fields/ where joy for ever dwells: hail horrors, hail/ infernal world, and thou profoundest hell/ receive thy new possessor: one who brings/ a mind not to be changed by place or time./ The mind is its own place, and in itself/ can make a heaven of hell, a hell of heaven./ What matter where, if I be still the same,/ and what I should be, all but less than he/ whom thunder hath made greater? Here at least/ we shall be free; the almighty hath not built/ here for his

23

envy, will not drive us hence:/ Here we may reign secure, and in my choice/ to reign is worth ambition though in hell:/ Better to reign in hell, than serve in heaven."[1]

In Milton's poetic depiction, the devil imagines God as "over against" creatures, dominating them by power and force; and likewise the devil imagines freedom to be simply having power and dominion. As the poet knew, this perversion—which is so often our perversion as well—completely inverts the reality of God. Blinded by pride and the violence it begets, human beings so often create "gods" in our own image: a violent and lustful Zeus, an arbitrary and implacable Judge, and so forth.[2] Freed from such idolatry by God's covenantal love as revealed in the Bible, we realize that the true God is he whose power is wisdom and whose freedom is self-giving love.

God freely creates us out of love and invites us, with wondrous mercy, to share eternally in the unfathomable dance of his wisdom and love. This is the true picture of reality; all others are painfully drab, meaningless, boring, and egotistical in comparison. When one discovers oneself to be a creature created by God, it is cause for rejoicing. To be a creature means that there is some purpose, some meaning of life. Otherwise, why would God have bothered to create? He either created for a goal, or else nothing would have moved him to create. We are caught up into this plan, and surely it must be an exciting and significant one. God creates, or gives being, and we depend continually upon this ongoing gift of being. Although we are used to thinking of ourselves as autonomous agents, we are actually recipients immersed in gift. Simply by creation, we have a relationship to God, who is not a finite, created being but rather is infinite, unlimited, uncreated Being. As the Creator of time and space, God is not temporal or spatial; he is sheer presence, infinite act-of-being. This recognition gives a deeper sense of meaning and solidity to our fragile lives.

Holiness

The excitement of God's plan for his creatures hinges upon holiness. When one thinks of holiness, however, two notions generally come to

1. John Milton, *Paradise Lost*, ed. Alastair Fowler, 2nd ed. (London: Longman, 1998), 75–76 (Book I, nos. 244–263).
2. The theme of the existential situation of idolatry, and rising from idolatry in Christ, is well explored in Dominique Barthélemy, O.P., *God and His Image: An Outline of Biblical Theology*, trans. Dom Aldhelm Dean, O.S.B. (New York: Sheed and Ward, 1966).

mind. The first is that perhaps there is no holiness. Plenty of people, religious and non-religious, exhibit self-righteousness; a brief glance at the newspaper, or into our own hearts, tells us that the world is a very troubled place. Interiorly, human beings often find unruly lust, paralyzing fear, greed, desire for hate-filled revenge, pride, and so forth. In our deeds and the deeds of those around us, we find various forms of selfishness, spite, lust, and violence. The second notion that comes to mind is almost equally troubling. Holiness may sound quite boring. Mark Twain famously joked that if Heaven was all it was said to be, he would choose Hell.

Yet, rather than a state of boring and static self-satisfaction, holiness is radical freedom from our selfish crimps and narrowness. The greatest ecstasy is to go out of oneself in the fire of divine wisdom and charity. Holiness is when we lose our violent pretenses to be God, and instead embrace the reality of creatureliness, of receiving everything from God. It is like being a child again in the best way; but it is also like being a mature adult in an unimaginably glorious way, because by becoming fully creatures again, children of God, we freely enter into the self-giving love who is God, and share in the full personhood of this unimaginably glorious dance of infinite wisdom and love. Holiness is not the drip of one moment succeeding another; it is the eternal and timeless fount of inexhaustible wisdom and love.

What does this have to do with the first two chapters of Genesis? As we will see, these first two chapters depict creation in terms of holiness: holy people dwelling in a holy land.

The Harmony of Creation

One can easily misread the first two chapters of Genesis.[3] Focusing on the external things, one might try to figure out where exactly was Eden (or is Eden) in relation to the Tigris and Euphrates Rivers (Gen. 2:10–14), or one might try to show that plants and trees could not have appeared before the sun and moon (Gen. 1:11–18). These approaches—the one seeking to prove, the other seeking to disprove—are simply flip sides of the same way of misreading the creation accounts.

---

3. For discussions of the genres, styles of writing, and interpretative development within the Bible, see such books as Robert Alter, *The Art of Biblical Narrative* (New York: Basic Books, 1981); James L. Kugel, *The Idea of Biblical Poetry: Parallelism and Its History* (Baltimore: Johns Hopkins University Press, 1981); G. B. Caird, *The Language and Imagery of the Bible* (Grand Rapids: Eerdmans, 1997 [1980]); Michael Fishbane, *Biblical Interpretation in Ancient Israel* (Oxford: Oxford University Press, 1985).

Since creation begins the march of time and God's unfolding plan, the narrative displays the rhythm of time, "there was evening and there was morning" (Gen. 1:5). Thus the first two chapters of Genesis testify to fundamental realities: God, who is not a creature, created everything that is (the doctrine of creation from nothing, *creatio ex nihilo*); there was a beginning of time and space; the universe as we know it developed over time rather than simply springing fully formed into being; human beings are radically different from the other animals.[4] At the center of Genesis 1 and 2, similarly, are spiritual realities such as holiness, goodness, harmony, order, justice. These spiritual realities do not negate the external realities of creation; rather, they expose the profound meaning, and the purpose or goal, that underlies and structures the physical realities. In depicting the creation of visible things, Genesis explains their origin in such a way as both to affirm the goodness of material and spiritual creation, and to make clear that their ultimate meaning is found in holiness, harmony, order, and justice.

This harmony and goodness is majestically enunciated in the opening verses of the first chapter of Genesis. As befits his radical difference from creatures, God speaks things into existence; all things come into existence (from nothing) by his word. Creation is a spiritual event, the work of the divine spirit who need not move to create. Logically prior to fiery explosions and external events is the "movement" of the divine spirit speaking his word of creation. Creation thus begins in the holy wisdom of God, who utters his word, which is full of creative meaning and power. Far from being irrational, creation is the harmonious expression of God's word, which has a meaning, and thus a goal and purpose. Governed by physical and moral laws, the order and design of creation displays the wisdom and intelligence of the Creator.

This harmonious creative expression builds progressively over the course of the "days," from inanimate creation to vegetative creation to animals and finally to rational animals, human beings. Creation possesses an order: it moves toward more and more complex forms of life. At the pinnacle of this order, we find the capacity for spiritual relationship. To some modern thinkers, "creation" appears to be simply a violent bang followed by propulsion and cooling of gasses; to others, creation above all involves the increasing complexity of chemical formations. Genesis

---

4. See St. Augustine, *The Literal Meaning of Genesis*, Vol. 1 (Books I-VI), trans. John Hammond Taylor, S.J. (New York: Newman Press, 1982). On creation "from nothing" see, e.g., J. C. O'Neill, "How Early Is the Doctrine of *Creatio Ex Nihilo*?" *Journal of Theological Studies* 53 (2002): 449–465. See also the *Catechism of the Catholic Church*, nos. 279–324. Cf. Joseph Cardinal Ratzinger, *'In the Beginning. . .': A Catholic Understanding of the Story of Creation and the Fall* (Grand Rapids: Eerdmans, 1995).

teaches deeper truths: creation proceeds not from violence but from the divine wisdom; creation, as a tabernacle or temple, possesses a mysterious inner order and harmony and finds its goal in spiritual relationship.[5]

But could Genesis's first account of creation be then a form of spiritualism or denigration of matter? On the contrary. Creation begins with light: "And God said, 'Let there be light'; and there was light. And God saw that the light was good" (Gen. 1:3–4). We take light for granted; but one can imagine that first light, first dawn, light arising from nothingness—how good it must have been! The goodness of the light, the first created reality, passes into a repeated series of creative acts in which God proclaims the goodness of what he has created by his word. Earth is singled out for its goodness: "God called the dry land Earth, and the waters that were gathered together he called Seas. And God saw that it was good" (Gen. 1:10). The pictures of Earth that we have gained from space travel in the last century demonstrate ever more clearly how beautiful and singular Earth is. When, by the continual creative causality of God's word sustaining the being of things, vegetation springs from Earth, God similarly "saw that it was good" (Gen. 1:12). The beauty of the sun, moon, and stars, which the divine Word creates and calls "good" (Gen. 1:18), further manifests the beauty of Earth, of its plants and trees.

On the fifth day God creates the first animals, specifically birds and fish. Now that creaturely life has arrived at self-motion, imitating the divine in a deeper way, for the first time God not only calls his creation good, but he also blesses it: "And God saw that it was good. And God blessed them, saying, 'Be fruitful and multiply and fill the waters of the seas, and let birds multiply on the earth'" (Gen. 1:21–22). The sixth day introduces the land animals, again called "good," and finally the rational animal, man.

Human beings, while animals, are nonetheless radically distinct from the other animals. The distinction consists in the way that human beings reflect the divine Word. Human beings have the intellectual power to know God and freely to love him; in human relationships, which are creative, we find an imaging of God's wisdom and love. Although the monkey and

---

5. See St. Basil the Great, *Hexaemeron*, in *Basil: Letters and Select Works*, Vol. 8 of the Second Series of Nicene and Post-Nicene Fathers, ed. Philip Schaff and Henry Wace (Peabody, MA: Hendrickson, 1995 [1895]), 52–107; St. Augustine, *Confessions*, trans. Henry Chadwick (Oxford: Oxford University Press, 1991), Book XIII; Joseph Cardinal Ratzinger, *'In the Beginning. . .'*, 27–39 (the section titled "Creation and Worship"); Michael Fishbane, *Text and Texture: Close Readings of Selected Biblical Texts* (New York: Schocken Books, 1979), 3–16. Joshua Berman, in *The Temple: Its Symbolism Then and Now* (Northvale, NJ: Jason Aronson, 1995), 13–19, draws out the connections between the creation account in Genesis 1–2 and the tabernacle/temple.

the human being are both animals, the human being images God in a profoundly deeper way: "Then God said, 'Let us make man in our image, after our likeness. So God created man in his own image, in the image of God he created him; male and female he created them. And God blessed them . . .'" (Gen. 1:26–28).[6] In human beings, whose personhood unites mineral, vegetative, and animal powers in the spiritual soul, the order and harmony of creation is wondrously exposed.[7] Creation finds its goal in spiritual relationship, without denigrating the non-rational creatures.

Does the creation of human beings on the sixth day constitute the high point of creation? Perhaps surprisingly, the answer is decisively no. The pinnacle of creation is nothing other than *God's own rest*. We might imagine God's "rest" on the seventh day as if God, worn out from his labors, were relaxing in an easy chair with a cool lemonade, freshly squeezed from the lemons he had made on day three. But, in fact, God's "rest" is his supreme holiness, his infinite wisdom and being. God's "rest" is himself. The dynamism of creation continues beyond creatures to include the goal or purpose of creation. The goal of creation, the culmination toward which the whole universe (by God's power) is mysteriously tending, is that "rest," the seventh day.[8]

The completion or fulfillment of creatures awaits their perfect sharing in God's own holiness. Genesis teaches, "So God blessed the seventh day and hallowed it, because on it God rested from all his work which he had done in creation" (Gen. 2:3). Creation cannot be understood apart from its goal. Its ultimate goal is to be made holy, to share in God's inexhaustible, timeless "rest" by loving as God loves, by becoming fully the temple of God. This goal pertains particularly to rational creatures, whose rational faculties enable them to enter into spiritual relationship. Since human beings are embodied and belong to the cosmos, with its mineral, vegetative, and animal life, the fulfillment of human beings will mean, in God's plan, the fulfillment of the entire cosmos.[9]

6. On the spiritual soul, see Ric Machuga, *In Defense of the Soul: What It Means to Be Human* (Grand Rapids: Brazos Press, 2002); *Catechism of the Catholic Church*, nos. 356–379. For the compatibility of evolutionary theory (absent philosophical materialism) and the theology of creation, see Stephen M. Barr, *Modern Physics and Ancient Faith* (Notre Dame, IN: University of Notre Dame Press, 2003).

7. See John Paul II, *Original Unity of Man and Woman: Catechesis on the Book of Genesis* (Boston: St. Paul Books and Media, 1981).

8. On God's Sabbath rest or perfect peace, see St. Augustine, *City of God*, trans. Henry Bettenson (New York: Penguin, 1984), Book XXII; see also St. Bonaventure, *The Journey of the Mind to God*, trans. Philotheus Boehner, O.F.M., ed. Stephen F. Brown (Indianapolis: Hackett, 1993), 37–39.

9. On the human vocation to eternal beatitude or happiness, see Servais Pinckaers, O.P., *The Sources of Christian Ethics*, trans. Mary Thomas Noble, O.P. (Washington, DC: Catholic University of America Press, 1995).

As manifested by its order, harmony, and wisdom, the creation is intended to be the "temple" of God's indwelling. This understanding of creation is later physically represented through the order, harmony, and wisdom of the temple in Jerusalem and ultimately will be spiritually established with the consummation of all things in heaven. The first account of creation, therefore, does not end until after the description of the seventh day, when the narrator can finally record, "These are the generations of the heavens and the earth when they were created" (Gen. 2:4).

Adam and Eve

At this point, the story of creation shifts to a narrative that has particularly to do with the first two human beings, Adam and Eve. The story indicates for us what it means for human beings to be holy people and dwell in a holy land. This holy land is Eden, and the holy people are Adam and Eve, the only two human occupants of Eden. As the second way of describing creation as a "temple," Eden is an extraordinarily attractive place full of abundance.[10] We read, "And the Lord God planted a garden in Eden, in the east; and there he put the man whom he had formed. And out of the ground the Lord God made to grow every tree that is pleasant to the sight and good for food, the tree of life also in the midst of the garden, and the tree of the knowledge of good and evil. A river flowed out of Eden to water the garden, and there it divided and became four rivers" (Gen. 2:8–10). To suppose either that Eden is straightforward "history," or mere fiction, would not do. There were two human beings—that is, rational animals—at the dawn of human existence. They lived somewhere on this earth, a place chosen and formed by divine Providence. Since sin means choosing against God, before they made this rebellious choice, they were sinless, or holy. There is no reason to suppose that they lacked unclouded intelligence, or were unable to know and love God.

We note first that man and woman are composed of a material element and a spiritual element: "the Lord God formed man of dust from the ground, and breathed into his nostrils the breath of life" (Gen. 2:7). In Eden, the man and the woman live in harmony and without sexual shame: "And the man and his wife were both naked, and were

10. On Eden as a temple, see Berman, *The Temple*, 21–34; Gordon Wenham, "Sanctuary Symbolism in the Garden of Eden Story," *Proceedings of the Ninth World Congress of Jewish Studies* (Jerusalem: World Union of Jewish Studies, 1986): 19–25. See also Gary Anderson, *The Genesis of Perfection* (Louisville: Westminster John Knox, 2001), chapter 2.

not ashamed" (Gen. 2:25). Being without sexual shame indicates that their bodily passions (emotions and desires) reflect the wisdom and love of their souls, rather than disturbing, by unruly desire, the order of wisdom and love. Thus, there need be no shame: all is ordered by wisdom and love. The unity of the man and woman is unparalleled. The man describes her as "bone of my bone and flesh of my flesh," and they are said to "cleave" together as "one flesh" (Gen. 2:23–24). While marriages after sin (under grace) seek to imitate and recover this original state, inevitably there is a significantly greater feeling of distance and division.[11]

Furthermore, the man and woman are not only rightly ordered to each other. They are also rightly (wisely and lovingly) related to their natural environment, as is described in the narrative by the man's ability to "name" all the animals. The giving of a true name signifies knowing the proper place and purpose of a creature. More importantly, their wisdom and love, the attributes of their embodied souls, relate them properly to God who is infinite wisdom and love. This good relationship to God becomes clear through the symbolic trees of knowledge and of life.[12] These two trees indicate that in creation one finds an ordering not of human making but instead inscribed in creation. This fundamental ordering is twofold: ontological and moral.

The ontological order consists simply in the fact that God alone causes life, as the infinite source of all finite being: this is symbolized by "the tree of life also in the midst of the garden" (Gen. 2:9). The moral order, symbolized by the "tree of the knowledge of good and evil," indicates that God's wisdom, not the decision of human beings, ultimately defines what is good and evil for human beings.[13] For example, it is not right for a wealthy man to steal from the poor, and no human law or human

11. Cf. John Paul II, *Blessed Are the Pure of Heart* (Boston: St. Paul Books and Media, 1983).

12. The *Catechism of the Catholic Church* consistently articulates a path for the truthful interpretation of the symbolic language of the first three chapters of Genesis. "Scripture presents the work of the Creator symbolically as the succession of six days of divine 'work,' concluded by the 'rest' of the seventh day. On the subject of creation, the sacred text teaches the truths revealed by God for our salvation, permitting us to 'recognize the inner nature, the value, and the ordering of the whole of creation to the praise of God'" (no. 337, citing *Lumen Gentium* no. 36). "The Church, interpreting the symbolism of biblical language in an authentic way, in light of the New Testament and Tradition, teaches that our first parents, Adam and Eve, were constituted in an original 'state of holiness and justice'" (no. 375). "The account of the fall in *Genesis* 3 uses figurative language, but affirms a primeval event, a deed that took place *at the beginning of the history of man*" (no. 390). "The 'tree of the knowledge of good and evil' symbolically evokes the insurmountable limits that man, being a creature, must freely recognize and respect with trust" (no. 396).

13. Cf. *Catechism of the Catholic Church*, no. 396.

will could ever make such an act right. In the story, God speaks his wise law to Adam and Eve by cautioning them not to disturb the "tree of the knowledge of good and evil."

Were they to disobey God and seek rebelliously to make their own the governance of good and evil, then the consequence of this would be internal rebellion and disorder within themselves, culminating in the breach of body and soul, namely death: "And the Lord God commanded the man, saying, 'You may freely eat of every tree of the garden; but of the tree of the knowledge of good and evil you shall not eat, for in the day that you eat of it you shall die'" (Gen. 2:16). So long as they do not disobey divine wisdom, Adam and Eve live in a state of holy wisdom and love, united in obedience to the source of all being, God.

Their holiness is measured by a fourfold harmony: between themselves and nature, between body and soul (no "shame"), between each other ("one flesh"), and between themselves and their Creator. Harmony and peace, not violence and competition for power, describe the original state of the first man and woman—hard as it is for us, as fallen people, to imagine. While we often imagine ourselves to be in a competitive power relationship with God and with other people, they recognized that divine wisdom actually gave them their being and liberated them for true excellence and love. As holy people, they experienced the fourfold harmony.

Correspondingly, they also lived in holy land. What do we mean by "holy land"? To identify the meaning of this concept, let us examine further descriptive language from Genesis 2 and 3. Genesis describes Eden as a garden specially planted by God for the first human beings to dwell in. God stocks Eden with "every tree that is pleasant to the sight and good for food" (Gen. 2:9). Eden also possesses its own river, bubbling fresh from the ground and watering the whole garden, making Eden a luxuriant place of wondrous life. Similarly, precious jewels are mentioned (apparently outside Eden, but generated by the life-giving power of the Edenic river), namely gold, "bdellium and onyx stone" (Gen. 2:11–12). Eden also contains plentiful birds and animals with whom man maintains good relations (Gen. 2:19–20); the serpent is not yet a problem. Most importantly, God is actively and beneficially present in Eden, continually caring for his creation, especially the man and woman. God speaks his wisdom to the man and the woman, and cares for them by making them partners in God's work. The description of Eve's creation has a mystical ring to it: "So the Lord God caused a deep sleep to fall upon the man" (Gen. 2:21). And God "walks" in Eden (Gen. 3:8).

In short, Eden is a place where God, who is spirit, profoundly dwells spiritually with human beings.[14] Genesis depicts the state of dwelling with God in terms of luxuriant and glorious life and of a river that generates life and wealth wherever it flows. Dwelling with God, man receives all kinds of beneficent gifts from God's active presence of wisdom and love. Thus, dwelling with God is described throughout the Bible in terms of material bounty. Our imagination responds more directly to this way of describing a spiritual condition. Moreover, since we are bodily creatures, living in communion with God does indeed have life-giving bodily results.[15] What we mean by "holy land," then, is the spiritual condition of dwelling with God, in the interior presence of God, a spiritual condition that elevates and perfects our bodily nature as well. Holy land is the divine indwelling that makes us "holy people" who live in God. People become holy by dwelling with God, in communion with his creative wisdom and love.[16] Holy people describes human beings who are without guilt or impurity, full of righteousness and justice, who can stand before God and each other without shame. As the covenantal history will make increasingly clear, "holy land" refers to the indwelling of God, to a place—ultimately man himself—made holy because God himself dwells there.

Do Adam and Eve experience the perfection of "holy people" in a "holy land"? Do they enjoy perfect holiness because God dwells perfectly in them? In one sense, the answer is yes. They are indeed without sin, and they rejoice in the perfect harmony and peace that sinless communion with God, divine wisdom and love, makes possible in their lives. Yet, in Eden, they have not yet achieved the fullness of the goal for which God created them. Recall what we noted above: the high point of creation is God's "rest," the seventh day. This gives us a significant clue about the destiny or goal of creation. Only when creation enters fully into the divine life of dynamic and inexhaustible "rest" will creation reach its apogee, its fulfillment. An infinitely more intense communion in God's holy life awaits Adam and Eve, if they continue to embrace God's love.

---

14. Cf. Wenham, "Sanctuary Symbolism in the Garden of Eden Story."

15. We are not spiritualizing away the material bounties that God promised Israel. God led Israel through the material realities to a hope for spiritual things; but the spiritual realities were part of the covenant with Israel from the beginning. Already for Israel the material bounties (e.g., the land flowing with milk and honey) symbolized their spiritual relationship with God, but of course not simply in a metaphorical sense. Similarly, for Christians, the descriptions of material bounty are not "mere" metaphors: they point to the sacramental life of the Church and the bodily glory of resurrected life.

16. See, e.g., St. Bernard of Clairvaux's glorious sermons on the Song of Songs: Bernard of Clairvaux, *On the Song of Songs*, Vols. I–IV, trans. Kilian Walsh, O.C.S.O., and Irene Edmunds (Kalamazoo, MI: Cistercian Publications, 1971–1980).

32

The Loss of Original Harmony

Genesis 1 and 2 thus promise more to come. In contrast, however, Genesis 3 describes the complete unraveling of "holy people, holy land." Eden is lost. As a result of the sin of Adam and Eve, the human race loses both its own righteousness and the indwelling of God. One must focus upon the interior spiritual realities that the story conveys, in order to understand the interior rebellion of Adam and Eve and its consequences.

Eve is tempted by the words of a rational creature. Since serpents are not rational animals, we can assume that this is a symbolic depiction of a fallen angel, as later biblical and postbiblical testimony affirms (e.g., Rev. 12:9 and Wis. 2:24). The devil/serpent suggests to Eve that God, far from being loving and wise, is in a competitive power relationship with creatures. God, according to the serpent, misled Adam and Eve into thinking that they would die were they to rebel against God's order of good and evil (symbolized, as we have seen, by the tree). On the contrary, says the serpent, "You will not die. For God knows that when you eat of it your eyes will be opened, and you will be like God, knowing good and evil" (Gen. 3:4-5).[17] In other words, God has demanded obedience under false pretences, and has succeeded in dominating Adam and Eve by making them think that they could not be gods for themselves. God's will stands against man's will; the more powerful God is, the weaker man is, and vice versa. If Adam and Eve want power to create the order of reality (good and evil) for themselves—ultimately an absurd prospect—all they have to do is rebel against God's authority. The devil thus insinuates that God's wisdom is nothing more than arbitrary power; once the human beings have thrown off God's yoke, then they will be "wise" (Gen. 3:6) with the same divine power.[18]

---

17. Cf. R. W. L. Moberly, "Did the Serpent Get It Right?" in his *From Eden to Golgotha: Essays in Biblical Theology* (Atlanta: Scholar's Press, 1992); for a survey of some patristic and other (including Milton's) theology of the Fall, see Anderson, *The Genesis of Perfection*, 99–116, as well as Anderson's historical-critical analysis of the account of the Fall in Appendix A of the same volume, 197–210.

18. Likewise, many of the shapers of "modernity" and "postmodernity" view God as the enemy of human "freedom," understood as autonomy. See Richard Bauckham's *God and the Crisis of Freedom: Biblical and Contemporary Perspectives* (Louisville: Westminster John Knox Press, 2002). See also Michael A. Gillespie, *Nihilism before Nietzsche* (Chicago: University of Chicago Press, 1995); Friedrich Nietzsche, *Thus Spoke Zarathustra: A Book for Everyone and No One*, trans. R. J. Hollingdale (New York: Penguin, 1969). Fyodor Dostoevsky masterfully depicts the sense of God as an enemy of human "autonomy" in his novel *The Devils*, trans. David Magarshack (New York: Penguin, 1971). The problem is addressed by Pope John Paul II in his encyclical *Veritatis Splendor* (1993).

Under the devil's influence, Eve and Adam freely arrive at the point where they reject God's command not to eat of this "fruit": "So when the woman saw that the tree was good for food, and that it was a delight to the eyes, and that the tree was to be desired to make one wise, she took of its fruit and ate; and she also gave some to her husband, and he ate" (Gen. 3:6). Rather than the wise and loving caregiver, God appears now as the one who was unjustly depriving human beings of nourishing wisdom. But of course this vision of God is a horribly false one. By choosing (illusory) power over love, Adam and Eve have sinned by pride. Intending to become arbiters of good and evil, they have created a god—an idol—in their own power-hungry image. They have rejected divine wisdom in favor of their disordered "wisdom." They have chosen the creature over the Creator.

This disordered act radically severs each aspect of the fourfold harmony, with disastrous consequences. Under each aspect, violence and injustice now reign where once was peace, harmony, and justice. Whereas they were once a holy people, they are so no longer; whereas they once dwelt with God in a holy land, they do so no longer.[19]

We have noted that the four aspects of harmonious justice or righteousness are between soul and body, between man and woman (or between neighbors), between human beings and nature, and between human beings and God. Having eaten the "fruit," in other words having rebelled interiorly and lost their communion with God, Adam and Eve become aware of their plight: "the eyes of both were opened, and they knew that they were naked; and they sewed fig leaves together and made themselves aprons" (Gen. 3:7). Their newfound shame indicates their awakening to the disorder they have brought upon themselves. They proceed to hide "from the presence of the Lord God" (Gen. 3:8). Their new interior disorder between their bodily desires and their rational souls, expressed by their shame, corresponds to a break in their communion with God. They no longer can stand openly either in the presence of each other, or in the presence of God. In the first mention of fear in the Bible, Adam and Eve are now afraid of God (Gen. 3:10). The image of a powerful tyrant to be feared eclipses the image of God as a wise and loving Father.[20] Human beings have severed themselves from the truth

---

19. For further discussion, see *Catechism of the Catholic Church*, nos. 385–412; Henri Blocher, *Original Sin: Illuminating the Riddle* (Grand Rapids: Eerdmans, 1999). Carol Harrison has shown how St. Augustine's understanding of sin enabled him to transform and Christianize the philosophical traditions that he had inherited: see Carol Harrison, *Augustine: Christian Truth and Fractured Humanity* (Oxford: Oxford University Press, 2000).

20. Cf. Pope John Paul II, *Crossing the Threshold of Hope*, trans. Jenny McPhee and Martha McPhee (New York: Knopf, 1995), 53.

about God. When God finds and questions them, their broken relationship with each other becomes clear: the bickering that characterizes fallen relations between human beings commences, as Adam blames Eve, who also denies responsibility (Gen. 3:12–13).

This broken human relationship, resulting from the interior rebellion against God, is poignantly expressed in the curse that Eve bears: self-giving love will be replaced by exploitative power on both sides. Eve will "desire" Adam, and Adam will "rule over" Eve; in both cases, each will approach the other from utilitarian rather than loving motives, seeing each other as tools to be used. The fruitfulness of the womb, of new life, will become bitterly painful. As is clear from the history of the male-female relationship, Eve will endure the brunt of this curse, but Adam too will suffer from his new tendency to see human relationships as opportunities for domination. The history of men using women for sexual purposes, of men seeking to dominate women, has caught up so many victims: victims of pornography, machismo, abuse, misogyny, abortion, divorce, and so forth. Women, too, have desired men in unloving ways, by seeking men for their money, power, and so forth. Because of the impulse to use rather than to love the other person, a sinful tendency shared by men and women, discord has established itself at the heart of human relationships. Not surprisingly, then, the history of human beings, whether male or female, using each other or seeking to dominate each other makes of history a litany of unjust war, strife, hatred, and violence of all kinds.[21]

The curse spoken to Adam involves the breach of the aspect of the original harmony that existed between human beings and nature. Since all aspects of human life are affected by the loss of wisdom that followed upon the disordered will-to-power, the fruitfulness of the earth under human cultivation is affected just as much as the fruitfulness of the womb in human procreation. No longer will nourishment be easily available, as it was in the bountiful garden. Instead, as God says, "cursed is the ground because of you; in toil you shall eat of it all the days of your life; thorns and thistles it shall bring forth to you; and you shall eat the plants of the field" (Gen. 3:17–18). In contrast to Eden, where "God made to grow every tree that is pleasant to the sight and good for food" (Gen. 2:9), the land will now bear "thorns and thistles." The very relationship between man and nature is distorted by the break of spiritual communion; no longer a place where God dwells intimately

21. Cf. Dietrich Bonhoeffer, *The Cost of Discipleship*, trans. R. H. Booth (New York: Macmillan, 1959); Mary Shivanandan, *Crossing the Threshold of Love: A New Vision of Marriage* (Washington, DC: Catholic University of America Press, 1999); William Brennan, *Dehumanizing the Vulnerable* (Chicago: Loyola University Press, 1995).

with man (holy land), the land becomes a place of material as well as spiritual aridity and barrenness. Human work and labor was originally harmoniously exercised as God had placed man in the garden "to till it and to keep it" (Gen. 2:15). Instead of becoming a pleasing sacrifice offered to God, work becomes an ultimately fruitless exercise when (dis-) ordered toward man's pleasure. As Ecclesiastes puts it, "I have seen everything that is done under the sun; and behold, all is vanity and a striving after wind. What is crooked cannot be put straight, and what is lacking cannot be numbered" (Eccles. 1:14–15).

It should be clear that "land" does not merely have a geographical meaning in these opening chapters of Genesis. The land, and its fruits, express human beings' spiritual relationship with God. Holy people and holy land correspond to each other, because the ultimate life-giving source is God, in his wisdom and loving care. Cut off by their own choice from spiritual communion with God, human beings no longer experience the easy fruitfulness upon which the transmission and sustenance of life depends. As we continue our reading of the Bible, therefore, we should expect that "land" will continue to have more than geographical significance; it will continue to signify the condition of spiritual communion with God.

Having lost their original justice or holiness, Adam and Eve are expelled from Eden. Put another way, now that they are no longer holy people, it is impossible for them to dwell in holy land, once one grasps the meaning of "holy land." The result of their pride is that "God sent him forth from the garden of Eden, to till the ground from which he was taken. He drove out the man; and at the east of the garden of Eden he placed the cherubim, and a flaming sword which turned every way, to guard the way to the tree of life" (Gen. 3:23–24). There can be no thought of "rediscovering" Eden. The angel with the flaming sword indicates how decisively human beings have cut themselves off from Eden, from communion with God in holiness.

Human beings, in their pride, have repudiated the spiritual element within them that, when their wills were pure, moved them to communion with God. God emphasizes that in repudiating their spiritual source, they have condemned themselves to subhuman, solely material existence: "In the sweat of your face you shall eat bread till you return to the ground, for out of it you were taken; you are dust, and to dust you shall return" (Gen. 3:19). The break of harmony between their bodies and souls means that their bodies, with their disordered desires, now govern; and that this condition of sin leads inevitably to a final breach between body and soul, the experience of death.

More awful than this is the reality that human sin has barred the way to the "tree of life." As we noted above, the tree of life symbolizes God's

36

presence in creation as the continual giver and source of creaturely being. In their pride, human beings now seek to become the source of being, to share in God's immortality by grasping it and claiming divine being for themselves. Were they able to grasp immortality for themselves, it would be a disordered, Godless immortality that would in fact be hell. God therefore "removes" himself from their sight by expelling them from dwelling in his presence: since their object is to become gods by their own power, the result is that their idolatrous concept of God (as power, rather than as wisdom and love) bars them from seeing God. They can only see their idol.

Thenceforth, human beings must await the coming of the "tree of life"; by humility, by not counting Godlikeness as something to be grasped or exploited for the ends of prideful power, the new "tree of life" (Jesus Christ) will be life-giving unto eternal life (cf. Phil. 2:5–11).[22]

East of Eden

With holiness replaced by destructive pride and desire to dominate, human beings commence the history of violence. The fourfold harmony of justice is now a fourfold disharmony of injustice.[23] We see this powerfully in the story of Adam and Eve's eldest son Cain. Cain, "a tiller of the ground" (Gen. 4:2), does not give God the offering he desires: "for Cain and his offering he had no regard" (Gen. 4:5). The land no longer bears, at least spiritually, the good fruit. As God had warned Adam, the land would become a place of "thorns and thistles." The first disharmony that we see, then, is between man and nature. But this disharmony represents much more fundamental breaks. In his anger against God, Cain experiences the intense inner disturbance resulting from the disorder between his body and soul. No longer guided by wisdom and charity, his passions have turned irrational and violent. This second disharmony, as God warns, breeds deadly violence: "The Lord said to Cain, 'Why are you angry, and why has your countenance fallen? If you do well, will you not be accepted? And if you do not do well, sin is crouching at the door; its desire is for you, but you must master it" (Gen. 4:6–7). Cain can yet master his irrationally violent passions, but "sin is crouching at the door."

22. On Christ's humility, which we are to imitate, see, e.g., St. Augustine, *The Trinity*, Book I; Bernard of Clairvaux, *The Steps of Humility and Pride*, trans. M. Ambrose Conway, O.C.S.O. (Kalamazoo, MI: Cistercian Publications, 1989).

23. Cf. *Catechism of the Catholic Church*, no. 400.

Indeed, the inner violence and disorder within Cain explodes into a murderous act of jealous rage against his own brother. Inviting Abel to go out into the fields with him, Cain "rose up against his brother Abel, and killed him" (Gen. 4:8).[24] The unholiness and injustice of the land and of the people could not be more manifest. The consequences of Adam and Eve's pride become crystal clear in the fields wet with the innocent blood of their son Abel, murdered by his own brother. Thus the third disharmony, between man and fellow man, introduces the history of irrational and oppressive violence that has plagued the human race.

Yet the root of it all, the worst and most fundamental breach, is the lie to God, the fourth disharmony: "Then the Lord said to Cain, 'Where is Abel your brother?' He said, 'I do not know; am I my brother's keeper?'" (Gen. 4:9). A murderer, Cain is a liar in the presence of God. This lie, rooted in violence, exposes the radical breach of communion between man and God; the lie cuts off all possibility of communication. Cain's sin manifests in all its horror the original lie, Adam and Eve's (prompted by the devil/serpent), which replaced divine wisdom with grasping for power and domination. Cain's naked assertion of brute power—his disdain for the brother he has murdered—demonstrates how far human beings have fallen from their original holiness as the image of God.[25]

In a plaintive cry, echoing his earlier words to Adam and Eve after their sin (Gen. 3:13), God himself proclaims man and the land unholy: "And the Lord said, 'What have you done? The voice of your brother's blood is crying to me from the ground. And now you are cursed from the ground, which has opened its mouth to receive your brother's blood from your hand. When you till the ground, it shall no longer yield to you its strength; you shall be a fugitive and a wanderer on the earth'" (Gen. 4:10–12). No longer a holy people, and thus cut off from "holy land," human beings are fugitives and wanderers, having lost their true homeland.

Has God abandoned humankind? Is there no hope left that human beings will ever attain the goal that God inscribed in creation, the goal of dwelling perfectly with God as holy people, embodying divine wisdom and love? On the contrary, God inscribes hope for salvation into his curse

---

24. Cain gets most of the attention in Genesis; the plight of the innocent man whom God loves (Abel) is depicted most profoundly, in the Old Testament, in the Book of Job; cf. Job 16:18, which seems to contain an allusion to Genesis 4:10, implicitly comparing Job to Abel.

25. See the discussion in John Paul II, *Evangelium Vitae* (The Gospel of Life) (Boston: St. Paul Books and Media, 1995). See also Ellen van Wolde, "The Story of Cain and Abel: A Narrative Study," *Journal of the Study of the Old Testament* 52 (1991): 25–41; Kenneth M. Craig Jr., "Questions Outside Eden (Genesis 4:1–16): Yahweh, Cain and Their Rhetorical Exchange," *Journal of the Study of the Old Testament* 86 (1999): 107–128.

of the serpent/devil. The serpent/devil's curse suggests that the tempter will not, in the end, destroy the goal for which rational creatures were created. God warns the serpent, "I will put enmity between you and the woman, and between your seed and her seed; he shall bruise your head, and you shall bruise his heel" (Gen. 3:15). It would be foolish to conclude that this warning intends to describe why human beings and snakes do not get along. Rather, at stake is whether the serpent/devil will win, will poison the land forever. God's promise is that the devil's "head" will be bruised, while the "heel" of Eve's "seed" shall be bruised. By the suffering of Eve's seed, the devil's "head," his plans as opposed to God's, will be crushed.[26]

In no way, then, does God abandon humankind, even though humankind abandons him. In their nakedness (again more than a literal nakedness, but a spiritual one), God himself clothes them: "The man called his wife's name Eve, because she was the mother of all living. And the Lord God made for Adam and for his wife garments of skins, and clothed them" (Gen. 3:20–21). Although humankind has turned away in pride from God, nonetheless God will clothe us anew. God will restore the "image of God" in us, renewing our justice and holiness and dwelling spiritually within us perfectly.

How is God going to restore and perfect us? How will God reverse our violence and disharmony, the horrible history of suffering, and make us holy? How are we to know him again, beyond the idols we have constructed in our power-hungry image? This history of salvation is described in the remainder of holy scripture, God's Word.

---

26. Cf. *Catechism of the Catholic Church*, nos. 410–411.

2

Abraham

Descendants and Land

This chapter begins with the history of sin and violence, and culminates in a promise—a covenant—between God and a man named Abraham. The events recorded in this part of the Bible can seem a bit anticlimactic, however, after the exciting events that occurred in Eden. After all, the desire for descendants and land is a fairly normal one in human life. We all like to talk about the time we had our first child or purchased our first house. Having children (descendants) and owning a house (land) seem to be the standard American dream. When we discover, as we will, that God took a definitive step in salvation history by promising Abraham descendants and land, we might be tempted to respond with a yawn and a "ho-hum." In fact, however, this promise of descendants and land signals the end to ordinary human life, because it radically begins the journey toward renewed holy people and holy land.

The Covenant with Noah

After Cain's murderous action decisively manifests the end of human holiness—the end of a people of justice who dwelt in the interior presence of God—life goes on, as we might expect, as normal. At least, life goes on as we have come to consider normal. Cain raises children and builds a city. Cain's descendants develop musical instruments, forge weapons and other tools of bronze and iron, and take pride in wreaking vengeance on their enemies (Gen. 4:23–24). Human culture appears to be proceeding well, with a relatively "normal" amount of violence and pride. No doubt, this is what a casual observer would have concluded. Yet, such "normalcy" is radically opposed to God's goodness, because it is the history of violence, injustice, and pride. We are accustomed to human culture being united with human violence and pride. It hardly gives us pause, even though it should.[1]

Despite the appearance of what we would call "normalcy," the question at the heart of the narrative, therefore, is how God will begin his work of restoring holiness to humankind. An important clue is the fact that after the murder of Abel, Adam and Eve conceive another son, Seth, who in many ways takes on Abel's role. Seth's line, his descendants, offers a path contrasting with Cain's line. After the birth of Seth's son, worship begins again: "At that time men began to call upon the name of the Lord" (4:26). Indeed, Seth has a descendant, Enoch, who "walked with God" and was taken up by God (Gen. 5:24). Three generations later, Seth's descendant Noah is described as "a righteous man, blameless in his generation; Noah walked with God" (Gen. 6:9). Thus, despite the death of Abel and the flourishing of Cain and his descendants, human holiness was never completely extinguished. God is going to work to repair human holiness through the line of Seth, who takes up the role of the righteous victim Abel.

God begins this work through Noah. But first of all any romanticism about the condition of humankind must be undermined. Our normal assumption is that if human culture is thriving, as represented by the material productivity of Cain's line, then things are going well. It comes as a shock to the unprepared reader, therefore, to learn of God's view of the situation: "The Lord saw that the wickedness of man was great in the earth, and that every imagination of the thoughts of his heart was only evil continually" (Gen. 6:5). Certainly, when we look inside our own hearts and our own apparently flourishing culture, we cannot deny the truth of this, even as we implore God in his mercy to convert us to himself. Yet, it gets worse in God's view.

In two distinct passages, which emphasize doubly, as it were, how bad things are, we find God's condemnation of the horrible injustice into which humankind has fallen. "And the Lord was sorry that he had made man on the earth, and it grieved him to his heart. So the Lord

---

1. See, e.g., the essays in *Must Christianity Be Violent?: Reflections on History, Practice, and Theology*, eds. Kenneth R. Chase and Alan Jacobs (Grand Rapids: Brazos Press, 2003).

said, 'I will blot out man whom I have created from the face of the ground, man and beast and creeping things and birds of the air, for I am sorry that I have made them'" (Gen. 6:6–7). There follows a similar plaint: "Now the earth was corrupt in God's sight, and the earth was filled with violence. And God saw the earth, and behold, it was corrupt; for all flesh had corrupted their way upon the earth. And God said to Noah, 'I have determined to make an end of all flesh; for the earth is filled with violence through them; behold, I will destroy them with the earth'" (Gen. 6:11–13).

We are tempted to protest against such descriptions. Surely, it could not have been so bad. After all, Cain's descendants were just making music and weapons! The Bible, however, will have none of our idealized view of ourselves.[2] History is indeed a grim picture: the violence that fills our hearts and our societies can be minimized only by the oppressors, as when a Stalin re-writes the Communist history books to blot out the slaughter of non-persons. In our comfortable houses, we can lose sight of how terrible and how deeply rooted injustice is. God's view, however, is the truthful one. Injustice, the loss of holiness, profoundly wounds and scars human relationships. Absolute chaos, destructive violence, came upon the world through the prideful deformation of the original human beings. This violence increases in intensity toward a situation where the violence, remarked upon by God in Genesis 6:11 and 6:13, threatens to dissolve and break down human existence completely.

What follows are two depictions of almost complete chaos. These depictions would be unbearable were they not marked, as well, by a sign of hope. The Bible begins, we recall, with depictions of extraordinarily beautiful order, harmony, and peace. The fourfold harmony that is original justice, and that we find depicted in the creation accounts, depends upon creatures' interior communion with God in love. When "the Spirit of God was moving over the face of the waters" (Gen. 1:2), intricate and delicate harmony and beauty emerged. In contrast, human dissolution and injustice unleash a violent chaos in human affairs that, far from uniting and bonding people together in harmony and peace, threatens the very existence of human communities. If human survival is a tenuous matter in the nuclear age, so it has always been: the violence of sin continually threatens the existence of the communities upon which

---

2. Cf. Stanley Hauerwas, *Unleashing the Scriptures*; idem, *A Community of Character: Toward a Constructive Christian Social Ethic* (Notre Dame, IN: University of Notre Dame Press, 1981); Karol Wojtyla, *Sign of Contradiction* (New York: Seabury Press, 1979). For a literary depiction of our condition, see C. S. Lewis's *Till We Have Faces: A Myth Retold* (New York: Harcourt Brace & Company, 1956).

human beings, individually and collectively, depend for survival.[3] Given the good order created by God, the disorder of sin and violence hardly go "unpunished": rather, by their very effects, they unleash their own punishment. Death and destruction follow upon human sin.

The Flood describes this deluge or absolute threat to creaturely existence. God sees the corrupt nature of humankind. We sometimes think lightly of our own corruption, because we have become used to it, but in fact corruption, the lack of true being that is caused by sin, indicates a radical loss of what we were meant to be, a radical loss of the existence that was intended for us. This corruption or loss of being is tending toward death, a loss of being.[4] Given this terrible plight, one might ask whether a good God would cause this loss of being. Yes and no. In one sense, God does not cause the loss of being; on the contrary, human sin and violence bring their own punishment. Yet, in another sense, God does cause the loss of being, since punishment belongs to God's good order: punishment restores the order of justice. Genesis speaks of God's causality in the punishment of sin: "For behold, I will bring a flood of waters upon the earth, to destroy all flesh in which is the breath of life from under heaven; everything that is on the earth shall die" (Gen. 6:17).

Genesis, however, also speaks of God's intervention, in the very midst of the absolute threat that human injustice poses to human existence, to bring about a restoration of humankind. In Noah, who descends from Seth, God finds a man of justice. Through this one man, God works to save humankind from complete dissolution: "Go into the ark, you and all your household, for I have seen that you are righteous before me in this generation" (Gen. 7:1). Even when man has slid from original justice and harmony to a dire situation where "the wickedness of man was great in the earth" (Gen. 6:5), God enters into a covenant, a permanent promise of relationship and blessing, with Noah and his descendants (Gen. 6:18). This covenant takes the rainbow as its symbol (Gen. 9:12–17). If the radical dissolution of the Flood embodies the very opposite of "holy land" (expressing the bitterly unstable and violent consequences of seeking to dwell in proud opposition to God's loving presence), the rainbow signifies the reality that harmony and beauty, not dissolution, will be the last word. Just as the harmonious rainbow follows the chaotic deluge, human beings shall once more be holy people dwelling harmoniously

3. For philosophical reflections on this biblical truth, see Alasdair MacIntyre, *Dependent Rational Animals: Why Human Beings Need the Virtues* (Chicago: Open Court, 1999).

4. See the presentation of this theme in St. Athanasius, *On the Incarnation* (Crestwood, NY: St. Vladimir's Orthodox Theological Seminary, 1993); cf. St. Augustine, *City of God*, Book XIV, chs. 12–15.

44

in and with God. Human beings will once more be his true image, filled with wisdom and love (holiness). On the chaotic flood of destructive violence that tends toward death and non-being, there will be an ark of God's salvation, an ark of justice established by God, that enables man not to be washed away but rather to dwell in God's land.

The covenant with Noah marks a first moment of new creation.[5] Just as God, after creating Adam and Eve, "blessed them" (Gen. 1:28) and commanded them to be fruitful and govern the earth, so now "God blessed Noah and his sons, and said to them, 'Be fruitful and multiply, and fill the earth'" (Gen. 9:1). Yet, although there are now powerful signs that God is at work to renew harmony and justice, it would be foolish to imagine that such a work could be easily done from within fallen humanity. In contrast to those who imagine that injustice is only a surface scratch upon the face of humanity, the Bible continually brings to the forefront the actual injustice, violence, and chaotic dissolution that profoundly wound and distort human history.

One might think that with Noah, the righteous man whom God had blessed, in charge, human history would now be a movement upward to holiness and harmony. The opposite is in fact the case. Noah cannot establish a holy people or a holy land. Instead, he falls into drunkenness and exposes his nakedness, the same "nakedness," or experience of sin, that Adam and Eve had experienced in their shame. His son Ham looks upon Noah's "nakedness," for which Noah curses Ham (cf. Lev. 20:11). Noah blesses his other two sons, Shem and Japheth, who had sought to cover their father's nakedness. This first movement toward new creation, in other words, does not bring about a new situation as regards justice.

In the story of Babel, the second great depiction of chaos caused by sinful pride, we see most clearly that the profound disharmony, violence, and dissolution continue unchanged after Noah. The descendants of Ham, who now take on the role in the narrative played earlier by the descendants of Cain, seek to establish themselves in the land without God: "Come, let us build ourselves a city, and a tower with its top in the heavens, and let us make a name for ourselves, lest we be scattered abroad upon the whole earth" (Gen. 11:4). This attempt to establish human beings apart from God—a human "name" over against God's name—displays the same pride of Adam and Eve, the same rejection of "holy land" or dwelling in and with God.[6] It obtains the same result,

5. See Michael Fishbane, *Text and Texture* (New York: Schocken, 1979), 33; Hans Urs von Balthasar, *The Glory of the Lord: A Theological Aesthetics*, Vol. 6, *Theology: The Old Covenant*, trans. Erasmo Leiva-Merikakis and Brian McNeil, C.R.V. (San Francisco: Ignatius Press, 1991 [1967]), 175–176.

6. See Fishbane (drawing on Martin Buber), *Text and Texture*, 34–38.

45

namely scattering and confusion, the dissolution of human community by punishment that human beings bring upon themselves. Rather than a Flood, this time the chaos is described in terms of lack of wisdom: "Therefore its name was called Babel, because there the Lord confused the language of all the earth; and from there the Lord scattered them abroad over the face of all the earth" (Gen. 11:9). Although made in the image of God, human beings could no longer understand each other. Their disordered will, their pride, results in the punishment of a blinded intellect. The punishment is intrinsic to the sin. Pride dissolves the harmony that makes possible the communion of wisdom and love.

Has anything changed after Noah? It almost seems that the answer is no. But in fact the story of Noah signals the beginning, in the very midst of human alienation from God and from each other, of God's work of reversing the Fall and restoring the holiness of human beings. Just as the story of Noah ends with a covenant symbolized by the harmony of a rainbow, so also the story of Babel leads into another covenant. As soon as the story of Babel concludes, we find the sentence, "These are the descendants of Shem" (Gen. 11:10). And a few verses later the genealogy of Shem's descendants arrives at a man named Abram (later called Abraham in Genesis 17).

The Covenant with Abraham

The blessing given to Abraham lays the foundation for the rest of salvation history. God commands Abraham, "Go from your country and your kindred and your father's house to the land that I will show you. And I will make of you a great nation, and I will bless you, and make your name great, so that you will be a blessing. I will bless those who bless you, and him who curses you I will curse; and by you all the families of the earth shall bless themselves" (Gen. 12:1–3).

The first thing to notice is that this promise of blessing will eventually encompass "all the families of the earth." The covenant with Noah, which God calls an "everlasting covenant" (Gen. 9:16), has the same mark of universality. Speaking of the rainbow, God says to Noah, "This is the sign of the covenant which I have established between me and all flesh that is upon the earth" (Gen. 9:17). All creation will be blessed by the Noahide covenant, in which God promises never again to allow destructive chaos to reign unchallenged upon the earth. By the rainbow, God signals that he intends to draw all creation once again into his harmony. The way that God intends to reverse the chaos of disharmony begins to become manifest shortly thereafter with God's promise to Abram. As with the covenant with Noah, the covenant with Abram will have a universal

46

impact: in some way, God reveals, all the families on earth, not simply Abram's family, will eventually be blessed by sharing in it.

The particular elements in the covenant with Abram, then, hearken back to Eden.[7] By obeying God, Abram will obtain a special land and many descendants. In the condition of original justice, Adam and Eve dwelt in holiness and harmony in God's presence, symbolized by the "holy land" of Eden. Now, God is promising Abram that his descendants will live in a land specially chosen by God and that his "name"—that is, his house or family, his descendants—will be "great." In a mysterious way, his descendants, and through his descendants all families on earth, will be restored to the condition enjoyed by Adam and Eve. They will receive the promise of the rainbow, the promise of harmony and peace.

God reiterates these two elements, land and people, to Abraham over and over again. Once Abram and Sarai (later renamed Sarah) have arrived in Canaan, immediately "the Lord appeared to Abram, and said, 'To your descendants I will give this land'" (Gen. 12:7). Soon afterwards, the Lord tells him, "Lift up your eyes, and look from the place where you are, northward and southward and eastward and westward; for all the land which you see I will give to you and your descendants for ever. I will make your descendants as the dust of the earth; so that if one can count the dust of the earth, your descendants also can be counted" (Gen. 13:14–16). Again, when Abram expresses concern that he is still childless, God tells him, "Look toward heaven, and number the stars, if you are able to number them. . . . So shall your descendants be" (Gen. 15:5).

With Abram, God begins a new family, a new and distinct people in whom God wills to accomplish the blessing of the world. The meaning of holiness is to be set apart for the worship of God. Abram is set apart from his polytheistic ancestors, and he consecrates the land to the worship of the true God. Thus, the description of earthly land and descendants carries more weight than one might at first imagine. The promise has Edenic overtones: God is going to accomplish something more than simply the establishment of another territorial nation. Rather, God is working to bless, that is, to accomplish in love the restoration of harmony for all families on earth through Abraham's family. In the end, territorial boundaries and familial boundaries will be transcended in some way insofar as all people, from all regions of the earth, will come to share in the blessing accomplished through Abraham's family.[8]

7. Cf. Fishbane, *Text and Texture*, 39.

8. Cf. Bailey Wells, *God's Holy People*, 185–207. On connections between Edenic blessing and the blessing of Abraham, cf. Umberto Cassuto, *A Commentary on the Book of Genesis*, 2 vols. (Jerusalem: Magnes, 1961, 1964): see especially Vol. 2, 124ff.

The promise is not, to repeat, simply about "mere" territorial land and descendants; it is about God's plan to renew the holiness of humankind. The promise's spiritual purpose is enhanced by the fact that God's blessing of Abraham is mediated. At the same time that he receives God's promise and blessing, Abraham receives a priestly and liturgical blessing. In this blessing, the liturgical gifts of bread and wine are offered up in praise of the God who has lifted up Abraham. Moreover, this priestly blessing comes from the king of Salem, pointing forward to the city of King David, Jerusalem.[9] After Abram has led a military conquest that ensures his ability to live in the land promised him by God, we read, "And Melchizedek king of Salem brought out bread and wine; he was priest of God Most High. And he blessed him and said, 'Blessed be Abram by God Most High, maker of heaven and earth; and blessed be God Most High, who has delivered your enemies into your hand!' And Abram gave him a tenth of everything" (Gen. 14:19–20). Entwined in the covenant with Abraham, therefore, is the kingly and priestly figure of Melchizedek, whose liturgical offering of bread and wine calls down divine blessing upon Abraham and Abraham's land. The liturgical offering that Melchizedek makes cannot be separated from the way that God's covenant with Abraham will be fulfilled. In contrast to Abraham's relationship with Melchizedek, king of Salem, is Abraham's utter rejection of the king of Sodom's offering (Gen. 14:21–24). Holiness—the blessing of right relationship with God—is impossible without the true worship of God.

Genesis twice describes the actual covenant made by God with Abraham, in Genesis 15 and 17. The story in Genesis 15 begins with the theme of trust in God: "Fear not, Abram, I am your shield; your reward shall be very great" (Gen. 15:1). Trust in God stands at the heart of any covenant with God, since it is only by trusting him as our source of strength and life that we can reverse the sin of pride. Although Abram obeyed God by moving his family to the land of Canaan, nonetheless his trust in God has weakened as he has remained childless. Without a child, he will not have the many descendants that comprise an integral part of God's promise to him. God takes Abram out to see the stars, and promises him again that his descendants will be as many as the stars. Despite the empirical evidence against it, Abram believes God: "And he believed the Lord; and he reckoned it to him as righteousness" (Gen. 15:6). Trust in God thus

---

9. Jon D. Levenson (*The Death and Resurrection of the Beloved Son: The Transformation of Child Sacrifice in Judaism and Christianity* [New Haven, CT: Yale University Press, 1993], 121) remarks, "The same cult-site almost certainly lies behind the use of the name 'Salem' (*salem*) in Gen 14:18, a name that otherwise occurs only in Ps 76:3, where it parallels 'Zion.'"

constitutes what is required in the recipient of a covenantal relationship with God, because such trusting faith is the opposite of pride.

We have so far encountered two clues about the holiness required on the part of the recipient of a covenantal relationship with God: a liturgical offering and faith. God now adds a third element: he seals the covenant with Abraham by means of a sacrificial offering. After the Fall, liturgical offerings share a sacrificial character so that the order of justice can be restored in human beings. When Abram, having believed the Lord's promise about descendants, proceeds to inquire about how he can know that he and his line will really possess the land promised by God, God responds, "Bring me a heifer three years old, a she-goat three years old, a ram three years old, a turtledove, and a young pigeon" (Gen. 15:9). This might seem a surprising response. It gets even stranger. Abram cuts each of the animals (except for the birds) in half and lays "each half over against the other" (Gen. 15:10). At sundown, God causes Abram to fall into a "deep sleep." Once we recall how God caused a "deep sleep" to fall upon Adam at the creation of Eve (Gen. 2:21), we recognize that this sacrificial imagery is also, mysteriously, marital imagery. By means of the sacrifice, God is making himself the marriage partner, as it were, of Abraham and his descendants.[10]

In his "deep sleep," Abraham experiences "a dread and great darkness" (Gen. 15:12). In this condition of "great darkness," Abraham hears God's promise that Abraham's descendants will be slaves in a strange land "for four hundred years," but shall then return to the promised land "with great possessions" (Gen. 15:13–14). The people are going to undergo a sacrificial trial, similar to the one that Abraham is undergoing in his "dread and great darkness," before they can enter into God's land. God then completes the sacrificial offering of the animals, and thereby solemnly seals the covenant with its promise of land and descendants: "When the sun had gone down and it was dark, behold, a smoking fire pot and a flaming torch passed between those pieces. On that day the Lord made a covenant with Abram, saying, 'To your descendants I give this land, from the river of Egypt to the great river, the river Euphrates, the land of the Kenites, the Kenizzites, the Kadmonites, the Hittites, the Perizzites, the Rephaim, the Amorites, the Canaanites, the Girgashites and the Jebusites" (Gen. 15:17–21).

Why does God seal the covenant with Abraham by a sacrifice? Are not sacrificial offerings simply relics of superstitious religion, which presumed an anthropomorphic god who would be pleased by the odor of

---

10. The marital theme in scripture will be explored in more detail as we progress.

roasting animal flesh?[11] It is true that sacrificial offerings do not change God. But sacrificial offerings do indeed change human beings, and indeed are required of human beings. Why? First, to offer something to one's Creator is an act of simple gratitude, an act of justice. The gifts do not change the Creator, but they change us. Simply put, we become just, and remain just, by doing acts of justice. At all times, it is a supreme act of justice to offer gifts to our Creator. Second, after human beings lost justice by the sin of pride, sacrificial offerings are even more necessary. Instead of giving what was due to God, Adam and Eve acted as if God (the giver of all blessings!) was their opponent.

Recall the symbolism of the forbidden fruit: Adam and Eve sought to establish themselves as the arbiters of the created order, rather than recognize the divinely established order of justice. They sought to grasp equality with God as if it were their due, rather than participate justly in God's gifts. They chose selfishness (pride) over self-giving (love).[12] In so doing, they disordered humankind; immediately, the external effects of interior disorder and radical disharmony became apparent. These effects, as Cain manifested most clearly, are so deeply ingrained that they are reversible only by profound interior sacrifice. Such a sacrifice is represented interiorly by Abraham's death to self in his dark night of "dread and great darkness," and exteriorly by the blood of animal sacrifice as the seal of covenantal relationship with God. Relationship with God, lost by injustice, can only be restored by a radical interior act of self-giving sacrifice, which will manifest itself exteriorly (in Jesus Christ) as a perfect covenantal sacrifice.[13]

The covenantal relationship by which God intends to renew humankind as holy people dwelling in and with him in holy land is further expressed in Genesis 17, which describes the covenant with Abraham a second time. Again we see the basic elements of people and land. Lest we imagine that the covenant is simply about mere people and land, however, God's first words to Abraham are "I am God Almighty; walk before me, and be blameless" (Gen. 17:1). Holiness, living in the presence of God and following his ways of perfect justice, constitutes the purpose of the covenant of people and land.

Recall also that God enters into relationship with Abraham with the intention of enabling not just Abraham's descendants, but also "all

---

11. For reflection on the place of animal sacrifice in the lives of ordinary ancient Jews, see E. P. Sanders, *Judaism: Practice and Belief 63 BCE—66 CE* (Philadelphia: Trinity Press International, 1994), 112–116.

12. This is the guiding theme of St. Augustine's *City of God.*

13. For further discussion see Matthew Levering, *Sacrifice and Community* (Oxford: Blackwell, 2005).

families of the earth" through Abraham, to participate in the blessing of holiness and justice. God's command, "walk before me, and be blameless," is far from a throwaway line: it shapes our entire understanding of what the land and descendants will ultimately mean. The covenant envisions the holiness and justice of all humankind, and in some way this holiness will come through Abraham. God promises in this sense that the covenant will be an "everlasting covenant" for Abraham's descendants and the land as an "everlasting possession," (Gen. 17:7–8), because he "will be their God" (Gen. 17:8). This presence of God making man holy ensures the "everlasting" character of the covenant. God tells Abraham, "Behold, my covenant is with you, and you shall be the father of a multitude of nations. No longer shall your name be Abram, but your name shall be Abraham; for I have made you the father of a multitude of nations. I will make you exceedingly fruitful; and I will make nations of you, and kings shall come forth from you" (Gen. 17:5–6). The covenant with Abraham will not be fulfilled until the "multitude of nations" and the "kings" arise. This covenant, therefore, is not complete in itself: God, in an as yet mysterious way, will bring forth supreme fruitfulness from Abraham by raising up kings and peoples that are sharers in his covenantal relationship of holiness with God.

Just as the covenant in Genesis 15 includes the element of sacrifice, so also the covenant in Genesis 17 mandates a particular liturgical action, one that involves a sacrificial aspect—circumcision. As we have seen, God promises Abraham, "I will be their God" (Gen. 17:8). The people that God intends to come from Abraham are to be the people of God. Their uniqueness will be measured by their holiness. In part, this means that this people must be a people of faith and of liturgical sacrifice. Faith and liturgical sacrifice will determine their identity as the holy people of God. By their sincere worship of the true God, offering themselves to him, they will become a people of self-giving love rather than selfishness and pride. To enter into this people of God, therefore, one must be initiated by obeying God and observing his commandment. The people of God must be marked out as bearers of God's promise of salvation, or transcendent justice and holiness, for the whole world. Thus God instructs Abraham, "So shall my covenant be in your flesh an everlasting covenant. Any uncircumcised male who is not circumcised in the flesh of his foreskin shall be cut off from his people; he has broken my covenant" (Gen. 17:13–14).

Abraham's Trials

Having received this covenantal relationship, it might seem that Abraham will now have an easy time of it, enjoying God's presence, until

51

his death at a ripe old age. Instead, however, he undergoes a series of increasingly intense and painful trials. First, like Noah before him, he seems to sin directly after receiving the covenant. Apparently not trusting that God will indeed give him a son, he has a child, Ishmael, with Sarah's maid at Sarah's invitation (Gen. 16). Furthermore, he twice passes off Sarah as his sister in order to avoid potential conflict with the ruler of the land where he is sojourning, a gambit that involves the risk that the ruler will marry Sarah (Gen. 12 and 20). The family and interpersonal discord that ensues shows once again, as with Noah, that God's covenantal work has not yet achieved the end for which he is gradually preparing Israel: humankind still lacks justice.

Second, "the Lord appeared to him by the oaks of Mamre, as he sat at the door of his tent in the heat of the day" (Gen. 18:1). This appearance of the Lord significantly takes the form of "three men" (Gen. 18:2). Abraham recognizes them as the Lord, and his attitude of hospitality and welcome displays the attitude of the man of prayer to God's direction. The visit begins with wonderful news: the Lord repeats his earlier promise that Sarah shall have a son, but this time adds that it will happen soon (Gen. 18:10). However, human discord again rears its ugly head. Showing that mercy and justice are not opposed, the Lord comes to bless Abraham's family, and then travels on to Sodom and Gomorrah to inflict just punishment. We generally avoid coming to terms with our desperate need for holiness, by ignoring or hiding the consequences of our sins. "Holiness" and "justice," in this way, come to seem abstract, impractical, or even merely boring. Abraham, however, is allowed no such luxury. God places him face-to-face with the horrible consequences of the disorder and disharmony of sin, namely death and destruction.

At the very moment of receiving the long-awaited news of a son, therefore, Abraham is confronted with the trial of witnessing the imminent punishment of sinners. This should come as no surprise: when God allows us to recognize that he has blessed us, he also inspires us to pray for others. The Lord says to himself, "Shall I hide from Abraham what I am about to do, seeing that Abraham shall become a great and mighty nation, and all the nations of the earth shall bless themselves by him? No, for I have chosen him, that he may charge his children and his household after him to keep the way of the Lord by doing righteousness and justice; so that the Lord may bring to Abraham what he has promised him" (Gen. 18:17–19). Holiness is no mere abstraction, but a life-or-death matter. The Lord intends to measure, and punish, the sin of Sodom and Gomorrah that very day.

As befits one who realizes that his blessing (the son God grants him) is a blessing-for-others, Abraham, in anguish, pleads for God to have mercy upon the whole people of Sodom and Gomorrah: "Wilt thou indeed destroy the righteous with the wicked? Suppose there are fifty righteous within the city; wilt thou then destroy the place and not spare it for the fifty righteous who are in it? Far be it from thee to do such a thing, to slay the righteous with the wicked, so that the righteous fare as the wicked! Far be that from thee! Shall not the Judge of all the earth do right?" (Gen. 18:23–25). God agrees to spare the whole city if even there are ten righteous people in the city; and God further enables Abraham's relatives (Lot and his family) to leave the city.

Yet the disorder of the city, characterized by the disordering of sexuality (thus a disorder that strikes at the center of human life, interpersonal relationships), is so great that in fact not even a single citizen is just. Even Lot and his family display the city's disorder: Lot's wife turns back in yearning for Sodom, and Lot gets drunk and has sexual intercourse with his two daughters (Gen. 19:32). Abraham, given a son by God, is thus witness to the horrible reality of humankind's disordered rejection of the merciful God, the same rejection made by Adam and Eve,which hideously mars the family of Abraham's cousin Lot.[14]

By these two trials, God makes clear that in this situation where at best people display varying degrees of injustice, there is a desperate need for justice; lack of justice brings upon itself its own dreadful punishment. The third great trial that God grants Abraham indicates how God intends to address, ultimately, this condition of injustice and disharmony. Having miraculously given Abraham and Sarah a son, Isaac, God commands Abraham to sacrifice Isaac: "Take your son, your only son Isaac, whom you love, and go to the land of Moriah, and offer him there as a burnt offering upon one of the mountains of which I shall tell you" (Gen. 22:2). Recall that sacrifice is integral to the covenant. Fidelity to the Creator must trump every created allegiance; one must be willing to give up all created goods in favor of union with God. This is the radical interior sacrifice that is required for creaturely justice, both before and after sin. Only such a trial could demonstrate that Abraham receives God's covenantal mercy as sheer gift, rather than as a this-worldly (self-serving) benefit.[15] In other words, only such a

14. Cf. John Henry Newman, "Abraham and Lot," in *Parochial and Plain Sermons* (San Francisco: Ignatius Press, 1987 [1891]), 483–491.

15. See, e.g., Jon D. Levenson, *The Death and Resurrection of the Beloved Son*, 126: "Abraham's willingness to heed the frightful command may or may not demonstrate faith in the promise that is invested in Isaac, but it surely and abundantly demonstrates his putting obedience to God ahead of every possible competitor. And if this is so, then if Abraham had failed to heed, he would have exhibited not so much a lack of faith in the promise as a love for Isaac that surpassed even his fear of God. He would, in other words, have elected Isaac his own son over Isaac the beloved son in the larger providential drama, the son whose very existence, from the moment of the angelic annunciation of his

trial could display that Abraham does not cling to the earthly land and descendants but instead clings to the true meaning of the covenant, spiritual holiness and justice.

Yet, it seems unbelievable that God could actually will for a man to sacrifice his son. In fact, as we would expect, God does not so will. God does indeed intend to address injustice by requiring faith and liturgical sacrifice, as we saw earlier, but the sacrifice will be primarily God's own. On the third day of their trip, Abraham takes Isaac apart to "worship" (Gen. 22:5) and tells Isaac, "God will provide the lamb for a burnt offering, my son" (Gen. 22:8). Displaying unwavering faith in God's goodness during this intense trial, Abraham binds Isaac and prepares to sacrifice him. An angel of the Lord stops him: "Do not lay your hand on the lad or do anything to him; for now I know that you fear God, seeing you have not withheld your son, your only son, from me" (Gen. 22:12). Abraham then sees a ram providentially caught in the thicket, and sacrifices the ram. The story concludes, "So Abraham called the name of that place The Lord will provide; as it is said to this day, 'On the mount of the Lord it shall be provided'" (Gen. 22:14).[16] God will provide the sacrifice; God will be the one to give up his Son, who willingly and freely goes to his death out of love in order to establish perfect justice.[17]

Jacob and His Family

Abraham's trials thus deepen further our understanding of how God intends to fulfill his covenantal promises, and of the meaning of these promises. The fulfillment, however, is still a long way off. As God had warned Abraham, Abraham's descendants must still undergo their own trial of slavery in a foreign land. Isaac marries Rebekah, who gives birth to the twins Esau and Jacob. By trickery and the help of his mother, Jacob steals his father's blessing from the firstborn Esau, and the covenantal promises descend through Jacob to his twelve sons. Twice, both times as he is crossing the sacred border of the promised land of Canaan, Jacob undergoes nighttime experiences by which God reveals more about his covenant.

---

impending birth, has run counter to the naturalness of familial life. The aqedah, in short, tests whether Abraham is prepared to surrender his son to the God who gave him." See also R. W. L. Moberly, "Living Dangerously: Genesis 22 and the Quest for Good Biblical Interpretation," in *The Art of Reading Scripture*, eds. Davis and Hays, 181–197.

16. Jon Levenson points out that this mountain may be an allusion to Mount Zion, the temple mount (Levenson, *The Death and Resurrection of the Beloved Son*, 118–119). Cf. 2 Chron. 3:1.

17. Cf. St. Augustine, *City of God*, Book XVI, ch. 32.

First, as Jacob is fleeing from his brother Esau out of the land of Canaan, Jacob dreams "that there was a ladder set up on the earth, and the top of it reached to heaven; and behold, the angels of God were ascending and descending on it!" (Gen. 28:12).[18] God stands above the ladder and reaffirms the covenantal promises about land, descendants, and blessing for all nations. This symbolic ladder joining heaven and earth adds the element of a perfect mediator to that of the sacrificial lamb of Abraham's near-sacrifice of Isaac. Jacob names the place "Beth-El," which means house of God. The vision confirms that God will bring his people to a place where he will unite them and dwell with them in the unity of heaven and earth.

Second, many years later, as Jacob is returning to the promised land once again in fear of Esau, Jacob wrestles all night with a mysterious "man," whom Jacob later identifies as God (Gen. 32:30). Jacob asks the one with whom he is struggling for two things: a blessing, and to know the stranger's name. Commending Jacob for his perseverance, the stranger gives Jacob the name "Israel" and blesses Jacob. Indeed, Jacob embodies the people of God in his profound perseverance and his unceasing desire to know God intimately. Jacob, who becomes Israel, personifies the people of Israel's vocation to be the instruments for God to reveal his name and his blessing to humankind. Human fidelity to the God of the covenants depends upon this firm yearning to enter into relationship with God; such a yearning for relationship with God belongs at the heart of the quest for holiness. For the rest of his life, Jacob walks with a limp, symbolizing extraordinary spiritual battle, that he acquired that night.[19]

Such moments of epiphany, however, are rare. Far greater is the continuous theme that runs through this section of the biblical narrative, namely the theme of injustice. Abraham's family is torn with strife as bitter as that of the family of Adam and Eve. Jacob cheats his brother Esau and is nearly killed by him; Jacob's father-in-law cheats Jacob, and Jacob in turn cheats his father-in-law (Gen. 29–31); Jacob's daughter Dinah is raped and Jacob's sons lead, under false pretenses, a vengeful and deadly rampage that threatens the very existence of Jacob's family in the land (Gen. 34–35); Jacob's favorite son Joseph is sold into slavery by his jealous brothers, who tell their father that Joseph is dead; Jacob's son Judah has sexual intercourse with his daughter-in-law Tamar who had disguised herself as a prostitute (Gen. 38: it is through this line

18. This ladder, interpreted as Christ (with the steps being his virtues), has fueled Christian mysticism through the centuries: see, e.g., St. John Climacus, *The Ladder of Divine Ascent*, trans. Colm Luibheid and Norman Russell (Mahwah, NJ: Paulist Press, 1982).
19. Cf. Fishbane, *Text and Texture*, 40–62.

that King David comes); Joseph is oppressed in Egypt as a slave and nearly dies when he is falsely accused by his master's lustful wife, but later rises to power and oversees a plan that saves lives but at the cost of making oppressed slaves of the entire Egyptian people (Gen. 39–47, especially 47:20–21); Jacob and his twelve sons end their days in Egypt, not in the promised land; and both Jacob and Joseph are mummified at their deaths (Genesis 48–50).

With all of its wickedness and human frailty, the story of Joseph manifests the truth that God will achieve his purposes through the very sins of human beings. Joseph summarizes the great mystery of divine providence when he addresses his brothers, "As for you, you meant evil against me; but God meant it for good" (Gen. 50:20). Even Joseph's slowness in revealing his true identity to his brothers serves as the occasion for Judah to make satisfaction for his previous sin. Judah, who had initiated the plan to sell Joseph into slavery (Gen. 37:26), ends up offering himself into slavery for the release of the youngest brother, Benjamin (Gen. 44:33–34). The conversion of Judah prepares Judah's role as the chosen line for God's blessing. From this brief inventory, it could hardly be clearer that despite the covenant with Abraham, God's plan of new creation, his plan to establish a holy people who dwell in and with him (holy land), has barely begun. Yet, it has begun. As we read in Jacob's deathbed blessing to his son Judah, from whom King David and the Christ will come: "The scepter shall not depart from Judah, nor the ruler's staff from between his feet, until he comes to whom it belongs; and to him shall be the obedience of the peoples" (Gen. 49:10).[20]

20. For a discussion of this section of Genesis, see Gordon J. Wenham, *Story as Torah: Reading the Old Testament Narrative Ethically* (Grand Rapids: Baker Academic, 2000), 39–41, 109–119.

3

Moses

Law and Tabernacle

The next stage of salvation history involves the gift of a law, or set of laws, and a tabernacle. In our present condition, however, law often seems something that binds and restricts us. We like laws only if they keep the neighbor's dog off our property, or prevent people from stealing our money or hurting our family. On this view, laws do not free us; rather, laws simply contain the violence, greed, domination, and lust that would break lose without laws. Similarly, we walk past tabernacles all the time (Catholic churches, for example, contain tabernacles in which Christ in the Eucharist is reserved), and pay them little notice. Since God is everywhere, tabernacles would not seem much different from other buildings and locales. Furthermore, God and law do not appear to fit together. If law simply confines and restricts us, the God of love must be different from a lawgiver.

Indeed, we generally think that because God wants us to be happy, in other words (so we often imagine) because God wants us to do what we want, God turns a blind eye to the foibles that involve us in violence, greed, domination, and lust, rather than self-giving love. In fact, as we will discover, law frees us and allows us to become the people we were intended to be, because law—at least, divine law—shows us the path of love, the path of holiness.[1] It is only a people formed in love by such a law that can worship God in truth and thereby delight in God's presence, signified by God's tabernacling in their midst.[2]

If the book of Genesis is dominated by the figures of Adam and Eve, Noah, Abraham, Isaac, and Jacob and his sons, the remaining books of the Torah—Exodus, Leviticus, Numbers, Deuteronomy—belong to Moses. Here the reader of the Bible faces a difficulty similar to that of the transition from Adam and Eve to Noah and Abraham. Let us review the terrain we have covered thus far. In the transition from the Fall to the covenant with Abraham, the question was, What does Eden have to do with a promise of land and descendants? What does a covenant in which God promises Abraham land and descendants have to do with the restoration of what was lost by sin?

Eden is a holy land in which holy people dwell. "Holy land" signifies the intimate interior dwelling in and with God that the righteous person enjoys, and "holy people" signifies the justice or righteousness in the person, a righteousness made possible by the indwelling of God. The Bible presents holiness in two ways: from the side of its cause, holiness comes from God's interior presence in the person within the relationship of true worship of God (holy land); from the side of its effect, holiness is the justice or righteousness manifested by the person and community (holy people). The Fall signals the loss of holiness, the loss of both holy land and holy people; it is no wonder that at the east "gate" of the garden of Eden there are now found "cherubim, and a flaming sword which turned every way, to guard the way to the tree of life" (Gen. 3:24).

Once we recognize the significance of Eden, then the significance of God's covenantal promise to Abraham of land and many descendants, from whom would flow blessing to the whole world, becomes clear. God is preparing the way not for simply a new nation-state among many other nation-states, but for a new "Eden," a new and universal holy land/holy people.

Now, however, we have reached a second key transition. What does the promise of land and descendants have to do with the Law and tabernacle given to Moses? It would seem that the addition of a Law and of a tabernacle is of lesser importance than the promise of land and

1. Cf. John Paul II, *Veritatis Splendor*; Russell Hittinger, *The First Grace: Rediscovering the Natural Law in a Post-Christian Age* (Wilmington, DE: ISI Books, 2003), 3–62.

2. For a discussion of the tabernacle, see Craig R. Koester, *The Dwelling of God: The Tabernacle in the Old Testament, Intertestamental Jewish Literature, and the New Testament* (Washington, DC: The Catholic Biblical Association of America, 1989); G. K. Beale, *The Temple and the Church's Mission: A Biblical Theology of the Dwelling Place of God* (Downers Grove, IL: InterVarsity Press, 2004).

descendants. In fact, the opposite is the case. The Law and the tabernacle/ark make clear that it is not land and descendants per se that God intends to provide; rather, it is "holy land," symbolized by God's presence with the people in the ark of the covenant that dwells in the tabernacle, and "holy people," informed and governed by divine Law. Far from Moses' work being a tangential accretion to the Abrahamic covenant, we find that Abraham's covenant needs to be understood in light of God's covenantal relationship through Moses with Abraham's descendants. God indicates this, as we recall, by including in the solemn covenant ritual with Abraham the story of Moses: "Know of a surety that your descendants will be sojourners in a land that is not theirs, and will be slaves there, and they will be oppressed for four hundred years; but I will bring judgment on the nation which they serve, and afterward they shall come out with great possessions" (Gen. 15:13–14).

Each covenant, in order to be understood, must thus be read in light of the covenants that follow. The covenant with Noah, promising universal blessing, should be understood in light of the covenant with Abraham, in which God reveals the particular path by which God is going to accomplish this blessing. Likewise the covenant with Abraham, with its promises of land and descendants, should be viewed in light of the covenant with Moses. Each succeeding covenant becomes, on the one hand, more *particular and narrow* (from broad universal blessing, to more narrow "land" and "descendants," to a particular nation with a particular Law and ark/tabernacle), and yet on the other hand, more *broad and bold*, as the motif of the establishment of universal holiness—a new Eden!—through Abraham's descendants (by whom all nations will be blessed) begins to manifest itself.[3]

The Slavery of Idolatry

The Book of Exodus opens with a description of the condition of the descendants of Jacob a few hundred years after Jacob's death: "But the more they were oppressed, the more they multiplied and the more they spread abroad. And the Egyptians were in dread of the people of Israel" (Exod. 1:12).[4] Pharaoh even commands that the Hebrew midwives kill the newborn males. The midwives forestall this command by trickery

3. On Christian readings of the Old Testament, see Richard B. Hays, "Reading Scripture in Light of the Resurrection," in *The Art of Reading Scripture*, eds. Davis and Hays, 216–238, especially the programmatic notes in 233–238.
4. Cf. James K. Hoffmeier, *Israel in Egypt: The Evidence for the Authenticity of the Exodus Tradition* (Oxford: Oxford University Press, 1996).

for some time, but eventually the Pharaoh issues a new command: "Every son that is born to the Hebrews you shall cast into the Nile" (Exod. 1:22). Into this situation, Moses is born, hidden in the reeds on the shore of the Nile, found by Pharaoh's daughter, and raised as her son (Exod. 2:10). Moses, however, knows himself to be a Hebrew, and defends Hebrews against Egyptian oppression, to the point of killing an Egyptian who was beating a Hebrew. Shortly after doing this, he flees for his life and becomes a shepherd in Midian, marrying the daughter of a priest of Midian (Exod. 3:1).

Both Moses and the entire people of Israel, then, are caught up into foreign cultures in which other gods are worshipped, and are subservient within these cultures. Note how Moses is raised within the Egyptian court and then marries into a Midianite priestly family. If we recall God's prophecy to Abraham in Genesis 15:13–14, it might seem then as though the story line is rather clearly set: Abraham's descendants, immersed and oppressed within a foreign land, will be led by Moses, himself immersed within the kingly and priestly culture of Egypt and Midian, to their own land in which Moses can exercise his own autonomous kingly and priestly authority. In other words, it might seem as though this is simply the story of an oppressed people gaining statehood and autonomous rule.[5]

Moses' encounter with God at Mount Horeb, also known as Mount Sinai, decisively changes this picture. God tells Moses, "I have seen the affliction of my people who are in Egypt, and have heard their cry because of their taskmasters; I know their sufferings, and I have come down to deliver them out of the hand of the Egyptians, and to bring them up out of that land to a good and broad land, a land flowing with milk and honey, to the place of the Canaanites, the Hittites, the Amorites, the Perizzites, the Hivites, and the Jebusites" (Exod. 3:7–8). God recognizes the economic and political sufferings that the Israelites, as slaves in Egypt, are enduring, and he promises to bring them to their own land that will flow "with milk and honey," in other words a rich land of comfort and material blessing.

Yet, before God says these words, he reveals himself to Moses in a different way at Mount Horeb, one that cuts at the root of idolatry. Specifically, God reveals himself as a God who is radically unlike any of the idols of the Egyptians, Midianites, or other nations. Recall that Adam and Eve, in their pride, idolatrously imagined themselves to be on par with God, as arbiters of justice. In other words, they gave honor and worship to themselves rather than to God their Creator, to whom

---

5. Jon D. Levenson warns against this kind of reductionist reading in his *The Hebrew Bible, the Old Testament, and Historical Criticism*, Chapter 6: "Exodus and Liberation."

worship is due, and from whom come all blessings of harmony, wisdom, and loving communion. To reverse original sin, God must deal above all with deeply ingrained idolatry.[6]

Idolatry, worshipping the creature over the Creator or imagining the Creator in creaturely terms (as if the Creator were a creature, as if God were "on our level" competing with us for resources), is the fundamental injustice, the fundamental disorder, from which all other manifestations of disorder and violence flow. With Abraham, God demands holiness (Gen. 17:1 and so forth), but does not go further than promising land and descendants and testing by means of the trials whether Abraham trusts in God or trusts in man—the latter trust being the mark of idolatry.

Now, at Mount Sinai/Horeb, God reveals to Moses far more of the characteristics of the one true God. In other words, it is only by knowing God, not by becoming wealthy and autonomous in their own land, that the people will be truly God's people and a people of blessing. It is only by knowing personal characteristics of the true God, the only existent one God, that the people will truly be separated from the Egyptians and Midianites. A relationship with the living God means knowing him, just like any other relationship; and knowing God means knowing God as radically not a creature and therefore as the radical source of all creatures. In order to be liberated from slavery—ultimately their slavery manifests the slavery of all humankind to sin—the Israelites must enter into the personal relationship of knowing and loving the living God.[7]

Idolatry, not geopolitical autonomy, is thus the central issue when God initiates the process of fulfilling his promises to Abraham by revealing himself to Moses at Mount Horeb.[8] The Israelites must become a holy people by knowing the true God (rather than worshipping an idolatrous concept of "god") and by loving God in justice; and the Israelites must come to dwell in a "holy land" in which God is powerfully present to them in true worship. Moses encounters God first in the burning bush: "And the angel of the Lord appeared to him in a flame of fire out of the midst of a bush; and he looked, and lo, the bush was burning, yet it was not consumed" (Exod. 3:2).

This image of a burning bush may seem rather odd: why would God choose a burning bush to manifest himself symbolically? What would a burning bush teach us about God? The fact that the bush burns with-

---

6. Failing to understand idolatry distorts Jack Miles's *God: A Biography* (New York: Vintage Books, 1995).

7. Cf. Exod. 12:12.

8. See St. Gregory of Nyssa, *The Life of Moses*, trans. Abraham J. Malherbe and Everett Ferguson (New York: Paulist Press, 1978); Nahum M. Sarna, *Exploring Exodus: The Origins of Biblical Israel* (New York: Schocken Books, 1996).

out change, without its energy being in any way consumed, is the key. The sun burns for billions of years and yet will die out eventually. God is such a perfect power, so perfect in his infinite act of being, that his act of being is pure act; it does not diminish or lessen or change, but rather is an active "to be" that is unchanging. Any other concept of God would be idolatrous, would conceive of God as existing in a creaturely manner. The first step against our almost unconscious idolatry has thus been taken.[9]

God then calls to Moses and commands him, "Do not come near; put off your shoes from your feet, for the place on which you are standing is holy ground" (Exod. 3:5). Is this God a new God, different from the God of Abraham? No. God informs Moses, "I am the God of your father, the God of Abraham, the God of Isaac, and the God of Jacob" (Exod. 3:6). As we have already seen, God then explains that he has heard the cry of his oppressed people and intends to deliver them from Egyptian slavery and lead them to the land, as he had promised Abraham. Moses, God makes clear, is to be the one who in this way fulfills the covenant with Abraham: "Come, I will send you to Pharaoh that you may bring forth my people, the sons of Israel, out of Egypt" (Exod. 3:10).

Moses receives the task of leading the people to the promised land. Once again God emphasizes that this land, while certainly a real land, signifies a spiritual condition of dwelling with God in worship. When Moses leads the people out of Egypt, their proximate destination will in fact be Mount Sinai, and their goal will be to worship. God says to Moses, "I will be with you; and this shall be the sign for you, that I have sent you: when you have brought forth the people out of Egypt, you shall serve God upon this mountain" (Exod. 3:12).

The exodus or journey to the land, therefore, is also and primarily a journey away from the idols of Egypt and toward knowing and loving the true God.[10] To dwell with God in worship (holy land), the people must be formed in justice and give what is due to God and each other. The first step is knowing who God is. The burning bush was the first symbolic revelation of the uncreated nature of the God of Abraham, Isaac, and Jacob; now Moses seeks, and receives, a second revelation. He asks God, "If I come to the people of Israel and say to them, 'The God of your fathers has sent me to you,' and they ask me, 'What is his name?' what shall I say to them?" (Exod. 3:13). Recall that Jacob, at the moment he

---

9. In *Exploring Exodus*, Sarna writes with regard to the burning bush, "Most commentators see in the fire that is self-sufficient, self-perpetuating, and wholly unaffected by its environment, a symbol of the transcendent, awesome, and unapproachable Divine Presence. The scriptures afford ample justification for this interpretation" (41).

10. Cf. Fishbane, *Text and Texture*, 121–140.

received the name Israel, was asking to know the divine name. Israel's paradigmatic stance is a profound desire to know the identity of God and to be in relationship with him. The divine name, Moses thus rightly expects, will reveal even more the depths of the divine identity and will enable Moses truly to lead the people to "holy land" and away from Egypt, which functions in the Bible as the paradigmatic locus of idolatry.

It should not surprise us that when God reveals his name, this name confirms and deepens what we learned from the symbolism of the burning bush: "God said to Moses, 'I am who I am.' And he said, 'Say this to the people of Israel, "I am has sent me to you"'" (Exod. 3:14). The path to holy land goes through this name. In order to dwell in and with God in worship, one must learn how to name him as the "I am" who sends—causes—everything. What would it mean to have as one's very identity "I am," in other words to be fully, simply, and exhaustively the meaning of the phrase "I am"?[11] The name requires that God is infinite and uncircumscribed "am," not bound by time or space, and that every finite and limited being receives its being from the infinite and unlimited "am." God is sheer "am," sheer being; in an infinite and therefore unfathomable way, he is the dynamic fullness of existence. In other words, he is the uncreated.[12] Worship of this "name" is the path that leads away from idolatry and to the "land" that God desires for his people.

Yet, once again we might ask whether this transcendent God, this God who seems so very great and majestic, is the same God as the one who

11. For philosophical reflection on the meaning of this name, see Ralph McInerny, *Characters in Search of Their Author* (Notre Dame, IN: University of Notre Dame Press, 2001).

12. Sarna remarks,

Whatever be the true etymology of the Tetragrammaton, and to this day it remains an enigma, God's response to Moses' question—'Ehyeh-'Asher-'Ehyeh—reflects a popular understanding that *YHVH* is to be interpreted in terms of the Hebrew stem *h-y-h*, 'to be.' Clearly, the name is not meant to be a mere identifying label. Such was not the main function of names in the ancient Near East. Rather, the name is intended to connote character and nature, the totality of the intricate, interwoven, manifold forces that make up the whole personality of the bearer of the name. In the present case, therefore, God's reply to Moses means that the Tetragrammaton expresses the quality of Being. However, it is not Being as opposed to nonbeing, not Being as an abstract, philosophical notion, but Being in the sense of the reality of God's active, dynamic Presence. Whether it means 'I Am That I Am,' or 'I Am Who I Am,' or 'I Will Be What I Will Be'—and it can mean any of these—God's pronouncement of His own Name indicates that the Divine Personality can be known only to the extent that God chooses to reveal His Self, and it can be truly characterized only in terms of itself, and not by analogy with something else. This is the articulated counterpart of the spectacle of fire at the Burning Bush, fire that is self-generating and self-sustaining. . . . Finally, in Exodus 3:15 God reaffirms the identification of *YHVH* with the God of the Patriarchs, and declares, 'This shall be My Name forever,

so tenderly makes his covenant with Abraham?[13] When Moses says "I am has sent me," does this refer to the same God who has been so present with Abraham, Isaac, and Jacob in history? Or is this God who names himself "I am" someone different, more aloof, from the God who names himself through the covenants? In fact, the two names signify the same God; it is only the God who is supreme, unchanging act, supreme presence, who can therefore be present intimately in every moment of history as Creator and redeemer. The idolatrous accounts of creaturely gods (Baal, Zeus, et al.) gave a false understanding of divine, uncreated being; but the idolaters were not wrong in their sense of the continual divine presence. Indeed, only the true God of Israel can truly be present. As soon as God has named himself "I am," we find in the very next verse, "God also said to Moses, 'Say this to the people of Israel, "The Lord, the God of your fathers, the God of Abraham, the God of Isaac, and the God of Jacob, has sent me to you": this is my name for ever, and thus I am to be remembered throughout all generations'" (Exod. 3:15).[14] As a historically present God, the God of Israel demands fidelity to the covenants. When Moses, formed by Egyptian and Midianite practices, is found to have failed to circumcise his son, God threatens Moses' life (Exod. 4:24) and Moses is spared only by his Midianite wife, Zipporah, who quickly circumcises their son and shows the family's fidelity to the covenant with Abraham.

The Exodus from Egypt

The plagues that follow underscore that this God, in contrast to the static and passive idols, is mighty in power and presence. As God tells Moses, "I know that the king of Egypt will not let you go unless com-

---

This My appellation for all eternity.' The character of God as just explained to Moses is absolute and unchanging. This immutability provides inflexible reliability that the promise of redemption will be realized. (*Exploring Exodus*, 52)

Cf. *Catechism of the Catholic Church*, nos. 212–213; St. Augustine, *The Trinity* (*De Trinitate*), trans. Edmund Hill (Brooklyn: New City Press, 1991), Book VII, ch. 3 (228); St. Thomas Aquinas, *Summa Theologiae*, I, q. 2.

13. Cf. Thomas Weinandy, *Does God Suffer?* (Notre Dame, IN: University of Notre Dame Press, 2000). For historical-critical analysis of the relationship of the religion of the patriarchs and the Mosaic covenant, see R. W. L. Moberly, *The Old Testament of the Old Testament: Patriarchal Narratives and Mosaic Yahwism* (Minneapolis: Fortress, 1992). Although we do not follow all of his particular judgments about patriarchal religion (for example, that it lacked a moral component), Moberly's book is intriguing for its evidence for the existence and distinctiveness of the patriarchs.

14. "The Lord" is the RSV's translation of the personal name YHWH by which Israel knew God.

pelled by a mighty hand. So I will stretch out my hand and smite Egypt with all the wonders which I will do in it; after that he will let you go" (Exod. 3:19–20). The Egyptian magicians, dependent upon a system of idol worship, can do nothing despite Pharaoh's pleas. That idolatry is the issue at stake is further underscored by the reason that Moses and his brother Aaron, who speaks to Pharaoh the words with which God inspires Moses (Exod. 4:16), consistently give to Pharaoh to explain their mission: "Thus says the Lord, the God of Israel, 'Let my people go, that they may hold a feast to me in the wilderness.' . . . The God of the Hebrews has met with us; let us go, we pray, a three days' journey into the wilderness, and sacrifice to the Lord our God, lest he fall upon us with pestilence or with the sword" (Exod. 5:1, 3). Moses and Aaron are not lying; in its deepest meaning, the "land" toward which the people are going is in fact marked out by the feast or sacrifice to the living God, by true worship. On hearing the testimony of Moses and Aaron, backed up by miraculous signs, the people of Israel believe "that the Lord had visited the people of Israel and that he had seen their affliction, [and] they bowed their heads and worshiped" (Exod. 4:31).

Nonetheless, the people still have weak faith. Frequently they complain against Moses and Aaron, and doubt that God intends to deliver them. Before the plagues, we find that the people of Israel "did not listen to Moses, because of their broken spirit and their cruel bondage" (Exod. 6:9). God nonetheless remains steadfast in his promise to the people of Israel that "I will take you for my people, and I will be your God; and you shall know that I am the Lord your God" (Exod. 6:7). A relatively undeveloped aspect of the covenant with Abraham here comes to the fore. Just as Abraham had interceded for Sodom and Gomorrah, so Moses becomes the intercessor or mediator between the people and God.[15] This intercession or mediation always is a trial. Moses often makes remarks such as, "O Lord, why hast thou done evil to this people? Why didst thou ever send me?" (Exod. 5:22). In his covenantal path by which he intends to create anew holy people who dwell in and with him, God increasingly reveals that this holiness of the whole people will be achieved through the trials of a mediator who suffers for and intercedes for the people.

Such mediation is signified ever more profoundly by the plagues, culminating in the tenth plague, which finally convinces Pharaoh to free the people from Egyptian slavery and allow them to go worship God. The ninth plague had signified, in a way similar to the chaos of the flood, the depths of the disorder and idolatry that plague Egypt: "there was thick

15. See Levenson, *Sinai and Zion*, 25; von Balthasar, *Theology: The Old Covenant*, 189–190.

darkness in all the land of Egypt three days," but there was light where the people of Israel dwelt (Exod. 10:22–23). This physical and spiritual darkness, suggestive of the condition of humankind after the Fall, is of course not efficacious in persuading Pharaoh to let the people go, since Pharaoh's condition of idolatrous spiritual darkness is precisely what prevents him from hearing God's word. The tenth plague, then, enacts the ultimate fruit of humankind's sinful condition: death. God promises, "About midnight I will go forth in the midst of Egypt; and all the first-born in the land of Egypt shall die, from the first-born of Pharaoh who sits upon his throne, even to the first-born of the maidservant who is behind the mill; and all the first-born of the cattle. And there shall be a great cry throughout all the land of Egypt, such as there has never been, nor ever shall be again" (Exod. 11:4–6). This plague, however, will not touch the people of Israel. Just as they experienced "light"—the presence of God—when the Egyptians dwelt in deep darkness, so likewise they will not undergo death.

Not dwelling with God (idolatrous land) and not being righteous (sinful people), the Egyptians experience in full the consequences of original sin, while the people of Israel are spared, signifying their part in God's plan to re-create holy land/holy people. They are not, however, spared because of their own righteousness in contrast to the Egyptians' wickedness. On the contrary, just like the sons of Jacob, the people of Israel are afflicted with the same sinful hardness of heart that afflicts all humankind. Instead, God spares them because of their participation in a covenantal ritual, the "Lord's passover" (Exod. 12:11). He commands them to slaughter a lamb, one for each household, and to eat it "with unleavened bread and bitter herbs" with "your loins girded, your sandals on your feet, and your staff in your hand; and you shall eat it in haste" (Exod. 12:8, 11). Each household is to take some of the blood of the sacrificial lamb and mark their doorposts and lintel with the blood. God says, "The blood shall be a sign for you, upon the houses where you are; and when I see the blood, I will pass over you, and no plague shall fall upon you to destroy you, when I smite the land of Egypt" (Exod. 12:13).

As this ritual indicates, the distinction between the Egyptians, who are mired in the idolatrous darkness of sin and death, and the Israelites is signified by the Israelites' participation in the saving blood of the sacrificial lamb. They are prepared to journey to the holy land, and the way by which they will become a holy people able to dwell with God in this "land" is through their sharing in the sacrificial blood, the blood of the covenant. The theme of mediation between the Israelites and God, a theme present in the figure of Moses, is thus augmented by the symbolism of a mediatorial sacrificial lamb by whose blood the

Israelites are set apart from the injustice of the idolatrous Egyptians. God commands the people of Israel to celebrate this passover ritual "throughout your generations . . . for ever" (Exod. 12:14). The people are now set apart for the Lord by two covenant rituals, circumcision and passover (Exod. 12:48).

After the tenth plague, God leads the people out of Egypt: "And the Lord went before them by day in a pillar of cloud to lead them along the way, and by night in a pillar of fire to give them light, that they might travel by day and by night" (Exod. 13:21). They are not yet, however, a holy people. Thus when Pharaoh chases them, they immediately berate Moses, "Is it because there are no graves in Egypt that you have taken us away to die in the wilderness? What have you done to us, in bringing us out of Egypt? Is not this what we said to you in Egypt, 'Let us alone and let us serve the Egyptians'?" (Exod. 14:11–12). In his mediatorial role, Moses responds that God will accomplish the freeing of his people from slavery to sin in Egypt; indeed, it is only God who can draw man away from sin and idolatry. Moses encourages them, "Fear not, stand firm, and see the salvation of the Lord, which he will work for you today. . . . The Lord will fight for you, and you have only to be still" (Exod. 14:13–14). God accomplishes this work by means of the miraculous crossing of the Red Sea, or the Sea of Reeds. In a celebration led by Moses' sister Miriam, the people rejoice in God's plan that is leading them toward holy land: "Thou wilt bring them in, and plant them on thy own mountain, the place, O Lord, which thou hast made for thy abode, thy sanctuary, O Lord, which thy hands have established" (Exod. 15:17).[16]

Yet, the people cannot turn toward God to dwell with him, unless God's power creates them anew. For the time being, they remain a sinful people. On the journey toward the promised land, toward the fulfillment of the covenant with Abraham, the people of Israel keep "murmuring" or grumbling against God. First, they complain because they have no water; God then provides them, through the mediation of Moses, with sweet water (Exod. 15:25). God here proclaims himself "the Lord, your healer" (Exod. 15:26). Next, they complain because they have no food: "Would that we had died by the hand of the Lord in the land of Egypt, when we sat by the fleshpots and ate bread to the full; for you have brought us out into this wilderness to kill this whole assembly with hunger" (Exod. 16:3). For the next forty years, while they are in the wilderness, God provides them with food from heaven, manna (Exod. 16:35). It is this food that sustains them on their journey through the

16. Cf. Brevard S. Childs, *The Book of Exodus: A Critical, Theological Commentary* (Philadelphia: Westminster Press, 1974), 230–239, 248–253.

wilderness to the promised land. Clearly, this healing water and bread from heaven, nourishing the people of God on their way to the land where they will dwell fully with God, signify something more than mere material food and water; indeed they symbolize God's revelation and presence as Israel's Redeemer.[17]

Divine Law and Divine Glory

The theme of "holy land," dwelling with God in sacrificial worship and relying in faith (through the mediator) upon his healing water and food from heaven for nourishment, powerfully shapes this part of the biblical narrative, as it will the New Testament as well. The Israelites are journeying by means of God's assistance toward the promised land. Yet, they are still sinful and still regularly complain bitterly against God, and so it might seem that the goal of "holy people" has been forgotten. In fact, however, God is about to draw them decisively toward holiness. He does this by leading the whole people to Mount Sinai/Horeb, where earlier he had revealed himself to Moses in the burning bush. Once they have encamped at the base of Mount Sinai, Moses climbs the mountain, and God gives him these words to speak to the people: "You have seen what I did to the Egyptians, and how I bore you on eagles' wings and brought you to myself. Now therefore, if you will obey my voice and keep my covenant, you shall be my own possession among all peoples; for all the earth is mine, and you shall be to me a kingdom of priests and a holy nation" (Exod. 19:4–6). The goal of Abraham's covenant is not ultimately geopolitical, but rather that Israel might become "a kingdom of priests and a holy nation"; and we recall from Abraham's covenant that the purpose of this holy people dwelling with God in priestly fashion, through sacrificial worship (holy land), is to bear blessing to all humankind.[18]

When Moses reports God's words to the people, they respond, "All that the Lord has spoken we will do" (Exod. 19:8). God then commands that the people consecrate themselves and wash their clothes (symbolizing inner purity), and "on the third day the Lord will come down upon Mount Sinai in the sight of all the people" (Exod. 19:11). On the morning of the third day, thunder, lightning, and a thick cloud indicate God's glorious presence on Mount Sinai; and this is followed by a trumpet blast, smoke, and fire upon the mountain. God's glorious holiness, depicted by this imagery, is entering into history. He calls Moses to the top of

17. Cf. Deut. 8:3, Amos 8:11, Neh. 9:13–15, Sir. 15:3, and elsewhere.
18. See Bailey Wells, *God's Holy People*, 27–57.

68

the mountain: Moses is once again in the role of mediator, because the people are not yet spiritually prepared to stand before God.

God then gives Moses a reflection of the divine glory, the divine holiness: the ten commandments. We are not accustomed to think of the glory of the Law; commandments generally seem mundane or simply burdensome to us.[19] Nonetheless, the only way that human beings, as the image of God, share in his glory is by sharing in his holiness, his truth and goodness. The ten commandments, also known as the Decalogue, are therefore paths of glory. The first three, or the first tablet, depict our holiness in relationship to God: in order to dwell with him, we must utterly renounce idolatry, avoid blasphemy, and worship him in accord with his due (the sabbath day, God's "rest"). The remaining seven, or the second tablet, depict our holiness in relationship to each other: honor our parents, do not kill, do not commit adultery, do not steal, do not lie, do not desire your neighbor's wife, do not desire your neighbor's goods (Exod. 20). These ten fundamental precepts describe the glorious pattern of holy people who are fit to dwell with God in holy land. We sometimes think that holiness is dull, but true holiness in a person is glorious—a resplendent and harmonious sharing in God's wisdom, goodness, and justice.

In the covenant with Abraham, God had promised Abraham land and descendants. Having given Moses the task of leading Abraham's descendants to the promised land, God has begun to shape Abraham's descendants into a "kingdom of priests and a holy nation" by giving them a Law, the ten commandments, that depicts the fundamental contours of human holiness. God also now gives the people other laws (Exod. 21–23) regulating economic, political, and cultic life in order to form this people, which otherwise could simply be a rabble, into a unity. In establishing them as a unified people, God continues his work of setting them apart from the idolatrous nations. The covenant with Moses, who is charged with leading the people into the land promised to Abraham, thus prepares the people to be holy and to dwell with God as a unified people with a unified worship.

In the Law, we find the pattern for "holy people"; the next step is for the Law to be ratified liturgically (holy land). God invites Moses, Aaron, Nadab, Abihu, and "seventy of the elders of Israel," representing the full community, to ascend the mountain and worship in his presence. Before doing so, Moses arranges for the entire people to ratify the Law and the covenant liturgically. After building an altar and presenting God with burnt offerings and peace offerings of sacrificial oxen, "Moses took half

19. See Levenson, *Sinai and Zion*, 42–50; von Balthasar, *Theology: The Old Covenant*, 31–73.

69

the blood and put it in basins, and half of the blood he threw against the altar. Then he took the book of the covenant, and read it in the hearing of the people; and they said, 'All that the Lord has spoken we will do, and we will be obedient'" (Exod. 24:7). The people agree to follow the Law: this obedience now becomes their covenantal obligation to God. They have entered into a structured relationship with God, not merely as individuals but as the people of God. Moses seals the covenant with the blood, which represents life-giving sacrifice to God: "And Moses took the blood and threw it upon the people, and said, 'Behold the blood of the covenant which the Lord has made with you in accordance with all these words'" (Exod. 24:8). The covenant is sealed by the sacrificial blood because the sacrifice represents what is owed in justice to God the Creator. Given the magnitude of his gifts of existence and blessing, we owe him all that we are, and even then the debt would not be repaid.

As with the sacrificial lamb of the Passover, so here too we find that dwelling with God, true worship of him, is mediated by sacrifice. Human selfishness and pride must be replaced with sacrificial self-giving to God in love, if we are truly to dwell in and with him. After Moses has sealed the covenant with the people, he ascends the mountain with Aaron, Nadab, Abihu, and the seventy elders. What follows is a depiction of the fruit of sacrificial self-giving to God, a foretaste of the true "holy land." The awesomeness, in the traditional sense of the word, of their experience on Mount Sinai is difficult to convey. Their encounter with God on the mountain finds expression in two images of profound intimacy: they see him, and they share a meal with him. Note that the one is not separated from the other: "they beheld God, and ate and drank" (Exod. 24:11).[20] From within this experience of a (sacrificial) meal, they "beheld" God.

This seeing constitutes an intellectual seeing, a knowing.[21] The inspired author uses imagery of precious jewels, indicating light, harmony, and brilliancy. We read that "they saw the God of Israel; and there was under his feet as it were a pavement of sapphire stone, like the very heaven for clearness" (Exod. 24:10). Furthermore, beholding God in and through the (sacrificial) meal leads Moses even further into the divine life. God draws Moses up higher: "Then Moses went up on the mountain, and the cloud covered the mountain. The glory of the Lord settled on Mount Sinai, and the cloud covered it for six days; and on the seventh day he called to Moses out of the midst of the cloud" (Exod. 24:16). Since we

20. For further discussion of the importance in the Old Testament of this experience of Israel's elders, see Walter Brueggemann, *Theology of the Old Testament: Testimony, Dispute, Advocacy* (Minneapolis: Fortress, 1997), 428–429.

21. Ibid.

know already that God's covenantal work intends to create humankind anew, to restore harmonious communion, we can see that the pattern of seven days indicates that God is accomplishing a new creation. More than this, however, the fact that Moses enters fully into God's presence, into the very depths of the mystery of God (revealed to Moses already as "I am"), on the seventh day means that Moses enters into the divine sabbath, the divine rest or perfect peace.[22] The ultimate goal of the sacrificial meal is to draw humankind into the divine peace. This endpoint, the pinnacle of the mountain of divine presence, means nothing less than that the "new creation" of humankind will not merely restore harmony and communion, but will grant humankind, by God's wondrous mercy and love, a supreme eternal sharing in God's own life.

Moses, in his mediatorial role, experiences a foretaste of this ultimate destiny. The Israelites, at the foot of the mountain, recognize that Moses is mystically suffering, or undergoing, the fire of God's presence. This fire separates Moses from worldly things: "Now the appearance of the glory of the Lord was like a devouring fire on the top of the mountain in the sight of the people of Israel. And Moses entered the cloud, and went up on the mountain. And Moses was on the mountain forty days and forty nights" (Exod. 24:17–18). On the mountain the Lord speaks to Moses and directs him to build the ark of the covenant and a tabernacle for the ark (Exodus 25–26), as well as an altar, a consecrated priesthood with instructions for offering the various kinds of sacrifices, and sabbath observance (Exodus 27–31). The earthly tabernacle is a copy of the true tabernacle of heaven. The Lord said to Moses, "And let them make me a sanctuary, that I may dwell in their midst. According to all that I show you concerning the pattern of the tabernacle, and of all its furniture, so shall you make it" (Exod. 25:8–9). The Law given in Exodus 20–23, which is directed to constituting a holy people, is now united in Exodus 25–31 with the cultic dwelling-place (the ark and the tabernacle) and the sacrificial priesthood that together will mediate God's presence in and with his people—in other words, it will manifest the reality of holy land, God dwelling in and with his people.

Exodus 24, therefore, serves as the great hinge between the chapters devoted to the Law and the chapters devoted to the liturgy: Moses' entering into the divine sabbath, the mysterious depths of God, through the sacrificial meal, exposes the unity of "holy people" and "holy land." It is the person who is made holy by sharing in the covenantal sacrifice who is fit, by God's mercy, to dwell eternally in the light of the divine life. In short, God leads the people of Israel out of Egyptian slavery to

22. Cf. Abraham Joshua Heschel, *The Sabbath* (New York: Farrar, Straus and Giroux, 1951).

the promised land not merely to give them earthly blessing but to enable them to share in his eternal sabbath, his eternal peace, as a new creation or holy people. This is why keeping the sabbath takes on such crucial importance: "You shall keep my sabbaths, for this is a sign between me and you throughout your generations, that you may know that I, the Lord, sanctify you. You shall keep the sabbath, because it is holy for you; every one who profanes it shall be put to death; whoever does any work on it, that soul shall be cut off from among his people" (Exod. 31:13–14). In this new creation, God is sanctifying the people; God is doing the great work. Against human pride, which continually seeks to grasp divine power, God gives Israel a Law that places God's work, not man's, at the center.

The Persistence of Idolatry

Yet, once again, as with the earlier covenants, the moment of covenantal consummation and blessing is also the moment of violation and sin.[23] On the very wedding night of her marriage to God, Israel commits adultery. We noted earlier that God's revelation to Moses was directed against human idolatry. At the very moment of receiving the covenant, however, the people fall back into the darkest abyss of idolatry: "When the people saw that Moses delayed to come down from the mountain, the people gathered themselves together to Aaron, and said to him, 'Up, make us gods, who shall go before us; as for this Moses, the man who brought us up out of the land of Egypt, we do not know what has become of him" (Exod. 32:1). Breaking all their earlier promises of fidelity, the people commission Aaron the priest of the covenant, and he willingly and expertly makes for them a golden calf, similar to the images of the gods worshipped in Egypt. The true God is forgotten; a false god receives the credit for God's work of salvation. The leaders of the people, fresh from beholding God and sharing a meal in his presence, proclaim, "These are your gods, O Israel, who brought you up out of the land of Egypt!" (Exod. 32:4).

Aaron then organizes sacrificial worship to the god imaged by the calf. Having journeyed from Egypt to Mount Sinai, they now return in spirit to Egypt and enter once again into idolatrous slavery. Aaron joyfully announces a priestly sacrifice to the image of the calf, whom Aaron identifies as God: "'Tomorrow shall be a feast to the Lord.' And they rose up early on the morrow, and offered burnt offerings and brought

---

23. We owe this insight to Gary Anderson.

72

peace offerings; and the people sat down to eat and drink, and rose up to play" (Exod. 32:6). This celebration mirrors, in a hideous mockery, the directives that God has given Moses for covenantal sacrifice. Descending from the mountain with the tablets of the Law, Moses and Joshua hear the noise from the people. Joshua thinks that the sound is war, which in fact it is: war against God. A civil war among the people breaks out, with Moses and the Levites on the side of God, and three thousand Israelites are killed; in addition to this punishment, a plague breaks out. The violence and disharmony that have marked the human condition since Adam and Eve arise in full force, despite the glorious manifestation of God and his Law, and despite the people's promise of fidelity.

Although the Mosaic covenant develops and deepens the covenants with Noah and Abraham, the Mosaic covenant thus does not accomplish God's ultimate goal of reconciling humankind to himself. Rather, the Mosaic covenant more profoundly reveals the inner disharmony, the injustice and alienation from God, at the heart of each human being. But the Mosaic covenant also signals the way forward. To the Abrahamic elements of land and descendants, God adds the promise of supreme union with God through participation in a sacrificial meal and through a mediator. God outlines the path of holiness through the Law, and God makes his presence more manifest in the ark of the covenant and the sacrificial liturgy. He is moving closer and closer to his people, even though the people remain plagued by the disharmony, violence, and idolatry of the Fall.

Moses the Mediator

After Sinai and the golden calf, Moses' mediatorial role becomes increasingly priestly as well as kingly, underscoring the reality that the promised land is not merely geopolitical but spiritual. He no longer functions primarily as the military leader and ruler; while remaining in those roles, he now appears fully as the priestly mediator of God's glory. In light of the people's idolatrous attempt to conflate God with a creature and draw him down to the creaturely level, God's presence appears in a "tent of meeting" set up outside the Israelite camp as they are journeying (Exod. 33). Moses now mediates the people's worship: "Whenever Moses went out to the tent, all the people rose up, and every man stood at his tent door, and looked after Moses, until he had gone into the tent. When Moses entered the tent, the pillar of cloud would descend and stand at the door of the tent, and the Lord would speak with Moses. And when all the people saw the pillar of cloud standing at the door of the tent, all the people would rise up and worship, every man at his tent door" (Exod. 33:8–10). Israel's worship becomes a participation in Moses' worship. God now speaks to Moses "face to face, as a man speaks to his friend" (Exod. 33:11).[24] Taught by God, Moses is presented as the model of a holy man, through whom the entire people gains access to God's favor and friendship, God's communion of love.

In this role of priestly mediator, Moses intercedes on behalf of the people and God promises Moses that God's "presence" will go with the people on their journey to the land (Exod. 33:12–17). Having received this promise, Moses begs to see God's "glory," and God grants that Moses may see his "back," but not his "face" (Exod. 33:18–23).[25] God once again appears to Moses on Mount Sinai, this time proclaiming as his "name" his attributes of steadfast love, mercy, and justice (Exodus 34). Moses receives the covenant anew. Indeed, God promises, "Behold, I make a covenant. Before all your people I will do marvels, such as have not been wrought in all the earth or in any nation; and all the people among whom you are shall see the work of the Lord; for it is a terrible thing that I will do with you" (Exod. 34:10). Descending once again from Mount Sinai with the tablets of the ten commandments, Moses' face shines with a reflection of God's glory, and Moses has to veil himself from the people of Israel (Exod. 34:35).[26] His priestly mediation has risen to the level of participation in God's light and life, the level of glorious "new creation."

Moses then directs the manufacture of the ark, priestly vestments, and tabernacle with its altar and laver (Exodus 35–40). In the future, God's presence will be mediated through his dwelling in the ark and tabernacle, and will be participated in by means of the priestly sacrificial liturgy.[27] After Moses has finished this work, we read that "the cloud covered the tent of meeting, and the glory of the Lord filled the tabernacle. And Moses was not able to enter the tent of meeting, because the cloud abode upon it, and the glory of the Lord filled the tabernacle" (Exod.

24. On human and divine friendship, see St. Augustine's *Confessions* and St. Aelred of Rievaulx, *Spiritual Friendship*, trans. Mary Eugenia Laker, S.S.N.D. (Kalamazoo, MI: Cistercian Publications, 1977); see also Donald X. Burt, O.S.A., *Friendship and Society: An Introduction to Augustine's Practical Philosophy* (Grand Rapids: Eerdmans, 1999).

25. The Book of Exodus implicitly indicates that the Mosaic covenant has limitations and points ahead to something greater. Even Moses, with whom God communes directly, cannot see God's glory/face. But through the Incarnation of the Word we behold God's glory (John 1:14; John contrasts the two covenants in verse 17). A Christian reading of the Old Testament should bring out how the Old Testament itself testifies to its own incompleteness. A "fulfillment" interpretation, on this reading, is the interpretation for which the Old Testament itself calls.

26. Cf. von Balthasar, *Theology: The Old Covenant*, 38–39.

27. On the ark and tabernacle, see Berman, *The Temple*, 35–56.

40:34–35). Here we have another foretaste of the holy land, which will be perfect worship accomplished by God's indwelling.

Leviticus, Numbers, Deuteronomy

The remainder of the Torah—Leviticus, Numbers, and Deuteronomy—extends and repeats the themes of the Mosaic covenant that we have found in Exodus.[28] As we will see, Leviticus contains Israel's liturgical manual for divine worship in the tabernacle and eventually the temple. Similarly, Deuteronomy highlights the Law through Moses' discourses or sermons, and thus provides directions for homiletics or preaching about the Exodus experience. Numbers, for its part, shows that both the liturgy and the homily are greatly needed! Let us briefly examine each book.

In painstaking detail, Leviticus describes the laws regulating the sacrificial offerings required of the people (especially the various sin-offerings, both for individual sin and for communal sin), ceremonial purity, economic and social justice, priestly service and vows, and the liturgical feasts and festivals (Leviticus 23; cf. Numbers 28–29).[29] These detailed laws correspond to every aspect of Israel's life and, in a way similar to the seven sacraments of the Church, make clear that Israel's entire existence is liturgical, that is, ordered to union with God through holy worship. In his mediatorial role, Moses inaugurates the priestly service of Israel; it is Moses who sacrifices the first bull for a sin offering (Lev. 8:15), the first ram for a burnt offering, and the ram of priestly ordination for Aaron and his sons. One might hope that the installation of a permanent priesthood, devoted to the worship of God, would lead to the eradication of sin.[30] However, Israel soon recognizes that sin will continue to infect her communal life. For one thing, even her priests are sinners. After their ordination, Aaron and his sons take on the priestly duties, but two of Aaron's four sons, Nadab and Abihu, deviate from the prescribed rite and are consumed by fire (Lev. 10:2): the rites are God-given, and only such rites honor God.

On the Day of Atonement, therefore, this day each year, Aaron has to sacrifice a bull for a sin offering for himself, along with a goat for a

---

28. See Bailey Wells, *God's Holy People*, 58–97.

29. For further discussion of Leviticus, see, for example, Mary Douglas, *Leviticus as Literature* (Oxford: Oxford University Press, 1999); Gordon Wenham, *The Book of Leviticus* (Grand Rapids: Eerdmans, 1979); Jacob Milgrom, *Leviticus: A New Translation with Introduction and Commentary*, 3 vols. (New York: Doubleday, 1991–2001).

30. Cf. Bailey Wells, "'Holy to YHWH': Priesthood according to Torah," in *God's Holy People*, 98–129.

sin offering for the sins of the whole people. As a hopeful sign that one day the people might be entirely cleansed from sin, God commands that on the Day of Atonement another goat will be sent forth out of the camp, "and shall bear all their iniquities upon him to a solitary land" (Lev. 16:22). Everything in Leviticus aims at this hoped-for communal holiness. The people are to become once again truly the image of God: "Say to all the congregation of the people of Israel, You shall be holy; for I the Lord your God am holy" (Lev. 19:2). Ethics (holy people) cannot be separated from sacrificial worship (holy land). Dwelling with God, which is manifested and made possible by worship, requires holiness of life.

Numbers picks up where the book of Exodus left off, and continues the description of Israel's journey toward the promised land. The journey of the twelve tribes, each of which is expected to contribute to the tabernacle, toward the land is measured by whether the people truly trust in the power of God's blessing.[31] Having set apart the tribe of Levi to serve as priests, God provides Aaron and his sons with a formal blessing to say over the people of Israel, "The Lord bless you and keep you: The Lord make his face to shine upon you, and be gracious to you: The Lord lift up his countenance upon you, and give you peace" (Num. 6:23–26). However, the murmuring and complaining against God that we found in the book of Exodus continues and even increases. Focused upon worldly things rather than upon the blessing of God, the people recall Egypt, and idolatry, nostalgically: "O that we had meat to eat! We remember the fish we ate in Egypt for nothing, the cucumbers, the melons, the leeks, the onions, and the garlic; but now our strength is dried up, and there is nothing at all but this manna" (Num. 11:4–6). They find meat in the form of quails, but it brings on the plague as divine punishment for their lack of trust; similar episodes of lack of trust happen throughout the journey (cf. Num. 21:4–7).

Not surprisingly, then, a series of uprisings against Moses occurs. First Aaron and Miriam, Moses' own siblings, speak out against him (Num. 12); later all the men sent out to reconnoiter the promised land, with the exception of Caleb and Joshua, declare that it will be impossible to conquer it, and for this lack of trust all these men die by the plague and the people are routed by the Amalekites and Canaanites in battle (Num. 13–14). It is for this rebellion that Israel is punished with forty years of wandering in the wilderness. Lastly Korah and Abiram challenge Moses' authority by declaring, "You have gone too far! For all the congregation are holy, every one of them, and the Lord is among them; why then do

31. On "Doxology and Trust," see chapter 5 of Patrick D. Miller, *They Cried to the Lord: The Form and Theology of Biblical Prayer* (Minneapolis: Fortress, 1994).

you exalt yourselves above the assembly of the Lord?" (Num. 16:3–4). This last rebellion results in the deaths of Korah and Abiram, followed by a plague that kills almost fifteen thousand people.

This (idolatrous) lack of trust in God affects the hearts of even Moses and Aaron. In front of the people, Moses boasts in his power of bringing water out of rock, rather than giving the honor to God who caused the miracle. For this act of prideful arrogance, God punishes Moses and Aaron by not allowing them to bring the people into the promised land (Num. 20:10–12). Although God enables Moses to accomplish a series of military conquests as he approaches the promised land, even these conquests are marred by the fact that the people of Israel begin to have sexual relations with the idolatrous peoples of the land, who worship Baal (cf. Num. 25). Moses nonetheless appears as God's instrument of justice, executing divine punishment for sins upon the native inhabitants of the land (Num. 31).

The dissension and violence that beset the people of Israel belies the hope of dwelling with God that God has set forth as the reason for his covenantal gift of descendants and land to Abraham. Despite the Law and liturgical sacrifices, the people are not holy; even Moses, the book of Numbers makes clear, is not holy. As we might expect, therefore, the centerpiece of Moses' homily in Deuteronomy, like the centerpiece of the liturgical cycle described in Leviticus, is the command to be holy. Moses urges, "Justice, and only justice, you shall follow, that you may live and inherit the land which the Lord your God gives you" (Deut. 16:20). This "land" is dwelling with God as a holy people, although it is also a physical land. Moses says, "And now, Israel, what does the Lord your God require of you, but to fear the Lord your God, to walk in all his ways, to love him, to serve the Lord your God with all your heart and soul, and to keep the commandments and statutes of the Lord, which I command to you this day for your good?" (Deut. 10:12–13). The holy God, moreover, manifests himself as love. Moses reminds the people repeatedly that God has chosen Israel out of sheer love (Deut. 6:4–5; 7:7–8; 10:14–11:1). Israel's task is to learn how to imitate this love: "For you are a people holy to the Lord your God; the Lord your God has chosen you to be a people for his own possession" (Deut. 7:6). The people are to be a people of mercy; every seventh year, all debts are to go free (Deut. 15).[32] They are to be a people of humility, and for this reason they will continue to be disciplined by God as a father disciplines his son (Deut. 8:5).

---

32. Cf. Moshe Weinfeld, *Social Justice in Ancient Israel and in the Ancient Near East* (Jerusalem: Magnes Press, 1995); Bruce V. Malchow, *Social Justice in the Hebrew Bible* (Collegeville, MN: Liturgical Press, 1996).

Although Moses is not allowed to enter into the promised land, symbolizing the fact that he is not the final mediator nor his law the final law, he gives in the book of Deuteronomy reasons for great hope.[33] He foretells the unification of worship at one place that God will "choose, to make his name dwell there" (Deut. 12:11). Similarly, he foretells that God will approve the Israelites' future desire to have a king. Moses advises the people that "you may indeed set as king over you him whom the Lord your God will choose" (Deut. 17:15), although he warns that this king must follow and establish the Law in everything, and must not oppress the people by acquiring numerous warhorses, wives, and wealth. In addition to foretelling the temple and king, Moses relates God's promise, "I will raise up for them a prophet like you [Moses] from among their brethren; and I will put my words in his mouth, and he shall speak to them all that I command him. And whoever will not give heed to my words which he shall speak in my name, I myself will require it of him" (Deut. 18:18–19). Such a prophet will be greater than Moses, who is the greatest prophet known to the inspired author: "And there has not arisen a prophet since in Israel like Moses, whom the Lord knew face to face" (Deut. 34:10).

As the people prepare to enter the promised land, where the covenant will go into effect, Moses solemnly renews the Sinai covenant at Moab (Deut. 29). This covenant binds all generations, and makes the people of Israel to be God's people: "You stand this day all of you before the Lord your God . . . that you may enter into the sworn covenant of the Lord your God, which the Lord your God makes with you this day; that he may establish you this day as his people, and that he may be your God, as he promised you, and as he swore to your fathers, to Abraham, to Isaac, and to Jacob. Nor is it with you only that I make this sworn covenant, but with him who is not here with us this day as well as with him who stands here with us this day before the Lord our God" (Deut. 29:10–15). In renewing the covenant, Moses warns that a cycle of covenantal blessing and curse will come upon the people. When they are faithful to the Lord, they will be blessed, and when they lose trust in the Lord and instead trust in their own human resources (cf. Deut. 8:11–14), they will experience the curses that follow from abandoning the covenant. Ultimately, this curse will be exile, alienation from God and the land (Deut. 29:21–28). Such exile will be tantamount to starvation, since "[m]an does not live by bread alone, but man lives by everything that proceeds out of the mouth of God" (Deut. 8:3). Yet God, faithful to his covenant, will draw them back from exile and nourish them again with his word.

33. Cf. Dennis T. Olson, *Deuteronomy and the Death of Moses: A Theological Reading* (Minneapolis: Fortress, 1994).

78

The promise of a new prophet, and a temple and king, makes clear that the history of God's salvific covenants will not end with Moses, just as it did not end with Abraham. The covenant with Moses does not yet restore humankind to justice, although the contours of God's plan are becoming clearer. Just as God, through Moses, added new elements to enable us to understand what he was doing in promising Abraham land and descendants, so also God will add new elements to deepen our understanding of the Mosaic people of Israel, now shaped as God's people by the Law and by God's presence in the ark of the covenant and the liturgy of the tabernacle. Yet, even when the fullness of God's covenantal plan is revealed by Christ Jesus, Moses' words will continue to impel us to holiness and conversion. As Moses says, "I have set before you life and death, blessing and curse; therefore choose life, that you and your descendants may live, loving the Lord your God, obeying his voice, and cleaving to him; for that means life to you and length of days, that you may dwell in the land which the Lord swore to your fathers, to Abraham, to Isaac, and to Jacob, to give them" (Deut. 30:19–20).[34] Let us choose life.

34. As Murphy points out in commenting upon Deuteronomy 30, "Walking in 'life,' or living in the land, is being related to God. . . . The people are enjoined to inhabit the Good; 'doing the good' is the basic analogy for the activity of being God" (Murphy, *The Comedy of Revelation*, 86).

4

David

King and Temple

Since the present chapter culminates in the gift of a king and a temple, we might begin by asking, should any people, even a people in a precarious situation against foreign invaders as Israel was, want a king and temple? Are not kings generally oppressive, and temples often centers of corruption? As the fourth-century BC Greek philosopher Aristotle pointed out in his evaluation of monarchy, "[T]he many are more incorruptible than the few; they are like the greater quantity of water which is less easily corrupted than a little. The individual is liable to be overcome by anger or by some other passion, and then his judgement is necessarily perverted; but it is hardly to be supposed that a great number of persons would all get into a passion and go wrong at the same moment."[1] No one familiar with the history of kingship, including (as we will see) the biblical history of Israel's kingship, would romanticize monarchical rule. It would seem, too, that a temple built by the king would be simply the centralized locale of a state-mandated religion. Why then would God's tremendous mercy and love be displayed by the gift of a king and a temple?

---

1. Aristotle, *Politics*, trans. Benjamin Jowett (New York: Random House, 1943), 160 (Book III, ch. 15, 1286a.32–37).

The task of a king is to represent the people, and to establish justice and righteousness among the people; a temple instantiates God's presence in the land by forming the whole people in true worship. Ultimately, the king and the temple will be one in Christ Jesus. The representative of the people who makes the people righteous (the king) will be the presence of God dwelling in and with the people (the temple).

The Promise of Reconciliation

Let us return to the biblical narrative. The descendants of Abraham have now arrived at the border of the promised land. In this land, through the ark of the covenant and the sacrificial liturgy of the tabernacle, God will dwell with them. Second, God has given them a Law intended to form them in holiness, causing them to be not merely a people, but a holy people. In other words, the people of Israel are intended to be "a kingdom of priests, a holy nation" (Exod. 19:6). Is the Mosaic covenant, then, enough? Does God need to go further, or has God now put in place sufficient instruments to accomplish his plan of salvation? We have already seen that Moses, in the book of Deuteronomy, suggests that something more is to come, namely a king and a unification of worship, and beyond that a great prophet. But why should there be something more to come? Would not the Mosaic covenant suffice to achieve the justice, peace, and communion that God is working to establish?

The answer is twofold. First, the Mosaic covenant, as is clear from the start, cannot achieve interior justice in the people of Israel. The Law indicates the pattern of such justice, but it does not bring it about. Thus, the same people who at Sinai receive and accept the truth of the ten commandments, beginning with the first commandment against having gods other than God, are the ones who at the first opportunity build a golden calf and offer worship and sacrifice to it. Likewise the very priests who offer the sacrifices, who themselves sin against God; two of the four sons of Aaron are consumed by fire because they did not follow the decreed ritual. On the Day of Atonement the chief priest must offer a whole bull for his sins and those of his family, and merely a goat for the entire people.

The second reason follows from the first. Sinful human beings thwart the achievement of reconciliation. By all accounts, neither the Law nor the tabernacle and the sacrificial liturgy achieve their purpose. Yet both the Law and the tabernacle liturgy represent the harmony that God intends to bring about. It seems, therefore, that the path of reconciliation must first be represented by God before God accomplishes reconciliation efficaciously. Just as the Bible's depiction of Eden symbolically displayed the elements of the fourfold harmony, the loving communion between God and humankind, so after the first human beings turn away from God in pride, the pattern of communal "turning to God" must be displayed. The covenants with Israel display this pattern, the pattern of reconciliation. The goal is always the same: a perfect interior communion of wisdom and love between God and humankind, which will be reflected in a perfect, visible communion of wisdom and love between human beings gathered together in and with God.

What are the symbolic elements we have seen thus far? As regards "holy people," being a community of righteousness, we have seen the gathering of a people, the descendants of Abraham. They are to "walk before [God], and be blameless" (Gen. 17:1). From them will come blessing to all nations (cf. Gen. 12:1–3). Since fallen people can be neither holy nor a visible communion without a law, God has given them a Law that binds them together and recalls them to the principles of justice. They are to be marked by faith (Abraham's complete trust in God), by perseverance in the desire to know God (Jacob's wrestling, Moses' shining face), by circumcision, and by the feast of Passover.

As regards "holy land," dwelling with God in his glorious presence, we have seen God's presence to his people grow in nearness and permanence. God revealed himself as "three men" to Abraham; to Jacob he reveals that in the promised land a permanent ladder between heaven and earth will be covenantally established; to Moses, with whom he talks as a "friend," he reveals his infinite and unlimited identity "I am," source of all being. In addition to revealing more and more of himself, God comes closer to Israel through his manifestation of his glory on Mount Sinai, a glory which he makes present to Israel in a permanent way in the ark of the covenant and in the tabernacle. Recall how "the cloud covered the tent of meeting, and the glory of the Lord filled the tabernacle" (Exod. 40:34). Because dwelling with God means undertaking the inner sacrifice of selfish desires, God institutes the sacrificial liturgy as a path through which Israel might, in faith, dwell more closely with him. At the same time, by mighty acts and through the mediatorial role of Moses, God leads them toward the land promised to Abraham.

What are the elements yet to be added? At the time of David, God makes a covenant in which we find the promise of a sacred kingship and a temple in which God will dwell, both of which Moses foretells in Deuteronomy. Before describing these new aspects to the story of "holy people, holy land," however, let us follow the developments that lead from Moses to David.

83

Joshua and New Creation

At his death, Moses passes the baton of leadership of the people of Israel to Joshua. Joshua, whose name means "the Lord saves," then, is the one who leads the people into the promised land. The book of Joshua can be likened to the first creation account. Recall the solemnity and harmony conveyed by the first creation account in Genesis 1. Solemnity and harmony likewise characterize the book of Joshua, which, as the completion of the Exodus, is the story of new creation, new "holy land."

The opening chapters of the book of Joshua present Joshua as another Moses.[2] Calling upon Joshua to live and rule according to the Mosaic Law and to shoulder Moses' task of guiding the people into the promised land, God tells Joshua, "No man shall be able to stand before you all the days of your life; as I was with Moses, so I will be with you; I will not fail you or forsake you" (Josh. 1:5). The tribes agree to obey Joshua, and Joshua leads them across the Jordan. Just as Moses lifted up his rod to part the Sea of Reeds, so also Joshua follows the ark of the covenant after the Jordan River parts when the priests enter it, carrying the ark (Josh. 3:13–17).[3] After crossing over, Joshua directs the circumcision of the entire people and the celebration of the feast of the Passover (Josh. 5). These are the two marks central to the people's liturgical participation in God's covenantal presence. Immediately thereafter the manna ceases, and the people from that time forward eat of the fruits of the land.

Cementing the impression that God is present in and with the people in the land, Joshua then meets the angelic "commander of the army of the Lord," who tells him the same thing that God had said to Moses at the burning bush on Mount Sinai, "Put off your shoes from your feet; for the place where you stand is holy" (Josh. 5:15). This holy land, the land of Canaan on the outskirts of Jericho, is thus none other than the extension of Mount Sinai, which constitutes the paradigmatic instance of spiritual holy land, God dwelling with man. Joshua is preparing to fight his first battle of conquest, laying the people of Israel's claim to the promised land, and God's power is going to accomplish the conquest for him.

2. For further discussion of the shaping of the texts of the Bible, with reference to Joshua 3, see Fishbane, *Biblical Interpretation in Ancient Israel*, 358ff. On Joshua as a new Moses, see Dale C. Allison, *The New Moses: A Matthean Typology* (Minneapolis: Fortress, 1993), 23–28.

3. One could also compare these miraculous parting of the waters (understood as harbingers of new creation) to God's parting of the waters in creation (Gen. 1:6–9).

The event that follows decisively identifies the land not merely geo-graphically but primarily as holy land, a place of spiritual new creation. While the people of Israel are laying siege to Jericho, God comes to Joshua and says, "See, I have given into your hand Jericho, with its king and mighty men of valor. You shall march around the city, all the men of war going around the city once. Thus shall you do for six days. And seven priests shall bear seven trumpets of rams' horns before the ark; and on the seventh day you shall march around the city seven times, the priests blowing the trumpets. And when they make a long blast with the ram's horn, as soon as you hear the sound of the trumpet, then all the people shall shout with a great shout; and the wall of the city will fall down flat, and the people shall go up every man straight before him" (Josh. 6:2–5). The symbolism of the numbers six and seven bears crucial significance. Just as God created man and thereby completed the labor of creation on the sixth "day," and rested on the seventh "day," so now for six days the Israelite soldiers are to work. Again, just as God created by his spiri-tual word, not by physical labor, so also the Israelite soldiers are to fight not by violence, but simply by solemnly circling the city in harmonious liturgical procession, following the ark of the covenant and the seven priests bearing the seven trumpets (Josh. 6:12). The "new creation" is being prepared.

Unlike the first creation, the new creation will be the perfect experi-ence of "holy land" or union with God, and therefore will not end at the natural level on the sixth day. Rather, the new creation will mean that human beings both emerge victorious over their sins (the "walls" that impede them from conquering the promised land), and attain a supernatural level of perfection by sharing in God's own life. In the new creation, human beings will share fully in the seventh day, in the full-ness of the harmonious divine life. In short, the repeated deployment of the perfect number seven—seven priests, seven trumpets, circling the city seven times—indicates the fullness, the perfection, of Israel's communion with God.

On the seventh day, after the seventh circle and the blowing of the seventh trumpet blast, the wall falls down flat and the people go "straight forward," unimpeded, to enter the first city of the promised land. As a scene of new creation, this account of conquest recalls Moses' experi-ence at the top of Mount Sinai in Exodus 24. Just as in the book of Joshua the people are circumcised and celebrate the Passover before conquering Jericho, so in Exodus 24 the people had been purified and the elders had shared a liturgical meal in the presence of God. Moses then ascended to the top of the mountain, where he spent six days in the divine cloud (the Holy Spirit, at work in new creation) before God called him to himself on the seventh day. In that scene of new creation,

85

of supernatural union with God on the holy land of Mount Sinai, Moses had received anew the Law with which to make a holy people. In the book of Joshua, it is not just Moses, but rather now the whole people who, obedient to the Law, are called by God into the holy land on the seventh day.[4]

Those who do not share in this covenantal relationship with God remain trapped in their sins. To remain in one's sins, as we have seen, is to remain alienated from God and on a path to well-deserved punishment and destruction. In the book of Joshua, this situation is depicted through the plight of those conquered by the people of God. Recall that this conquest is the divine punishment of sin: God foretold to Abraham that his descendants would not occupy the land for four hundred years, "for the iniquity of the Amorites is not yet complete" (Gen. 15:16).[5] We have already

4. Cf. Richard D. Nelson, *Joshua: A Commentary* (Louisville: Westminster John Knox Press, 1997), 94.

5. Divinely sanctioned warfare is one of the greatest stumbling-blocks for modern readers of the Old Testament. Throughout our chapters, we note that sin itself calls down the just punishment of death. By rebelling in pride against the Giver of life and being, human beings have turned away from the source of life and love, and have turned toward death and pride. The punishment of turning away from God is death.

The Old Testament teaches in the strongest possible terms that all of us, by divine justice, are condemned by our sins to death; in the order of Providence this death may come about through the various means that characterize our intrinsic disharmony, including war, which at times in the Bible functions as the execution of the just penalty of death that we all deserve. Until we understand the gravity of our sins and that in our pride we really do deserve death—and this is the purpose of the Old Testament's pedagogy—we cannot understand what St. Paul means when he cries out, "Wretched man that I am! Who will deliver me from this body of death? Thanks be to God through Jesus Christ our Lord! . . . There is therefore now no condemnation for those who are in Christ Jesus. For the law of the Spirit of life in Christ Jesus has set me free from the law of sin and death. For God has done what the law, weakened by the flesh, could not do: sending his own Son in the likeness of sinful flesh and for sin, he condemned sin in the flesh, in order that the just requirement of the law might be fulfilled in us, who walk not according to the flesh but according to the Spirit" (Rom. 7:24–8:4).

One should also note that in the Old Testament predication to God of emotion, intention, will, and intellection is at times metaphorical rather than analogical predication. Proper interpretation of such predication requires attention to the genre and historical context of the writing, as well as sufficient metaphysical erudition to avoid interpreting language about the transcendent God in such a way that "God" becomes a creaturely idol. For example, we read both that "the Lord was sorry that he had made man on the earth, and it grieved him to his heart" (Gen. 6:6) and God is "the Father of lights with whom there is no variation of shadow due to change" (Jas. 1:17). Either God changes his mind and grieves in a human way (and thus is a creaturely idol), or he does not change; if the latter, then the former predication to God of repentance and grief has to be understood as metaphorical, in accord with the genre of writing. The danger of a false literalism in divine predication is similarly present in the interpretation of such passages as "Thus says the Lord of hosts, 'I will punish what Amalek did to Israel in opposing them on the

seen, in the Flood, Babel, and Sodom and Gomorrah, what it means for iniquity or sin to be "complete." Sin breaks down community by corrupting and weakening it from within: when a community has reached a certain degree of corruption, it is due, as it were, for destruction because of its inner weakness and the violent inner forces that are tearing it apart from within. The people of Israel, in conquering the land, are the instruments of this punishment of destruction: "they utterly destroyed all in the city" of Jericho (Josh. 6:21). The point is that, in fact, only sharing, through holiness, in God's saving covenant spares human beings from the death and destruction that comes from sin, from alienation from God.

Yet, the people of Israel are still not holy people. Just as when Moses received the commandments on Mount Sinai, only to come down the mountain to find rank idolatry thoroughly consuming the people, so also after the great triumph at Jericho, symbolic of holy people dwelling in holy land, Joshua finds his triumphant army breaking the covenant and returning to sinful ways. When this happens, other nations are the instruments of the punishment of Israel. After the victory at Jericho, some of the Israelite soldiers take forbidden booty, which was all devoted to the Lord, and the people of the small city of Ai rout the Israelite army (Joshua 7).[6] Completely forgetting God's power and their trust in him, "the hearts of the people melted, and became as water" (Josh. 7:5). Joshua tears his clothes and prostrates himself in prayer before the ark of the covenant, where God dwells liturgically with his people ("holy land").

In answer to Joshua's intercessory prayer for the people, God says, "Israel has sinned; they have transgressed my covenant which I commanded them; they have taken some of the devoted things; they have

---

way, when they came up out of Egypt. Now go and smite Amalek, and utterly destroy all that they have; do not spare them, but kill both man and woman, infant and suckling, ox and sheep, camel and ass'" (1 Sam. 15:2–3).

Modern readers of scripture tend to agree that such passages must be read with strict literalism as fully expressing the divine will, in this instance that Israelite soldiers must slaughter babies. Yet, as the comparison of Genesis 6 and James 1 shows, interpretation of speech about God in the Bible cannot coherently proceed along the lines of simplistic literalism. The point being made in 1 Samuel, as elsewhere, is that only within God's covenant of mercy can human beings escape the destruction merited by sin. On the interpretation of biblical speech about divine attributes, including the divine will, see, e.g., St. John of Damascus, *The Orthodox Faith*, trans. Frederic H. Chase Jr., Book IV, chs. 17–19 (373–385, especially 384–385), in idem, *Writings* (Washington, DC: Catholic University of America Press, 1958); St. Thomas Aquinas, *Summa Theologiae* I, q. 1, a. 9; q. 3, a. 1; q. 19, a. 7. On metaphysically deficient Enlightenment modes of reading scripture, one might begin with Hans W. Frei, *The Eclipse of Biblical Narrative: A Study in Eighteenth and Nineteenth Century Hermeneutics* (New Haven, CT: Yale University Press, 1974).

6. On this sin, see David Noel Freedman, *The Nine Commandments*, 104–108; cf. Nelson, *Joshua: A Commentary*, 95–106.

stolen, and lied, and put them among their own stuff. Therefore the people of Israel cannot stand before their enemies; they turn their backs before their enemies, because they have become a thing for destruction. I will be with you no more, unless you destroy the devoted things from among you. Up, sanctify the people" (Josh. 7:11–13). Joshua does so, and Israel renews its march of conquest by God's power. God commands Joshua, "Stretch out the javelin that is in your hand toward Ai; for I will give it into your hand" (Josh. 8:18). Joshua stretches out the javelin until Ai is utterly destroyed.

The same elements are present here, then, that we found with Moses when he was leading the people out of Egypt. The people are weak of faith and fall quickly into sin, despite their repeated professions of fidelity to the covenantal Law. Conquering enemies and entering into (or progressing toward) the promised land depends upon covenantal fidelity; and falling away from the covenant means falling into the same death and destruction that awaits the sinful communities and leaders such as Pharaoh. These accounts are not simply geopolitical narratives of military conquest. On the contrary, the narrative repeatedly makes clear that the "land" toward which the people are truly moving is holiness; holiness—covenantal fidelity—is the measure of every geopolitical description.

For modern readers used to secular history, the main spiritual (covenantal) point of the biblical narrative is easily lost. Those of us living in material comfort in wealthy nations have trouble recognizing the gravity of the fallen human condition, the terrible disorder brought about by sin. Remaining in one's sins, remaining in the fallen state of disorder and disharmony, means following the path of bodily death and spiritual destruction, both for the individual and for the community in whose corruption he or she participates. God's covenantal presence with the people of Israel aims at reversing this deadly condition, and ultimately at reversing it for all nations, who will be blessed through Israel. This reality is depicted in the book of Joshua. Thus after the victory at Ai, Joshua constructed an altar according to Moses' directions, and "they offered on it burnt offerings to the Lord, and sacrificed peace offerings. And there, in the presence of the people of Israel, he wrote upon the stones a copy of the law of Moses" (Josh. 8:31–32) and read aloud the entire Law (Josh. 8:35). The covenantal order has been reestablished, and the people are victorious in the land, dwelling liturgically with the living God.

Renewal of the Covenant at Shechem

After conquering the initial portion of the promised land, Joshua gives each of the twelve tribes its portion, its inheritance, that it will have to go out and conquer. Joshua then calls all the elders of Israel to him at Shechem. He reminds them that their presence in the land depends not on geopolitical considerations, but on holiness, on love of God: "Therefore be very steadfast to keep and do all that is written in the book of the law of Moses. . . . For the Lord has driven out before you great and strong nations; and as for you, no man has been able to withstand you to this day. One man of you puts to flight a thousand, since it is the Lord your God who fights for you, as he promised you. Take good heed to yourselves, therefore, to love the Lord your God" (Josh. 23:6, 9–11).

If they keep the covenant, Joshua notes, they will be blessed, but if they transgress the covenant by falling into the idolatrous ways of the native peoples who remain in the land, or by returning to the false gods worshipped by many of the Israelites in Egypt (e.g., the golden calf), then divine punishment will cause them to "perish quickly from off the good land" (Josh. 23:16; cf. 24:14). Echoing Moses' command to choose between life and death, Joshua proclaims: "Now therefore fear the Lord, and serve him in sincerity and in faithfulness; put away the gods which your fathers served beyond the river, and in Egypt, and serve the Lord. And if you be unwilling to serve the Lord, choose this day whom you will serve, whether the gods your fathers served in the region beyond the river, or the gods of the Amorites in whose land you dwell; but as for me and my house, we will serve the Lord" (Josh. 24:15).

The people of Israel declare unanimously that they, too, will serve the Lord. Joshua warns them, however, that serving the living God requires sacrifice and holiness, because "he is a holy God" (Josh. 24:19) and cannot be served by sinners; rather, God will punish sin. Nonetheless, the people promise to serve and obey the Lord, even despite the potential consequences. They promise to be measured not by earthly success, but by holiness. Joshua thereby renews the covenant (Josh. 24:25) between God and the people of Israel, the descendants of Abraham, now that they are truly dwelling in the promised land.

As we saw with the Mosaic covenant and the golden calf, here once again the moment of consummation is also the moment of violation. The first chapter of Judges recounts that, of the twelve tribes, only Judah actually conquers the land apportioned it by Joshua. The remaining tribes all fail to drive out the inhabitants of the land and thus succumb to the temptation to reject the divine law and imitate the ways of the nations, especially in idolatrous worship. After Joshua and his generation died, "there arose another generation after them, who did not know the Lord or the work which he had done for Israel. And the people of Israel did what was evil in the sight of the Lord and served the Baals; and they forsook the Lord, the God of their fathers, who had brought them out of the land of Egypt; they went after other gods, from among the gods of the peoples who were round about them, and bowed down to them; and they provoked the Lord to anger" (Judg. 2:10–12).[7] God is holy, but fallen humanity is not holy. Sin incurs, by its very nature, the punishment of alienation from God (God's "anger") and radical disorder, disharmony, and lack of peace.

This simple truth recurs throughout the Old Testament. Although God is working covenantally to reverse the situation, his covenants also enable us to see how far fallen human beings are from being able to live as a holy people. By revealing the elements of a *holy people* (e.g., a holy Law, mediator, faith, sacrificial liturgy), and by foreshadowing *holy land* through liturgical time and place (Mount Sinai, the tabernacle/ark), the covenants give hope; and yet they do not change the fallen nature of the recipients. Neither the people of Israel nor their leaders (e.g., Moses) are holy, and thus the reconciliation, the restoration of harmony and communion, has not yet been truly achieved. The people require a holy mediator, whose holy humanity will reconcile human beings with God.

The Judges: Blessing and Curse

The book of Judges, then, displays over and over again the cycle of curse and blessing that Moses in Deuteronomy had foretold.[8] When the people fall away from God, their unity crumbles and they are conquered. In this condition of alienation, they cry out again to God, and he answers their prayers by sending the blessing of a "judge" or military leader who temporarily unifies the twelve tribes and who functions, like Abraham, Moses, and Joshua, as a mediator between Israel and God. None of the judges, however, possesses the holiness or greatness of the earlier figures. Although individual judges (e.g., Gideon, Samson) sometimes accomplish great military feats, the people do not become a people formed by the Law, and few of the judges have a relationship with God. Because of the weakness of the judges, God does not enable Israel to retain the control of the land established by Joshua: "Because this people have transgressed my covenant which I commanded their fathers, and have not obeyed my voice, I will not henceforth drive out

7. On the Canaanite worship of Baal, see Bernhard W. Anderson, *Understanding the Old Testament*, abriged 4th ed. (Upper Saddle River, NJ: Prentice Hall, 1998), 167–175.

8. For theories about the historical provenance of the book of Judges, see Baruch Halpern, *The First Historians* (University Park: Pennsylvania State University Press, 1996).

before them any of the nations that Joshua left when he died" (Judg. 2:20–21).[9]

The people of Israel's control of the land is continually breaking down, and their condition vis-à-vis the "land," as we would expect, mirrors their relationship with God. Israel falls into terrible distortions of the Law. Thus, violating the laws regarding liturgical sacrifices, the judge Jephthah vows that if God gives him victory over the Ammonites, he will sacrifice as a burnt offering to God the first person who greets him on his homecoming: he sacrifices his daughter (Judg. 11:39).[10]

Eventually, the disorder in Israel becomes as bad as, or even worse than, that of Sodom and Gomorrah. Just as did the men of Sodom, the Benjaminites in Gibeah seek to rape a male stranger. The stranger, a Levite and thus from the priestly tribe, escapes, but instead the Benjaminites rape and kill the Levite's female concubine. The Levite divides her into twelve pieces and sends the pieces "throughout all the territory of Israel" (Judg. 19:29), signifying the spiritual condition of the people in the land. Although the other tribes punish the Benjaminites severely in the resulting civil war, the horrific rape and consequent civil war depicts the spiritual condition of Israel only a few generations after Joshua.[11] The book of Judges concludes poignantly, "In those days there was no king in Israel; every man did what was right in his own eyes" (Judg. 21:25).

In short, the history of the judges traces, through the cycle of curse and blessing, the downward spiral from unity in dwelling with God (the people's covenantal profession of fidelity) to civil war in which God's presence cannot be discerned. If the book of Joshua holds out the promise of "holy land," harmonious dwelling with God, the book of Judges represents the very opposite, due to the lack of a holy ruler or mediator.

Samuel, the Last Judge

The lack of a holy ruler or mediator is soon augmented by the lack of a unified place of worship in Israel and indeed by the loss in battle of the ark of the covenant itself. The story of the last "judge," however, points

9. For insightful analysis of "The Rhetorical Function of Judges," see Wenham, *Story as Torah*, 45–71. Wenham also provides a detailed exploration of the story of Gideon, 119–127.

10. On the sin of Jephthah, see Tammi J. Schneider, *Judges* (Collegeville, MN: Liturgical Press, 2000), 176–186, although Schneider somewhat misses the radical critique present in the text.

11. On this horrific sin and the civil war that follows, see Freedman, *The Nine Commandments*, 114–118.

the way forward in both regards. This final judge is Samuel. Samuel's mother, Hannah, was barren before conceiving Samuel. She prayed to the Lord at Shiloh, where the ark of the covenant resided under care of the priest Eli, and the Lord heard her prayer. Her song of rejoicing, her *magnificat* (1 Sam. 2), parallels the song led by the Israelite women after crossing the Sea of Reeds; and her son indeed is instrumental in another triumphant period of Israel's history. Not surprisingly, during Samuel's childhood, "the word of the Lord was rare in those days; there was no frequent vision" (1 Sam. 3:1).

Samuel grows up in Eli's house. Due to the spiritual corruption of Eli's sons, paralleling the corruption we read about in the book of Judges, God tells both Eli and young Samuel, to whom God speaks directly, that God will take away the priesthood from Eli. Before becoming judge, Samuel is a prophet; the Lord reveals to him, "Behold, I am about to do a thing in Israel, at which the two ears of every one that hears it will tingle. On that day I will fulfill against Eli all that I have spoken concerning his house, from beginning to end. And I tell him that I am about to punish his house for ever, for the iniquity which he knew, because his sons were blaspheming God, and he did not restrain them" (1 Sam. 3:11–13). Soon after, the people of Israel are routed in battle by the Philistines, who capture the ark of the covenant and kill the two sons of Eli.

At this low point, then, Israel lacks both a ruler and any divine worship. The situation, however, turns for the better. The Philistines are quickly willing to return the ark of the covenant, because God brings devastation and diseases upon the Philistines holding the ark (1 Sam. 6). To sinners, God's presence always is felt as a danger and threat, because God's holiness judges the guilty. With the ark restored to Israel's territory, even though to a Gibeonite rather than Israelite city, covenantal worship is once again possible.

Samuel now takes on the role of military ruler or judge. He proclaims blessing to Israel, "If you are returning to the Lord with all your heart, then put away the foreign gods and the Ashtaroth from among you, and direct your heart to the Lord, and serve him only, and he will deliver you out of the hand of the Philistines" (1 Sam. 7:3). Israel renounces the idols, and Samuel—who by now functions in prophetic, priestly, and kingly roles—offers burnt offerings to the Lord and organizes a military attack that initiates a series of military defeats of the Philistines. For many years afterward, from his home city of Ramah, Samuel "administered justice to Israel" (1 Sam. 7:17), thereby fulfilling the kingly office, since the purpose of the ruler is to establish justice by ensuring that the Law is followed.

Yet, Samuel's effort in his old age to make his sons "judges" in his footsteps fails. Samuel's sons, like Eli's, are corrupt. The elders of Israel therefore request that Samuel appoint them a king. While acquiescing to this request, God warns that the elders of Israel have a false understanding of kingship. A king, God warns through Samuel, will enslave the people by requiring them to sustain a standing military and kingly pomp. The people no longer recognize that the true leader of Israel is God. In fact, no "holy people" or "holy land" is possible except under *divine kingship*; human kings will continually fall short of their necessary office of establishing the fullness of justice (holiness) in the land.

By failing to request God as their king, the people have misunderstood the nature of their needs as God's people, who are called to be holy people and dwell perfectly with God. Thus, as God tells Samuel, "they have not rejected you, but they have rejected me from being king over them" (1 Sam. 8:7; cf. 1 Sam. 12).[12] Even so, God requires Samuel to accede to the people's request. By means of the human kingship, God will add another covenantal piece of the puzzle, foreshadowing the ultimate means of reconciling humankind to God. Israel will indeed be established in justice by a human king, but not by the kind of worldly king described in God's warning here to the people:

> These will be the ways of the king who will reign over you: he will take your sons and appoint them to his chariots and to be his horsemen, and to run before his chariots. . . . He will take your daughters to be perfumers and cooks and bakers. He will take the best of your fields and vineyards and olive orchards and give them to his servants. He will take the tenth of your grain and of your vineyards and give it to his officers and to his servants. He will take your menservants and maidservants, and the best of your cattle and your asses, and put them to his work. He will take the tenth of your flocks, and you shall be his slaves. (1 Sam. 8:11–17; cf. Deut. 17:14–20)

This warning is suggestive of the greatest king of Israel, the son of David, King Solomon, the temple builder, in whose times the people dwelt in peace. If the people trust in such merely human kings to establish them in the land, they will be exiled, cut off from God's presence. Only a divine Davidic king will be able to establish the holiness that the people seek, so that they may dwell eternally in the land of God's presence.

King Saul

God first leads Samuel to Saul, who reluctantly accepts Samuel's commission to anoint him king over all the tribes of Israel. Saul's humil-

---

12. For theological discussion, see, e.g., Martin Buber, *The Kingship of God*, trans. Richard Schiemann (New York: Harper and Row, 1967).

ity commends him. When Samuel first comes to him, Saul asks, "Am I not a Benjaminite, from the least of the tribes of Israel? And is not my family the humblest of all the families of the tribe of Benjamin? Why then have you spoken to me in this way?" (1 Sam. 9:21). But Saul easily succumbs to a fatal pride, lack of trust in God.[13] Having gathered an army to fight the Philistines, Saul is waiting for Samuel to arrive to offer the sacrifices to God; but when Samuel does not arrive on time, Saul offers the sacrifices to God himself.

Lacking the authority to function in this priestly role, Saul has thus sinned against God. Samuel warns Saul that as punishment, "your kingdom shall not continue" (1 Sam. 13:14). Saul opportunistically disobeys the Lord again, as regards booty from a victory over the Amalekites (1 Sam. 15:9), and Samuel reiterates his warning. It would be impossible for God to reverse humankind's fallen condition, whose core is pride, by means of a proud king. Samuel upbraids Saul, "Behold, to obey is better than to sacrifice, and to hearken than the fat of rams. For rebellion is as the sin of divination, and stubbornness is as iniquity and idolatry. Because you have rejected the word of the Lord, he has also rejected you from being king" (1 Sam. 15:22–23). Later in Saul's life, this pride, which seeks to manipulate events to serve his own will rather than God's, is displayed as a condition verging on madness: "Now the Spirit of the Lord departed from Saul, and an evil spirit from the Lord tormented him" (1 Sam. 16:14).

After Saul's actions with regard to the Amalekites make clear his sickness of pride, God sends Samuel to consecrate David, the youngest of Jesse's sons, who serves as a shepherd to his father's flock. Departing from Saul, God's Spirit fills David: "Then Samuel took the horn of oil, and anointed him in the midst of his brothers; and the Spirit of the Lord came mightily upon David from that day forward" (1 Sam. 16:13).[14] David serves Saul in his court, and performs mighty acts of battle even as a youth, as his conquest of the Philistine hero Goliath indicates. David's humility is expressed, like Abraham's, in his total trust in God. As David tells Goliath, "This day the Lord will deliver you into my hand . . . that all the earth may know that there is a God in Israel, and that all this assembly may know that the Lord saves not with sword and spear; for the battle is the Lord's and he will give you into our hand" (1 Sam. 17:46–47).

David refuses to manipulate events opportunistically against God's will. When Saul, threatening David's life, compels David (by now Saul's son-in-law) to flee the court, David establishes himself with his supporters

13. Cf. Newman, "Saul," in *Parochial and Plain Sermons*, 500–508.
14. Cf. Newman, "The Call of David," in *Parochial and Plain Sermons*, 1583–1590.

in the wilderness, where David twice has Saul trapped and spares Saul's life. David refuses to kill "the Lord's anointed" (1 Sam. 24:6, 26:9), for such Saul still is. Even while David, with his band of guerrilla fighters, clearly stakes out a claim to the kingship, he does not directly challenge Saul.[15]

The kingship of Saul comes to an end in a battle with the Philistines. On the night before his death, Saul even turns to witchcraft for assistance. By the aid of a medium, against God's Law, Saul calls forth the spirit of Samuel from the dead, only to be rebuked by Samuel, who prophesies that Saul, despite his machinations, will lose the kingdom the very next day. Three of Saul's sons are killed in the battle, including David's great friend Jonathan, and Saul, gravely wounded, commits suicide, a final act of unholy manipulation rather than submissive trust in God's will. Though firmly lamenting Saul's death, David then wages a lengthy civil war against Saul's son Ishbosheth to obtain the kingship over all Israel (2 Samuel 2–3). David reigns first for seven years over the tribal territory of Judah at Hebron; finally, due to the incompetence of Ishbosheth combined with the malignancy of David's general Joab, David becomes king of all Israel. "All the elders of Israel came to the king at Hebron; and King David made a covenant with them at Hebron before the Lord, and they anointed David king over Israel" (2 Sam. 5:3). David would reign for thirty-three more years in the new capital city of Jerusalem.

King David

To solidify his kingdom, David inaugurates his kingship over Israel by doing three things. First, eager to establish a royal city that would have ties neither to Judah, where he had reigned for seven years, nor to the other tribes, where the house of Saul had reigned, David conquers the city of the Jebusites, Jerusalem, one of the cities of the promised land that had not been conquered by Joshua. David establishes his royal city in Jerusalem, which is also thenceforth called "Zion, that is, the city of David" (2 Sam. 5:7). Second, led by God, he soundly defeats the Philistines. Third, having established his royal city and his hold on the land of Israel, he moves to centralize Israel's worship by bringing the ark of the covenant to Jerusalem.

Yet, God serves notice to David that this move cannot mean that David is taming God, as if God were now to serve David rather than

15. On the literary artistry of the narratives about David, see Alter, *The Art of Biblical Narrative*.

the other way around. During David's first attempt to bring the ark to Jerusalem, his men were carrying the ark by its poles and "David and all the house of Israel were making merry before the Lord with all their might, with songs and lyres and harps and tambourines and castanets and cymbals" (2 Sam. 6:5). However, one of David's men, Uzzah, took hold of the ark to steady it because the oxen had stumbled: "And the anger of the Lord was kindled against Uzzah; and God smote him there because he had put forth his hand to the ark" (2 Sam. 6:7). God's presence cannot be used or manipulated by kings, military leaders, or priests; rather, God must be approached in reverence for the divine power. As it were, it is God, not man, who safeguards God. After three months, David makes another attempt to bring the ark of the covenant into the city of David, and this time he succeeds. It is crucial to note that David—like Melchizedek, the archetypal king of Salem, and unlike Saul—is not only king, but also performs priestly functions. Throughout the journey to Jerusalem, David offers sacrifices before the ark and dances, clothed in an ephod, in front of the ark. When the ark arrives at its tent in Jerusalem, David offers burnt offerings and peace offerings, and blesses the people "in the name of the Lord of hosts" (2 Sam. 6:18).

The Davidic Covenant

In the history of God's covenantal work to reconcile human beings to himself, the name David now joins those of Moses, Abraham, and Noah. Recall that the covenantal movement is one from general to particular. God begins simply by promising that Eve's seed would crush the head of the "serpent" and by promising, in the covenant with Noah, blessing to all human beings as signified by the harmony and peace of the rainbow after the stormy chaos of the flood. In a general way, these two original covenants make clear that God will reconcile fallen human beings to himself and restore the original harmony.

The covenant with Abraham gives us our first clue as to how God will do this: land and descendants who are to imitate Abraham in faith and holiness, and thereby bring blessing to all nations. The covenant with Moses specifies it further: not merely land and descendants, but descendants formed as a holy people by a holy Law, and "land" formed by the holy presence of God dwelling in the midst of the people liturgically at Mount Sinai, in the ark of the covenant, and in the sacrificial liturgy. As shown by the book of Judges, however, Law without a king to establish obedience to the Law is not efficacious: without a government, each person does whatever he or she feels like doing, and profound violence and disharmony ensue.[16] Furthermore, without a stable and unified locus of divine presence and divine liturgy, the people fall into idolatry and the manipulation of God, rather than dwelling in and with God.

The covenant with David thus adds two things, both foretold by Moses: a divinely ordained kingship and a divinely ordained temple. The task of the king is to establish justice, perfect reconciliation ("holy people"), by ensuring obedience to the divine Law; the meaning of the temple is that God's name dwells most perfectly in the land, and that the land is truly a "holy land" or place where human beings dwell liturgically with God in an intimate fashion.

When David first proposes to build a temple for God, God replies to David through the prophet Nathan that David will not make God a "house"; rather God will make David a "house," meaning a royal line of kings. God promises, "I will raise up your offspring after you, who shall come forth from your body, and I will establish his kingdom for ever. I will be his father, and he shall be my son. When he commits iniquity, I will chasten him with the rod of men, with the stripes of the sons of men; but I will not take my steadfast love from him, as I took it from Saul, whom I put away before you. And your house and your kingdom shall be made sure for ever before me; your throne shall be established for ever" (2 Sam. 7:12–16). David, in amazed response, glorifies God.[17]

The Davidic covenant as here promised has several crucial aspects: 1) his kingdom will know peace and rest from its enemies; 2) the king will have a father-son relationship with God, as a son of God; 3) the king will inherit a perpetual throne; and 4) the king will build a temple for God. The difficulty, as we will see, with this covenant is that each of these four elements will be lost during the times of the Davidic kings. God will eventually be shown to be faithful to each element, but it will be many years later.[18]

There is a certain irony to the fact that with the Davidic covenant God now has chosen to use a human king as the instrument for the fulfillment of his promises to Abraham and to Moses. In 1 Samuel 8, as we saw, God showed that Israel's request for a human king was a rejection of the Lord as king over them. Under God's covenantal design, he chooses the instrument of rejection to become the instrument of fulfillment. As Psalm 118 says, "the stone which the builders rejected has become the cornerstone. This is the Lord's doing and it is marvelous in his eyes."

16. On the Old Testament's view of violence as corresponding to that of the New Testament, see Wenham, *Story as Torah*, 147–149.

17. For a theology of the Davidic covenant emphasizing cultic liturgy, see Levenson, *Sinai and Zion*.

18. See St. Augustine, *City of God*, Book XVII, chs. 12–13 (742–743).

Shouldn't this be "our eyes"? This reveals the merciful wisdom of God who is instructing his people and leading them from the very midst of this sin and iniquity back into a righteous relationship with him.

Solomon's Temple

God's covenantal promise of a temple built by David's son comes true during the reign of David's son Solomon. When Moses built, according to the divine pattern, a tabernacle for God in the wilderness and "the cloud covered the tent of meeting, the glory of the Lord filled the tabernacle" (Exod. 40:34) so powerfully that Moses could not even enter it. Likewise, during the consecration of the temple in Jerusalem, after the priests had installed the ark of the covenant in the inner sanctuary of the temple, "a cloud filled the house of the Lord, so that the priests could not stand to minister because of the cloud; for the glory of the Lord filled the house of the Lord" (1 Kings 8:10–11). Jerusalem, because of the temple, has become true "holy land."[19] Solomon proclaims to God, "I have built thee an exalted house, a place for thee to dwell in for ever" (1 Kings 8:13). Yet Solomon recognizes that God dwells bodily in no place, because God is not bodily. As Solomon says, God dwells "in thick darkness" and "heaven and the highest heaven cannot contain thee; how much less this house which I have built!" (1 Kings 8:12, 27). How then does God dwell in the temple in Jerusalem? How is a particular land holy, since God, the "I am," sheer Being (Exodus 3), is everywhere yet is contained nowhere? Solomon, careful to consecrate the temple in a way befitting the God who revealed himself to Moses on Mount Sinai, distinguishes himself from the idolaters by asking, "But will God indeed dwell on the earth?" (1 Kings 8:27).

The answer is that God dwells in the temple, the holy land, because the temple is a place of true worship. Wherever God is worshiped in a way befitting his glory, God's name, his full identity, is present in the worshippers. Because God has given Israel instructions on how to worship him and avoid idolatry, the temple is true holy land. Those who direct their prayers to God through the mediation of the temple are

19. For scholarship on Israel's theology of God's presence in the temple, see, in addition to Levenson's *Sinai and Zion*, T. N. D. Mettinger, *The Dethronement of Sabaoth: Studies in the Shem and Kabod Theologies* (Lund: CWK Gleerup, 1982); Ben C. Ollenburger, *Zion, City of the Great King: A Theological Symbol of the Jerusalem Cult* (Sheffield: Sheffield Academic Press, 1987); G. K. Beale, *The Temple and the Church's Mission: A Biblical Theology of the Dwelling Place of God* (Downers Grove, IL: InterVarsity, 2004); Jon D. Levenson, *Theology of the Program of Restoration of Ezekiel 40–48* (Missoula, MT: Scholars Press, 1976); Jerome T. Walsh, *1 Kings* (Collegeville, MN: Liturgical Press, 1996).

truly united with God. Those outside the historical and geographical sphere of the temple thus can still become united with God through the true path of the temple. In his speech at the consecration of the temple, Solomon prays to God "that thy eyes may be open night and day toward this house, the place of which thou hast said, 'My name shall be there,' that thou mayest hearken to the prayer which thy servant offers toward this place. And hearken thou to the supplication of thy servant and of thy people Israel, when they pray toward this place; yea, hear thou in heaven thy dwelling place; and when thou hearest, forgive" (1 Kings 8:28–30). Because of the true worship offered in the temple, the temple mediates God's presence and enables the whole people to dwell with God. The land thus becomes "holy land," a land where human beings dwell in and with God. God is transcendent, and yet he is intimately present.

The responsibility of the Davidic king, then, is to represent the people before God (by his own holiness) and to establish the people in holiness. As Solomon says, "Now therefore, O Lord, God of Israel, keep with thy servant David my father what thou hast promised him, saying, 'There shall never fail you a man before me to sit upon the throne of Israel, if only your sons take heed to their way, to walk before me as you have walked before me'" (1 Kings 8:25). The Davidic king's responsibility, like Abraham's, is to "walk before me [God], and be blameless" (Gen. 17:1). If the Davidic king perfectly observes the Law, then the people will have the opportunity to become holy and the land will become holy. David and Solomon are both kings who also possess a priestly function; they both offer sacrifices to God and mediate between human beings and God. Thus, having consecrated the temple by which the land is made holy, Solomon concludes his speech by praying that the people will be holy:

> The Lord our God be with us, as he was with our fathers; may he not leave us or forsake us; that he may incline our hearts to him, to walk in all his ways, and to keep his commandments, his statutes, and his ordinances, which he commanded our fathers. Let these words of mine, wherewith I have made supplication before the Lord, be near to the Lord our God day and night, and may he maintain the cause of his servant, and the cause of his people Israel, as each day requires; that all the peoples of the earth may know that the Lord is God; there is no other. Let your heart therefore be wholly true to the Lord our God, walking in his statutes and keeping his commandments, as at this day. (1 Kings 8:57–61)

To be holy means to observe the Law, beginning with the truth that there is only one God, and to trust entirely in this God. God has chosen to reveal himself to "all peoples of the earth" in and through Israel. Led by King Solomon, the people offer sacrifices and feast for seven days, indicating their full entrance into holy land, God's dwelling-place.

Corrupt Kings

Nonetheless, the covenantal history is not yet consummated or fulfilled. The people still are not holy, and therefore still are not truly and permanently reconciled to God in harmony and peace. After both the covenant with David, and Solomon's renewal of the covenant at the dedication of the temple, the people sin grievously. The pattern of blessing and sin continues. Directly after God has made covenant with him, David horribly violates the Law by taking another man's wife (Bathsheba) to himself and ordering the man, Uriah, to be killed (2 Sam. 11).[20]

As a consequence of David's corruption, his whole family, like Adam's and Jacob's, falls into violent division. One of David's sons, Amnon, rapes David's daughter Tamar; in revenge, David's son Absalom kills Amnon. Absalom then rebels against King David and, in a brutal civil war, drives David from Jerusalem.[21] Although David regains his kingship, it is at the price of Absalom's life; and David's cry, "O my son Absalom, my son, my son Absalom! Would I had died instead of you, O Absalom, my son, my son!" (2 Sam. 18:33) rends our hearts. David also has to face rebellion from the ten tribes that had originally followed the house of Saul (2 Sam. 20), as well as frequent war against the Philistines. Yet David continues to proclaim, "This God—his way is perfect; the promise of the Lord proves true; he is a shield for all those who take refuge in him" (2 Sam. 22:31).

For his part, Solomon, the son of David and Bathsheba, claims the kingship only after a bitter struggle against his brother Adonijah and the general Joab. Upon gaining the kingship, Solomon executes both of them (1 Kings 2).[22] Solomon marries the daughter of Pharaoh, and eventually Solomon's kingship comes to resemble Pharaoh's, that is to say, the epitome of the nations from which Israel was to be set apart.

At first Solomon "loved the Lord," and humbly asks God to grant him wisdom to be able to establish justice: "And now, O Lord my God, thou hast made thy servant king in place of David my father, although I am but a little child; I do not know how to go out or come in. And thy servant is in the midst of thy people whom thou hast chosen, a great people, that cannot be numbered or counted for multitude. Give thy

20. Cf. John Barton, *Ethics and the Old Testament* (Harrisburg, PA: Trinity Press International, 1998), 19–36.

21. On David's sins, see, e.g., David Noel Freedman, *The Nine Commandments: Uncovering the Hidden Pattern of Crime and Punishment in the Hebrew Bible*, ed. Astrid B. Beck (New York: Doubleday, 2000), 130–135. For examination of the civil war, see R. N. Whybray, *The Succession Narrative: A Study of II Samuel 9–20 and I Kings 1 and 2* (London: SCM Press, 1968), 17; cf. Walsh, *1 Kings*.

22. Cf. Whybray, *The Succession Narrative*; Walsh, *1 Kings*.

servant therefore an understanding mind to govern thy people, that I may discern between good and evil; for who is able to govern this thy great people?" (1 Kings 3:7–9). Solomon clearly understands the purpose of kingship in Israel, namely establishing a holy people; God therefore grants him both wisdom and riches.

As Solomon's kingship, however, is founded upon violence against his brother, so also Solomon's palace and fortifications, as well as the temple, are built with "forced labor" (1 Kings 9:15), recalling the Israelites' slavery in Egypt. In fact, as noted above, Solomon's deeds exactly fulfill Samuel's original warning to the people of Israel that a king would take their children, take their land, and take the fruits of land (1 Samuel 8).[23] God himself warns Solomon that "if you turn aside from following me, you and your children, and do not keep my commandments and my statutes which I have set before you, but go and serve other gods and worship them, then I will cut off Israel from the land which I have given them; and the house which I have consecrated for my name I will cast out of my sight; and Israel will become a proverb and a byword among all peoples" (1 Kings 9:6–7).

Indeed, Solomon, though famous for his wealth and wisdom (cf. 1 Kings 10:23–24), falls away from God. His many wives are from the countries and peoples round about Israel, despite Moses' warning not to intermarry with the people of the land. In his old age, "his wives turned away his heart after other gods" (1 Kings 11:2), and despite his majestic words at the dedication of the temple, Solomon ended by building shrines in Israel for his wives' worship of the goddess Ashtoreth, Milcom of the Amorites, Chemosh of Moab, and Molech of the Ammonites, among others.[24] Filled with worldly wisdom and worldly riches, Solomon becomes a worldly, idolatrous king, as Samuel had warned. Rather than a "holy land," devoted to dwelling with God, Solomon builds a typical kingdom of this world. All such kingdoms, however, are doomed to corruption and destruction, since their foundation is, unlike God, passing away.

The Davidic covenant, therefore, seems to have led to an impasse. The kings are not holy, and so they do not establish justice (holiness) among the people by ensuring obedience to the Law. The majority of the Davidic line actively leads the people astray. Lacking holy people, there can be no holy land; without right worship, the temple is simply a building doomed to destruction, and God cannot be present there. As a result of Solomon's sins, the unity of Israel (the unity of the holy people and holy land) is broken upon his death. Abraham's descendants never

---

23. For discussion of the complexities of Solomon, cf. Baruch Halpern, *The First Historians*, chapter 7: "Dr. Faustus or Mr. Hyde?: The Problem of Solomon ben-David."
24. For further discussion, see Walsh, *1 Kings*, 133–149.

again live under one Israelite king. Through the prophet Ahijah (1 Kings 11), God tells the rebel leader Jeroboam that after Solomon's death (c. 920 BC), Jeroboam will rule over the ten northern tribes while Solomon's son Rehoboam, the Davidic king, will rule in Jerusalem only over the two southern tribes. From this point on the ten northern tribes will be called "Israel" and the two southern tribes will be called "Judah."

After Solomon's death, because of Rehoboam's arrogant refusal to reduce the forced labor and the taxes, the division occurs and the rebellion succeeds. The first act of Jeroboam, now king of the northern kingdom of Israel, is to build golden calves for the people of the ten tribes to worship, placing them in the shrines of Dan and Bethel which are in the northern kingdom, so that his people will no longer go to the temple in Jerusalem (1 Kings 12).[25] The end of holy people is the end of holy land; the golden calf, bane of the Mosaic covenant, seemingly has emerged victorious over the Davidic covenant as well. The selfish pride of the Fall, and the violence and disharmony it causes, appears still in control of human history.

Elijah the Prophet

In the midst of this collapse and the chaos, there are still signs that God is working to bring his covenantal plan to ultimate fulfillment. Even as both "Israel" and "Judah" are heading toward exile—the covenantal curse that follows from alienation from God (cf. Deuteronomy 28)—God inspires prophets who signal God's power. One such man is Elijah (1 Kings 17–22), a prophet in Israel, who struggles against King Ahab and Queen Jezebel, a worshipper of Baal.[26]

Elijah challenges the prophets of Baal to a test of strength at Mount Carmel. Here Elijah says to the people, "How long will you go limping with two different opinions? If the Lord is God, follow him; but if Baal, then follow him" (1 Kings 18:21). In contrast to the unity of the people for the Lord in Joshua's time, the people do not respond. But Elijah then demonstrates the Lord's power. In contrast to the false god Baal, who can do nothing, God kindles the sacrificial offerings; "when all the people saw it, they fell on their faces; and they said, 'The Lord, he is God; the Lord, he is God'" (1 Kings 18:39). Acting with the power of God to enact justice, Elijah executes the false prophets of Baal for

25. Cf. John Henry Newman, "Jeroboam," in *Parochial and Plain Sermons*, 519–529; St. Augustine, *City of God*, Book XVII, ch. 21 (758); Walsh, *1 Kings*, 171–201.

26. On the sins of Ahab and Jezebel, see Freedman, *The Nine Commandments*, 141–146.

their idolatry. Yet, even this has little or no effect upon the idolatry of the people, despite Elijah's exhortations to the people to commit themselves to fidelity to the Lord.

Despairing over the inefficacy of his efforts, Elijah then retreats to Mount Horeb/Sinai, where like Moses he encounters the Lord. Instead of the dramatic revelation that Moses experienced, however, Elijah finds the Lord in "a still small voice" (1 Kings 19:12). The meaning of this "still small voice" is that although God seems weak during this period of rebellious kings, his providence continues to act powerfully in and through the people of Israel. After Elijah is taken up to heaven (2 Kings 2), his work is continued by his disciple Elisha, whose miraculous works include reviving the dead, feeding one hundred men from several loaves, cleansing a leper, and striking a regiment with blindness (2 Kings 4–6). Despite such prophets, Israel remains plagued by idolatry, violence, and disorder.[27]

The Slide toward Exile

There are some good kings, especially among the Davidic kings in Judah. Under King Jehoash, for example, Jehoiada the priest "made covenant between the Lord and the king and people, that they should be the Lord's people, and also between the king and the people" (2 Kings 11:17). The altars to Baal are torn down, and King Jehoash authorizes repairs to the temple.

Yet, other Davidic kings commit horrible acts. Thus, some years after Jehoash, King Ahaz "even burned his son as an offering, according to the abominable practices of the nations whom the Lord drove out before the people of Israel" (2 Kings 16:3). Ahaz also attempts to model the temple worship upon that of the king of Assyria.

The curse of exile therefore becomes inevitable for the broken land of Israel and Judah. In 722 BC, Assyria exiles Israel from the land: the people are forced to move to cities in Assyria (2 Kings 17:6), and native Assyrians are brought to inhabit Israel (2 Kings 17:24), bringing into being the mixed religion—syncretism—of the Samaritans (2 Kings 17:29–34). The people of Israel is thus tragically broken apart. The narrative catalogues the idolatrous acts that brought about this punishment that breaks apart the very people of God: "And they forsook all the commandments of the Lord their God, and made for themselves

27. On Elijah, see Walsh, *1 Kings*, 225–289, although Walsh misinterprets Elijah as a failure rather than an exemplar of God's providential ordering of history even in the worst of times.

molten images of two calves; and they made an Asherah, and worshiped all the host of heaven, and served Baal. And they burned their sons and daughters as offerings, and used divination and sorcery, and sold themselves to do evil in the sight of the Lord, provoking him to anger" (2 Kings 17:16–17, cf. 17:34–41).

Because of the prayers of the good King Hezekiah and the intervention of the great prophet Isaiah, Judah is spared at that time (2 Kings 18–19). But a century and a half later, in 587 BC, Judah too goes into exile, due in large part to the idolatry of Hezekiah's son Manasseh, who reigns for fifty-five years and, among other things, "burned his son as an offering, and practiced soothsaying and augury, and dealt with mediums and with wizards" (2 Kings 21). Despite the good efforts of his grandson King Josiah, who reads aloud the whole Law to the people after it is discovered, dusty and unused, in the temple, Judah cannot avoid exile at the hands of the Babylonians. Josiah does everything he can:

> And the king went up to the house of the Lord, and with him all the men of Judah and all the inhabitants of Jerusalem, and the priests and prophets, all the people, both small and great; and he read in their hearing all the words of the book of the covenant which had been found in the house of the Lord. And the king stood by a pillar and made a covenant before the Lord, to walk after the Lord and to keep his commandments and his testimonies and his statutes, with all his heart and all his soul, to perform the words of the covenant that were written in this book; and all the people joined in the covenant. (2 Kings 23:2–3)

Josiah commands that the altars of the false gods be destroyed, and he organizes the first keeping of the feast of Passover since the days of the judges.

The accumulated weight of infidelity, however, renders Josiah's efforts impotent. After Josiah's death, his own son becomes an idolater. In the end, the Davidic kings, like the kings of the northern kingdom "Israel," fail utterly in their mission of mediating holiness to the people. The covenantal curses are fulfilled. From all appearances, the covenants are rendered meaningless. The covenant with David, which seemed to specify the ways in which the holiness promised by the covenant with Moses would be established, lies in apparent shambles. To the shock and horror of the people of Judah, who had believed that the covenant meant that by God's power the physical temple would stand forever and a Davidic king would reign in Jerusalem from the time of David onward without fail, a Babylonian general breaches the walls of Jerusalem. "And he burned down the house of the Lord" (2 Kings 25:9). The Davidic king was blinded and taken to Babylon, and the people were exiled to Babylon. From all appearances, the quest for "holy people" and "holy land" thus came to an end due to the impossibility of making the people holy.

The Hope of Israel

But the appearances were misleading. True, the people, like all the peoples on earth, were not holy; but God was preparing to accomplish reconciliation nonetheless. God would do so through the people that he both prepared and humbled, as incapable of being holy on their own. As we will see, the prophets, the most significant of them writing before or during the exile in 587 BC, teach that the people of Israel must await a divine Davidic king who will be holy, who by his sacrifice will reconcile the whole world to God, and who will fulfill the Law and establish a new covenant that enables each one of us to share in his fulfillment of the Law. This new covenant will include all the nations, and thus blessing will indeed, as God promised, flow forth from Abraham to all the nations. When this Davidic king arrives, the day of God's triumph will be at hand and the people's exile finally over; the land will be purified and made holy, and the people will once again be gathered together in the new, glorious temple on Mount Zion. The whole world will be created anew when the king returns to Zion.[28]

Until that time, the people of Israel have to wait and to hope. In 539 BC, Babylon itself is conquered by Persia; and the next year King Cyrus of Persia signs an edict allowing the Jews to return to Jerusalem, though without a Davidic king. They rebuild the temple, though not nearly to its former splendor; the aged Jews who had seen the former temple weep. In the fifth century BC, Ezra the priest leads a second group of exiles back to Jerusalem from Babylon, and he institutes religious reforms based upon the book of Deuteronomy. In the fourth century BC, Alexander the Great conquers the Persian Empire and Israel passes from Persian to Greek hands. By the second century BC, Greek culture has become dominant even among many Jews (1 Macc. 1). When Antiochus Epiphanes, who earlier robbed and defiled the temple, commands that all the territories under his rule must upon penalty of death adopt Greek worship and customs, the family of Mattathias Maccabeus wages a successful rebellion. In the first century BC, the Romans conquer the territory of Israel; yet the ultimate restoration is not far away.

---

28. For further reflection on the theological significance of Zion, see Levenson, *Sinai and Zion.*

In this period of waiting—between the exile in 587 and the advent of Christ Jesus—much of the Wisdom literature of Israel takes shape, inspired, according to Israel's tradition, by the writings of King David and King Solomon.[29] Here is the place, therefore, to comment, if all too briefly, upon the theological significance of such writings as Job, the Proverbs, Ecclesiastes, the Song of Songs, the Wisdom of Solomon, and Sirach (the latter two present in the Catholic Bible). We are able simply to indicate their place within the schema of charity or holiness that we have sketched to this point, the covenantal development of "holy people" and "holy land."

Although a holy man, Job sees his children, health, and possessions obliterated. Although his foolish friends seek to convict him of sin against God, and his wife urges him to despair, Job maintains his innocence in the presence of God. The Proverbs seem to teach that if only human beings are holy, God's presence will be richly with them. On this view, "holy people" will necessarily bring about the manifold blessings of "holy land," and indeed the Proverbs are right that holiness is a blessed path. The book of Job, however, makes powerfully and unmistakably clear that "holy land," dwelling in and with God, will come about only through the radical mystery of God's Providence, which is too wonderful for Job to understand. In the midst of the agony of his suffering and his desire for justice, Job can still testify, "For I know that my Redeemer lives, and at last he will stand upon the earth; and after my skin has been thus destroyed, then from my flesh I shall see God, whom I shall see on my side, and my eyes shall behold, and not another" (Job 19:25–27).

Job's extraordinary lament, charging God with failure to defend his holy one (cf. Job 29–31), leads to God's stirring rebuttal that God, and God alone, will appoint the day of his new creation, just as God alone governed creation. "Then the Lord answered Job out of the whirlwind: 'Who is this that darkens counsel by words without knowledge? Gird up your loins like a man, I will question you, and you shall declare to me. . . . Where were you when I laid the foundation of the earth? Tell me, if you have understanding. Who determined its measurements—surely you know! Or who stretched the line upon it? On what were its bases sunk, or who laid its cornerstone, when the morning stars sang together, and all the sons of God shouted for joy?'" (Job 38:1–7). Astonished and awed by the presence of God whom creatures cannot control or master, Job responds with repentance, thereby indicating his willingness to rely on God, rather than on his own holiness, for salvation (Job 42).

29. For more extensive discussion, see, e.g., Leo G. Perdue, *Wisdom and Creation: The Theology of Wisdom Literature* (Nashville: Abingdon, 1994).

Job receives anew the blessings of God's presence after his repentance, which comes about through his encounter "in the whirlwind" with the living God who is not "tame."[30]

As the experience of Job prefigures, the indwelling of God will come about only through the misunderstood suffering of a righteous man; but how this will be, and why, is entirely beyond Job. The point is that Israel must trust in God's Providence for the ultimate establishment of his indwelling or "holy land" (the blessings that Job loses and, at the end of the book, re-acquires). Obedience to the Deuteronomic covenant cannot *earn* the establishment of God's indwelling. A holy man cannot earn God's indwelling. Rather, God's indwelling will be accomplished as a radical gift, through the mode of the suffering of an innocent man.

Ecclesiastes, the message of Qoheleth ("the Preacher"), repeats throughout the theme that "I have seen everything that is done under the sun; and behold, all is vanity and a striving after wind. What is crooked cannot be made straight, and what is lacking cannot be numbered" (Eccles. 1:14–15). Qoheleth tests everything—knowledge, pleasure, cultivation of property, wealth, even cynicism—and finds that everything "is vanity." As he emphasizes over and over again, given the sinful brokenness and the temporal fleetingness of human existence, nothing created can satisfy the human desire for meaningfulness and justice. Whether a consummation will ever come about, breaking through the apparent "vanity" and meaningless "striving" of created things, is entirely in God's hands. Only God can bring about justice. Human beings can only wait with desire and dependence upon God. God "has put eternity into man's mind, yet so that he cannot find out what God has done from the beginning to the end" (Eccles. 3:11). Our lives are in the hands of the Creator, and Qoheleth calls us to meditate upon this utter dependence "before the silver cord is snapped, or the golden bowl is broken, or the pitcher is broken at the fountain, or the wheel broken at the cistern, and the dust returns to the earth as it was, and the spirit returns to God who gave it" (Eccles. 12:6–7).

Qoheleth remarks most upon the lack of permanent justice (holy people), whereas the Song of Songs focuses upon union with the beloved (holy land). Only divine indwelling brings human beings to fulfillment. The Song of Songs begins, "O that you would kiss me with the kisses of your mouth!" (Songs 1:2), and the continual theme is desire for ful-

30. On Job, see St. Thomas Aquinas, *The Literal Exposition on Job: A Scriptural Commentary Concerning Providence*, trans. Anthony Damico (Atlanta: Scholars Press, 1989). See also Francesca Murphy's evocative reading in *The Comedy of Revelation*, 151–181.

fillment in the arms of the beloved. The lover belongs entirely to the beloved and vice versa (Songs 2:16).[31]

The Wisdom of Solomon, like Proverbs and Sirach, takes up the theme of righteousness. Echoing Proverbs, Wisdom states that "the souls of the righteous are in the hand of God, and no torment will ever touch them" (Wis. 3:1). Yet, Wisdom hardly can be accused of having an overly optimistic viewpoint as regards the material blessings experienced by the righteous in this life. On the contrary, Wisdom prophesies the death of the innocent man at the hands of the unrighteous. In a lengthy passage which deserves to be quoted in full, Wisdom presents the unrighteous, denying God's Providence and life after death and thereby discerning only pleasure and power, as saying,

Short and sorrowful is our life, and there is no remedy when a man comes to his end, and no one has been known to return from Hades. Because we were born by mere chance, and hereafter we shall be as though we had never been; because the breath in our nostrils is smoke, and reason is a spark kindled by the beating of our hearts. When it is extinguished, the body will turn to ashes, and the spirit will dissolve like empty air. Our name will be forgotten in time, and no one will remember our works; our life will pass away like the traces of a cloud, and be scattered like mist that is chased by the rays of the sun and overcome by its heat. For our allotted time is the passing of a shadow, and there is no return from our death, because it is sealed up and no one turns back. Come, therefore, let us enjoy the good things that exist, and make use of the creation to the full as in youth. Let us take our fill of costly wine and perfumes, and let no flower of spring pass by us. Let us crown ourselves with rosebuds before they wither. Let none of us fail to share in our revelry, everywhere let us leave signs of enjoyment, because this is our portion, and this is our lot. Let us oppress the righteous poor man; let us not spare the widow nor regard the gray hairs of the aged. But let our might be our law of right, for what is weak proves itself to be useless. Let us lie in wait for the righteous man, because he is inconvenient to us and opposes our actions; he reproaches us for sins against the law, and accuses us of sins against our training. He professes to have knowledge of God, and calls himself a child of the Lord. He became to us a reproof of our thoughts; the very sight of him is a burden to us, because his manner of life is unlike that of others, and his ways are strange. We are considered by him as something base, and he avoids our ways as unclean; he calls the last end of the righteous happy, and boasts that God is his father. Let us see if his words are true,

31. See St. Bernard of Clairvaux, *On the Song of Songs*, Vols. I-IV, trans. Kilian Walsh, O.C.S.O., and Irene Edmunds (Kalamazoo, MI: Cistercian Publications, 1971–1980); Jacob Neusner, *Israel's Love Affair with God: Song of Songs* (Valley Forge: Trinity Press International, 1993).

and let us test what will happen at the end of his life; for if the righteous man is God's son, he will help him, and will deliver him from the hand of his adversaries. Let us test him with insult and torture, that we may find out how gentle he is, and make trial of his forbearance. Let us condemn him to a shameful death, for, according to what he says, he will be protected. (Wis. 2:1–20)

Through such an innocent man, God will prove his righteousness, and reveal his loving Providence, by making his people holy. Furthermore, God will do so in a way that brings about the indwelling of God's Wisdom in human hearts. The book of Wisdom, like Proverbs, thus personifies the Wisdom of God as the source through which justice and salvation will come (Wis. 7–12; cf. Prov. 8, Sir. 24).

Sirach offers a way to sum up our exposition of the historical narratives of God's covenants in the Old Testament. "Let us now praise famous men," Sirach says, "and our fathers in their generations. The Lord apportioned to them great glory, his majesty from the beginning" (Sir. 44:1–2). Sirach goes on to recount briefly the lives of such figures as Adam, Noah, Abraham, Moses, Joshua, Samuel, David, Elijah, Hezekiah, and Josiah. He then concludes: "May he [God] entrust to us his mercy! And let him deliver us in our days!" (Sir. 50:24).

5

Psalms and Prophets

New King, New Temple, New Covenant

Israel was called to be a holy people in God's presence. In and through Israel, God was going to reverse the Fall and unite humankind to himself. By the end of 2 Kings, however, it appears that this plan has failed. Israel is in exile from the promised land, has no Davidic king on the throne, and the temple has been destroyed.

Despite appearances, however, God's covenantal plan has not failed. God will indeed return to Zion as king, will purify the land by fulfilling the Law and establishing justice, and will vindicate his people by drawing all nations to perfect union with himself in his new temple. Both before and after the exile, Israel clung firmly to this hope and expectation. Even after Israel returned to the geographical land of Israel, Israel still was in spiritual exile, as signified by the empty Davidic throne and the recognition that God's presence had not returned powerfully to the second, reconstructed temple. And, except for a brief period under the Maccabees, the people of Israel were continuously a subject people occupied by mighty foreign powers.

The books of the psalms and the prophets show that God's promise to restore his people in holiness is not to be accomplished easily. God's promise is wholehearted: He will judge Israel's enemies; he will bring Israel again to dwell in his holy land; and he will return to Zion. He will do this by bringing to fulfillment his covenantal work in history. Since

God is pure love, everything he does in the succession of covenants aims at slowly teaching man how to return to God's infinite mercy and love. Clearly, God is not the one who needs the covenants; God is infinite, unchanging love. Rather, human beings need to change, to convert or turn again toward God, the source of life and love. God's covenants reveal that from within human history, he is going to restore the order of justice, the right order of human beings to God.

Demonstrating his boundless mercy and self-giving love, God is not going to accomplish this by an act of power and domination over human beings, as it were commanding or compelling them to "love" him or to turn to him as their own true source of happiness. Rather than by an act of power, God is going to restore the order of justice between human beings and God from the side of human beings, within human history, and by an act of self-gift.

This self-gift, the contrary of pride, will be made by a human being for all other human beings, and will restore justice. It will then be clear that despite the profundity of humankind's sins, God's mercy greatly exceeds the forces of injustice. Love, not prideful power and domination, will triumph in human history; the true reality of God will be once and for all revealed. This fullness of mercy, proclaimed in the psalms and the prophets, will ultimately be revealed in the righteousness of Jesus Christ, the incarnate Son of God.

In the psalms and prophets of Israel, we find once again a people aching to be holy,[1] a penitent people both crying out for God's deliverance and praising him for his holy gifts, and a people eager for a holy ruler who will shape the whole land to the pattern of temple-holiness. Similarly, the psalms and prophets reveal to us the promise of a divine Davidic king and shepherd who, on the triumphant Day of the Lord, will conquer sin by bearing it sacrificially. This will be a Day of new covenant in which God's Spirit will transform the hearts of sinners, a Day of healing water pouring forth from the new temple, fructifying all nations by uniting them to the worship of the Lord in Zion, a Day in

---

1. Because of the Old Testament's frankness about the sins of even such figures as Moses and David, as well as of the entire people (the Golden Calf, the Exile), it may seem by this point that we have overlooked the real desire of the people of Israel to be holy. In fact, only a people aching to be holy can recognize its sins. God is leading Israel toward the fulfillment of its hopes, and insofar as many of the people remain faithful to this hope (a "faithful remnant" according to the prophecies of Isaiah and Zephaniah, along with the book of Lamentations and the Psalms), they already participate implicitly by the Holy Spirit in its fulfillment in Christ. It should be noted that Israel's condition of sojourning and falling short is hardly unknown to Christians. Christians sojourn in Christ by the grace of the Holy Spirit, but do so as a penitential people, profoundly aware of our sinfulness even as we rejoice in the healing and deifying presence of Christ and his Spirit.

which the land and temple are made anew, and everything becomes a sharer in the holiness of God's dwelling in the temple.

In short, the psalms and prophets, in different ways, lead us to expect that God is going to do something that builds upon his earlier covenants and fulfills—and radicalizes—them. This new covenant will follow the covenantal path that we have already seen, the path of faith, mediation, sacrifice, healing, law, king, and temple; that is, the path of restoring and perfecting what was lost in Eden, namely holy people who are holy because God dwells in them (holy land).

Songs of Holiness: The Psalms

The psalms' frequent motifs of flourishing, success, and triumph over enemies must thus be understood in the context of a holy people spiritually dwelling with God. Psalm 137, for example, includes crushing the heads of the enemies' children, but was never excluded from the Jewish or the Christian canon. Those who pray Psalm 137 do not seek the slaughter of noncombatants, but seek the complete and utter destruction of all spiritual enemies, including their own sinfulness.[2] May God show no mercy on our sinfulness, but perfectly expunge it from us so we can enjoy him forever!

As the hymnbook of ancient Israel, the psalms anticipate the fulfillment of the covenants in Jesus Christ and his mystical Body, the Church.[3] Through the psalms, God teaches Israel how to attain in prayer the perfect dwelling with God in holiness, the fulfillment of holy people and holy land. The psalms are divine instruction in how to pray and in what to hope for: the perfection of justice in the people through the king (holy people) and through the presence of God in the temple (holy land).[4]

Psalm 2 presents in richly developed form the theme of a saving Davidic king: in response to the injustice of the peoples, who reject "the Lord and his anointed" (Ps. 2:2), God "will speak to them in his wrath, and terrify them in his fury, saying, 'I have set my king on Zion,

2. See St. Athanasius, *The Letter to Marcellinus*, in R. C. Gregg, ed. and trans., *Athanasius: The Life of Anthony and the Letter to Marcellinus* (New York: Paulist Press, 1980).

3. See St. Augustine, *On the Psalms*, 2 vols., trans. Scholastica Hebgin, O.S.B., and Felicitas Corrigan, O.S.B. (Westminster, MD: The Newman Press, 1960–1961). For a study suggesting that the final form of the Psalter is eschatological in outlook, see David C. Mitchell, *The Message of the Psalter: An Eschatological Programme in the Book of Psalms* (Sheffield: Sheffield Academic Press, 1997).

4. For an account of how Israel's psalms functioned within biblical Israel, see Patrick D. Miller, *They Cried to the Lord*. See also Gregory Vall, "Psalm 22: *Vox Christi* or Israelite Temple Liturgy?" *The Thomist* 66 (2002): 175–200.

my holy hill.' I will tell of the decree of the Lord: He said to me, 'You are my son, today I have begotten you'" (Ps. 2:5–7). The king reigns in Zion, the temple mount ("holy hill"). As the representative or embodiment of Israel (God's son), the king will establish justice for all nations. The same point is made in Psalm 110, although this psalm identifies the king as also a priest. The psalm begins, "The Lord says to my lord: 'Sit at my right hand, till I make your enemies your footstool.' The Lord sends forth from Zion your mighty scepter. Rule in the midst of your foes! Your people will offer themselves freely on the day you lead your host upon the holy mountains" (Ps. 110:1–3). From Zion, the "holy land" sanctified by God's dwelling in the temple, the king comes forth to establish justice and exercise triumphant judgment upon sin. This king is a priest, and therefore establishes perfect justice not only between human beings but also between humankind and God. Although the king is not a Levite, nonetheless God tells him, "You are a priest forever after the order of Melchizedek" (Ps. 110:4), the "king of righteousness" who preceded the Levitical priesthood.[5]

The triumphant king will share in the divine throne, and will mediate this sharing to others. As Psalm 45 says, "Your divine throne endures for ever and ever. Your royal scepter is a scepter of equity; you love righteousness and hate wickedness" (Ps. 45:6–7). The throne of this king is divine, yet the king is a man: "I will address my verses to the king; my tongue is like the pen of a ready scribe. You are the fairest of the sons of men; grace is poured upon your lips; therefore God has blessed you for ever" (Ps. 45:1–2). The king, full of grace, will win a victory of justice, and he will marry the virgin bride and lead her to his palace. We read, "The princess is decked in her chamber with gold-woven robes; in many-colored robes she is led to the king, with her virgin companions, her escort, in her train. With joy and gladness they are led along as they enter the palace of the king" (Ps. 45:13–14). The "palace" and the "divine throne" are the same: sharing in God's holiness by dwelling with him, which is the fulfillment of human happiness, "joy and gladness." The bride is Israel, and the king is the mediator who enables her and her children to share the divine life. Thus the king will make his sons to be "princes in all the earth" (Ps. 45:16), sharers in his kingship. The marriage between God and Israel will draw all human beings into God's own life of holiness. As Psalm 37 says, such holiness in truth and love is the fulfillment of our heart's desire for happiness, "Take delight in the Lord, and he will give you the desires of your heart" (Ps. 37:4).

5. See St. Augustine, *City of God*, Book XVII, ch. 17 (748–749).

Psalm 119 sings of the form or pattern of justice that the king establishes, namely the Law. In this psalm, which contains numerous short prayers in praise of the Law, we hear the ardor of the Israelites to fulfill the Law. They long for the Law's perfect establishment in their hearts and actions, because they recognize that to fulfill the Law is none other than to share in God's own holiness. They want holiness because it is a participation in the life of the holy God. To fulfill the Law means to be deified, to imitate the divine life. Indeed, such holiness is the only true "life"; all else is vanity and passing away. "Deal bountifully with thy servant, that I may live and observe thy word. Open my eyes, that I may behold wondrous things out of thy law. I am a sojourner on earth; hide not thy commandments from me! My soul is consumed with longing for thy ordinances at all times" (Ps. 119:17–20; cf. Ps. 40). To follow the Law, to share in God's holiness, is to "live."

God, through the king, will be the one who delivers the people of God. The psalmist proclaims, "The Lord is the strength of his people, he is the saving refuge of his anointed. O save thy people, and bless thy heritage; be thou their shepherd, and carry them forever" (Ps. 28:8–9). As shepherd and king of the people, God will make the people holy by installing them in his holy land, by enabling them to dwell in safety in and with him. Psalm 27 emphasizes that the victory is won not through military might or other geopolitical measures, but by those who dwell in and with God in the temple. "Though a host encamp against me, my heart shall not fear; though war arise against me, yet I will be confident. One thing have I asked of the Lord, that will I seek after; that I may dwell in the house of the Lord all the days of my life, to behold the beauty of the Lord, and to inquire in his temple. For he will hide me in his shelter in the day of trouble; he will conceal me under the cover of his tent, he will set me high upon a rock" (Ps. 27:3–5; cf. Ps. 26). At the defeat of his enemies—the defeat of injustice and sin—the psalmist will celebrate by joyfully offering sacrifices in God's "tent" (Ps. 27:6). When the holy people is finally established, the celebration itself will be the "holy land."

Dwelling in God's "temple" or "tent" (liturgically and sacrificially) enables one to know God intimately, face-to-face, and thereby to share in his holiness. "Thou hast said, 'Seek ye my face.' My heart says to thee, 'Thy face, Lord, do I seek.' Hide not thy face from me" (Ps. 27:8–9). Many of the psalms center on the desire to enter the temple and dwell with God. The righteousness of the people is always intertwined with the ability to experience the dwelling of God. Psalm 24 describes how the king of glory enters the gates of the temple. Only the one who has "clean hands and a pure heart" can enter the divine presence (Ps. 24:4; cf. Ps. 84).

God's covenantal promise that he will give Israel holiness and an intimate sharing in his life resounds through the psalms, despite the fact that the promise has not yet been fulfilled: "Remember thy word to thy servant, in which thou has made me hope. This is my comfort in my affliction that thy promise gives me life. Godless men utterly deride me, but I do not turn away from thy law. When I think of thy ordinances from of old, I take comfort, O Lord" (Ps. 119:49–52). The psalm awaits God's merciful action to save and vindicate his people, "Let thy mercy come to me, that I may live; for thy law is my delight. Let the godless be put to shame, because they have subverted me with guile; as for me, I will meditate on thy precepts" (Ps. 119:77–78). Those who love the Law are waiting for God to bring it to fulfillment; the Law, in itself, is not a final end. Rather, the people of Israel plead for the full arrival of God's justice: "I long for thy salvation, O Lord, and thy law is my delight. Let me live, that I may praise thee, and let thy ordinances help me. I have gone astray like a lost sheep; seek thy servant, for I do not forget thy commandments" (Ps. 119:174–176).[6]

Psalm 27 powerfully announces this same hope, "I believe that I shall see the goodness of the Lord in the land of the living! Wait for the Lord; be strong, and let your heart take courage; yea, wait for the Lord!" (Ps. 27:13–14). Likewise, in Psalm 118, a psalm of thanksgiving for deliverance, the psalmist describes his trial and God's saving power, "All nations surrounded me; in the name of the Lord I cut them off! They surrounded me, surrounded me on every side; in the name of the Lord I cut them off! They surrounded me like bees, they blazed like a fire of thorns; in the name of the Lord I cut them off! I was pushing hard, so that I was falling, but the Lord helped me. The Lord is my strength and my song; he has become my salvation" (Ps. 118:10–14). As we read on, we find that this final salvation is yet to happen, although the psalmist knows that it will happen. He prays, "Open to me the gates of righteousness, that I may enter through them and give thanks to the Lord" (Ps. 118:19).

Psalm 118 contains a wondrous mixture of thanksgiving for God's victory combined with prayer that God will win the victory. The victory is not in doubt, but neither is it yet won. Through Israel, a people rejected by the nations, God will achieve his salvation and build the perfect temple. The small "stone" that is Israel will be the foundation for the entire holy land. "The stone which the builders rejected has

---

6. For this reason, many of the psalms are penitential. Only the repentant can recognize their need for a redeemer to establish them in justice. See the profound work of St. John Fisher, bishop of Rochester who was beheaded in 1535, *Exposition of the Seven Penitential Psalms* (San Francisco: Ignatius Press, 1998).

become the head of the corner. This is the Lord's doing; it is marvelous in our eyes. . . . Save us, we beseech thee, O Lord! O Lord, we beseech thee, give us success!" (Ps. 118:22–25).

The Lord Promises His Faithfulness: The Prophets

If the themes of king and temple, law and liturgy, penitence and deliverance, holiness and sharing in God's intimate life are prominent in the psalms, they are if anything even more central in the writings of the prophets. Here we will address certain aspects of the writings of eight of the prophets: Isaiah, Jeremiah, Ezekiel, Daniel, Joel, Amos, Zechariah, and Malachi.[7] We will place special emphasis on the writings of Isaiah, which powerfully portray the establishment of holiness in the people and the new creation in which God fully dwells.

Isaiah: The Servant

The Book of Isaiah contains three trajectories for the establishment of a holy people: through the suffering servant, by God himself, and through the Davidic king, or Messiah. God will bring all three together in the New Covenant in the form of a suffering divine Messiah. Indeed, Christian readers have often viewed Isaiah as "the fifth Gospel" because of its insistence upon the integration of these three ways of establishing holiness.[8]

---

7. For various contemporary modes of interpreting the prophets, see Abraham J. Heschel, *The Prophets* (New York: Harper & Row, 1962); Joseph Blenkinsopp, *A History of Prophecy in Israel: From the Settlement in the Land to the Hellenistic Period* (Philadelphia: Westminster Press, 1983); Norman Podhoretz, *The Prophets: Who They Were, What They Are* (New York: Free Press, 2002); Willem A. VanGemeren, *Interpreting the Prophetic Word: An Introduction to the Prophetic Literature of the Old Testament* (Grand Rapids: Zondervan, 1990).

8. See John F. A. Sawyer, *The Fifth Gospel: Isaiah in the History of Christianity* (Cambridge: Cambridge University Press, 1996). Sawyer provides a valuable sourcebook but woefully lacks understanding of Christian theological reading of Isaiah, to the point of offering almost a parody of Christian reading. For commentaries on Isaiah, see especially Christopher R. Seitz, *Isaiah 1–39* (Louisville: Westminster John Knox Press, 1993); Brevard S. Childs, *Isaiah* (Louisville: Westminster John Knox, 2001); idem, *The Struggle to Understand Isaiah as Christian Scripture* (Grand Rapids: Eerdmans, 2004). Our theological reading of the prophets, as with our other chapters, may be supplemented by works that address such questions as authorship, redaction, and so forth. For our purposes, these questions are put to the side in order to focus upon the theological meaning whose intelligibility—assuming that pre-critical readers were able to understand the Bible's message—cannot *depend* upon strictly historical-critical issues.

117

Let us begin with the trajectory of the servant. God knows the Servant and calls him "from the womb," and the Servant's words will bring judgment upon sin (Isa. 49:1–2). The Servant is the representative and embodiment of Israel (Isa. 49:3); and this is true even though the Servant's task is to restore Israel to God, to end its spiritual exile.[9] Through the Servant, God's promise of accomplishing (through the righteousness of Israel as embodied by the Servant) the healing of the whole world will be fulfilled: "It is too light a thing that you should be my servant to raise up the tribes of Jacob and to restore the preserved of Israel; I will give you as a light to the nations, that my salvation may reach to the end of the earth" (Isa. 49:6). Through the Servant, God will make Israel his bride, establishing an intimate union between humankind and God, and Israel's "children" will be blessed and raised up by all nations, as all nations are gathered into this intimate relationship with God (Isa. 49:8–26).

God is thus preparing the "day of salvation" (Isa. 49:8) in which all prisoners, enslaved to sin, will be liberated and all will be reconciled to God, nourished by his sacred food and restorative water (Isa. 49:9–10). God's love for humankind as represented by Israel is poignantly expressed: "'Can a woman forget her sucking child, that she should have no compassion on the son of her womb?' Even these may forget, yet I will not forget you. Behold, I have graven you on the palms of my hands; your walls are continually before me" (Isa. 49:15–16). How will God, through the Servant, manifest his powerful saving love? He will not do it through violence or military power. God's land has always had love, holiness, as its goal, not the geopolitical ends of worldly kingdoms.

Thus the Servant will manifest God's love by his self-humbling. As the reverse of the selfish pride of Adam and Eve, the Servant will reconcile humankind to God by his self-giving love and his trust in God. This humility will cause fallen human beings, who regard only power, to abuse him. In Isaiah's prophecy, the Servant speaks, "The Lord God has opened my ear, and I was not rebellious, I turned not backward. I

---

9. Indeed, one referent of the term "servant" is the group of exiles who will return and live out Israel's true identity and vocation as a faithful remnant. The "Servant," in our reading, is never separate from the faithful people (Christ is the Head of his mystical Body). Jon Levenson points out, "The identification of Jesus with the suffering servant of the Book of Isaiah thus became a mainstay of Christian exegesis. It was not shaken until the twelfth century, when Andrew of St. Victor, anticipating modern critical study, interpreted the servant as a representation of the Jewish people as they suffered during the Babylonian exile" (Levenson, *The Death and Resurrection of the Beloved Son*, 201). Andrew of St. Victor's interpretation does not contradict the patristic Christian interpretation, but rather exposes how supremely Jesus, as suffering servant, embodies and represents Israel.

gave my back to the smiters, and my cheeks to those who pulled out the beard; I hid not my face from shame and spitting" (Isa. 50:5–6). In this apparent powerlessness, the Servant has great power; his power is the power of holiness, to unite humankind with God and to judge sins (Isa. 50:7–11).

God therefore urgently proclaims to sinners that the Servant will bear their sins; they will endure the "wrath" of God no longer, for the Servant will reconcile them to God. The powers of sin and death will be destroyed, because God will rescue from them all those who cling to the salvation won by the Servant (Isa. 51:22–23). The work of the Servant will bring about a new creation, the achievement of God's covenantal plan to create human beings anew. "Listen to me, my people, and give ear to me, my nation; for a law will go forth from me, and my justice for a light to the peoples. My deliverance draws near speedily, my salvation has gone forth, and my arms will rule the peoples; the coastlands wait for me, and for my arm they hope. Lift up your eyes to the heavens, and look at earth beneath; for the heavens will vanish like smoke, the earth will wear out like a garment, and they who dwell in it will die like gnats; but my salvation will be for ever, and my deliverance will never be ended" (Isa. 51:4–6). The new creation in justice and holiness will be the answer to all prayers, a cause of tremendous celebration and "everlasting joy" (Isa. 51:11).

Yet, the Servant will be hard to recognize at first. Certainly God will prepare his way, so that many, witnessing the words and deeds of the Servant, will "see the return of the Lord to Zion" (Isa. 52:8). Certainly, too, in the end, even if not at first, God will make clear the identity of his Servant: "Behold, my servant shall prosper, he shall be exalted and lifted up, and shall be very high. As many were astonished at him—his appearance was so marred, beyond human semblance, and his form beyond that of the sons of men—so shall he startle many nations; kings shall shut their mouths because of him; for that which has not been told them they shall see, and that which they have not heard they shall understand" (Isa. 52:13–15). The pagan nations, who have not received the covenants and prophecies, will nonetheless recognize him when he is "exalted and lifted up." Yet, his suffering will cause many to fail to believe that God's Servant has accomplished salvation: "Who has believed what we have heard? And to whom has the arm of the Lord been revealed?" (Isa. 53:1). The Servant will have no "beauty" or "comeliness," will be "despised and rejected," and will be "a man of sorrows, and acquainted with grief" (Isa. 53:2–3). Yet, his holy and innocent suffering, as the sacrificial love of God's Servant (reversing the sin of pride), will reconcile humankind to God, and thereby bear our sins: "Surely he has borne our griefs and carried our sorrows; yet we esteemed him stricken, smitten by

119

God, and afflicted. But he was wounded for our transgressions, he was bruised for our iniquities; upon him was the chastisement that made us whole, and with his stripes we are healed. All we like sheep have gone astray; we have turned every one to his own way; and the Lord has laid on him the iniquity of us all" (Isa. 53:4–6). It will be God's will, as well as the will of the Servant, to accept this sacrificial suffering in love so as to unite humankind to God's own life.

Rather than selfishly grasping at the power of divinity, as did Adam and Eve, the Servant will reveal that divinity is self-giving love, and that to share in the divine life is only possible through the path of self-giving love. The Servant will open this path for all, and intercede for sinners as the mediator: "[H]e bore the sin of many, and made intercession for the transgressors" (Isa. 53:12). After the Servant has accomplished his work, Israel, the bride of God, will have many "children." All those who share in the Servant's work will become children of God and will belong to the bride, Israel: "For your Maker is your husband, the Lord of hosts is his name; and the Holy One of Israel is your Redeemer, the God of the whole earth he is called" (Isa. 54:3). The covenant with Noah will be fulfilled, and permanent blessing will fill the earth (Isa. 54:9–10). The Servant will establish Israel in justice (Isa. 53:10–11). In the "everlasting covenant" of joy and peace, all will bathe in the healing waters of God and receive his holy bread (Isa. 55:1–3,12).[10]

GOD THE REDEEMER

The next trajectory within Isaiah arises with the prophecy that God himself will establish holiness. Although the Servant will suffer and is clearly a human being, Isaiah 59 indicates that the Redeemer, the Servant, can only be God. All humankind is alienated from God. The prophet warns Israel that "your iniquities have made a separation between you and your God, and your sins have hid his face from you so that he does not hear. For your hands are defiled with blood and your fingers with iniquity; your lips have spoken lies, your tongue mutters wickedness. No one enters suit justly, no one goes to law honestly; they rely on empty pleas, they speak lies, they conceive mischief and bring forth iniquity" (Isa. 59:2–4). The people have sunk themselves in bitter violence, destruction, and lack of peace (Isa. 59:6–8). We have seen the truth of this charge displayed after the initiation of every covenant. It follows that "justice is far from us, and righteousness does not overtake us" (Isa. 59:9). The people, blinded by sin, live in darkness and act like animals (Isa. 59:9–11). Yet, even as their sins pile up, the people desire

---

10. On the Servant, see St. Augustine, *City of God*, Book XVIII, ch. 29 (796–797).

justice, and desire union with God: "We all growl like bears, we moan and moan like doves; we look for justice, but there is none; for salvation, but it is far from us" (Isa. 59:11).

According to the prophet, when God sees that there is "no justice," God recognizes that "no man" can reverse the situation, since all human beings are caught up in sin (Isa. 59:15–16). Therefore, God's "own arm brought him victory, and his righteousness upheld him. He put on righteousness as a breastplate, and a helmet of salvation upon his head; he put on garments of vengeance for clothing, and wrapped himself in fury as a mantle" (Isa. 59:16–17). God himself will vindicate his righteousness by vindicating the truth of his covenantal promises. He will establish justice and reconcile human beings to himself as he has promised he would do, even if his covenantal partner (Israel, representing humankind) is unable on her own to achieve justice. God will take it on himself to make Israel holy. He will send his permanent spirit and word upon the people: "'And he will come to Zion as Redeemer, to those in Jacob who turn from transgression, says the Lord. And as for me, this is my covenant with them, says the Lord: my spirit which is upon you, and my words which I have put in your mouth, shall not depart out of your mouth, or out of the mouth of your children, or out of the mouth of your children's children, says the Lord, from this time forth and for evermore'" (Isa. 59:20–21).

When God accomplishes this work, Israel shall be a light to the nations, and all nations will stream to Israel and serve Israel. Indeed, Israel will be a "land" dwelling in the everlasting light of God's own holiness: "Your sun shall no more go down, nor your moon withdraw itself; for the Lord will be your everlasting light, and your days of mourning shall be ended. Your people shall all be righteous; they shall possess the land forever, the shoot of my planting, the work of my hands, that I might be glorified" (Isa. 60:20–21). God alone can accomplish the restoration of holiness.

Isaiah 63 also gives indication that God himself will be the Servant. Isaiah 63 begins as a dialogue between a questioner and the redeemer of Israel, who explains himself in the same terms as we found applied to God in Isaiah 59. The questioner asks, "Who is this that comes from Edom, in crimsoned garments from Bozrah, he that is glorious in his apparel, marching in the greatness of his strength?" The redeemer answers, "'It is I, announcing vindication, mighty to save.'" The questioner then asks, "Why is thy apparel red, and thy garments like his that treads in the wine press?" The redeemer answers, "'I have trodden the wine press alone, and from the peoples no one was with me. . . . For the day of vengeance was in my heart, and my year of redemption has come. I looked, but there was no one to

121

help; I was appalled, but there was no one to uphold; so my own arm brought me the victory, and my wrath upheld me" (Isa. 63:1–4). The year of redemption belongs to God alone, and he alone triumphs over sin. God alone is the one treading "the wine press," in other words accomplishing the harvest of human history by bringing judgment upon sin and saving his people.

The book of Isaiah combines images of the redeemer as the human Servant, with images of the redeemer as God. The prophecy has no need to reconcile the two sets of images, since both will be true.

THE DAVIDIC KING

In addition to the two images of the human redeemer and the divine redeemer is the image of the redeemer king. The third trajectory for the establishment of righteousness in the people is through the promise of the coming Davidic king. The king is the Lord's anointed ("messiah"), so this trajectory often is summarized under the rubric of the "messianic promises," although the term "messiah" itself occurs only once in Isaiah (Isa. 45:1). The redeemer will be a Davidic king filled with the Spirit of God: "There shall come forth a shoot from the stump of Jesse, and a branch shall grow out of his roots. And the Spirit of the Lord shall rest upon him, the spirit of wisdom and understanding, the spirit of counsel and might, the spirit of knowledge and the fear of the Lord" (Isa. 11:1–2).

In accord with the role of kingship, he will establish true justice and make the people holy (Isa. 11:3–4), and as a result the land will be holy land, filled with peace. The wolf and the lamb shall lie down together, symbolizing the absence of violence that comes about when all dwell in and with God by knowing God intimately: "They shall not hurt or destroy in all my holy mountain; for the earth shall be full of the knowledge of the Lord as the waters cover the sea" (Isa. 11:9). All the nations will seek the glorious dwelling-place in God that is mediated by the Davidic king (Isa. 11:10). This king will have both human and divine names: "For to us a child is born, to us a son is given; and the government will be upon his shoulder, and his name will be called 'Wonderful Counselor, Mighty God, Everlasting Father, Prince of Peace.' Of the increase of his government and of peace there will be no end, upon the throne of David, and over his kingdom, to establish it, and to uphold it with justice and with righteousness from this time forth and for evermore. The zeal of the Lord of hosts will do this" (Isa. 9:6–7). The king will establish a holy people dwelling in the holy land of peace, harmony, and righteousness. We will see in the new covenant that the king, the Servant, and God are one.

The image of the promised messiah thus leads to the broad prophecy concerning the new creation of a holy land. Isaiah uses other powerful imagery to describe this holy land. He speaks of a "day" of the Lord, in which the Lord will establish perfect justice. The fallen order of the world will be reversed, and all will be newly created. Isaiah hearkens back to Exodus 24, when the elders of Israel beheld God and ate and drank in his presence on Mount Sinai. He prophesies that on the triumphant "day" when justice is established and sin punished, "Then the moon will be confounded, and the sun ashamed; for the Lord of hosts will reign on Mount Zion and in Jerusalem and before his elders he will manifest his glory" (Isa. 24:23). On the triumphant "day," God will again prepare a feast on his "holy mountain," but this time for "all peoples," not just for the elders of Israel (Isa. 25:6). The day in which justice is established—that is, the day that establishes the holy people—also inaugurates a perfect dwelling with God.

The Hebrew word for day, *yom*, can also mean "age, or period of time." It will be a "continuous day of the Lord" as the prophet Zechariah phrases it. The day of the Lord therefore is not a singular twenty-four hour day, but a new age in which God's kingdom of holiness will be established. All nations will be able to dwell with God through the mediation of Israel, which will be vindicated: "And he will destroy on this mountain the covering that is cast over all peoples, the veil that is spread over all nations. He will swallow up death for ever, and the Lord God will wipe away tears from all faces, and the reproach of his people he will take away from the earth" (Isa. 25:7–8). In this salvation that brings all peoples into union with God, human beings will find eternal life. Dwelling in holiness with God, those who have died will live forever. "Thy dead shall live, their bodies shall rise. O dwellers in the dust, awake and sing for joy! For thy dew is a dew of light, and on the land of the shades thou wilt let it fall" (Isa. 26:19). The Lord will judge all humankind together (Isa. 26:21).

Isaiah emphasizes the joyful newness and rebirth that God's salvation, by defeating the idols, will bring about. When God executes his judgment, the old fallen creation will pass away: "All the host of heaven shall rot away, and the skies roll up like a scroll" (Isa. 34:4). The justice of God's Servant, filled with the divine Spirit, will create anew the world. No longer will the world be filled with idolatry; the world, created anew, will now rejoice in God's presence.[11]

The Servant represents and embodies Israel. God says, "Behold my servant, whom I uphold, my chosen, in whom my soul delights; I have

---

11. For discussion of Isaiah's ethical vision, see John Barton, *Understanding Old Testament Ethics: Approaches and Explorations* (Louisville: Westminster John Knox Press, 2003), 130–153.

put my Spirit upon him, he will bring forth justice to the nations" (Isa. 42:1). The work of the Servant signals the end of the deafness and blindness of idolatry: "I am the Lord, that is my name; my glory I give to no other, nor my praise to graven images. Behold, the former things have come to pass, and new things I now declare; before they spring forth I tell you of them" (Isa. 42:8–9; cf. Isa. 48). The joyful newness of the perfect "holy land" comes from knowing God. Whereas we sometimes take "knowing God" for granted, in fact it is the glorious announcement of a personal relationship with one's Creator. God's servant, embodying Israel, will spread the good news about God's true identity: "Before me no god was formed, nor shall there be any after me. I, I am the Lord, and besides me there is no savior" (Isa. 43:10–11).[12]

Knowing and loving the true God, the holy people will shout for joy now that they are freed from the weight of proud idolatry. "Sing to the Lord a new song, his praise from the end of the earth! . . . let the inhabitants of Sela sing for joy, let them shout from the top of the mountains. Let them give glory to the Lord, and declare his praise in the coastlands" (Isa. 42:10–12). In the new creation, the wilderness will bloom, the desert will be watered, the lame will "leap like a hart," the blind see, the deaf hear, and the dumb "sing for joy" (Isa. 35:6). The perfect worship offered by the holy people in Zion constitutes the path to God. On this peaceful "Holy Way," all those redeemed by the Lord will convert ("return") from selfish pride to love for God and joyful union with him. "And the ransomed of the Lord shall return, and come to Zion with singing; everlasting joy shall be upon their heads; they shall obtain joy and gladness, and sorrow and sighing shall flee away" (Isa. 35:10).

God promises that all Israel, through his Servant, will be filled with his Spirit and be children of God (Isa. 44:3–5). In the new creation, this holy people will dwell in a new Jerusalem, a new temple (Isa. 44:28). God will marry his bride Israel (Isa. 62:4–6), which will be called by a new name and vindicated before the entire world (Isa. 62:2); the people of Israel "shall be called The holy people" and the land of Israel "a city not forsaken" (Isa. 62:12). As God says at the end of the prophecy of Isaiah, "For behold, I create a new heavens and a new earth; and the former things shall not be remembered or come into mind. But be glad and rejoice for ever in that which I create; for behold, I create Jerusalem a rejoicing, and her people a joy" (Isa. 65:17–18). The holy land will enjoy perfect peace and harmony, and "all flesh" will worship God in the everlasting new creation (Isa. 66:23).

12. See Christopher Seitz, *Zion's Final Destiny* (Minneapolis: Fortress, 1991).

Jeremiah: The New Covenant

Jeremiah suffers intensely as Israel descends into exile in 587 BC, because he dares to warn against Israel's misguided belief that the covenant with David would protect her from being conquered. But his prophecy is far from negative overall. He prophesies a "new covenant." The latter specifies for us the "new thing" that we read about in Isaiah. Jeremiah prophesies against the rulers and false prophets of Israel, whom he calls wicked shepherds. In their stead, God will raise up a holy Davidic king: "Behold, the days are coming, says the Lord, when I will raise up for David a righteous Branch, and he shall reign as king and deal wisely, and shall execute justice and righteousness in the land. In his days Judah will be saved, and Israel will dwell securely. And this is the name by which he will be called: 'The Lord is our righteousness'" (Jer. 23:5–6). By means of the "righteous Branch," God will gather all the exiled Israelites back to the land of Israel (Jer. 23:8; cf. Jeremiah 30–31), in a new exodus.[13]

Forgiving the sins of the people and treating Israel once more as a "virgin," God will begin anew: "Again I will build you, and you shall be built, O virgin Israel!" (Jer. 31:4). Israel had become an adulteress in committing idolatry. When God returns to Zion and ends the exile, he will make a "new covenant" with the people (Jer. 31:31), and will permanently marry the people to himself in an intimate and profound union.

This covenant will differ from the earlier covenants in that, as God says, "I will put my law within them, and I will write it upon their hearts; and I will be their God, and they shall be my people. And no longer shall each man teach his neighbor and his brother, saying 'Know the Lord,' for they shall all know me, from the least of them to the greatest, says the Lord; for I will forgive their iniquity, and I will remember their sin no more" (Jer. 31:33–34). Human beings will be moved inwardly to perform God's Law, and this perfect love will be joined to a perfect knowledge of God, since in order to love God we must know him. So that our wills can be healed, God will forgive our sins and reconcile us to himself. All of this will be accomplished by the Branch, the Davidic king.[14]

Ezekiel: God and Zion

Active around the same time as Jeremiah, Ezekiel graphically depicts the withdrawal of God from Zion and Israel and then, just as graphi-

---

13. On the theme of a new exodus, see Michael Fishbane, *Text and Texture*, 121–140.
14. For an introduction to Jeremiah, see R. E. Clements, *Jeremiah* (Atlanta: John Knox Press, 1988); cf. St. Augustine, *City of God*, Book XVIII, ch. 33 (804–805).

cally, depicts the coming return of the Lord.[15] Ezekiel's vision of God, which occurs while he is among the exiles in Babylon in the early sixth century BC, both deepens and challenges our understanding of God as the "I am," the name revealed to Moses and underscored by Isaiah's warnings against idolatry.

Ezekiel sees "a great cloud, with brightness round about it, and fire flashing forth continually, and in the midst of the fire, as it were gleaming bronze. And from the midst of it came the likeness of four living creatures" (Ezek. 1:4–5). The four creatures each have four faces (man, lion, ox, eagle) and four wings; by each creature is a wheel. At the center of "the living creatures there was something that looked like burning coals of fire, like torches moving to and fro among the living creatures; and the fire was bright, and out of the fire went forth lightning. And the living creatures darted to and fro, like a flash of lightning" (Ezek. 1:12–14). Above the living creatures was a shining crystalline sky, and above that was "a throne, in appearance like sapphire; and seated above the likeness of a throne was the likeness of a human form" (Ezek. 1:26). The human form possesses the likeness of bronze and of fire, and the brightness of a rainbow (Ezek. 1:27–28). When Ezekiel sees this vision, he falls down to worship. God speaks the divine word to him and fills him with the Spirit, and then gives him his prophetic mission (Ezek. 2:2–3).

What can we learn from the imagery of the vision?[16] First, against any temptation to imagine the unchanging God as static, the powerful images of movement in the vision remind us that God is "unchanging" because God, in his eternal present, is the perfect fullness of action. In this way our understanding of the revelation to Moses is deepened. Second, we must grapple with the mystery that on God's throne there appears a human form. It is this human form that is associated with the rainbow, the Noahide sign of blessing to all humankind. Calling to mind the two sets of passages in Isaiah about the redeemer—one identifying him as God alone, the other as the human servant—we must ask whether, in the mystery of salvation, there can be a union of divinity and humanity.

God then feeds Ezekiel a scroll filled with the record of "lamentation and mourning and woe" (Ezek. 2:10). At God's command, Ezekiel eats the scroll, "and it was in my mouth as sweet as honey" (Ezek. 2:3). The scroll of bitterness, indicative of human history, is sweet because God, despite everything, will bring good from human wickedness. After

15. For commentary on Ezekiel, see, e.g., Daniel I. Block, *The Book of Ezekiel*, 2 vols. (Grand Rapids: Eerdmans, 1997); Henry McKeating, *Ezekiel* (Sheffield: JSOT, 1993).

16. Cf. Bailey Wells, "'For the Sake of My Holy Name': The Context of Ezekiel," in *God's Holy People*, 160–184.

Israel's destruction, God will redeem Israel. When Ezekiel has eaten the scroll, God introduces him to the fullness of Israel's sin, the reason for the "lamentation and mourning and woe." The corruption of the people (unholy people) is reflected by the corruption of their worship (unholy land). God warns Ezekiel about the corruption of the people, "Because the land is full of bloody crimes and the city is full of violence, I will bring the worst of the nations to take possession of their houses; I will put an end to their proud might, and their holy places shall be profaned" (Ezek. 7:23–24).

To show Ezekiel the extent of the corruption of their worship, the Spirit of God carries Ezekiel "in visions of God [recalling Ezekiel's earlier vision] to Jerusalem," to the temple (Ezek. 8:1–4). As God leads Ezekiel deeper and deeper into the temple, Ezekiel discovers increasingly horrible abominations. In the outer court, the seventy elders of Israel along with the chief priest, in a horrifying parody of Exodus 24 and 32, are offering incense to idols in the shape of animals. This vision represents what the elders, believing that "the Lord has forsaken the land" (Ezek. 8:12), are doing in their own homes. Within the temple's north gate, Ezekiel finds the women of Israel weeping for a foreign god. Finally, in the inner court, Ezekiel discovers twenty-five men "worshiping the sun in the east" (Ezek. 8:16). The temple has become the locus of idolatry; the people have returned themselves completely to Egyptian slavery in spirit.

The great reversal of the Exodus will now commence since the unholy people have defiled the land. The same nation that in the Exodus left Egypt to enter the promised land will now be exiled again into another Egypt. As he had earlier punished with plagues the unholy idolaters of Egypt, God brings the punishment of destruction, the fulfillment of the curses associated with the covenant (the outcome of alienation from the wisdom of the life-giving God), upon Israel. God gives Ezekiel a vision of executioners: "Then he cried in my ears with a loud voice, saying, 'Draw near, you executioners of the city, each with his destroying weapon in his hand'" (Ezek. 9:1).

Yet, with the executioners of divine justice, there stands an executioner of divine mercy. From the threshold of the temple, God calls to this man, "Go through the city, through Jerusalem, and put a mark upon the foreheads of the men who sigh and groan over all the abominations that are committed in it" (Ezek. 9:4). This "mark" is the Hebrew letter "tau," the last letter of the Hebrew alphabet, which is formed in the shape of an X.[17] In the vision, those who bear the mark are spared from

17. See the note on this verse in *The New Oxford Annotated Bible*, with the Apocrypha, expanded ed. (Revised Standard Version) (Oxford: Oxford University Press, 1977), 1008.

punishment for sin; those who lack the mark are executed, because they remain in their sins. This mark spares the Israelites just as the blood of the Passover lamb spared the Israelites in Egypt. After placing the cross upon the people who are to be spared, the executioner of mercy returns and enters into the glory of the Lord, manifested by the cloud and brightness in the temple. He there receives burning coals from the altar under God's throne, to distribute to God's holy people. It is this divine fire that will be cast upon the earth by God's mediator of mercy in his new Passover.

Ezekiel then sees the fullest possible expression of the failure of the covenants with Moses and David to bring about a holy land. God, who had promised to place his name upon the temple, now departs from the temple. The glory of the Lord that had so filled the temple that the priests could not stand to minister, now departs. The departure is described with solemnity and order, making clear that God is not fleeing, but rather that he is accomplishing, in a mysterious way, his wise plan. "And the glory of the Lord went up from the cherubim to the threshold of the house; and the house was filled with the cloud, and the court was full of the brightness of the glory of the Lord" (Ezek. 10:4).

From the threshold, the cherubim lift their wings to ascend, the glory of the Lord going with them. At the east gate of the temple, the gate that belongs to the Lord, they pause. Then they move "straight forward" and the glory of the Lord leaves the temple. Ezekiel next sees them standing "upon the mountain which is on the east side of the city" (Ezek. 11:23), and then his vision ends. The Lord has departed by this path; he will return by this path. God promises to gather the exiles back to Jerusalem, to cleanse the city of idols, and to end the exile of his people by giving "them one heart, and [putting] a new spirit within them; I will take the stony heart out of their flesh and give them a heart of flesh, that they may walk in my statutes and keep my ordinances and obey them; and they shall be my people, and I will be their God" (Ezek. 11:19–20). By this inner gift of the Spirit, God will finally make his people holy, and purify their land.

The End of Exile: The New Temple

Ezekiel provides glorious prophetic descriptions of the new holy people and holy land that God will establish by creating the people and the temple anew. In Ezekiel 37, we find the description of the valley of "very dry" bones, representing the people of Israel long dead in their sins and cut off from the life-giving source, God. God asks Ezekiel, "Son of man, can these bones live?" (Ezek. 37:3) When Ezekiel replies that God alone knows the answer, God inspires him to prophesy that the Lord will newly create the bones by clothing them with flesh and breathing the breath of life into them. Israel will be created anew by God's Spirit! God says to Ezekiel, "Son of man, these bones are the whole house of Israel. Behold, they say, 'Our bones are dried up, and our hope is lost; we are clean cut off'" (Ezek. 37:11). Against such hopelessness, God instructs Ezekiel to prophesy that God will indeed fulfill his promise to make Israel a holy people, filled with the "life" of God's Law and presence: "Thus says the Lord God: Behold, I will open your graves, and raise you from your graves, O my people; and I will bring you home into the land of Israel. And you shall know that I am the Lord, when I open your graves, and raise you from your graves, O my people. And I will put my Spirit within you, and you shall live, and I will place you in your own land; then you shall know that I, the Lord, have spoken, and I have done it, says the Lord" (Ezek. 37:12–14). When God ends her exile and newly creates her, Israel will be a holy people filled with his Spirit.

Similarly, God shows Ezekiel two sticks, representing the broken and divided "Judah" and "Israel," and promises that their unity will be restored. When he ends Israel's exile, he "will make them one nation in the land, upon the mountains of Israel; and one king shall be king over them all; and they shall be no longer two nations, and no longer divided into two kingdoms. They shall not defile themselves any more with their idols and their detestable things, or with any of their transgressions; but I will save them from all the backslidings in which they have sinned, and will cleanse them; and they shall be my people, and I will be their God" (Ezek. 37:22–23). The brokenness of disharmony, violence, and division, the plagues of humankind since the Fall, will be healed in Israel by God. He will purify the people and make them a holy, harmonious unity.[18]

To these images of holy people dwelling in unity as God's people, Ezekiel adds a rich description of "holy land," specifically a vision of the rebuilt temple. After the destruction of the temple, Ezekiel is brought "in visions of God to the land of Israel" (Ezek. 40:2), and here he sees a vision of the new temple. Ezekiel gives a lengthy, painstakingly detailed account of the exact measurements of every part of the new temple. These detailed measurements in the prophecy need not be taken literally, but rather indicate the holy order and harmony of the new temple: it has been framed by the wise God.

Before he enters into the inner court of the temple, Ezekiel has a vision of the return of God to the temple at the east gate, from which God had departed. "And behold, the glory of the God of Israel came from the east; and the sound of his coming was like the sound of many waters;

18. See St. Augustine, *City of God*, Book XVIII, ch. 34 (806).

129

and the earth shone with his glory" (Ezek. 43:2). God will return and Israel will indeed become the perfect holy land, where God dwells in and with his holy people. God tells Ezekiel, "Son of man, this is the place of my throne and the place of the soles of my feet, where I will dwell in the midst of the people forever. And the house of Israel shall no more defile my holy name" (Ezek. 43:7). God then gives instructions about the priesthood and the sacrificial liturgy. At the east gate of the temple, Ezekiel finds that "water was issuing from below the threshold of the temple toward the east (for the temple faced east)" (Ezek. 47:1). This water becomes a deep river fructifying the desert and making the salt water fresh, providing a continual flow of abundant life and healing. Such will be the healing and life-giving water that flows from the side of God's new temple, when God dwells perfectly in and with man.

THE END OF EXILE: THE NEW KING

A final element of Ezekiel's prophecy needs to be mentioned: how will God bring about this new creation of Israel, this holy people and holy land? Just as we saw with Isaiah, God's chosen instrument will be the Davidic king. God will bring about the new creation of Israel in holiness by sending a Davidic king who will establish perfect justice and a new, eternal covenant. God promises, "My servant David shall be king over them; and they shall all have one shepherd. They shall follow my ordinances and be careful to observe my statutes. They shall dwell in the land where your fathers dwelt . . . and David my servant shall be their prince for ever. I will make a covenant of peace with them; it shall be an everlasting covenant with them; and I will bless them and multiply them, and will set my sanctuary in the midst of them for evermore" (Ezek. 37:24–26). The Davidic king will mediate to the people God's eternal covenant. The king, as the loving shepherd of the people, will establish perfect justice, mercifully reconciling the people to God. The king will make it possible for them to dwell with God, by establishing the perfect temple: "My dwelling place shall be with them; and I will be their God, and they shall be my people. Then the nations will know that I the Lord sanctify Israel, when my sanctuary is in the midst of them for evermore" (Ezek. 37:27–28).

The Davidic king will be the mediator of this new covenant, and yet at times in the prophecy Ezekiel speaks as if God will accomplish the work alone. Condemning the wicked leaders or "shepherds" of Israel, God says, "Behold, I, I myself will search for my sheep, and will seek them out. As a shepherd seeks out his flock when some of his sheep have been scattered abroad, so I will seek out my sheep" (Ezek. 34:11–12). As shepherd, God will end the exile of his "sheep," the people of Israel,

130

and feed them "upon the mountain heights of Israel" (Ezek. 34:14). God emphasizes, "I myself will be the shepherd of my sheep, and I will make them lie down, says the Lord God. I will seek the lost, and I will bring back the strayed, and I will bind up the crippled, and I will strengthen the weak, and the fat and the strong I will watch over; I will feed them in justice" (Ezek. 34:15–16). God will be the shepherd, and he will also be the judge. "Behold, I, I myself will judge between the fat sheep and the lean sheep" (Ezek. 34:20). Yet, following upon this promise is the promise that "I will set over them one shepherd, my servant David, and he shall feed them: he shall feed them and be their shepherd" (Ezek. 34:23). Will the Davidic king be the shepherd, or will God be the shepherd?

It seems clear that God is going to work through the Davidic king; but will God work in such a way that the Davidic king's action is literally God's action? The prophecy, like Isaiah's, leaves open the question of how God and the new Davidic king will be related. God promises that "I am about to act" in order to "vindicate the holiness of my great name, which has been profaned among the nations, and which you [Israel] have profaned among them; and the nations will know that I am the Lord, says the Lord God, when through you I vindicate my holiness before their eyes" (Ezek. 36:22–23). God will vindicate his righteousness and truthfulness, by fulfilling his covenantal promises, making Israel holy and dwelling in and with them. He will do this through the work of the Davidic king. Since the exile is preeminently a spiritual condition of alienation from God, God will end the exile by reconciling sinners to himself through water and the Spirit: "I will sprinkle clean water upon you, and you shall be clean from all your uncleannesses, and from all your idols I will cleanse you. A new heart I will give you, and a new spirit I will put within you; and I will take out of your flesh the heart of stone and give you a heart of flesh. And I will put my spirit within you, and cause you to walk in my statutes and be careful to observe my ordinances. You shall dwell in the land which I gave to your fathers, and you shall be my people, and I will be your God" (Ezek. 36:25–28). By water and the Spirit, through the mediation of the Davidic king, God will cause the people to be holy and to dwell in and with him, holy land.

Daniel: Sharing in God's Throne

Daniel, one of the latest prophets, sees a vision of the divine court: "As I looked, thrones were placed and one that was ancient of days took his seat; his raiment was white as snow, and the hair of his head like pure wool; his throne was fiery flames, its wheels were burning fire. A stream of fire issued and came forth from before him; a thousand thousands served him, and ten thousand times ten thousand stood before him; the court sat in judgment" (Dan. 7:9–10). The record of all human history lays open, and sin is conquered and judged. Then the conqueror arrives: "behold, with the clouds of heaven, there came one like a son of man, and he came to the Ancient of Days and was presented before him" (Dan. 7:13). The human being who has conquered enters into the divine throne, and receives divine authority. Again we have the mystery of union between divinity and humanity that we have already seen suggested in Isaiah and Ezekiel. According to the vision in Daniel 7, "And to him was given dominion and glory and kingdom, that all peoples, nations, and languages should serve him; his dominion is an everlasting dominion, which shall not pass away, and his kingdom one that shall not be destroyed" (Dan. 7:14). Daniel then learns that the "saints of the Most High," the holy people, will share forever in this divine kingdom.[19] Likewise, Daniel finds that there will be a final judgment in which the dead, if they have been written in the book of life, will rise to share eternally in the divine kingdom (Dan. 12:1–3).

Hosea: The Marriage of God and Man

Hosea's prophecy explores the intimate union that God, who executes judgment upon sin, wills to achieve between himself and humankind. The prophet compares this union—the dwelling of God in man and man in God—to a marriage: "And in that day, says the Lord, you [Israel] will call me, 'My husband,' and no longer will you call me, 'My Baal.' . . . And I will betroth you to me for ever; I will betroth you to me in righteousness and in justice, in steadfast love, and in mercy. I will betroth you to me in faithfulness; and you shall know the Lord" (Hos. 2:16, 19–20). The union, or holy land, will be so intimate that we will know and love the Lord as in a marriage covenant, in which the partners are equals. By God's mercy and power, we will know and love him as he knows and loves us. To know the transcendent Creator in this way is a union beyond our imaginings. This is the God of mercy!

The Triumphant Day of the Lord

The books of Joel, Amos, Zechariah, and Malachi bring to the forefront the "day" of God's victory over sin. This will be a day of judgment.

---

19. If one interprets the "saints of the Most High" to be the "one like a son of man," one adduces further evidence of the unity of Christ and his Church (that is, the faithful remnant described in Daniel and elsewhere) in the mystical Body.

Joel proclaims, "Blow the trumpet in Zion; sound the alarm on my holy mountain! Let all the inhabitants tremble, for the day of the Lord is coming, it is near, a day of darkness and gloom, a day of clouds and thick darkness!" (Joel 2:1–2). In the face of the coming day of judgment, the people must repent; and in response, God will renew the land. "Fear not, O land; be glad and rejoice, for the Lord has done great things!" (Joel 2:21). Israel will become the source of bountiful blessing to all peoples: "So you shall know that I am the Lord your God, who dwell in Zion, my holy mountain. And Jerusalem shall be holy and strangers shall never again pass through it. And in that day the mountains shall drip sweet wine, and the hills shall flow with milk, and all the stream beds of Judah shall flow with water; and a fountain shall come forth from the house of the Lord" (Joel 3:17–18). The day will be one of judgment upon the nations, but will accomplish the vindication of Israel; her covenants will be fulfilled, and she will nourish all the nations with her restorative food and drink. God's Spirit will fill the people and make them holy. Speaking of the holy land after the day of judgment, God says, "And it shall come to pass afterward, that I will pour out my spirit on all flesh" (Joel 2:28).

Amos likewise warns about the day of judgment of sin, "'And on that day,' says the Lord God, 'I will make the sun go down at noon, and darken the earth in broad daylight. I will turn your feasts into mourning, and all your songs into lamentation; I will bring sackcloth upon all loins, and baldness on every head; I will make it like the mourning for an only son, and the end of it like a bitter day'" (Amos 8:9–10). The worldly order—which is really the disorder of sin—will be judged and turned upside down, causing destruction for those who cleave to the worldly order.[20] Sinners will attempt to hide from God, and will discover its impossibility. Yet, the day will also, as in Joel, be a day of triumph. Out of the judgment, a triumphant new Israel will arise: "In that day I will raise up the booth of David that is fallen and repair its breaches, and raise up its ruins" (Amos 9:11).

Zechariah prophesies that the day will be the day of the Davidic king, the day of the Lord's return to Zion and to his temple to end the exile and restore the land, that is to say to restore Israel's communion with God. "Rejoice greatly, O daughter of Zion! Shout aloud, O daughter of Jerusalem! Lo, your king comes to you; triumphant and victorious is he, humble and riding on an ass, on a colt the foal of an ass. . . . On that day the Lord their God will save them, for they are the flock of his people; for like the jewels of a crown they shall shine on his land" (Zech. 9:9,

20. For analysis of Amos's oracles against the nations, see John Barton, *Understanding Old Testament Ethics*, 77–129.

16). Zechariah prophesies that God will send to the people of Israel a shepherd, armed with two staffs, "grace" and "union" (Zech. 11:7). The shepherd will desire to unite the people and to heal them. However, they will reject him and his grace, along with the union he offers. They will value his work at the price of thirty shekels (Zech. 11:12), which he will have cast into the treasury (Zech. 11:13). Yet, on that day, on which the shepherd is rejected, God will also bring about the triumph of Israel. The land of Israel will be purified, and all its inhabitants will share in the glory of the Davidic king, which will be a divine glory: "On that day the Lord will put a shield about the inhabitants of Jerusalem so that the feeblest among them on that day shall be like David, and the house of David shall be like God, like the angel of the Lord, at their head" (Zech. 12:8). Israel, led by God, will conquer the other nations in Jerusalem (Zech. 12:9, 14:2). God will fight for Israel "as on a day of battle," and he will place his feet upon the Mount of Olives, through which he will make a path for the holy people to come to him (Zech. 14:3–5).[21]

Even so, this day will not be a day of rejoicing for Israel, as one would have supposed it would. Instead it will be a day of weeping for their sin against the shepherd. God says, "I will pour out on the house of David and the inhabitants of Jerusalem a spirit of compassion and supplication, so that, when they look on him whom they have pierced, they shall mourn for him, as one mourns for an only child, and weep bitterly over him, as one weeps over a first-born" (Zech. 12:10). God will remove the idols from the land of Israel, and will heal them with the water that takes away sins: "On that day there shall be a fountain opened for the house of David and the inhabitants of Jerusalem to cleanse them from sin and uncleanness" (Zech. 13:1). From thenceforth, "there shall be continuous day" (Zech. 14:7).

The day of the Lord's victory will last forever as its fruits are continually celebrated. Living water, causative of new creation, will flow forth from Jerusalem (Zech. 14:8). All nations will worship the true God, and God, having reconciled all peoples to himself by establishing justice, will be king over all: "And the Lord will become king over all the earth; on that day the Lord will be one and his name one" (Zech. 14:9; 14:16–17). All blessings will flow from the king. The covenant curse will be ended, the land inhabited, and sinners judged (Zech. 14:11–15). The whole land will be holy, and all will offer a fitting sacrifice to the Lord; there will be no need for traders selling and buying in the temple "on that day" (Zech. 14:21). God himself will provide the sacrifice.

We will conclude with the prophet Malachi. He adds a further sign of the arrival of the day of judgment: "Behold, I will send you Elijah

21. See St. Augustine, *City of God*, Book XVIII, ch. 35 (807).

134

the prophet before the great and terrible day of the Lord comes. And he will turn the hearts of fathers to their children and the hearts of children to their fathers, lest I come and smite the land with a curse" (Mal. 4:5). Israel will be prepared for the coming of the "day," and many will repent. On the "day," God will return to his temple. As God says, "Behold, I send my messenger to prepare the way before me, and the Lord whom you seek will suddenly come to his temple; the messenger of the covenant in whom you delight, behold, he is coming, says the Lord of hosts. But who can endure the day of his coming, and who can stand when he appears?" (Mal. 3:1–2)[22]

The Eyes of Faith

Once Jesus has come and inaugurated his kingdom in the Church, Christians can look back and see how all of the promises and prophecies come together in the person, work, and mission of Jesus Christ. This is clearly the apostolic form of preaching as carried out by St. Peter and St. Paul and as recorded in Acts. Nonetheless, one should avoid the false conclusion that this continuity, recognized by the apostles after the gift of the Holy Spirit came upon them, means that the prophecies and the promises of the old covenant so perfectly depicted Jesus Christ that it would be impossible to miss his coming. In fact, the Old Testament could, in God's providence, have been fulfilled in several different ways. The themes of holy people and holy land do not require a Christian interpretation of the Old Testament.[23]

Yet, once Jesus Christ has suffered, died, and risen from the dead, sending his Spirit upon those who believe, we can recognize how the theme of holiness in the Old Testament becomes fully understandable in light of the perfect judgment of sin that God has accomplished in Christ, who comes to Zion as true king and true temple, on his victorious Day of the Cross. As the *Catechism of the Catholic Church*, following St. Augustine, teaches, "the New Testament lies hidden in the Old and the Old Testament is unveiled in the New."[24] The New Testament is "hidden" in the Old. As Isaiah says in chapter 63, "Behold, says the Lord, I am doing something new." What exactly the new covenant will be requires God's decisive action in history, which occurs in Jesus Christ. To this history we now turn.

---

22. Cf. ibid., 808–810.
23. See for example Levenson, *Sinai and Zion*.
24. *Catechism of the Catholic Church*, no. 129.

135

6

Gospel of Matthew

The King and His Kingdom

Could a people living in their own land be in exile? It seems not. After all, if one is a New Yorker and lives in New York, then by definition one is not in exile from New York. For five centuries before the time of Jesus, the inhabitants of Israel and Judah had been back in the land from which the Assyrians and Babylonians, respectively, had exiled them. Certainly, numerous Jews had not yet returned, instead remaining as foreigners in the cities of what came to be known as the "diaspora." Many Jews, however, had returned to the land of Joshua and David. Yet, many among them who reflected theologically upon their situation still considered themselves to be in exile in their own land.[1] How could this be?

---

1. On the ongoing exile, see N. T. Wright, *The New Testament and the People of God* (Minneapolis: Fortress, 1992); idem, *Jesus and the Victory of God* (Minneapolis: Fortress, 1996). For support of Wright's position, see Craig A. Evans, "Jesus and the Continuing Exile of Israel," in Carey C. Newman, ed., *Jesus and the Restoration of Israel: A Critical Assessment of N. T. Wright's Jesus and the Victory of God* (Downers Grove, IL: InterVarsity Press, 1999), 77–100. Wright's account of Judaism after Christ needs more nuance. See Douglas Harink, *Paul among the Postliberals: Pauline Theology beyond Christendom and Modernity* (Grand Rapids: Brazos Press, 2003), 151–207. On Israel and the Church, see Richard John Neuhaus, "Salvation Is from the Jews," and George Lindbeck, "The Church as Israel: Ecclesiology and Ecumenism," in *Jews and Christians: People of God*, eds. Carl E. Braaten and Robert W. Jenson (Grand Rapids: Eerdmans, 2003), 65–77 and 78–94, respectively.

Imagine that your family has lived in the same city for years. The things that you love about the city—the coffee shop at the corner, the park, the great community theater, the tree-lined streets—have been there all your life. Then you go away for a few years and come back to find that nothing of what you love about your city remains. Strangers have moved in; there is no longer even a city mayor, because the "city" is now merely a suburb of a sprawling metropolis. The coffee shop has been turned into a liquor store; the park has become a parking lot; the community theater no longer is operational, having been replaced by a community bowling alley; the trees lining the streets had to be chopped down when the city replaced all the underground water and gas pipes.

Imagine, then, that you continue living in the city for the rest of your life. The city, however, never gets back the qualities that you loved in your youth. From a beautiful, cultured city, the city is now permanently, it seems, a rundown place where beer and bowling are the staples of what social life remains. You continue to live in the city, then, but it is not "your" city; it is not the city as it should be, as it once was. You are in "exile" in your own home.

The Jews who had returned to the promised land were in this situation. In their case, the exile was far more poignant. Rather than missing the friendly coffee shop and the tree-lined streets, they were missing their king and their temple. Although a new temple had been built, it could not rival Solomon's, and the return of God to his new temple, prophesied in Ezekiel's ecstatic vision, had not happened. The Jews who had returned were in "exile" because they remained cut off, alienated from, the covenantal relationship in which God had sworn to uphold them. Because of their sins, their failure to be "holy people" and their consequent loss of "holy land" (as foretold in Deuteronomy and by the prophets), they had been exiled, and the everlasting Davidic king and the glory of the temple were still, despite their return to the land, absent.

Thanks to their scriptures, especially the prophets, however, the Jewish people in Jesus' time had hope that things were going to change and that their spiritual exile would soon end. Those Jews who pondered their situation theologically were actively and expectantly awaiting God's return as redeemer of his people. They awaited a Davidic king, shepherd, and Messiah[2] who, on the triumphant Day of the Lord, would conquer sin by bearing it sacrificially; they awaited a Day of new covenant in which God's Spirit would transform the hearts of sinners; they awaited a Day of healing water pouring forth from the new temple, fructifying all nations by uniting them to the worship of the Lord in Zion; they awaited a Day

---

2. Cf. John J. Collins, *The Scepter and the Star: The Messiahs of the Dead Sea Scrolls and Other Ancient Literature* (New York: Doubleday, 1995).

of judgment on God's enemies in which the land and temple would be "cleansed," made anew, and everything would become a sharer in the holiness of God. In short, they awaited their vindication: the fulfillment of their covenantal relationship with God, the fulfillment of their status as his chosen people, the inauguration of a true holy people in holy land. By the time of Jesus, such expectations were shared by many Jews, but there was significant disagreement among various Jewish groups about what exactly was going to happen, how it would be brought about, and what it would mean for the people.[3]

It is the message of the Gospels—indeed it is the gospel itself—that Jesus of Nazareth, son of Mary, wondrously fulfilled the promises and covenants of God. The Gospels and other writings of the New Testament reveal Jesus to be the divine king and to be the perfect temple; in and by Jesus, the people are made holy and the holy land is finally established. Our theological introduction will focus upon two of the Gospels: Matthew and John.[4]

Why these two? Together, through their distinct approaches to the identity of Jesus, the Gospels of Matthew and John express and make manifest the perfect fulfillment of holy people and holy land. Matthew focuses upon Jesus' identity as the returning divine Davidic king, who represents the people before God and who establishes perfect justice ("holy people") as the new, greater Moses. John focuses upon Jesus' identity as the perfect temple, the locus of perfect worship from whom flows the life-giving water. As John shows so clearly, it is Jesus who as the divine Son, in union with his Father and the Spirit whom they send, dwells within believers and thereby gives believers eternal life in God the Trinity ("holy land").

The Gospel of Matthew: End of Exile

At the very outset of his Gospel, Matthew announces Jesus as the Davidic king. The exile has ended and the king has arrived to accomplish the salvation promised by God. Matthew begins with a genealogy that

3. Again see N. T. Wright, *The New Testament and the People of God*, and *Jesus and the Victory of God*. For contrasting views, see the essays in Paul Copan and Craig A. Evans, eds., *Who Was Jesus?: A Jewish-Christian Dialogue* (Louisville: Westminster John Knox Press, 2001).

4. By commenting on John and on one of the synoptic Gospels, medieval theologians sought to gain a deep theological insight into the mysteries revealed by Jesus Christ. For research into the genesis of the four Gospels, see Martin Hengel, *The Four Gospels and the One Gospel of Jesus Christ: An Investigation of the Collection and Origin of the Canonical Gospels*, trans. John Bowden (Harrisburg, PA: Trinity Press International, 2000).

identifies Jesus as a descendant of Abraham through the line of David. Not only is the content of the genealogy significant, but so is the formal structure. Just as John's Gospel begins with "In the beginning," so also Matthew's gospel begins with the (new) creation.

Matthew divides the genealogy into three sections of fourteen generations each: "So all the generations from Abraham to David were fourteen generations, and from David to the deportation to Babylon fourteen generations, and from the deportation to Babylon to the Christ fourteen generations" (Matt. 1:17). In the ancient world, numbers were seen to have great significance. Fourteen is two times seven, with the number seven signifying the perfection of creation. Following the symbolism of the seven days of creation, new creation—entrance into the holy land—is signified by a pattern of six followed by a decisive seventh in which the people attain a sharing in God's triumphant "rest."[5]

Matthew's genealogy shows that Jesus is the culmination of the new creation that God has been working out through his covenants. The first set of fourteen generations begins with Abraham, the second set with David, and the third set with the beginning of the exile. These three sets of fourteen correspond to six sets of seven, which is significant given the number symbolism prevalent in Israel. The birth of Jesus (Matt. 1:18) signals the end of exile and the arrival of the seventh seven, the day of the Lord. The formal structure of the genealogy is thus suggestive of what the content displays, namely that Jesus is the Davidic king who will instill justice into his people and lead them into the temple of the new creation by offering creation back to God his Father.

The Divine King versus the Worldly King

Matthew's next task is to establish the *manner* of Jesus' kingship. What will his kingship accomplish? What kind of king will he be?

As we saw in our first chapter, on Eden, people tend to imagine God as "over against" themselves. The claim of autonomy posits human power against God's. The fundamental sin, the sin of pride, is to imagine oneself as God's competitor. This creates an imaginary "power struggle,"

---

5. For a brief summary of the debate over the meaning of the genealogy, see Donald Senior, *Matthew* (Nashville: Abingdon, 1998), 37. Senior notes that scholars have argued that "Matthew was simply pointing to the symmetry of fourteen as a multiple of 'seven,' which in Semitic gematria (in which Hebrew characters are also numbers) conveyed perfection or completion" (37). For discussion of the pattern of new creation in Luke, Paul, and John, see Paul S. Minear, *Christians and the New Creation: Genesis Motifs in the New Testament* (Louisville: Westminster John Knox Press, 1994).

in which people try to grasp the prerogatives of God. Becoming disordered through this prideful grasping for divine power, people fall into the violence, lust, greed, and lies that we saw in the Old Testament's clear-sighted depiction of the history of sin.

This interior spiritual disorder causes us to live a lie, as if God were in fact our opponent. In fact, of course, God is a God of gift; everything created is his gift. He is infinite; creatures are finite. Creatures receive existence; creatures exist by sharing finitely, through God's loving and free (and continual) act of creating or giving being, in the pure infinite Act that is God. God's power is expressed and known as self-giving wisdom and love.

Jesus will exercise this divine manner of kingship. As "Emmanuel," God with us (Matt. 1:23), Jesus will rule by his self-gift, by his wisdom and love. His rule will accomplish justice not through force, but through self-giving love that will reverse the original sin of pride and, with wondrous mercy, restore the order of justice between humankind and God. In contrast, worldly kingship as exercised in the fallen world often involves, as we have seen even in the case of David and Solomon, violence and stamping out one's enemies.

Jesus, the humble, true king of his people Israel, is thus contrasted at his birth with the worldly king Herod, who rules Israel by domination and injustice.[6] After Joseph has learned in a dream that Mary, a virgin, is with child "of the Holy Spirit; she will bear a son, and you shall call his name Jesus, for he will save his people from their sins" (Matt. 1:20–21), we find that Herod responds by attempting to kill Jesus. Having heard from "wise men from the East" that the "king of the Jews" has been born, Herod gathers the religious leaders and asks where the king, the messiah, was to be born. When the religious leaders, relying upon the prophecy of Micah 5:2, answer that the Davidic king will be born in Bethlehem, Herod "sent and killed all the male children in Bethlehem and in all that region who were two years old or under" (Matt. 2:16).

Even though Joseph succeeds in fleeing with Mary and Jesus to Egypt, one might think that this slaughter of the innocent demonstrates the supremacy of violent worldly kings over the kingship of Jesus. Matthew, however, sees more deeply: he notes that this slaughter, in its implications, fulfills Jeremiah's prophecy, "A voice was heard in Ramah, wailing and loud lamentation, Rachel weeping for her children; she refused to be consoled, because they were no more" (Matt. 2:18; Jer. 31:15). This prophecy comes from the most famous passage in Jeremiah—chapter 31, the promise of the new covenant. The very next verse in Jeremiah

6. Cf. Senior, *Matthew*, 44.

states: "Thus says the Lord: 'Keep your voice from weeping, and your eyes from tears; for your work shall be rewarded, says the Lord, and they shall come back from the land of the enemy" (Jer. 31:16).[7] Jesus' kingship, by vindicating God's promises, will raise up and glorify the righteous. The power of Jesus' kingship will be self-giving love, which will, in the end, appear victorious over the forces of violence.

The Anointed King

After the narratives of Jesus' birth, flight into Egypt, and settling in Nazareth, the story of Jesus' public ministry begins with John the Baptist preaching repentance and baptizing in the wilderness by the river Jordan. That John and Jesus begin at the Jordan River overflows with significance. Israel had wandered in the wilderness for forty years before finally ending the exodus by crossing the river Jordan and entering the promised land. At that point, their leader Joshua, whose name means "the Lord's salvation" in Hebrew,[8] completed the journey begun by Moses and inaugurated the conquest of the promised land at Jericho. Now a new leader, "Jesus," the Greek form of Joshua, will be anointed to lead Israel on a new Exodus out of the wilderness of sins and into the promised holy land, the kingdom of God or new creation. The fact that John begins offering purification and repentance in the river Jordan, and not in the temple, confirms the idea that Israel was still in exile even while the second temple, built after the exiled people were allowed to return, was still standing.[9] Jesus will submit at the river Jordan to the baptism of this prophet clothed in camel hair who ate locusts and wild honey.

The river Jordan had also been the stage for the greatest of the prophets in Israel. There the prophet Elijah passed on his spirit of prophecy to his disciple Elisha. Elisha had asked for and received a double portion of the spirit of Elijah (2 Kings 2). Although Elijah is the more famous prophet, Elisha had greater miraculous powers, even the power to raise the dead. Similarly John the Baptist, whom Jesus identifies with Elijah (Matt. 17:12), is the great prophet who passes on

---

7. The larger context of Jeremiah 31, as well as of Hosea 11:1 ("Out of Egypt have I called my son") which is quoted in Matt. 2:15, points to the end of the exile, thereby suggesting once again that Matthew sees Jesus' birth as ending the exile of the people of Israel.

8. Cf. Senior, *Matthew*, 41.

9. N. T. Wright (*Jesus and the Victory of God*, 161) observes that "John's family was priestly, and his activity of offering a baptism of forgiveness out in the desert presented a clear alternative to the Temple."

his spirit of prophecy in a double portion to a much greater successor. "I baptize you with water for repentance, but he who is coming after me is mightier than I, whose sandals I am not worthy to carry; he will baptize you with the Holy Spirit" (Matt. 3:11). Elisha received the spirit of Elijah, but the baptism of Jesus reveals him to be greater than Elisha since he receives directly the Spirit of God, which comes down in the form of a dove and rests on him.[10] While Jesus builds on the preaching of John the Baptist, he does not receive the spirit of John, but the Spirit of God himself.

The baptism of Jesus manifests him as the Davidic king. Recall that the prophet Samuel anointed David as king over Israel, and Zadok the priest and Nathan the prophet anointed David's son Solomon as king (1 Kings 1:34).[11] Although John the Baptist is known as a prophet, he is also of the priestly line of Aaron through his parents Zechariah and Elizabeth. John anoints Jesus as the king over Israel. Requesting this baptismal anointing, Jesus says that John should baptize him "in order to fulfill all righteousness" (Matt. 3:15). As the true king who will instill justice in his people, Jesus' goal, in contrast to Herod's, is now made crystal clear: "to fulfill all righteousness." He will reverse the disorder of original sin, and will establish a holy people in holy land, as God had promised in his covenants with his people.

At Jesus' baptism, God declares Jesus to be the Davidic king when he says from heaven: "This is my beloved Son, with whom I am well pleased."[12] The first half is a quotation of Psalm 2:7; the second half is from Isaiah 42:1.[13] The combination of these two sources, which we discussed in chapter five, is powerful. Psalm 2, praising the coronation of the new king emphasizes the relationship of the king as a son of God and the triumph of the Lord and his anointed over his enemies. Isaiah 42.1 begins a servant song, which concludes, that "I have put my Spirit upon [my servant], he will bring forth justice to the nations." The voice from heaven thus shows Jesus to be the Davidic king with the status as the Lord's anointed, the Son of God, the servant of God upon whom rests the Holy Spirit. This exalted divine kingship aims at the fulfillment of holy people, the establishment of justice in Israel by restoring harmony to the people of God themselves and driving out all of their enemies. Jesus is manifested as the Davidic king, the servant of Israel

10. Many commentators connect the Spirit's manifestation in the form of a dove with the dove sent forth by Noah (Gen. 8:12), another indication of new creation.

11. For this parallel, see N. T. Wright's suggestive remarks in *Following Jesus: Biblical Reflections on Discipleship* (Grand Rapids: Eerdmans, 1995), 24.

12. The name "David" in Hebrew means "beloved."

13. See Senior, *Matthew*, 56.

who, according to many of the prophecies, will lead and govern Israel and, through Israel, all of the other nations in perfect justice.

The Justice of the Holy People

What does it mean to instill a people with justice? Consider the meaning of the word "justice." One might think of the civil rights movement of the 1960s in the United States. The ending of segregation was a triumph of justice. By recognizing that the dignity of the human person is not limited to white-skinned people, justice was instilled in our nation to a greater degree. The current pro-life movement continues the cry for justice. Just as African Americans deserve full participation in American society, so the unborn members of our society deserve the protection of the law.[14] By condoning and supporting the murder of the innocent, our nation lacks the fullness of justice.

Jesus Christ, as the new son of David, seeks to instill justice in the new kingdom he is proclaiming. We will see that Jesus' justice includes—and goes far beyond—the justice of human laws. Justice is rooted in the obedience of God's law, not as an external rule code, but as a path leading to participating in God's own holiness. As we saw in chapter four, the kings of the Old Testament failed because, as worldly kings, they perverted their authority by using it to serve their own selfish ends. David committed adultery with Bathsheba and had her husband murdered. Solomon multiplied his foreign wives and concubines and eventually came to worship their false gods. By contrast, immediately after his anointing as king at his baptism, Jesus goes into the wilderness where he fasted for forty days. Jesus rebukes the temptations of earthly food, earthly fame, and earthly rule and thereby resists the temptations to which we so often succumb.[15] Unlike worldly kings, Jesus shows himself to have the personal righteousness that makes it possible for him to instill righteousness in his kingdom.

14. See two works by the biblical scholar Michael J. Gorman: *Abortion and the Early Church: Christian, Jewish and Pagan Attitudes in the Greco-Roman World* (Eugene, OR: Wipf and Stock, 1998 [1982]) and, with Ann Loar Brooks, *Holy Abortion?: A Theological Critique of the Religious Coalition for Reproductive Choice* (Eugene, OR: Wipf and Stock, 2003). See also Michael T. Mannion, ed., *Post-Abortion Aftermath* (Kansas City, MO: Sheed & Ward, 1994).

15. On the experience of prayer and fasting as necessary for sharing in Christ's salvific sacrifice, see the meditation of Alexander Schmemann, *Great Lent: Journey to Pascha*, rev. ed. (Crestwood, NY: St. Vladimir's Seminary Press, 1974). On the three aspects of Christ's temptation, see the interpretation of Fyodor Dostoevsky, *The Brothers Karamazov*, trans. Richard Pevear and Larissa Volokhonsky (San Francisco: North Point Press, 1990), especially "The Grand Inquisitor," 252ff.

The task of the holy king is to create a holy people, and to represent that people before God. As was the case with the first son of David, King Solomon, the wisdom he requests and is granted is not for his own sake, but for that of his people (cf. 1 Kings 3:3–14). After Jesus resists the temptations of the devil, he begins to call together the disciples, Simon Peter and Andrew, James and John (Matt. 4:18–22). Through the authority that Jesus will share with the apostles, this event marks the beginning of the visible extension of the kingdom.

At his baptism, God the Father declares Jesus to be his Son, the Davidic king who has authority to govern as the Lord's anointed. Jesus exhibits this authority by casting out demons and healing physical illnesses (Matt. 4:23, 8–9), thereby signaling the greater spiritual healing that is the forgiveness of sins. Jesus also exercises his authority as the anointed king by his preaching and teaching. At the end of the Sermon on the Mount, "the crowds were astonished at his teaching, for he taught them as one who had authority, and not as their scribes" (Matt. 7:28–29). The Sermon on the Mount manifests true justice by showing the people the way of living as children of God in the world. Jesus appears not only as the new Moses teaching a new divine law, but also as the new David instituting the new law in his kingdom.

In his baptism, Jesus is proclaimed as the Son of God; in the Sermon, Jesus teaches that those who enter his kingdom will share in his sonship. This communication of sonship contrasts with the Old Testament Davidic king who was called to be a son of God, but did not have the power to share that sonship with the members of his kingdom.[16] From the introductory beatitudes onward, the Sermon focuses on divine filiation. The seventh beatitude—often considered by the Fathers of the Church to be the final and highest one—says, "Blessed are the peacemakers, for they shall be called sons of God" (Matt. 5:9).[17] The first sixteen verses of the Sermon conclude with an exhortation to live out the gift of divine filiation: "Let your light so shine before men, that they may see your good works and give glory to your Father who is in heaven" (Matt. 5:16). Indeed, what may be the toughest commandment of the Sermon is identified with the new reality of divine sonship, "But I say to you, Love your enemies, and pray for those who persecute you, so

16. For similar reflections, see Wright, *Jesus and the Victory of God*, 646f.
17. On the Sermon on the Mount, see Michael Dauphinais, "Languages of Ascent: Gregory of Nyssa's and Augustine of Hippo's Exegeses of the Beatitudes," *Nova et Vetera* 1 (2003): 141–163; St. Gregory of Nyssa, *The Lord's Prayer and the Beatitudes*, trans. Hilda C. Graef (New York: Paulist Press, 1954). See also Dale C. Allison, *The Sermon on the Mount: Inspiring the Moral Imagination* (New York: Crossroad, 1999); on the Mosaic background see idem, *The New Moses*, 172–194.

that you may be sons of your Father who is in heaven" (Matt. 5:44–45). "You, therefore, must be perfect, as your heavenly Father is perfect" (Matt. 5:48).

Jesus concludes his instructions on right almsgiving, right praying, and right fasting with the promise, "and your Father who sees in secret will reward you" (Matt. 6:4, 6, 18). He teaches his disciples to pray, "Our Father who art in heaven . . ." (Matt. 6:9). He encourages them to be free of all anxiety: "Look at the birds of the air: they neither sow nor reap nor gather into barns, and yet your heavenly Father feeds them" (Matt. 6:26). Jesus combines the demanding challenge of the Sermon with an insistence on the extraordinary generosity of the Father: "If you then, who are evil, know how to give good gifts to your children, how much more will your Father who is in heaven give good things to those who ask him!" (Matt. 7:11). In the new kingdom of God proclaimed by Jesus, all his followers will share in his kingship, which means sharing in his sonship.

The gift of divine sonship fulfills the deepest longings of human beings who were originally created in grace. To be a son of God means to have the fourfold harmony of rightly loving God, one's neighbor, oneself, and the whole created order. It also means to enter into the temple of the Father by means of right relationship to him. This gift is indeed good news. Jesus begins his Sermon with the proclamation of beatitude or of blessings upon those who have entered into his kingdom of holiness. Another word for beatitude is happiness, not the subjective happiness associated with pleasure, but the objective state of happiness.

This objective happiness of human beings consists in knowing and loving God, who alone is most knowable and lovable. When God converts us from sin and turns us toward himself in Jesus Christ, he rewards us with the ability to know and to love him more than ourselves. Only God can satisfy our hearts! As St. Augustine says, "You stir man to take pleasure in praising you, because you have made us for yourself, and our heart is restless until it rests in you."[18] In the Beatitudes, Jesus thus promises true fulfillment and everlasting happiness to all those who enter into his kingdom of divine sonship.

By viewing the Sermon on the Mount in terms of sharing in Jesus' kingship and his sonship, we avoid one of the prevalent traps in the interpretation of the Sermon. There has been a tendency to interpret the Sermon as a list of rules.[19] At some points in Church history, the Sermon has been seen as a list of rules only for an elite, instead of for

18. St. Augustine, *Confessions*, Book I, 3. See also Romano Guardini, *The Lord*, trans. Elinor Castendyk Briefs (Washington, DC: Regnery, 1954), 79–86.
19. Cf. Pinckaers, *The Sources of Christian Ethics*, 134f.

every baptized Christian. This approach, however, misinterprets the role of law within the Old Testament context. The Law was not a mere list of rules to be kept or not; rather it was a way, a path, to holiness and dwelling with God.[20] As we saw in our fifth chapter, Psalm 119 summarizes this view of the law, "Thy word is a lamp to my feet and a light unto my path" (Ps. 119:105). Psalm 19 says, "the law of the Lord is perfect, reviving the soul" (Ps. 19:7). The focus of the law is not on doing certain actions, but on becoming a certain kind of person. Certain actions are necessary, but the aim is the cultivation of the virtues so that the person shares in the self-giving holiness of God. "You shall be holy; for I the Lord your God am holy" (Lev. 19:2).

Jesus' followers must be perfect as their Father is perfect. He says to them, "unless your righteousness [justice] exceeds that of the scribes and Pharisees, you will never enter the kingdom of heaven" (Matt. 5:20). The righteousness described here is God's own holiness, and thus can only descend upon people by grace insofar as they enter into right relationship with him. By becoming children of the Father through the gift of the Holy Spirit, Jesus' followers share in the righteousness and justice of the Son.[21] The Sermon extends to all people an invitation to become children of God and thus be a holy people, a light unto the nations. We have seen Jesus as the king instilling justice through teaching the new law of the kingdom. Now we will see how he instills justice in his holy people by conquering Israel's enemies.

Rest from Israel's Enemies

The Davidic king was supposed to end Israel's exile, gather her into a unity, and grant her eternal rest from her enemies. Even Solomon, following upon David's conquests, had secured rest for the land. God had promised to give Israel a central sanctuary only after he has given Israel "rest from all your enemies" (Deut. 12:10), and this temple had been built during the peace and unity achieved by Solomon.[22] The promised "rest" from enemies harkens back to the Sabbath rest, the culmination of creation, and suggests that the establishment of Israel in the land is a new creation, perfect holy land.

As the Davidic king, Jesus grants Israel rest from her enemies: he brings about the true holy people as a new creation. Some of the Jews of Jesus' day thought they only had one enemy—Rome. The domination

20. Cf. Wright, *Jesus and the Victory of God*, 287f.
21. The Greek *dikaiosune* can be translated as both "righteousness" and "justice."
22. See Levenson, *Sinai and Zion*, 96.

of the Roman Empire provided the Jewish people with relatively little self-governance. Yet, Jesus announces to the people that they are to love their enemies. If the Davidic king was returning to Zion to restore Israel and end her exile, why was he not conquering Israel's enemies? Why was Jesus not granting Israel rest from her enemies by driving out the Romans, just as Judas Maccabeus had driven out the Greeks two hundred years before?

Jesus commands them to make peace with their earthly enemies because he has come to bring rest from the more deadly spiritual enemies. As the angel of the Lord said to Joseph at the beginning of Matthew, "You shall call his name Jesus, for he will save his people from their sins" (Matt. 1:21). The Romans oppressed Israel, but even when Israel was free from external oppressors, as she was under King Solomon, she continued to be oppressed by sin and thus eventually, through exile, lost her land as well.

The end of the exile, the restoration of the "land," thus depends not on defeating the Roman soldiers but on radical holiness. Jesus manifests his power over the forces of evil in the world through his healing miracles and the casting out of demons. He grants the leper rest by cleansing him so that he can return to full participation in his community (Matt. 8:1–4). Jesus displays his authority over the Romans when he heals the servant of the Roman centurion (Matt. 8:5–13). The paralyzing illness of the centurion's servant and the fever of Peter's mother-in-law (Matt. 8:14–16) flee before the power of Jesus.

Jesus' power to heal physical illnesses symbolizes his power to forgive sins. The encounter with the paralytic reveals this clearly. Jesus first forgives the man's sins and then says, "That you may know that the Son of man has authority on earth to forgive sins. . . . Rise, take up your bed and go home" (Matt. 9:6). That the authority to forgive sins has now come on earth is a sign that the new covenant is on the verge of being established. In Jeremiah 31, the prophet speaks of the new covenant in conjunction with the forgiveness of sins: "I will forgive their iniquity, and I will remember their sin no more" (Jer. 31:34). Thus, when Jesus speaks of the Son of Man having authority on earth to forgive sins, he is suggesting that he is inaugurating the new covenant prophesied by Jeremiah.[23]

Immediately afterwards Jesus calls Matthew the tax collector to follow him, and Jesus then eats with tax collectors and sinners. Jesus has authority to bring back the sinners because he is inaugurating a new age of the forgiveness of sins. As the king who can instill justice, Jesus

23. Wright, *Jesus and the Victory of God*, 268–274.

has the power to bring sinners into his kingdom and make them holy people. Jesus replies to the Pharisees, "Go and learn what this means, 'I desire mercy, and not sacrifice.' For I came not to call the righteous, but sinners" (Matt. 9:13).[24] Those who consider themselves righteous cannot become righteous, because the only true righteousness is that which Jesus grants through the forgiveness of sins. Because forgiveness comes through the Davidic king, the promised redeemer, there is no righteousness outside of the kingdom of God.[25]

The spiritual enemies of Israel include more than the sinfulness of the people. Satan and his demons actively work to ensnare the people of God. Jesus shows his kingly authority over the forces of Satan by casting out demons. At the country of the Gadarenes, he casts demons out of two demoniacs and sends the demons into a herd of swine that then drown in the sea (Matt. 8:28–34). Jesus grants rest to the people possessed by demons, but the whole city begs him to leave. In doing so, the city puts the material wealth of the herd above the worth of the two demoniacs who are now at peace. Peace is a precondition for justice since it indicates the tranquility from external enemies and internal anxieties necessary for giving God and other people the love that is due them. Jesus' kingship will not bring material blessings—at least not at first—but will bring the infinitely greater blessing of the justice restored to the human person. St. Augustine and St. Thomas will echo this point by saying that the justification of the sinner is a greater miracle than the creation of the universe.

After Jesus has established his authority over sins, diseases, and demons, he shares this authority with the twelve apostles (Matt. 10:1–2). David established his kingdom by uniting the twelve tribes of Israel. Jesus begins to build up his kingdom by calling twelve apostles symbolizing the fullness of the united kingdom of Israel. There is no attempt to recreate the twelve tribes in terms of physical descent; instead Jesus establishes his spiritual kingdom through the twelve apostles. Jesus accomplishes the unity that David could not. His followers are not to be known for following particular apostles, whether Peter, or Paul, or James, but for following him (cf. 1 Cor. 1:12–13). The apostles, with Peter as their head as we will see in Matthew 16, form the means by which the members of his kingdom will enjoy his kingship. After his anointing as king at his baptism and his triumph over Satan in the wilderness, Jesus

24. On the Pharisees, see Günter Stemberger, *Jewish Contemporaries of Jesus: Pharisees, Sadducees, Essenes*, trans. Allan W. Mahnke (Minneapolis: Fortress, 1995); Wright, *The New Testament and the People of God*.

25. Cf. *Catechism of the Catholic Church*, nos. 846–848. Only Christ justifies sinners, but this does not mean that only Christians—let alone all Christians—are righteous.

has proclaimed the arrival of the kingdom and healed the diseased and possessed. In other words, he has inaugurated his holy people. Now his apostles will do what he has been doing. They will preach the kingdom and heal the diseased and possessed (Matt. 10:7–8).

Jesus does not restrict his kingship, but instead shares it with his apostles. Their authority, as a participation in Christ's kingship, is not about power or domination. Rather, they are called to be kingly by imitating his humble service and sacrifice. In turn, believers must humbly receive the truth of Christ from the Church, as the apostolic kingdom, rather than seeking in pride to be united to Christ as isolated individuals.

Sharing in Christ's kingship means humbly receiving, rather than arrogantly usurping.[26] Thus Christ says to his apostles, "He who receives you receives me, and he who receives me receives him who sent me" (Matt. 10:40). God is the ultimate king who shares his authority with Jesus the anointed king who shares his authority with the apostles. The authority to guide the flock, granted to the apostles by Christ, does not serve the apostles' self-aggrandizement, but instead allows more and more people to share in the self-giving kingship of God by becoming his sons and daughters, filled with his Spirit of wisdom and love. Despite the failure of both the apostles and the whole flock to live up always to their kingly vocation, the Church's apostolic structure does not impede our union with God. Rather, Christ makes clear that the ongoing apostolic ministry in the Church is the divinely ordained means by which we can humbly have personal access to God our Father through Christ Jesus in the Holy Spirit.[27]

The Anointed but not yet Enthroned King[28]

When Jesus was walking through the grain fields on the Sabbath, his disciples became hungry and ate some of the grains of wheat. The Pharisees (who appear to have been spying on them) object to Jesus, "Look, your disciples are doing what is not lawful on the sabbath." Jesus defends himself on the grounds that David and those who were with him ate the bread of the Presence, which was not lawful for them to eat.

---

26. See Joseph Cardinal Ratzinger, *Called to Communion: Understanding the Church Today*, trans. Adrian Walker (San Francisco: Ignatius Press, 1996), 137, 160.

27. For further discussion, see Vatican II, *Lumen Gentium*; cf. Avery Dulles, S.J., *The Priestly Office: A Theological Reflection* (New York: Paulist Press, 1997); Rudolf Schnackenburg, *The Church in the New Testament*, trans. W. J. O'Hara (New York: Seabury Press, 1965).

28. Cf. Wright, *Jesus and the Victory of God*, 535.

Contrary to a common interpretation, this passage is not primarily about Jesus' anti-legalism. The passage reveals that Jesus is claiming the authority of the Davidic king, thereby showing where he stands vis-à-vis the Pharisees. Jesus had referred to the time when David and his followers were on the run from King Saul (1 Samuel 21). As we saw in our fourth chapter, David had already been anointed as king by Samuel (1 Samuel 16) but was not yet enthroned. Saul and his men were hunting down David as an apparent threat to his kingdom. Even with Saul trying to kill him, David does not take advantage of his chance to kill Saul, but instead says "I will not put forth my hand against my lord; for he is the Lord's anointed" (1 Sam. 24:10).

David the anointed, but not yet enthroned, king respects the temporarily legitimate authority of King Saul. The point of Jesus' reference to David and the bread of the presence becomes clear: Jesus the anointed, but not yet enthroned, king respects the temporarily legitimate authority of the scribes and Pharisees, even while unmasking its hypocrisy and simultaneously predicting its destruction. Jesus will later say, "The scribes and Pharisees sit on Moses' seat; so practice and observe whatever they tell you, but not what they do; for they preach, but do not practice" (Matt. 23:2). The overall message of the reference to David, however, is one of prophetic denunciation. Just as God abandoned Saul and was with David, so likewise God has abandoned the scribes and Pharisees and is now with Jesus.

Jesus and Peter

At Caesarea Philippi, Jesus asked his disciples, "Who do men say that the Son of Man is?"[29] Simon Peter gives the true answer, "You are the Christ, the Son of the living God." Jesus responds, "Blessed are you, Simon Bar-Jona! For flesh and blood has not revealed this to you, but my Father who is in heaven. And I tell you, you are Peter (*petros*), and on this rock (*petra*) I will build my church and the powers of death shall not prevail against it. I will give you the keys of the kingdom of heaven, and whatever you bind on earth shall be bound in heaven, and whatever you loose on earth shall be loosed in heaven" (Matt. 16:17–20). The

29. On the title "Son of Man" as a claim to divine status, see Craig A. Evans, "Jesus' Self-Designation 'The Son of Man' and the Recognition of His Divinity," in *The Trinity: An Interdisciplinary Symposium on the Trinity*, eds. Stephen T. Davis, Daniel Kendall, S.J., and Gerald O'Collins, S.J. (Oxford: Oxford University Press, 1999), 29–47; Joel Marcus, "Son of Man as Son of Adam," *Revue Biblique* 110 (2003): 38–61; and "Son of Man as Son of Adam, Part II," *Revue Biblique* 110 (2003): 370–386.

Catechism of the Catholic Church teaches that although the title Son of God was given to the kings of the Old Testament, in this context Peter's confession also refers to the transcendent nature of Christ's divine sonship, since Jesus says that God the Father has revealed it to him.[30]

Sometimes interpreters of Peter's confession see a dichotomy between Jesus as the Davidic king and Jesus as the eternal Son of God. This dichotomy crumbles, however, when one recalls the prophetic streams covered earlier in this book that indicate that God will restore his people *both* by himself (Isa. 59; Ezek. 34; Zech. 14) *and* through David (Jer. 33; Ezek. 37). Only because Jesus is the eternal Son of God can he be the perfect Davidic king. In other words, Jesus is the Davidic king par excellence since he is son of God not by adoptive grace but by his eternal nature.[31]

Now that his kingship has been recognized and proclaimed by Peter, Jesus reveals more fully the plans of his kingdom. He will build his Church on Peter, whose new name means "rock." Just as King Solomon, according to Jewish tradition, built the temple of God on the foundation rock (where the Muslim Dome of the Rock lies today), so also Jesus is building his temple on his "rock." Jesus proclaims that the "gates of Hades will not prevail against" his temple on its foundation rock of Peter.[32] The powers of sin and death will be conquered through the new sacrifices that will be offered in the new temple, the Church.

After saying that he will build the temple of the Church on Peter, Jesus then gives him the keys of the kingdom of heaven. Jesus thus gives Peter his authority so that justice will be instantiated within the Church even when Jesus is no longer present in human form on earth. To understand the image of the keys of the kingdom, recall that the king would often have a royal steward who would oversee the daily operations of the kingdom. In Isaiah 22:15–25, God says that he is going to

30. *Catechism of the Catholic Church*, no. 443.

31. For various views of Jesus' identity, see, in addition to the works of Wright, Ben F. Meyer, *The Aims of Jesus* (London: SCM Press, 1979); Rudolf Schnackenburg, *Jesus in the Gospels: A Biblical Christology*, trans. O. C. Dean Jr. (Louisville: Westminster John Knox Press, 1995); Larry W. Hurtado, *One God, One Lord: Early Christian Devotion and Ancient Jewish Monotheism*, 2nd ed. (New York: T. & T. Clark, 1998); Richard J. Bauckham, *God Crucified: Monotheism and Christology in the New Testament* (Grand Rapids: Eerdmans, 1999); Ben Witherington III, *Jesus the Sage: The Pilgrimage of Wisdom* (Minneapolis: Fortress, 1994); Luke Timothy Johnson, *The Real Jesus* (New York: HarperSanFrancisco, 1996); idem, *Living Jesus: Learning the Heart of the Gospels* (New York: HarperSanFrancisco, 1999); Thomas G. Weinandy, O.F.M. Cap., *Jesus the Christ* (Huntington, IN: Our Sunday Visitor, 2003).

32. On Peter's confession and the foundation of the Church, as well as Jewish and Hellenistic legends about the foundation stone, see Ben F. Meyer, *Christus Faber: The Master Builder and the House of God* (Allison Park, PA: Pickwick, 1992).

replace a wicked royal steward with a faithful one.[33] The royal steward is "over the household" (Isa. 22:15). The royal steward has an office (Isa. 22:19), a robe and authority (Isa. 22:21). He is a father to the people of Jerusalem (Isa. 22:21), and "the key of the House of David" is placed on his shoulder. "He shall open, and none shall shut; and he shall shut and none shall open" (Isa. 22:22). By virtue of his office, the royal steward exercises not his own authority, but the authority of the king.

In this light, Jesus is the Davidic king who is establishing an office of the royal steward beginning with Peter. In the community of disciples, Peter has the keys to open and shut, to bind and to loose. In the Old Testament kingdom this was principally the power to instill justice in the people by carrying out punishment of offenses. In the new kingdom it will be the power proper to the new covenant: forgiveness of sins, the sacramental communication of Christ's merciful love. Peter exercises not his own authority, but the authority of Jesus the king. Jesus willingly extends his own authority as the Son of Man (Matt. 9:6) to Peter and the other apostles through him (cf. Matt. 18:18). Most importantly, this "kingly" authority is not power and domination, but rather is mercy and forgiveness.[34]

The Transfiguration of the Lord

After the establishment of Peter as the royal steward of the kingdom and the prediction of his suffering, death, and Resurrection, Jesus took Peter, James, and John up Mount Tabor to reveal to them his true glory. "And he was transfigured before them, and his face shone like the sun, and his garments became white as light" (Matt. 17:2). Through the

33. For the comparison with Isaiah 22, see Senior, *Matthew*, 191. For a brief treatment of the royal steward in ancient Israel, see Roland de Vaux, *Ancient Israel: Its Life and Institutions* (New York: McGraw-Hill, 1961), 129–131.

34. Interpreting this text, Joseph Ratzinger emphasizes the element of forgiveness:

This seems to me to be a cardinal point: at the inmost core of the new commission, which robs the forces of destruction of their power, is the grace of forgiveness. It constitutes the Church. The Church is founded upon forgiveness. Peter himself is a personal embodiment of this truth, for he is permitted to be the bearer of the keys after having stumbled, confessed and received the grace of pardon. . . . Behind the talk of authority, God's power appears as mercy and thus as the foundation stone of the Church. (Ratzinger, *Called to Communion*, 64)

For discussions of the priesthood and the Petrine office, see, e.g., John Paul II, *Crossing the Threshold of Hope*, Chapter 1: "'The Pope': A Scandal and a Mystery"; Matthew Levering, ed., *On the Priesthood: Classic and Contemporary Texts* (Lanham, MD: Rowman and Littlefield, 2003).

glorification of his own humanity, Jesus shows the three apostles the glory to be shared by all members of his kingdom. He is the righteous and glorious king of the holy kingdom. "And behold, there appeared to them Moses and Elijah talking with him" (Matt. 17:3).

The conversation with Moses and Elijah has profound significance. As is often noted, Moses stands for the law and Elijah stands for the prophets, both of which point to Jesus as their fulfillment. As we have seen in earlier chapters of this book, Moses and Elijah, moreover, alone in the Old Testament saw the glory of God directly. In Exodus 33, Moses stood on Mount Sinai and asked the Lord to show him his glory. The Lord passed in front of Moses showing him his goodness and his glory, yet covered Moses' eyes so that he could not see the Lord's face (Exod. 33:21–23). Elijah also saw the Lord on Mount Sinai. In 1 Kings 19, Elijah cried out to the Lord asking for deliverance, and that Lord told him to "stand upon the mount before the Lord" (1 Kings 19:11). There came a great wind, an earthquake, and a fire, but the Lord was not in these; the Lord revealed himself to Elijah in "a still small voice" (1 Kings 19:12). Elijah covered his face because no man can see God face to face and live.

In light of these two theophanies, we can see more clearly the implications of the Transfiguration. Moses and Elijah were the only two men that the Old Testament records as having witnessed the glory of God on a mountain. Now Moses and Elijah stand on the mountain witnessing Jesus Christ. Matthew records that, "A bright cloud overshadowed them, and a voice from the cloud said, 'This is my beloved Son, with whom I am well pleased; listen to him'" (Matt. 17:5). As the Son, Jesus shares the Father's glory. The sacred humanity of Jesus is now the face of God that Moses and Elijah can behold.[35]

Peter, James, and John also stand in the place of Moses and Elijah and now carry on their prophetic leadership in the new covenant. The king of the new covenant now has manifested his full glory as the eternal Son in human nature. The king will share his glory with his kingdom, composed of those who imitate him in self-giving love. As he tells the rich young ruler who asks him how to inherit eternal life: "If you would be perfect, go, sell what you possess and give to the poor, and you will have treasure in heaven; and come, follow me" (Matt. 19:21).[36] The fullness of his eternal glory, however, will remain hidden until it is partially revealed in his Resurrection and fully manifested when he comes to establish perfectly his kingdom at the end of the world.

35. For further theological implications, see Christoph Schönborn, O.P., *God's Human Face: The Christ-Icon*, trans. Lothar Krauth (San Francisco: Ignatius Press, 1994).

36. Cf. John Paul II, *Veritatis Splendor*, nos. 6–28; see also the profound scene in Fyodor Dostoevsky, *The Brothers Karamazov*, 43–44.

154

The Day of the Lord

Desiring to celebrate the feast of Passover in Jerusalem, Jesus enters triumphantly into the city. Beginning at the Mount of Olives, Jesus rides on an ass into Jerusalem (Matt. 21:1–11). King Solomon had ridden David's mule into Jerusalem when he was anointed king over Israel and Judah (1 Kings 1:33–35). However, Jesus' entry foretells the arrival of something much greater than the "rest" accomplished by Solomon. By fulfilling the prophesies of Zechariah, Jesus makes clear that the Day of the Lord has now arrived. As we recall, Zechariah 9:9 prophesies, "Behold, your king is coming to you, humble, and riding on an ass, on a colt the foal of an ass." Zechariah also prophesied that the Lord himself "shall stand on the Mount of Olives" before he goes to fight Israel's enemies (Zech. 14:4). Furthermore, on the "Day" on which he stands on the Mount of Olives, "there shall be continuous day" (Zech. 14:7), "living waters shall flow out from Jerusalem" (Zech. 14:8), "the Lord will become king over all the earth; on that day the Lord will be one and his name one" (Zech. 14:9), all nations shall worship the Lord in Jerusalem (Zech. 14:16), and everything will be made holy so that there will no longer be need for the traders who facilitate animal sacrifice in the temple (Zech. 14:21).[37]

The crowds anticipate the glorious Day of the Lord. They greet Jesus with the unmistakable cry, "Hosanna to the Son of David! Blessed is he who comes in the name of the Lord! Hosanna in the highest!" (Matt. 21:9). The Davidic king has returned to Jerusalem to defeat Israel's enemies and accomplish the promised salvation. As the divine Davidic king, not a worldly king, he returns not to a palace, but to the temple. He thus accomplishes the return of God's glory to the temple.

Arriving at his temple, he forcibly "drove out all who sold and bought in the temple, and he overturned the tables of the money-changers and the seats of those who sold pigeons" (Matt. 21:12). Why does he do this? Far from a random act of violence, his actions in the temple signify the ending of the animal sacrifices, which are no longer needed because he himself is the new temple. It is his sacrifice that will unite human beings to God, and it is by sharing in the temple of his body that human beings will now properly worship God. In cleansing the temple of the traders, Jesus says, "It is written, 'My house shall be called a house of prayer'; but you make it a den of robbers" (Matt. 21:13).[38] The first half of this

---

37. Cf. Hans Urs von Balthasar, *Theo-Drama, Theological Dramatic Theory*, Vol. 5: *The Last Act*, trans. Graham Harrison (San Francisco: Ignatius Press, 1998), 40–46.

38. It would be a mistake to read this prophetic denunciation as anti-Judaism. See William R. Farmer, ed., *Anti-Judaism and the Gospels* (Harrisburg, PA: Trinity Press International, 1999).

verse is from Isaiah 56:7 and recalls the inclusion of the Gentiles in the worship of the temple, which will now occur through Jesus' sacrifice. The second half is from Jeremiah 7:11, the context of which castigates the people of Judah for imagining that the physical temple of Israel will not be destroyed despite their moral corruption. Jesus' sacrifice will bring to perfection and reconstitute the temple of God.

By cleansing the temple of the money-changers and animal traders, Jesus shuts down the sacrifices of the temple for the day. This one-day closure prefigures a permanent cessation of sacrifices in the temple. We read, "Jesus left the temple and was going away, when his disciples came to point out to him the buildings of the temple. But he answered them, 'You see all of these, do you not? Truly, I say to you, there will not be left here one stone upon another, that will not be thrown down'" (Matt. 24:1–2).[39] The destruction of the temple occurred before the generation hearing Jesus had passed away—in AD 70 at the hands of the Romans. The physical temple was not an end in itself; its liturgy and sacrificial offerings were ordered to the consummation of perfect holiness that Jesus Christ himself embodies. Only the spiritual temple that is his mystical Body, the Church, can by his Spirit and through his once-and-for-all sacrifice loose people from their sins and instill them with justice.

In Jesus' great prophetic discourse in Matthew 24, his prophecy of the destruction of the temple is intertwined with his prophecy of the end of the world. Having inaugurated the triumphant Day of the Lord, Jesus identifies this Day with the end of the world, even though human history, with its normal patterns, will continue onward for a period of time until all is brought to final completion. The Day of the Lord marks the end or fulfillment of human history; all that remains is for humankind to share in his fulfillment. As Zechariah prophesied, on the Day of the Lord, which is inaugurated by Jesus' entrance into Jerusalem and his temple, God will truly become king over all the earth, since Jesus will reconcile all humankind to God (Matt. 28:18). Sin will be completely judged, since the king himself will bear our sin: all creation will thus be made sacred to God through Jesus' sacrifice.[40]

From Jesus, the new temple, will flow forth cleansing water to all the earth (Matt. 28:19), and his eucharistic sacrifice will constitute a continuous Day because humankind will forever receive its fruits. The return of the king will thus mark the end of the old temple and the old creation. Indeed, seen in this light, the temple is a microcosm of the universe

39. See Wright, *Jesus and the Victory of God*, 333–336.
40. For discussion of Adam's authority over the cosmos and of Jesus as the new Adam, see Joel Marcus, "Son of Man as Son of Adam," and "Son of Man as Son of Adam, Part II."

(literally, a micro-cosmos) and the universe is a macro-temple.[41] Just as the Son of Man has authority over the physical temple and speaks of its destruction, so the Son of Man has authority over the cosmos and can speak of its destruction: the new king and the new temple (Jesus himself) ushers in a new heavens and new earth, as Isaiah had prophesied.

In proclaiming his kingly power after his triumphal entry, Jesus also warns those who oppose him that their path is one of destruction. Yet, he does so with great sadness, arising from his deep mercy. Even in preaching dreadful woe to the rulers in Jerusalem, he declares, "O Jerusalem, Jerusalem, killing the prophets and stoning those who are sent to you! How often would I have gathered your children together as a hen gathers her brood under her wings, and you would not!" (Matt. 23:37).[42] Jesus concludes by saying that not only will they come to destruction, but so will their temple: "Behold, your house is forsaken and desolate" (Matt. 23:38).[43]

In three parables about the kingdom of heaven in Matthew 25, Jesus urges his hearers to prepare for the full inauguration of his kingdom by faithfully imitating his self-giving love, and he again warns urgently against the consequences of failing to love.[44] The parable of the wise and foolish maidens ends with the five foolish maidens, who had fallen asleep and been unprepared, being shut out from the bridegroom's marriage feast (cf. Hosea). The parable of the talents concludes with the servant who hated his master and buried his talent, rather than lending it abundantly to others, being cast "into the outer darkness; there men will weep and gnash their teeth" (Matt. 25:30).

In the third and final parable, Jesus simply speaks of the Son of Man coming in his glory and separating the sheep at his right from the goats at his left. Here he refers to himself directly as the king and invites those who have practiced mercy to inherit eternal life: "Then the King will say to those at his right hand, 'Come, O blessed of my Father, inherit the kingdom prepared for you from the foundation of the world; for I was hungry and you gave me food, I was thirsty and you gave me drink, I was a stranger and you welcomed me, I was naked and you clothed

41. On the theme of the temple as a micro-cosmos in the Old Testament, see, e.g., Levenson, *Sinai and Zion*, 111–145; Joshua Berman, *The Temple*, 10–19; G. K. Beale, *The Temple and the Church's Mission*.

42. See P. W. L. Walker, *Jesus and the Holy City: New Testament Perspectives on Jerusalem* (Grand Rapids: Eerdmans, 1996).

43. On this theme of judgment (that accomplishes the long-awaited restoration), see Steven M. Bryan, *Jesus and Israel's Traditions of Judgement and Restoration* (Cambridge: Cambridge University Press, 2002).

44. For discussion of Jesus' parables, see Craig L. Blomberg, *Interpreting the Parables* (Downers Grove, IL: InterVarsity Press, 1990).

me, I was sick and you visited me, I was in prison and you came to me" (Matt. 25:34–36). Only practicing the works of mercy prepares one to receive God's mercy; those who have not so loved cannot enter his kingdom, but rather are condemned to eternal fire. Members of the kingdom must thus meet the ethical demands of the covenant to care for the "widows and orphans" in the language of the Old Testament or "the least of these my brethren" (Matt. 25:40) in the New. By these teachings in Matthew 25, Jesus establishes his kingdom around imitation of his kingship, founded upon self-giving love. Those who follow and imitate the pride, arrogance, and violence of worldly kings have no place in the kingdom of God.

"This is My Blood of the Covenant"

If the kingdom proclaimed by Jesus demands such perfect holiness, then how can anyone hope to enter? In analyzing the Sermon on the Mount, we indicated that the disciples of Jesus can only become perfect as their heavenly Father is perfect by receiving God's righteousness as his adopted sons. But how is the righteousness of the Son of God passed on to his followers, that is, how are they adopted as sons with their sins purified? Jesus has already said that he came to call sinners, not the righteous. The king's role is to establish justice in his kingdom, and so Jesus as king must find a way to establish justice in his kingdom, a justice that he has already emphasized does not lie within the would-be members of his kingdom. How is it that Jesus' kingdom, composed of sinners, becomes a true holy people?

Here the place of sacrificial offerings to God once more becomes central. Sacrifice is the very opposite of the pride by which Adam and Eve selfishly sought to be like "god." Sacrifice belongs, as we have seen, at the heart of the covenants with Abraham, Moses, and David. The animal sacrifices of the Exodus are especially important, since the Exodus is intended to be a journey away from idolatry and toward holy land, toward dwelling with God by true worship. The sacrifice of the Paschal lamb spared the Israelites the destruction that is the consequence of sin (the tenth and ultimate plague). Furthermore, after receiving the Law at Mount Sinai, Moses offered sacrifice to God and consecrated the people: "And Moses took the blood and threw it upon the people, and said, 'Behold the blood of the covenant which the Lord has made with you in accordance with all these words'" (Exod. 24:8). Recall that Moses, with Aaron and his sons as well as seventy elders of Israel, then ascended Mount Sinai where "they beheld God, and ate and drank"

(Exod. 24:11). The saving presence of God is connected with this sacrificial meal, as well as with the Passover meal.

The path toward a holy people, a holy kingdom, is thus already set forth in the Old Testament. Even so, what Jesus is about to do goes far beyond what could have been expected. On the eve of his sacrificial death, he institutes a new sacrificial meal that will truly and fully unite human beings with the divine Redeemer. The king himself will become the new Passover sacrifice for his new kingdom.[45] By receiving Christ in the Eucharist, believers will be united and transformed into God's holy people, the mystical Body of Christ, the new temple. Like the blood of the Paschal lamb in Egypt, Christ's sacrifice will thereby separate out his holy people from the destruction that is the consequence of sin. His self-giving love will renew the world, and by sharing in his sacrifice, those who belong to his kingdom will be transformed into his kingly image.

Jesus tells his disciples, "You know that after two days the Passover is coming, and the Son of man will be delivered up to be crucified" (Matt. 26:2).[46] At the evening of the Passover meal, he revealed himself to be the Passover sacrifice. "Take, eat; this is my body. . . . Drink of it, all of you; for this is my blood of the covenant, which is poured out for many for the forgiveness of sins" (Matt. 26:26–28).[47] Just as the covenant with Moses was sealed by "the blood of the covenant" that was sprinkled on all those who entered it (Exod. 24:8), so also the new and perfect covenant between humankind and God will be ratified by sacrifice, the opposite of Adam and Eve's pride. In his words at the last supper, Jesus reveals how the perfect justice necessary to enter his kingdom will be established. His blood will be the blood of the new covenant, poured out for the forgiveness of sins. The body and blood present at the first Eucharist are the body and blood to be shed on the cross. The Eucharist and the crucifixion cannot be separated. At the last supper, Jesus explains the true meaning of the sacrifice he will offer on the next day. He not only shows its true meaning as a sacrifice for the forgiveness of sins; he also shows his apostles, and through them

45. See the reflections on this topic of Wright, *Jesus and the Victory of God*, 557–563.

46. For further discussion, see Donald Senior, C.P., *The Passion of Jesus in the Gospel of Matthew* (Collegeville, MN: Liturgical Press, 1990); Wright, *Jesus and the Victory of God*, 540–611.

47. See Jerome Kodell, O.S.B., *The Eucharist in the New Testament* (Wilmington, DE: Michael Glazier, 1988); Peter Stuhlmacher, "The New Testament Witness Concerning the Lord's Supper," in *Jesus of Nazareth, Christ of Faith*, trans. Siegfried Schatzmann (Peabody, MA: Hendrickson, 1993), 58–102; Ben F. Meyer, *One Loaf, One Cup: Ecumenical Studies of 1 Cor 11 and Other Eucharistic Texts* (Macon, GA: Mercer University Press, 1993).

all of his followers, the true means through which they can share in that sacrifice—the Eucharist.[48]

The new covenant established at the Last Supper and consummated on the cross is continued through the Eucharist of the Church. As the Davidic king, Jesus brings the power to forgive sins to its perfection through his sacrifice on the cross. Now sinners can indeed, by faith in Jesus and the sacraments of faith, become holy people and thus enter into his kingdom (holy land).

The disciples, led by Peter, think that they are already holy and insist that Jesus need not undergo his suffering alone. After the last supper is ended, they sing a hymn and go with Jesus to the Mount of Olives. Recall Zechariah 13:3–4, "Then the Lord will go forth and fight against those nations as when he fights on a day of battle. On that day his feet shall stand on the Mount of Olives which lies before Jerusalem on the east. . . ." The Day has arrived; the Lord is here. Jesus warns his disciples, however, that he will perform his saving sacrifice alone. He alone can establish justice and reconcile all people to God: "Then Jesus said to them, 'You will all fall away because of me this night; for it is written, "I will strike the shepherd, and the sheep of the flock will be scattered" (Zech. 13:7). But after I am raised up, I will go before you to Galilee'" (Matt. 26:31–32). Peter responds proudly, "'Though they shall all fall away because of you, I will never fall away'" (Matt. 26:33). Jesus prophesies Peter's threefold denial, but Peter and all the disciples are obstinate: "'Even if I must die with you, I will not deny you.' And so said all the disciples" (Matt. 26:35).

Yet, Peter, James, and John fail even to remain awake with Jesus during his agonizing hours of prayer in the Garden of Gethsemane, where the Lord expresses in prayer his sorrow and his conformity to his Father's will. On the great Day of the Lord, the disciples fail. Only Christ, God incarnate, is able to bear the world's history of sin. As we read in Isaiah 59:15–16, "The Lord saw it, and it displeased him that there was no justice. He saw that there was no man, and wondered that there was no one to intervene; then his own arm brought him victory, and his righteousness upheld him." Arising from his prayer, Jesus awakens his disciples. The time has arrived: "Behold, the hour is at hand, and the Son of man is being betrayed into the hands of sinners. Rise, let us be going; see, my betrayer is at hand" (Matt. 26:45–46). Judas identifies Jesus with a kiss, a mark of love that, in this context, horribly displays humankind's lack of real love.[49]

48. For further discussion of the Eucharist, see John Paul II, *Ecclesia de Eucharistia* (2003); Matthew Levering, *Sacrifice and Community* (Oxford: Blackwell, 2005).

49. For discussion of Christ's Agony in the Garden, see St. Thomas More, *The Sadness of Christ*, trans. Clarence Miller (Princeton: Scepter, 1993).

The Passion of Christ

Barely a few days after his triumphant entry into Jerusalem as the Son of David who returns to the temple and enacts its messianic cleansing, then, Jesus is betrayed by his own disciples, arrested, and condemned to death with the guilty. The return of the Davidic king to Zion to accomplish the triumphant Day of the Lord, as foretold by so many prophets, turns out to be the Day of greatest humiliation and sacrifice. At his arrest, "all the disciples forsook him and fled" (Matt. 26:56). Peter follows him, only to deny three times any relationship with him (Matt. 26:69–75). Surely this humiliating death does not befit the divine Redeemer of whom Isaiah prophesies, "The Lord saw it, and it displeased him that there was no justice. He saw that there was no man, and wondered that there was no one to intervene; then his own arm brought him victory, and his righteousness upheld him. He put on righteousness as a breastplate, and a helmet of salvation upon his head; he put on garments of vengeance for clothing, and wrapped himself in fury as a mantle" (Isa. 59:16–17). We expect God to do this as a warrior.

As we have seen, however, Jesus at the Last Supper prepares the disciples for his sacrificial death, and celebrates his Eucharist with them. Even before entering Jerusalem in triumph, he had warned his disciples, who were arguing over who would have the privilege of sitting on Jesus' right and left hands in his kingdom: "You know that the rulers of the Gentiles lord it over them, and their great men exercise authority over them. It shall not be so among you; but whoever would be great among you must be your servant, and whoever would be first among you must be your slave; even as the Son of man came not to be served but to serve, and to give his life as a ransom for many" (Matt. 20:25–28). Unlike a worldly ruler, who relies upon power and domination, the divine Davidic king conquers by love. God, in the righteous man Jesus Christ, truly conquers sin by his sacrificial love on the cross, the triumphant Day of the Lord. Humankind's pride is reversed by Christ's self-giving love.

As we saw in our first chapter, pride disorders the relationship between humankind and God, and this disorder culminates in the punishment of death. As suffering Servant and divine conqueror, therefore, Christ on the cross freely accepts death and thereby, in his perfect love for each one of us, pays this penalty and heals (re-orders) humankind from within. Where there once was a fatal lack of justice, now there is, in Christ, a bridge of saving justice (holiness!) between humankind and God. God in Christ reveals the true nature of divine kingship and divine righteousness: humility and self-giving love.[50]

---

50. Quoting Galatians 2:20, the *Catechism of the Catholic Church* affirms that Jesus did not die for a vaguely conceived "humankind," but rather died out of love for each one

Christ suffers a punishment so brutal that even the Romans would not use it on their own citizens. On the cross he cries out, "My God, my God, why hast thou forsaken me?" (Matt. 27:46). Contrary to some interpretations, this does not entail that Jesus was completely abandoned by God the Father, for this would mean that the eternal Son was completely alienated from the eternal Father. In the Old Testament context of kingship, which we have seen is pervasive in Jesus' ministry, the expression "My God, my God, why hast thou forsaken me?" would be recognized as the first line of Psalm 22, a psalm of distress and crying out that ends in final deliverance. Psalm 22 concludes, "Yea, to him shall all the proud of the earth bow down. . . . Posterity shall serve him; men shall tell of the Lord to the coming generation, and proclaim his deliverance to a people yet unborn, that he has wrought it" (Ps. 22:29–31). In the full context of Psalm 22, we see that even on the cross Jesus is not completely abandoned. More precisely, we see that his supreme humility on the cross is the sign of his divine kingship. By quoting Psalm 22, Jesus reveals that his horrific suffering expresses the nature of his kingship, which is so different from the character of worldly kings who attempt to establish justice by domination. Psalm 22 indicates that Jesus will be delivered and established in his proper place as the rightful king.[51]

Even those who torture him and put him to death manifest the truth of Jesus' enthronement. Pilate's soldiers beat him as a mock king: "they stripped him and put a scarlet robe upon him, and plaiting a crown of thorns they put it on his head, and put a reed in his right hand. And kneeling before him they mocked him, saying, 'Hail, King of the Jews!'" (Matt. 27:28–29). Unbeknownst to them, their violence in reality begins to crown him as king, because God's true power is perfectly expressed in self-giving love. The crucifixion, although apparently a great defeat, in fact is the victorious road to his enthronement in the Resurrection. Above Jesus was placed a sign that read, "This is Jesus the King of the Jews" (Matt. 27:37). God's providence embraces and overcomes the sin and violence of man. Even in their violence, they still proclaim, unintentionally of course, the truth of what is actually happening—Jesus is becoming the king, not only of the Jews, but of the universe. This but manifests the truth that even human sins do not fall outside of God's

---

of us: "Jesus knew and loved each and all during his life, his agony, and his Passion and gave himself up for each one of us: 'The Son of God . . . loved me and gave himself up for me'" (no. 478). On Christ's knowledge and Christ's death, see *Catechism*, nos. 472–474, 598–618. See also Matthew Levering, *Christ's Fulfillment of Torah and Temple* (Notre Dame, IN: University of Notre Dame Press, 2002); Joel B. Green and Mark D. Baker, *Recovering the Scandal of the Cross: Atonement in New Testament and Contemporary Contexts* (Downers Grove, IL: InterVarsity Press, 2000).

51. See St. Augustine, *City of God*, Book XVII, ch. 17, 749–750.

providence, for God can bring good out of them. The greatest good of the resurrected kingdom comes from the greatest evil of the crucifixion. When at his death "the curtain in the Temple was torn in two, from top to bottom; and the earth shook" (Matt. 27:51) and the realms of death are stirred, we can see that what the prophets foretold as the cataclysmic Day of the Lord, in which all previous divisions would be overcome and all people would be measured by Christ, has now taken place. The curtain that separated the people from the Holy of Holies in the temple is no more; God's presence now manifests itself directly to the people. Their exile has ended. Indeed, the cross is the place of divine (kingly) judgment on sin; Christ's love judges the world and Christ himself endures the judgment, the radical disharmony of suffering and death. His cross ends forever the exile of humankind from God.

The Resurrection gloriously proclaims this deliverance. The deliverance of the king, and thereby of his people, from the power of sin and death begins to manifest itself when Mary Magdalene and the other women come to care for the dead body of Jesus on the dawn of the first day. The reference to dawn of the first day leads the reader back to the first day of creation; this is truly the dawn of the new creation. The angel of the Lord said to the women, "Do not be afraid; for I know that you seek Jesus who was crucified. He is not here; for he is risen as he said" (Matt. 28:5–6).[52] God has delivered Jesus! With Jesus' deliverance from death, the new creation, holy people in holy land, has begun. Jesus has finally been fully enthroned as the king. As we might have expected from the divine king, whose power is expressed in self-gift, the cross was the first stage of his coronation, completed in the Resurrection. A new kingdom with a new king has been established, a kingdom in which righteousness and eternal life are given to all who enter it under the blood of the covenant.

The kingdom should not be viewed as spiritual as though it were in opposition to a physical kingdom. It would be incomplete to say that in the Old Testament the kingdom was physical and in the New Testament it is spiritual. The ultimate meaning of the Old Testament promises was directed toward the holiness of the people dwelling perfectly with God. In the New Testament, the physical Resurrection of Jesus as well as the resurrection of the body for believers shows that Jesus' kingdom remains physical. The difference is that in the kingdom proclaimed

52. See *Catechism of the Catholic Church*, nos. 638–655. See also N. T. Wright, *The Resurrection of the Son of God* (Minneapolis: Fortress, 2003), along with the valuable review of this book by Gary A. Anderson, "The Risen Christ," *First Things* 137 (Nov. 2003): 51–54. Anderson raises an important concern about the relationship of historical reconstruction to the theological task.

and established by Jesus, the physical restoration of the kingdom must await the end of history. Members of Jesus' kingdom cannot expect to be spared physical death and suffering—indeed Jesus says they must embrace it by taking up their cross and following him. But members of Jesus' kingdom can expect to be spared eternal physical death and suffering. The kingdom he proclaims is not merely a spiritual kingdom, but is a spiritual and physical kingdom that has yet only been established in part.

Evangelization

Upon his death and Resurrection, Jesus is firmly enthroned as the Davidic king who now reigns over the kingdom of God. At what is often called "The Great Commission," Jesus says to the eleven remaining apostles, "All authority in heaven and on earth has been given to me. Go therefore and make disciples of all nations, baptizing them in the name of the Father and of the Son and of the Holy Spirit, teaching them to observe all that I have commanded you; and lo, I am with you always, to the close of age" (Matt. 28:18–20). The resurrected Jesus is the enthroned king with complete authority over heaven and earth; the waters of baptism, as Ezekiel had foretold, are the healing waters flowing from the new temple, his Church, and fructifying the whole earth. He is the king of the universe. Yet, his purpose is to share his kingship with the members of his Church, those who are united to him in self-giving love.

Jesus possesses all authority, but possesses it so as to share it. He sends his apostles out to bear that authority in the world, in order to expand and bring to completion his kingdom. The apostles are to "make disciples," baptizing them in the name of the Father, Son, and Holy Spirit and teaching them to obey Jesus' commandments. Jesus gives the apostles the ability, by word and sacrament, to communicate his holiness to believers. To become a disciple and to be baptized is to enter Jesus' kingdom. Through the sacrament of baptism, believers are initiated into the new covenant of Jesus Christ. Through the sacrament of the Eucharist, as we have seen, believers continue to participate in the new covenant. Members of the kingdom receive righteousness from Jesus through the teachings and sacraments of the apostolically structured Church. Because of this righteousness, believers are able to obey all that Jesus has commanded, even though we often fall short. Our obedience, as well as the justice that comes from perfect obedience, is not our own, but rather is freely received from Jesus as the great king who instills justice within each member of his kingdom.

Are the themes of king and kingdom (the establishment of holy people) likewise at the center of Luke-Acts and Mark? Yes, but in different ways. Thus Luke-Acts presents the themes of king and kingdom as reconfigured around God's *mercy* effected through the life, death, and Resurrection of Jesus and the gift of the Holy Spirit at Pentecost that, as God's indwelling in the Church, makes possible the preaching of the apostles. For Luke-Acts, the formation of a holy people in Christ is above all the fruit of God's tremendous mercy. While the theme of divine mercy is of course present in Matthew as well, Luke places it at the center of his Gospel and of the life of the holy people (Acts). For instance, Luke relates that Jesus on the cross says, "Father, forgive them; for they know not what they do" (Luke 23:34) and that Jesus promises the repentant thief who is being crucified with him, "Truly, I say to you, today you will be with me in Paradise" (Luke 23:42). Luke similarly presents the parable of the Prodigal Son (Luke 15:11–32) as well as Mary's Magnificat, which glorifies the Lord by proclaiming that "his mercy is on those who fear him from generation to generation" (Luke 1:50).

Mark, too, focuses upon the establishment of the holy people, but he does so by emphasizing the dramatic actions of Jesus as the Son of God and thereby inculcating a sense of the *urgency* of the call to conversion and holiness. In Mark, everything is done "immediately" (Mark 1:10, 12, 18, 20, 21, 23, 29, 30, 42, and so forth), driving the narrative on toward its stunning climax. In an unexpected way, like a flash of lightening, Jesus has established God's holy people; we must respond.

The themes of holy people and holy land are found in all the Gospels. Yet, in comparison to the emphasis of the Synoptic Gospels on king and kingdom (the establishment of holy people), the Gospel of John focuses on temple and divine indwelling (the establishment of holy land). Let us now explore the Fourth Gospel.

7

Gospel of John

The Temple of the Trinity

John's Gospel begins boldly by echoing the first line of Genesis, "In the beginning. . . ." The true meaning of the creation story in Genesis is bound up with the story of Jesus. Genesis 1–3 is an open-ended story because by the end man and woman are exiled from the garden, the temple where God dwelled with them. They have lost the righteousness with which they were created. They now are ashamed of themselves and afraid of God. They have become an unholy people dwelling in an unholy land, a land no longer indwelt by God. As proclaimed by John, the story of Jesus is thus the story of restoring and perfecting creation by reestablishing a holy land in which God dwells with his holy people. The remaking of a holy people will occur through Jesus Christ, the incarnate Son of God. As we will see, Jesus reveals his body to be the new and perfect temple of God.

Trinitarian Foundations of Glory

"In the beginning was the Word, and the Word was with God, and the Word was God. He was in the beginning with God; all things were made through him, and without him was not anything made that was made" (John 1:1–3). John steps back behind the first chapter of Genesis and reveals what Genesis leaves implicit—that the Word of God, the pattern by which God created the heavens and the earth, is a distinct person within the one Godhead, yet fully equal to God. At the heart of the Jewish tradition is the radical distinction between God the Creator and the universe he made. Thus the greatest sin is that of idolatry, worshipping parts of the creation instead of its Creator. The Word of God, whom John will soon identify as the one who became incarnate in Jesus Christ, is placed squarely on the Creator-side of the distinction between Creator and creation. The Word was with God, the Word was God, and through the Word all things were made. The Word is "with God," and so the Word is distinct from God; yet the Word "was God," and so the Word is God.[1] Here we already have a hint of the divine "persons," each of whom is fully God, in the one God. Furthermore, the Word "was in the beginning with God; all things were made through him," and so the Word is the Creator.[2] When in the fourth century a priest named Arius argued that the Word was created, summarizing it in the slogan, "There was when the Word was not," St. Athanasius, and the Council of Nicea, could remind him that John teaches the very opposite.[3]

If John identifies the Word with God, however, surely he could not mean that the Word truly became man?[4] Once one has grasped the eternal glory of God, it is difficult to imagine how such a glorious God could wish to be intimate with humankind, let alone become a man! Aristotle, knowing nothing of God's revelation to Israel, conceived of God as "thinking of Himself through all eternity."[5] In a sense, Aristotle was right. In knowing himself in the Word, God knows all creatures. Aristotle, however, did not conceive of God as the loving Creator. In this sense, Aristotle turned out to be completely wrong.

Throughout the history of the Old Testament, as we have seen, God showed his desire to reverse the disharmony in humankind caused by sin,

1. See St. Augustine, *Homilies on the Gospel of John*, in Nicene and Post-Nicene Fathers, First Series, Vol. 7, ed. Philip Schaff (Peabody, MA: Hendrickson, 1995 [1888]), Tractates I-III (7–25); St. Thomas Aquinas, *Commentary on the Gospel of Saint John*, Part I, trans. James A. Weisheipl, O.P., and Fabian R. Larcher, O.P. (Albany, NY: Magi Books, 1980), 31–63. See also Ben Witherington, III, *John's Wisdom: A Commentary on the Fourth Gospel* (Louisville: Westminster John Knox Press, 1995), 19, 47–59.

2. Leon Morris, *The Gospel according to John*, rev. ed. (Grand Rapids: Eerdmans, 1995), 65–66; cf. Marianne Meye Thompson, *The God of the Gospel of John* (Grand Rapids: Eerdmans, 2001).

3. See St. Athanasius, *On the Incarnation*; cf. the texts contained in William G. Rusch, ed., *The Trinitarian Controversy* (Philadelphia: Fortress Press, 1980).

4. G. K. Chesterton is particularly good at addressing this question. See Chesterton, *Orthodoxy: The Romance of Faith* (New York: Image Books, 1990 [1908]).

5. Aristotle, *Metaphysics*, trans. Hippocrates G. Apostle (Grinnell, IA: Peripatetic Press, 1979), Book XII, ch. 9 (210).

and to dwell intimately again in a relationship of love with his people. From the time of Moses until David, God dwelt in the tabernacle, or tent of meeting. The glory cloud, or *kabod*, signified the Lord's presence.[6] At the completion of the tabernacle under Moses, the Book of Exodus describes how "the cloud covered the tent of meeting, and the glory of the Lord filled the tabernacle. And Moses was not able to enter the tent of meeting, because the cloud abode upon it" (Exod. 40:34–35). From Solomon until the Babylonian exile, God's "name," as we have seen, dwelt in the temple. At the dedication of Solomon's temple in 1 Kings 8, the pattern of Exodus is repeated: "when the priests came out of that holy place, a cloud filled the house of the Lord, so that the priests could not stand to minister because of the cloud; for the glory of the Lord filled the house of the Lord" (1 Kings 8:10–11). God's dwelling is a spiritual presence or union with his people; the Bible does not imagine God as physically confined to a place as if he were a creature. At each of these climatic moments through his covenants, therefore, God was beginning to reverse the disharmony of creation. The land would no longer be alienated from God, and God would again dwell with his people and consecrate them to himself.

Yet, this reversal could not take place from the side of humankind. Israel, like all peoples, kept falling back into idolatry and pride. Recall how the prophet Ezekiel describes the terrifying vision of the glory of the Lord leaving the temple (Ezek. 11:23). Although the covenants revealed more and more clearly God's plan for the salvation of his people, nonetheless Israel, like all peoples, was not yet holy. Israel thus violated the covenants that represented God's dwelling with Israel and Israel's dwelling with God, and Israel went into exile. The land was desolate because of the people's lack of holiness. Even with the rebuilding of the temple in the fifth century BC and with the much later rededication of the temple under the Maccabees (second century BC), the glory cloud never reappears in the temple. The reversal of disharmony, the renewal and consummation of God's dwelling with his people, would require a mighty and amazing act of God. To fulfill the purpose of his covenants, God would need to dwell fully with his people in holy land. A God of domination and power would have no interest in doing this, but the God of Israel, who seeks out his sinful creatures and desires their conversion, would.

6. For discussion of the manifestation of divine glory, see Hans Urs von Balthasar, *The Glory of the Lord: A Theological Aesthetics*, Vol. 1, *Seeing the Form*, trans. Erasmo Leiva-Merikakis (San Francisco: Ignatius Press, 1982). See also David B. Hart, *The Beauty of the Infinite: The Aesthetics of Christian Truth* (Grand Rapids: Eerdmans, 2003).

Once one recalls that God's glory has never returned to the temple after the Babylonian exile, the full meaning of John 1:14 becomes clearer: "And the Word became flesh and dwelt among us, full of grace and truth: we have beheld his glory, glory as of the only Son from the Father."[7] The Greek literally should be translated, "the Word became flesh and pitched his tent [tabernacled] among us." The Lord who dwelt in the tabernacle and then the temple in the form of a cloud now dwells with us in Jesus.[8] The formless cloud has given way to the form of human flesh. The expression "flesh" here stands for the entire human person of body and soul. Against the Apollinarian heresy that denied a rational soul in the human nature of Jesus, the Fathers of the Church often pointed to Psalm 65:2, "To thee shall all flesh come on account of sins."[9] Clearly, "all flesh" does not indicate only human bodies coming to God, but rather the human race, the members of which are made up of a body and a rational soul.

John's teaching is similar to Colossians 1:15, which describes Jesus as "the image [icon] of the invisible God." Because God now dwells in the tabernacle/temple of Jesus, those who see the human form of Jesus "have beheld his glory." Now we see the full import of John beginning with the Word of God as the Creator and not as a creature. The one through whom all things were created is the same one who has dwelt with us in Jesus Christ. Creation indeed has been renewed because God again dwells with man. The new creation is a communion in the Trinity's superabundant life of wisdom and love. Since wisdom and love enlighten our spirit, John describes the fount of new creation in terms of "life" and "light": "In him was life, and the life was the light of men. . . . The true light that enlightens every man was coming into the world" (John 1:4, 9).[10]

This renewal of creation (perfect holy land, dwelling with God) is accomplished through the gift of divine filiation. Throughout John, Jesus is revealed as the Son who enjoys full union with his Father. The Incarnation of the Word offers human beings the ability to share in

7. For discussion of the glory that Adam had before the Fall, which Jesus the new Adam, recovers, see Marcus, "Son of Man as Son of Adam" and "Son of Man as Son of Adam, Part II."

8. For connections with the Old Testament figure of Wisdom, see Witherington, *John's Wisdom*.

9. See St. Augustine, *Expositions on the Book of Psalms*, the Oxford translation, Vol. 8 of Nicene and Post-Nicene Fathers, First Series (Peabody, MA: Hendrickson, 1995 [1888]), Psalm 65 [64], no. 5 (269).

10. On the symbolism of light, see St. Thomas Aquinas, *Commentary on John*, Part I, 58–63, 69–76; Craig R. Koester, *Symbolism in the Fourth Gospel: Meaning, Mystery, Community* (Minneapolis: Fortress, 1995), chapter 4.

the unique communion of Son and Father by becoming children of God.[11] John 1:12 focuses on this gift of divine filiation when describing the power Jesus has communicated to man: "But to all who received him, who believed in his name, he gave power to become children of God" (John 1:12). That God's power or grace is needed for human beings, by faith, to become children of God manifests a central truth of John—because of sin human beings have forfeited their divine filiation. Man was created to share in the glory of God, and now God is restoring that glory. In the Incarnation, "we have beheld his glory, glory as of the only Son from the Father" (John 1:14). By becoming children of God, human beings are restored in the harmony of original justice and can behold the indwelling glory of God. The themes of holy people and holy land reflect two different aspects of the one saving reality of our divine filiation. At Jesus' Resurrection, he shows that the gift of divine filiation has now been fully given. Jesus says to Mary Magdalene, "I am ascending to my Father and *your* Father, to my God and *your* God" (John 20:17, emphasis added).[12] The cross will be shown to have been the true sacrifice for sin that has now opened the way for human beings to share in the eternal glory of the Father and the Son.

The Sacrificial Priest King

The remainder of John 1 carefully, yet subtly, delineates how the Word made flesh who now dwells with us will restore us so that we are able to dwell with him. This comes in three stages: the Lamb of God, the king of Israel, and the temple. John the Baptist proclaims, "Behold, the Lamb of God, who takes away the sin of the world!" (John 1:29). Drawing on the promised lamb from the sacrifice of Isaac (Genesis 22) and the Passover lamb of the exodus (Exodus 12), Jesus is identified as the sacrificial lamb who will free the people from their sins and lead them into the promised land of Abraham's blessing. In other words, Jesus himself embodies the sacrificial cult of the temple: in the Lamb, human beings can dwell with God in true worship. John the Baptist makes clear that this dwelling with the Father in the Son will occur through the Holy Spirit: "John bore witness, 'I saw the Spirit descend as a dove from heaven, and it remained on him. I myself did not know him; but he who sent me to baptize with water said to me, 'He on whom you see

11. See Kurz, "Beyond Historical Criticism: Reading John's Prologue as Catholics," in Johnson and Kurz, *The Future of Catholic Biblical Scholarship*, 159–181.
12. See Marianne Meye Thompson, *The Promise of the Father* (Louisville: Westminster John Knox Press, 2000).

the Spirit descend and remain, this is he who baptizes with the Holy Spirit.' And I have seen and have borne witness that this is the Son of God" (John 1:32–34). It is the Holy Spirit who enables us to recognize Jesus as the Son.[13]

To follow Jesus, therefore, means to dwell with God who is Father, Son, and Holy Spirit.[14] Jesus shows us that following him means dwelling in the Trinity when two of John's disciples begin to follow him. Turning, Jesus asks, "What do you seek?" (John 1:38). Their reply at first seems quite strange. "And they said to him, 'Rabbi' (which means Teacher), 'where are you staying?'" Why would they care where he was staying? Once we recall the evangelist John's pregnant words from earlier in the first chapter of his Gospel, however, their question takes on a much deeper meaning: "No one has ever seen God; the only Son, who is in the bosom of the Father, he has made him known" (John 1:18). Where is Jesus staying? In the bosom of the Father. He dwells there, and he will enable his followers to dwell in the Father with the Son. He therefore answers, "Come and see" (John 1:39), and they dwell with him that day. Jesus' first disciples also identify him as the Davidic king. Andrew says to his brother Peter, "We have found the Messiah (which means Christ)" (John 1:41). Messiah or Christ is a title meaning the anointed one in Hebrew and Greek, respectively. Nathanael likewise says, "Rabbi, you are the Son of God! You are the King of Israel!" (John 1:49).

Jesus does not deny the names given him by John the Baptist and the disciples, but he adds to them his own. When he says to Nathanael, "Truly, truly, I say to you, you will see heaven opened, and the angels of God ascending and descending upon the Son of man" (John 1:51), he recalls the dream that Jacob had when Jacob was leaving the promised land to seek his fortune, a dream of a ladder upon which the angels of God were ascending and descending. Jacob describes this place, at the northern boundary of the promised land, as the meeting of heaven and earth and names it "Bethel" which means "house of God," another name for the temple: "And he was afraid, and said, 'How awesome is

13. On the Holy Spirit in the New Testament, see St. Basil the Great, *On the Holy Spirit*, trans. David Anderson (Crestwood, NY: St. Vladimir's Seminary Press, 1997); Gordon D. Fee, *God's Empowering Presence: The Holy Spirit in the Letters of Paul* (Peabody, MA: Hendrickson, 1994).

14. On the Trinity and the New Testament, see Gordon D. Fee, "Paul and the Trinity: The Experience of Christ and the Spirit for Paul's Understanding of God," in his *To What End Exegesis?* (Grand Rapids: Eerdmans, 2001), 330–350; C. Kavin Rowe, "The God of Israel and Jesus Christ: Luke, Marcion, and the Unity of the Canon," *Nova et Vetera* 1 (2003): 359–380; idem, "Biblical Pressure and Trinitarian Hermeneutics," *Pro Ecclesia* 11 (2002): 295–312; idem, "Luke and the Trinity: An Essay in Ecclesial Biblical Theology," *Scottish Journal of Theology* 56 (2003): 1–26; Witherington and Ice, *The Shadow of the Almighty*.

this place! This is none other than the house of God, and this is the gate of heaven" (Gen. 28:17). By claiming this image for himself, Jesus reveals himself to be the temple, the true promised land, uniting man with God as prefigured in the dream of Jacob. This dream characterized the vocation of the people of Israel to be a people who dwelled with God. Jesus will make his people holy, and enable them to enter the holy land where he dwells in the Father's bosom, by offering himself as the sacrificial lamb in the temple which he is.

What John 1 implies, John 2 makes explicit. Jesus is the temple, the locus of the covenantal marriage of God and humankind. First, "[o]n the third day" (John 2:1)—the day of resurrection, consummation—there takes place a marriage at Cana in Galilee. Jesus and his mother Mary are present. When she tells him that the wine has run out, he warns her that his "hour" has not yet come. Nonetheless, she instructs the servants, "Do whatever he tells you" (John 2:5). Mary thus reveals herself as the perfect disciple of her son. By obeying Jesus, the faithful servants of Israel will witness a great sign of the new covenant, the wine of purification from sin.[15] Jesus commands that six stone jars, normally used for "the Jewish rites of purification" at the temple, be filled with water. When the servants draw liquid from the jars, it is wine: "the steward of the feast called the bridegroom and said to him, 'Every man serves the good wine first; and when men have drunk freely, then the poor wine; but you have kept the good wine until now" (John 2:9–10). This sign, by which Jesus "manifested his glory" (John 2:11) and caused his disciples to believe in him, signifies the temple marriage of God and humankind, a marriage procured by the forgiveness of sins accomplished by the Messiah's sacrificial blood, the good wine of the new covenant.[16]

Second, on the feast of Passover, Jesus goes to Jerusalem and enters the physical temple. There he makes a whip of cords and drives out from the temple the moneychangers, those selling animals for sacrifice, and the animals themselves. He says to them, "Take these things away; you shall not make my Father's house a house of trade" (John 2:16). The disciples see in Jesus the fulfillment of Psalm 69, "Zeal for thy house will consume me" (John 2:17; Ps. 69:9). When the Jewish authorities in the temple ask Jesus, "What sign have you to show us for doing this?" Jesus answers them, "Destroy this temple, and in three days I will raise it up" (John 2:19). Although Jesus leaves the meaning of his words for his listeners to discover, John immediately lets his readers in on the mystery: "he spoke

15. See Francis J. Moloney, *The Gospel of John* (Collegeville, MN: Liturgical Press, 1998), 66–68, 72.

16. For discussion of the wedding feast at Cana, see Ignace de la Potterie, *Mary in the Mystery of the Covenant*, trans. Bertrand Buby (New York: Alba House, 1992), 157–208.

of the temple of his body" (John 2:21). The first two chapters of John thus clearly reveal Jesus as the temple. The Bible throughout shows that man's deepest desire is to dwell with God, and now John shows that the temple in which one can find merciful forgiveness of sins (image-restoration, holy people) and behold the Trinity in covenantal union (image-perfection, holy land) is Jesus Christ.[17]

Living Water: Baptism

In John 3, Nicodemus comes to Jesus by night and questions him. Jesus quickly begins to instruct him on how one is to enter the kingdom of God. "Unless one is born anew, he cannot see the kingdom of God" (John 3:3). The word "anew" is *anothen* in the Greek and can also mean from above. Nicodemus mistakenly thinks Jesus meant that Nicodemus must be born a second time "anew" or "again," but Jesus implies that the meaning "from above" is the right one. One cannot see the kingdom unless one is born from above. Jesus states clearly that he has come from above when he says the Son of Man has "descended from heaven" (John 3:13). As the eternal Son now made man, he has been born from above, and there is no other way for human beings to share in communion with the Father unless they also are born from above.

How then can one be born from above? "Truly, truly, I say to you, unless one is born of water and the Spirit, he cannot enter the kingdom of God. That which is born of the flesh is flesh, and that which is born of the Spirit is spirit" (John 3:5–6). Jesus is instructing Nicodemus in the mystery of the Word become flesh: the Word was not born of the flesh, that is, not simply from natural human descent, but born of the Spirit. The kingdom of God is that communion with the Father that was previously only shared by the Son. If human beings are to enter the kingdom, Jesus is saying they must likewise be born of the Spirit. John said as much when he said, "But to all who received him, who believed in his name, he gave power to become children of God; who were born, not of blood nor of the will of the flesh nor of the will of man, but of God" (John 1:12). This birth "from above" or "of God" must be accomplished through birth "of water and the Spirit." It will not do to interpret this as "spiritual water."[18] The visible water is the sign of the invisible birth in the Spirit. Water was

17. On image-restoration and image-perfection, see Romanus Cessario, O.P., *The Godly Image: Christ and Salvation in Catholic Thought from Anselm to Aquinas* (Petersham, MA: St. Bede's Publications, 1990). See also Richard B. Hays, "Reading Scripture in Light of the Resurrection," 216–238.
18. As is done by, among others, Leon Morris in *The Gospel according to John*, 193.

already a ritual sign of repentance, as seen in the baptism of John (John 1:26). Jesus reveals to Nicodemus that he will give a greater baptism than John, and it will be greater because the visible sign of water will contain the invisible power of the Spirit. Jesus' baptism will be of water and the Spirit and will communicate the forgiveness of sins, enabling the recipient to enter the kingdom of God as a child of God.

Since the forgiveness of sins that the sacrament of baptism communicates is accomplished by the cross of Jesus, his conversation about baptism soon turns to the cross. Jesus explains to Nicodemus that the Son of Man must be lifted up, as Moses lifted up the serpent in the wilderness (John 3:14). This "lifting up" forms the context of the famous John 3:16, "For God so loved the world that he gave his only Son, that whoever believes in him should not perish but have eternal life." As long as human beings remain in exile or alienation from God, they cannot share in the loving communion with God as Father that, as we saw in the Old Testament, God wills to give them. Jesus implies to Nicodemus, then, that he will open up the way to true communion with the Father in eternal life through his own sacrifice on the cross. The merciful forgiveness and reconciliation achieved by the cross is then applied to the sinner through the baptism of water and the Spirit received in faith in the Son.[19] Faith in Jesus the mediator and baptism in water and the Spirit are the route to eternal life. When the divine Word has become human flesh in order to redeem human beings so they can dwell with him, it is appropriate that redemption won by the incarnate Lord continues to be offered under the visible, tangible forms of the sacraments: otherwise, we risk spiritualizing away the Lord's ongoing desire to be incarnationally present with us.

The Samaritan woman at the well in John 4 continues Jesus' unveiling of the gift of baptism. "There came a woman of Samaria to draw water. Jesus said to her, 'Give me a drink'" (John 4:7). In a parallel story from Genesis, Abraham's steward, sent to find a wife for Isaac, decides, "Let the maiden to whom I shall say, 'Pray, let down your jar that I may drink,' and who shall say, 'Drink, and I will water your camels'—let her be the one whom thou [God] hast appointed for thy servant Isaac" (Gen. 24:14).[20] In light of Genesis 24, Jesus' encounter with the Samaritan woman thus hints at a courtship scene; but the courtship here is the spiritual marriage of God and sinners brought about by the forgiveness of sins. To her surprise, Jesus identifies her sin: "You are right in saying, 'I have no husband'; for you have had five husbands,

---

19. Cf. *Catechism of the Catholic Church*, nos. 1213–1228.

20. The parallel is mentioned in Raymond E. Brown, S.S., *The Gospel according to John (I–XII)* (New York: Doubleday, 1966), 170.

and he whom you now have is not your husband; this you said truly" (John 4:17–18). Her history of infidelity recalls the prophet Hosea of the Northern Kingdom (whose capital was Samaria), whom God commands, "Go, take to yourself a wife of harlotry and have children of harlotry, for the land commits great harlotry by forsaking the Lord" (Hos. 1:2). Hosea's prophecy concludes, "I will heal their faithlessness; I will love them freely, for my anger has turned from them. I will be as the dew to Israel; he shall blossom as the lily" (Hos. 14:4–5).

Jesus proceeds to show the woman of Samaria how this prophecy will be fulfilled. He says to her at the well, "If you knew the gift of God, and who it is that is saying to you, 'Give me a drink,' you would have asked him and he would have given you living water" (John 4:10). "Living water" is flowing water, as opposed to stagnant, or standing, water: stagnant water eventually poisons, whereas living water continually renews and gives life. As Jesus says, speaking of the water of the well, "Every one who drinks of this water will thirst again, but whoever drinks of the water that I shall give him will never thirst; the water that I shall give him will become in him a spring of water welling up to eternal life" (John 4:13–14). The spiritual marriage between humankind and God, the new creation of fallen humanity, will come about by means of the water that flows from Jesus, who proclaims himself to be the Messiah, the Christ (John 4:25–26).

The image of living water leading to eternal life evokes the temple scene of Ezekiel 47. In this vision, as we saw in our chapter on the prophets, Ezekiel describes water flowing from the temple getting deeper and deeper until it became a river that could not be passed through. The river of water will flow into the stagnant sea. Normally the fresh water is sullied by the stagnant water, as when one pours fresh water from a pitcher into a glass half-full of putrid water. But here a miracle occurs because the flowing water transforms the stagnant water. Ezekiel describes the result, "And wherever the river goes every living creature which swarms will live and there will be very many fish, for this water goes there, that the waters of the sea may become fresh" (Ezek. 47:9). God's creation, burdened by alienation from God (Gen. 1–3), is renewed and restored through the waters from the temple. It is the prophecy of a new creation.

At the Feast of Tabernacles (cf. Lev. 23:42–43) in John 7, Jesus claims this prophecy for himself. On the Feast of Tabernacles, which recalls and celebrates the journey of the exodus, Solomon consecrated the temple (1 Kings 8:2). Because of the large number of animal sacrifices (cf. Num. 29) during the feast, blood and cleansing water would pour forth from the temple. Additionally, Moses commanded that every seven years, at the time of the feast, the entire Torah should be read to the people at the place of God's choosing, associated by Jewish tradition with the temple (cf. Deut. 31:9–13).[21] In John 7, Jesus goes to the temple in the middle of the Feast of Tabernacles and teaches the new law. In response to his hearers' amazement at his authoritative teaching, Jesus answers, "My teaching is not mine, but his who sent me; if any man's will is to do his will, he shall know whether the teaching is from God or whether I am speaking on my own authority" (John 7:15–17).[22]

Jesus then declares that the living water, fulfilling the goal of the Exodus, is now present in himself. "On the last day of the feast, the great day, Jesus stood up and proclaimed, 'If any one thirst, let him come to me and drink. He who believes in me, as the scripture has said, "Out of his heart shall flow rivers of living water"'" (John 7:37–38). The "his heart" here can be taken for the disciple's heart as well as Jesus' heart.[23] When believers are united to Jesus by baptism and the Spirit, they share in his Wisdom (cf. Sir. 15:3) and his Spirit flows from them as well.[24] John clarifies that he said this "about the Spirit, which those who believed in him were to receive; for as yet the Spirit had not been given, because Jesus was not yet glorified" (John 7:39).

Jesus has already identified himself as the temple in John 1:51 and 2:19–21; in the context of the Feast, the image of living waters flowing out of his heart makes clear that the new creation foretold in Ezekiel 47 has arrived. The prophet Zechariah repeats this theme, substituting Jerusalem for the temple: "On that day [the day of the Lord] living waters shall flow out from Jerusalem" (Zech. 14:8).[25] As he promised the woman at the well, now Jesus promises all the Jews at the Feast of Tabernacles that he will satisfy their thirst with living water. The river flowing out of the temple renewed the life in the stagnant sea. The flowing water from the temple of Jesus will renew the life of sinners. The members of his mystical Body will become the temple in Jesus and thus no longer share in sin, but in life. As we have seen with Jesus' discussion of baptism, the

21. Michael Strassfeld, *The Jewish Holidays*, 125–126.
22. On faith, biblical exegesis, and theology, see R. W. L. Moberly, "How Can We Know the Truth? A Study of John 7:14–18," in *The Art of Reading Scripture*, ed. Ellen F. Davis and Richard B. Hays (Grand Rapids: Eerdmans, 2003), 239–257.
23. See Gordon D. Fee, "Once More—John 7:37–39," in his *To What End Exegesis?* 83–87.
24. St. Thomas Aquinas points out the connection between spiritual drink and the enlightenment of Wisdom, as described in Sirach 15:3. See St. Thomas Aquinas, *Commentary on John*, 433.
25. Jesus' image here also recalls the water that flowed from the rock struck by Moses to satiate the thirst of the people of Israel on their journey toward the promised land, during which they were sustained by heavenly gifts of water and bread. St. Paul identifies this rock as Christ (1 Cor. 10:4).

gift of the Spirit flowing from his heart also foreshadows the sacrifice of the cross. On the cross, water and blood will literally flow from his heart (John 19:34), manifesting his status as the new rock for the new Exodus and, above all, the new temple for the new kingdom.[26]

Human beings are creatures of endless yearnings, ultimately longing for God their Father—God alone, who is infinite and inexhaustibly rich life, can satisfy. Without full communion with God, human beings are eternally thirsty and hungry for more. The entrance into this communion is through the water of baptism. The symbolism of water is rich and multi-layered, but the sacramental symbolism of being born of water and the Spirit (John 3), of the living water and the Samaritan (John 4), and of the living water flowing from the heart of Jesus (John 7) is evident.

Living Bread

Once one recognizes that Jesus is the new temple of the new kingdom, it follows that only those who enter this eternal temple can attain eternal life. Eternal life consists in dwelling with the almighty God and Creator. Anything else would be described better as eternal death, since, apart from enjoying God, man will be eternally frustrated. We have seen how Jesus reveals baptism in water and the Holy Spirit, accompanied by belief in him, as the entrance into his kingdom. Baptism and faith are the door to the kingdom, but how does one abide in the kingdom? How does one remain in God, the promised land, rather than experience the curse of exile caused by sin? Jesus reveals his incarnational plan for how his disciples will abide in him and he in them—the Eucharist.[27]

John 6 begins with the miracle of the loaves and fish. Recall that Elisha the prophet had miraculously fed one hundred men from twenty loaves (2 Kings 4:42–44). With five barley loaves and two fish, Jesus feeds a crowd of more than five thousand. After the meal, he commands his disciples to gather what is left over: "Gather up the fragments left over, that nothing may be lost" (John 6:12). They fill twelve baskets. The symbolism of the number twelve points to the Church founded on the twelve apostles as the restoration and fulfillment of the twelve tribes of Israel: all shall be fed by Christ through his Church, and not

26. Cf. Kevin Vanhoozer, "Body-piercing, the Natural Sense and the Task of Theological Interpretation: A Hermeneutical Homily on John 19:34," *Ex Auditu* 16 (2000): 1–29.

27. For a theological and doctrinal presentation, see John Paul II, *Ecclesia de Eucharistia*. For exegetical commentary, see Francis J. Moloney, S.D.B., *The Gospel of John* (Collegeville, MN: Liturgical Press, 1998), 221–224.

one of those chosen by Jesus shall be lost. Because of the miracle, the crowd recognizes Jesus as "the prophet who is to come into the world" (cf. Deut. 18:15) and desire to make him king (John 6:14–15). After he escapes to Capernaum, miraculously walking across the water to meet his disciples and identifying himself to them as the divine "I am" (John 6:20), he warns the crowd that they are just seeking him for earthly food. Just as earthly water cannot long satisfy, so also earthly food cannot. But Jesus will give the food that "endures to eternal life" (John 6:27).[28]

Jesus unveils the various meanings of this food in stages.[29] First, it is to believe in the one whom God has sent (John 6:29). Second, Jesus identifies himself as "the bread of life" (John 6:35) that has "come down from heaven" (John 6:33). At this level, the bread of life can be seen as the wisdom of God, which comes from on high. As he has throughout the Gospel, Jesus claims for himself the personification of Wisdom.[30] The bread of life thus has a sapiential dimension (cf. Sir. 15:3). Jesus is the true wisdom. "Every one who sees the Son and believes in him should have eternal life" (John 6:40). Third, Jesus calls himself the "living bread" and identifies this bread as his "flesh" (John 6:51). The manna given in the wilderness did not protect those who ate it from death, but the living bread, the flesh of Jesus, will give eternal life. We have already seen that the image of living water recalls the new creation that was to come from the new temple. Since his body is the temple, to enter the temple one must enter his body. By offering his flesh, that is, his body, to be consumed, Jesus allows his followers to dwell with God in the new temple. When some of his hearers object, Jesus intensifies his language, "Truly, truly, I say to you, unless you eat the flesh of the Son of man and drink his blood, you have no life in you; he who eats my flesh and drinks my blood has eternal life" (John 6:53–54).[31] This new temple is the indwelling of the Father, the source of eternal life. Now the bread is revealed to be both wisdom from on high and the eucharistic flesh. The sapiential and eucharistic dimensions are intertwined since the Word and Wisdom of God has become flesh and tabernacled among us. Jesus shows that this tabernacling is not limited to his historical life on earth but will be made available to each generation of believers through the Eucharist.[32]

28. See Johnson and Kurz, *The Future of Catholic Biblical Scholarship*, 203–218, 219–236.

29. See Brown, *The Gospel according to John (I–XII)*, 257–304.

30. This is the emphasis of Witherington III, *John's Wisdom*.

31. Indicating the intensification of Jesus' teaching, the Greek verb changes from "eat" (*phago*) to "gnaw" (*trogo*).

32. For a profound meditation on the Eucharist, see Thomas Merton, *The Living Bread* (New York: Farrar, Straus & Giroux, 1956).

The glorious divine communion of the Father and the Son is made available to believers as the Son dwells in them and they in him. Jesus explains this mystery of indwelling, "He who eats my flesh and drinks my blood abides in me, and I in him. As the living Father sent me, and I live because of the Father, so he who eats me will live because of me" (John 6:56–57). The flesh gives life insofar as the flesh is the divine tabernacle. This is what Jesus means when he says, "It is the spirit that gives life, the flesh is of no avail; the words I have spoken to you are spirit and life" (John 6:63). Jesus reveals that his flesh cannot save if his flesh is merely understood as human flesh, rather than understood in the light of faith that Jesus provides by giving us his Spirit. If we do not understand the flesh of Jesus in the light of faith, we will fail to see that the human flesh of Jesus gives eternal life because the Word was made flesh. A temple is only holy because God indwells it. The flesh of Jesus possesses the power of eternal life only because God indwells it. By receiving the Spirit, we will recognize that the Word of God, who is the life-giving spirit, indwells the flesh of the earthly Jesus and thus indwells the eucharistic flesh of Jesus.

The sacramental vision of baptism and Eucharist are used by Jesus to intensify the revelation that his body is the new temple. Through his conversations with Nicodemus and the Samaritan woman, and now at the synagogue in Capernaum, Jesus shows that one must pass through certain realities in order to enter the new temple that gives eternal life. One must receive the living water of baptism and the living bread of the Eucharist. These two are the sacramental means through which God restores human beings in holiness and dwells with them. Baptism and the Eucharist remake us as holy people dwelling in a holy land.

The Good Shepherd

What happens if one rejects this new temple? John 8 shows that one loses this unique communion with the Father that takes away one's sins.[33] One remains enslaved in one's sins. "Truly, truly, I say to you, every one who commits sin is a slave to sin. . . . If the Son makes you free, you will be free indeed" (John 8:34, 36). Of the Jews who do not accept him, Jesus has strong words: "You are of your father the devil, and your will is to do your father's desires" (John 8:44). This does not imply that the Jews of Jesus' day or the Jews throughout the centuries have knowingly rejected this communion with the Father. As Peter in

33. Cf. the interpretation given by Witherington and Ice, *The Shadow of the Almighty*, 49.

180

Acts 3:17 says, "I know that you acted in ignorance [in crucifying the Holy and Righteous One], as did also your rulers." The Jews spoken of in John 8 stand for all those who recognize the unique communion offered in Jesus and yet reject it. Because they do not see their own sinfulness (cf. the attempt to stone the woman caught in adultery, John 8:2–11) and thus do not welcome Jesus' announcement of the forgiveness of sins, they cannot participate in Jesus' fulfillment of the journey of the exodus. They remain in slavery to sin.

Far from being the enemy of his hearers, Jesus emphasizes, "I am the good shepherd. The good shepherd lays down his life for his sheep" (John 10:11). He will gather together his people and nourish and care for them, "There shall be one flock, one shepherd" (John 10:16). This image of the good shepherd has led to wonderful portraits of Jesus as a humble shepherd, but this unfortunately misses the main point of Jesus claiming this title. The image of the shepherd here is not agrarian, but royal[34]; it is not simply pastoral, but messianic, which means related to the coming Davidic king, the messiah, through whom God will restore Israel. To uncover the roots of this image we must turn again to the prophet Ezekiel.[35]

In Ezekiel 34, the Son of Man is told to "prophesy again the shepherds of Israel" (Ezek. 34:1). Instead of feeding the sheep, the kings of Israel have been feeding themselves. Even worse, God charges that because of the violence and wickedness of the kings, the sheep have become food for the shepherds. "Thus says the Lord God, Behold, I am against the shepherds" (Ezek. 34:10). God, however, promises that he will seek out his sheep and bring them to graze on the mountains of Israel. Because the human kings have failed to be the faithful instrument for God's authority, God must become the shepherd himself. God says through his prophet Ezekiel, "I myself will be the shepherd of my sheep" (Ezek. 34:15). God also says in the same context, "I will set up over them one shepherd, my servant David, and he shall feed them" (Ezek. 34:23). God will be the shepherd through the new Davidic king.

The new shepherd, who is both God and the Davidic king, will lead the flock into the true holy land, the land where God dwells. In Ezekiel 37, God promises to set up David as king, "they shall all have one shepherd" (Ezek. 37:24). In this new covenant with the new David, God promises, "I will set up my sanctuary in the midst of them for evermore.

34. Citing an article by Moshe Weinfeld, Jon Levenson remarks, "The ancient image of the king as shepherd expresses the perennial idea that the ruler is to be the servant of his people: his exaltation above his subjects is inseparable from his selfless devotion to their welfare" (Levenson, *The Death and Resurrection of the Beloved Son*, 145).

35. As does St. Thomas Aquinas in his *Commentary on the Gospel of St. John*, Part II, trans. James Weisheipl, O.P., and Fabian Larcher, O.P. (Petersham, MA: St. Bede's Publications, 1999), 124–135.

My dwelling place shall be with them; and I will be their God, and they shall be my people" (Ezek. 37:26–27). In order to accomplish his plan, God needs a David who will be free from all sinfulness and be able to be the perfect mediation of the divine presence. This David comes on earth when the Word became flesh. Now the Davidic king mediates perfectly the presence of God, since the Son is fully one with the Father. As Jesus says, "I and the Father are one" (John 10:30). This corresponds to the earlier statement of John, "No one has ever seen God; the only Son, who is in the bosom of the Father, he has made him known" (John 1:18). But the Davidic king alone, even if perfect, remains incomplete. The king makes the people holy, but the Davidic king must establish the holy land, the sanctuary in which God dwells perfectly with human beings. The prophecy from Ezekiel explicitly connects the one shepherd with the everlasting "sanctuary" (Ezek. 37:26), or temple.

Therefore when Jesus says, "I am the good shepherd," he claims to fulfill all that was prophesied by Ezekiel. He is God himself who said, "I myself will shepherd them." He is the new Davidic king established by God as the "one shepherd." Through his kingly authority, Jesus is establishing the everlasting sanctuary where God will dwell with his people. This new sanctuary will be neither in Samaria nor in Jerusalem. Jesus has said, "the hour is coming, and now is, when the true worshippers will worship the Father in spirit and truth" (John 4:23). The new sanctuary thus includes both that God will eternally dwell with human beings and that we will eternally worship him. Jesus reveals that this can only take place in the sanctuary of his body.[36] Only in the body of Jesus can man again dwell with God in bliss. Although John has not yet explicitly said that the body of Jesus is the Church, it has been implied throughout. If believers want eternal life, they must enter the body of Jesus through belief in him, through baptism of water and the spirit, and through feeding on his eucharistic flesh.[37]

36. Cf. *Lumen Gentium* nos. 1–8, in Austin Flannery, O.P., ed., *Vatican Council II*, Vol. 1: *The Conciliar and Post Conciliar Documents* (Northport, NY: Costello, 1975), 350–358.

37. In his *On the Trinity* (Book VIII, 12–16; PL 10, 246–249), St. Hilary of Poitiers remarks,

We believe that the Word became flesh and that we receive his flesh in the Lord's Supper. How then can we fail to believe that he really dwells within us? When he became man, he actually clothed himself in our flesh, uniting it to himself forever. In the sacrament of his body he actually gives us his own flesh, which he has united to his divinity. This is why we are all one, because the Father is in Christ, and Christ is in us. He is in us through his flesh and we are in him. With him we form a unity that is in God. The manner of our indwelling in him through the sacrament of his body and blood is evident from the Lord's own words: 'This world will see me no longer but you shall see me. Because I live you shall live also, for I am in my Father,

Indwelling of God in the Temple, in the Body of Christ

The mystery of the indwelling of God in the Body of Christ is most clearly depicted in the discourse that Jesus gives in the upper room, on the eve of his Pasch, in John 13–17. In John there is no scene of the institution of the Eucharist, but this lengthy discussion presumably would have been at the last supper when the Eucharist was instituted. Jesus begins by rising from the supper, taking off his outer garments, and washing the feet of his disciples, a task of the lowliest of house servants. Afterwards he puts on his outer garments, sits again at the table and then asks his disciples, "Do you know what I have done to you? You call me Teacher and Lord; and you are right, for so I am. If I then, your Lord and Teacher, have washed your feet, you also ought to wash one another's feet" (John 13:12–14). The action of the foot washing is symbolic of his life among human beings, in which he overturns our worldly understanding of kingship by manifesting the radical power that is self-giving love. He explicitly tells his disciples that he has given them an example.[38] The disciples are to imitate his service and thus mediate his presence. "If you know these things, blessed are you if you do them" (John 13:17).

Moral obedience and purity, therefore, belong to receiving the indwelling of God and sharing in the divine kingship that establishes true justice.[39] As Psalm 24 succinctly states, "Who shall stand in [the Lord's] holy place? He who has clean hands and a pure heart" (Ps. 24:3–4). Apart from doing what the Lord commands, human beings cannot find happiness, or blessedness. Moral purity is not an end in itself, but rather is

---

you are in me, and I am in you.' If it had been a question of a mere unity of will, why should he have given us this explanation of the steps by which it is achieved? He is in the Father by reason of his divine nature, we are in him by reason of his human birth, and he is in us through the mystery of the sacraments. This, surely, is what he wished us to believe; this is how he wanted us to understand the perfect unity that it achieved through our Mediator, who lives in the Father while we live in him, and who, while we live in him, and who, while living in the Father, lives also in us. This is how we attain to unity with the Father. Christ is in very truth in the Father by his eternal generation; we are in very truth in Christ, and he likewise is in us. . . . [T]he point is that Christ is the wellspring of our life. Since we who are in the flesh have Christ dwelling in us through his flesh, we shall draw life from him in the same way as he draws life from the Father.

38. For further discussion, see Marianne Meye Thompson, "'His Own Received Him Not': Jesus Washes the Feet of His Disciples," in *The Art of Reading Scripture*, eds. Davis and Hays, 258–273.

39. On this point, see Michael J. Gorman, *Cruciformity: Paul's Narrative Spirituality of the Cross* (Grand Rapids: Eerdmans, 2001); Romanus Cessario, O.P., *Introduction to Moral Theology* (Washington, DC: Catholic University of America Press, 2001), 152–153.

the intrinsic means through which one enters the dwelling of the Lord and shares in the Lord's life. Psalm 17 says, "As for me, I shall behold thy [God's] face in righteousness; when I awake, I shall be satisfied with beholding thy form" (Ps. 17:15).

The response of the believer to the invitation of Jesus unites faith and works of love. To believe in Jesus cannot be separated from keeping his commandments, especially his new commandment to love one another as he has loved them (John 14:34). Jesus states, "He who has my commandments and keeps them, he it is who loves me; and he who loves me will be loved by my Father, and I will love him and manifest myself to him" (John 14:21). Keeping the commandments has become the mode of the indwelling of God.

By means of the foot washing, Jesus has also passed onto his apostles, and thus to his Church, his unique role as the temple of God. There is no contradiction here. Jesus' role remains unique since the apostles only share in it as those who receive it from him. Jesus says to the apostles, "Truly, truly, I say to you, he who receives any one whom I send receives me; and he who receives me receives him who sent me" (John 13:17, 20). The pattern evolves: God's presence mediated through Jesus; Jesus' presence mediated through the apostles inspired by the Holy Spirit. (The word apostle means "one who is sent.") In terms of our encounter with God, the pattern reverses: the apostles, inspired by the Holy Spirit, mediate Jesus; and Jesus mediates the Father. This reality can be schematized as follows: God → Jesus → the Apostles → believers—and—believers → the Apostles → Jesus → God.[40]

By way of intensifying the mystery, in John 14, Jesus shifts from the language of receiving the Father, to that of seeing the Father. Just before Jesus' death and Resurrection, Phillip asks Jesus, "Lord, show us the Father, and we shall be satisfied" (John 14:8). Jesus answers, "Have I been with you so long, and yet you do not know me, Philip? He who has seen me has seen the Father" (John 14:9). To have seen Jesus is to have seen the Father. In other words, Jesus is saying that to have seen Jesus with faith in him is to have entered the sanctuary and seen the face of God (cf. Ps. 27:8–9).

John 15 depicts this through the image of the vine and the mystery of friendship with God. Recalling the language of "abiding" that dominated the eucharistic discourse of John 6, Jesus uses the image of the vine and the branches, from Isaiah 5, to show that he is the true Israel, into whom his disciples are incorporated. His disciples share fully in his holy relationship with the Father. "I am the true vine, and my Father is the

---

40. Cf. J.-M. R. Tillard, O.P., *Church of Churches: The Ecclesiology of Communion*, trans. R. C. De Peaux, O. Praem. (Collegeville, MN: Liturgical Press, 1992).

vinedresser. . . . I am the vine and you are the branches. He who abides in me, and I in him, he it is that bears much fruit, for apart from me you can do nothing" (John 15:1, 5). This image captures the two pronged relation in John: Those who accept Jesus can share in his life-giving and glorifying relationship with the Father; those who, knowing what they are freely rejecting, reject Jesus and his love can "do nothing" and will end in death and frustration. But those who believe in Jesus as the divine Son of God and keep his commandments can come to know the fulfillment of the God-given desire for happiness.

Jesus tells the disciples this underlying meaning to his revelation: "These things I have spoken to you, that my joy may be in you, and that your joy may be full" (John 15:11). Jesus desires that our joy may be full. For those who by God's grace want the true happiness that is self-giving love, Jesus reveals himself to be "the way, and the truth, and the life; no one comes to the Father, but by me" (John 14:6). Human beings often find their greatest earthly happiness in the true friendship of deep relationships in which the person delights in the good of the friend. Jesus fulfills the deepest desires of human beings by elevating them, in the Holy Spirit, to become friends of God, who delight in God's infinite goodness. To such a delight, there can be no limit. Jesus has made the joy of his disciples "full."

The image of friendship emphasizes the reality of the Church's mediation of divine glory. As friends, the disciples share fully in the communion of the Son with the Father. "No longer do I call you servants, for the servant does not know what his master is doing; but I have called you friends, for all that I have heard from my Father I have made known to you" (John 15:15). The immediate context of this friendship with God is Jesus' new commandment to "love one another as I have loved you" (John 15:13).[41] As friends, they are to love as he has loved them. The converse is true also, only if they love as Jesus loved, can they be his friends. If we recall that the whole of John 13–17 takes place at the Last Supper, then the language of Jesus concerning making the disciples his friends takes on deeper meaning. By receiving his flesh and blood, the disciples have the Son abiding in them and can truly love as he loved. The "abiding" that Jesus describes in John 15:4–10 belongs to the "abiding" made possible by the Eucharist: "He who eats my flesh and drinks my blood abides in me, and I in him. As the living Father sent me, and I live because of the Father, so he who eats me will live because of me" (John 6:56–57).

In a succession of passages about the coming Counselor (Paraclete), or Spirit of Truth, Jesus promises his disciples the Holy Spirit, who will

---

41. See St. Thomas Aquinas, *On Charity (De Caritate)*, trans. Lottie H. Kendzierski (Milwaukee: Marquette University Press, 1984).

sustain the communication of divine life in the Church organized apostolically. "I will pray to the Father, and he will give you another Counselor, to be with you for ever, even the Spirit of truth" (John 14:16–17). "The Counselor, the Holy Spirit, who the Father will send in my name, he will teach you all things, and bring to your remembrance all that I have said to you" (John 14:25; cf. John 15:26). It is the Holy Spirit in the Church that allows the Church to mediate successfully the divine presence. The infallibility of the Church in solemn teaching on Christian faith and moral life stems from Jesus' gift of the Holy Spirit who "will teach you all things."[42] The true tabernacling of God with human beings could not be accomplished merely through Jesus living in Galilee. To have seen Jesus is to have seen the Father, but if Jesus was limited to his historical body, then only a few could ever see the Father.

When Jesus ascends bodily to the Father after his Resurrection, his mystical Body will be the tabernacling of God among human beings. "Nevertheless I tell you the truth; it is to your advantage that I go away, for if I do not go away, the Counselor will not come to you; but when I go, I will send him to you" (John 16:7). When Jesus' physical body ascends to heaven, the Spirit now indwells his Church and enables his members to share in his glory.[43] "When the Spirit of truth comes, he will guide you into all the truth; for he will not speak on his own authority, but whatever he hears he will speak, and he will declare to you the things that are to come. He will glorify me, for he will take what is mine and declare it to you" (John 16:13–14). The Spirit is sent from the Father and the Son into the world to continue the presence of God in the world.[44] The mission of the Spirit extends the mission of the Son: In the Spirit, the Church is the Body of Christ, the new and perfect temple indwelt with God.

In the great high priestly prayer of Jesus in John 17, this indwelling of God is manifested through the themes of God's glory, God's name, God's love, and his unity. The glory that the Son shared with the Father from the beginning, he now shares with all believers (John 17:5, 22). The Father's "name" (the very divine identity), proclaimed by the Son, is now given to the disciples (John 17:6, 22).[45] The love shared between

42. See Vatican Council II, *Lumen Gentium* no. 25.
43. For theological reflection upon Christ's ascension, see Douglas Farrow, *Ascension and Ecclesia: On the Significance of the Doctrine of the Ascension for Ecclesiology and Christian Cosmology* (Grand Rapids: Eerdmans, 1999).
44. For a theological exposition of the holy Trinity, see Gilles Emery, O.P., *Trinity in Aquinas* (Ypsilanti, MI: Sapientia Press, 2003).
45. As St. Athanasius says, "For the Son of God became man so that we might become God" (*On the Incarnation*, no. 53, quoted in the *Catechism of the Catholic Church*, no. 460).

the Father and the Son is now communicated to those who believe in the Son (John 17:26). Also, the believers are now brought up into the unity of the Father and the Son (John 17:22–23). In the Old Testament, Israel was meant to have access to God's name and glory that dwelt in the one temple. Now in the New Testament, the Church as the new Israel has access to God's name and glory in the one Jesus Christ. Because the glory, name, love, and unity of God have come down through the Word's dwelling among us, man now can rise up, be born from above (John 3), and participate in the eternal glory, name, love, and unity of God. John's Christology cannot be separated from his ecclesiology or vice versa. Both depict the wonderful indwelling of God in Christ and through Christ in the Church.

The one shepherd, Christ, must lead the one flock, the Church (John 10:16; Ezek. 34:22–23). This unity is mystical since it is humanity's participation in unity of the Trinity. Yet, this unity must also be visible since it is the sign of God's unity to a fallen world. Jesus prays "that they may be one (*ut unum sint*) even as we are one, I in them and thou in me, that they may become perfectly one, so that the world may know that thou hast sent me and hast loved them even as thou hast loved me" (John 17:22–23).[46] The unity of the heavenly temple of the Father and the Son has descended to earth in Jesus who now gives all believers access to this unique communion with the Father. The visible unity of the Church, prayed for by Jesus, is the visible sign of the mystical unity of the Body of Christ. In the Spirit, the members are unified with each other, with the Son, and with the Father.

Water and Blood Flowing from the Temple

Jesus is rejected by his people and condemned to death by the high priest and Pontius Pilate. The chief priests show their complete denial of Jesus' kingship (God's kingship) when they say to Pilate, "We have no king but Caesar" (John 19:15). On the cross the one who promised living water to quench thirst forever, now says, evidencing his wondrous mercy and desire for the salvation of humankind, "I thirst" (John 19:28).[47] On the day of preparation for the Feast of the Passover, when thousands of lambs would be being slaughtered in the temple, Jesus the Lamb of God is slain as the king of the Jews. So they could remove the bodies in order to observe the Sabbath in purity, the Jewish authorities ask to have the legs broken to bring about swiftly the death of the crucified men.

46. Cf. John Paul II's encyclical *Ut Unum Sint* (1995).
47. See the interpretation of St. Thomas Aquinas, *Commentary on John*, Part II, 577.

Jesus, however, having been beaten, tortured, and humiliated, was already dead, and so the soldier did not break his legs. The legs of the Passover lamb could not be broken (Exod. 12:46), and thus Jesus is revealed to be the new Passover Lamb, slain yet with bones unbroken. John records that, "One of the soldiers pierced his side with a spear, and at once there came out blood and water" (John 19:34). The flowing out of blood and water confirmed the death of the man Jesus. The symbolism of the imagery, however, runs much deeper.[48] In John 7, Jesus said that streams of living water would flow from the side of the Son of Man. Now his prophecy is fulfilled. The body of Jesus is both the sacrifice and the temple. Fulfilling the early identification of the mission and person of Jesus in John 1:15–51, Jesus now has become the priest-king who offers himself as the sacrificial lamb in the temple, which he is. This water and blood symbolize the living water and the living flesh and blood promised by Jesus in John 4 and 6. The living water of baptism and living flesh and blood of the Eucharist will literally flow from his body, the Church, as it is filled with the Holy Spirit after Jesus' Resurrection.

On the cross, Jesus gives Mary to the beloved disciple, John. In giving Mary, his mother, to John, Jesus gives Mary to be the mother of disciples. Again we see the profound unity between Jesus and his disciples, between the historical body of Jesus and the Church. As Mary was the mother of the historical body of Jesus, now that she has received the disciple John, she has become the mother of the mystical Body of Jesus as well.[49] After performing this act, Jesus tastes the vinegar on hyssop that the soldiers offer him in response to his thirst. The hyssop reminds us that Jesus is the true Passover Lamb. Moses had commanded, "Take a bunch of hyssop and dip it in the blood which is in the basin, and touch the lintel and the two doorposts with the blood which is in the basin. . . . For the Lord will pass through to slay the Egyptians; and when he sees the blood on the lintel and on the two doorposts, the Lord will pass over the door, and will not allow the destroyer to enter your houses to slay you" (Exod. 12:22–23).[50] Moreover, as was foreshadowed by the prophet Ezekiel who consumes the scroll of lamentation that

---

48. See Vanhoozer, "Body-piercing."

49. Cf. John Paul II, *Mother of the Redeemer* (*Redemptoris Mater*), nos. 23, 44. Ignatius Press has published an edition of this encyclical with an introduction by Joseph Cardinal Ratzinger and commentary by Hans Urs von Balthasar: *Mary, God's Yes to Man* (San Francisco: Ignatius Press, 1988). For discussion of Marian theology in light of the central biblical texts, see Joseph Cardinal Ratzinger, *Daughter Zion*, trans. John M. McDermott, S.J. (San Francisco: Ignatius Press, 1983). See also David S. Yeago, "The Presence of Mary in the Mystery of the Church," *Nova et Vetera* 2 (2004): 147–168.

50. Donald Senior, C.P., *The Passion of Jesus in the Gospel of John* (Collegeville, MN: Liturgical Press, 1995), 116–118.

nonetheless tastes sweet (Ezekiel 3), Jesus now in the bitterness of his Passion brings human history to its intended, "sweet" fulfillment. "When Jesus had received the vinegar, he said, 'It is finished'; and he bowed his head and gave up his spirit" (John 19:30). "It is finished" would be better translated as "fulfilled" or "consummated" in order to express its triumphant note.[51] Jesus' cross has brought to fulfillment God's saving work, ongoing since Adam and Eve, to restore and transform creation. From this moment forward, all human history, in Christ's mystical Body the Church, is taken up into new creation.

The Body Invisible and Visible

After the mysterious glorification of Jesus on the cross, he is visibly glorified as the Son of God in his Resurrection. But as we have seen through the whole drama of the believer's participation in God, Jesus does not keep his glory to himself but shares it with his apostles. More specifically, Jesus communicates his glory by communicating his identity as the Son of God to all believers. Mary Magdalene is the first to see the risen Jesus. Jesus reveals to her the full mystery of divine filiation, of becoming children of God: "I am ascending to my Father and your Father, to my God and your God" (John 20:17). The power to become children of God, announced in John 1:12, has now become a reality with the Resurrection of Jesus.

The theme of divine filiation unites the parallel themes of holy people and holy land. Holy people indicates that human beings regain the righteousness and justice with which God created them. To become a holy people, the shame and fear that arose in Genesis 3 must be cleansed. This shame and fear arose precisely because human beings lost their relationship of divine sonship with God. With original sin the Fatherhood of God is obscured and replaced with an image of God as a master and tyrant. To share in Jesus' sonship allows human beings to see again God as loving Father and to stand before him without fear and without shame.[52] Divine filiation also includes the theme of holy land by indicating the presence of the Father to the children of God. As children they have returned from a godless, unholy land, to the dwelling place of God. God the Father now dwells with them. Through becoming children of God, believers are made a holy people by participating in the perfect justice of the Son and are brought into a holy land by participating in the perfect union of the Son

51. Cf. Moloney, *The Gospel of John*, 504.
52. John Paul II has explored these themes in *The Theology of the Body* and *Crossing the Threshold of Hope*.

with the Father: "See what love the Father has given us, that we should be called children of God; and so we are" (1 John 3:1). No mere metaphor, the divine filiation brought about by the grace of the Holy Spirit forms the deepest mystery of the Christian revelation of salvation.

Jesus appears to the apostles in the upper room and reiterates their foundational calling as apostles to share in his own mission from the Father: "Peace be with you. As the Father has sent me, even so I send you" (John 20:21). But they are not merely sent in Jesus' name, for now they receive the very indwelling of God that has made Jesus the temple of God—the Holy Spirit. John records that "when he had said this, he breathed on them, and said to them, 'Receive the Holy Spirit. If you forgive the sins of any, they are forgiven; if you retain the sins of any, they are retained'" (John 20:22–23). Jesus gives his apostles the Holy Spirit for the forgiveness of sins. Sin must be removed before man is capable of dwelling with God. The very indwelling of the Holy Spirit that makes the Church as the Body of Christ the true holy land is the same power that makes the Church the true holy people. The authority of the apostles, and through them the Church, does not obstruct one's personal relationship with God as Father. The whole of John now can be seen to point to the gift of the visible authority of the Church as the visible means of entering into the mystical indwelling of the Father and the Son. The sacraments of baptism, the Eucharist, and now confession allow people to receive the forgiveness of sins necessary to share in Jesus' unique communion with the Father.

Jesus emphasizes the visible character of the Body of Christ when he appoints Peter as the shepherd of his flock in John 21. At the time of Jesus' trial, Peter had denied him three times. After his Resurrection, Jesus comes to Peter and asks him three times, "Do you love me?" Each time Peter replies "yes," and Jesus tells Peter to "Feed my sheep" (John 21:15–17). Jesus institutes Peter, whose threefold denial is replaced by his threefold affirmation of love, as the visible shepherd of his visible flock. Jesus has already claimed for himself the role of the Davidic king as the good shepherd, the one shepherd. Building on the foundation of the Last Supper discourse (John 13–17), we can see that just as the Son mediates the presence of the Father, so the apostles, and specifically Peter now, mediate the presence of the Son. God the Father is the shepherd. Jesus, the Word made flesh, is the shepherd. Peter, having been humbled by his weakness and converted once again to the Lord, is the shepherd. After the ascension of the historical body of Christ, Peter heads the visible Body of Christ. The visible Church needs a visible head, even though the Church is filled with the invisible Holy Spirit. More precisely, because the Church is filled with the invisible Holy Spirit, the Church needs a visible head in Peter.

190

It belongs to the dignity of Christ's body to be visible in human history. Thus, what was true for Peter remains true for his office. And yet, Peter's role is kingly in the sense of Christ's kingship, not of worldly kingship. In exercising his rightful authority, Peter will suffer and serve. As Jesus warns him, "'Truly, truly, I say to you, when you were young, you girded yourself and walked where you would; but when you are old, you will stretch out your hands, and another will gird you and carry you where you do not wish to go.' (This he said to show by what death he was to glorify God.)" (John 21:18). Christ then gives Peter, and the Church, his watchword: "Follow me" (John 21:19).

The same themes of divine indwelling and divine filiation continue through the Johannine epistles (1, 2, 3 John). John, in particular, emphasizes how believers share in eternal life with God, who is love, and have fellowship with the Father and the Son. As in the Gospel of John, this divine indwelling results from knowing and loving God through the new covenant in Christ Jesus. "See what love the Father has given us, that we should be called children of God; and so we are. The reason why the world does not know us is that it did not know him. Beloved, we are God's children now; it does not yet appear what we shall be, but we know that when he appears we shall be like him, for we shall see him as he is" (1 John 3:1–2).

8

Romans

The Righteousness of God and the Body of Christ

The letters of St. Paul, addressed to particular pastoral situations and aimed at expressing the good news about the crucified and risen Lord, teach us about our relationship to Jesus both as individuals and as a people gathered into Israel's Messiah. The letters give us concrete insight into the holiness and worship required in discipleship to Jesus as the living Lord. We will focus upon the Letter to the Romans. In patristic times, St. Augustine's meditation on Romans led him to articulate the doctrine of original sin and the corresponding doctrine of the initiative of God's grace in the conversion of believers.[1] Romans thus stands at the heart of the Church's longstanding theological controversy over grace and justification. Romans profoundly articulates the biblical theme of God's bringing about a "holy people" fit to dwell in and with him. The Letter to the Romans proclaims how people become righteous by sharing in God's new covenant in Jesus Christ.[2]

1. Cf. St. Augustine, *Anti-Pelagian Writings*, ed. Philip Schaff, Nicene and Post-Nicene Fathers, First Series, Vol. 5 (Peabody, MA: Hendrickson, 1995 [1887]). This volume includes thirteen distinct works by St. Augustine.
2. For insightful essays on the letter to the Romans, see Sven K. Soderlund and N. T. Wright, eds., *Romans and the People of God: Essays in Honor of Gordon D. Fee on the*

A Covenantal People

Romans has sometimes been read primarily as an explanation of how the individual believer is saved. For Jews and Christians, however, salvation first concerns a community, namely, the people of God. Individuals are saved, of course, but they are not saved as individuals, but as members of the community. In God's plan for the salvation of the human race he does not save individuals by themselves, but brings them into a personal relationship with himself as members of his holy, covenanted people. As we have seen, the Christian revelation is above all the establishment of the new covenant in Jesus Christ—the marriage of God and humankind—by which, as Hosea prophesied, our sins are forgiven (Luke 24:47) and we are adopted as children of God (John 1:12). The new covenant is established by the sacrifice of Jesus on the cross and completed in his Resurrection. To be saved thus means to be in this perfect covenantal relationship with God.

In order to illumine this new covenant of God's holy people, the letter to the Romans focuses upon how God through Christ makes us just or righteous, or how God fills us with justice and righteousness. (Justice and righteousness can be used interchangeably since both are used to translate the same Greek word, *dikaiosune*.) It is impossible to understand how God includes us in the covenant without also asking how this justice continues to manifest itself among members of the covenant. The second follows from the first. The reality of the Body of Christ (holy land) reveals what our justification (holy people) accomplishes. Our justification is our actual entrance into the Body of Christ in which we share in his perfect justice. We become a holy people who can dwell in God's presence.

The Obedience of Faith

Romans begins and concludes with a peculiar expression, the "obedience of faith" (Rom. 1:5; 16:26). According to Paul, and the gospel he has received from God, the Gentiles are now brought into the obedience of faith. Formerly, the Jews alone knew the obedience of faith in virtue of the covenant of Moses symbolized by circumcision. Then comes the gospel of Jesus Christ "who was descended from David according to the flesh and designated Son of God in power according to the Spirit of holiness by his resurrection from the dead" (Rom. 1:3–4). The central

Occasion of His 65th Birthday (Grand Rapids: Eerdmans, 1999); Jouette M. Bassler, ed., *Pauline Theology*, Vol. 3, *Romans* (Atlanta: Scholars Press, 1997).

message of Romans is that because of Jesus Christ now both Jews and Gentiles share in the obedience of faith.

The fact that Paul, who had been a zealous Pharisee, speaks of the obedience of faith gives us insight into how the Jews and early Christians understood salvation. Contrary to some oft-repeated misunderstandings, the Jews did not believe in works-righteousness, that is, that their obedience to the law earned them the right to salvation.[3] Instead, Judaism, as we have seen, firmly believed that the election of the Jews was an unmerited blessing from God (cf. Deut. 9:4–7). Obedience to the law was the free response to God's invitation to holiness. The initiative for salvation came squarely from the side of God, not the Jews themselves. By saying that the Jews have already been under the obedience of faith, Paul shows that the key for the Jews' membership in the covenant was the faith in God expressed through obedience to his law. Jesus Christ perfectly embodied this obedience of faith and thus fulfilled the law.[4] It is by faith in him that both Jews and Gentiles now receive the unmerited gift of justification. As Paul says, "For I am not ashamed of the gospel: it is the power of God for salvation to every one who has faith, to the Jew first and also to the Greek. For in it the righteousness of God is revealed through faith for faith; as it is written, 'He who through faith is righteous shall live'" (Rom. 1:16–17).[5]

Having set forth the "righteousness of God" as revealed in the faithfulness of Christ for the salvation of both Jews and Gentiles, Paul next provides an analysis of the state of the Gentiles prior to their inclusion in the new covenant.[6] Even in their state apart from the revelation of the law of Moses, the Gentiles were capable of coming to know that God exists and that he alone ought to be worshipped. Paul states that "Ever since the creation of the world his invisible nature, namely his eternal power and deity, has been clearly perceived in the things that have been made" (Rom. 1:20; cf. Wis. 13:1–3). This classic formulation of natural theology teaches that by reflecting on the visible universe human beings

3. N. T. Wright states, "[Among first century Jews] 'justification by works' has nothing to do with individual Jews attempting a kind of proto-Pelagian pulling themselves up by their moral bootstraps, and everything to do with the definition of the true Israel in advance of the final eschatological show down," *What Saint Paul Really Said: Was Paul of Tarsus the Real Founder of Christianity?* (Grand Rapids: Eerdmans, 1997), 119.

4. On the obedience of faith, see Douglas Campbell, "Romans 1:17—A Crux Interpretum for the PISTIS CHRISTOU Debate," *Journal of Biblical Literature* 113 (1994): 265–285.

5. Our discussion relies largely upon Richard B. Hays, *Echoes of Scripture in the Letters of Paul* (New Haven, CT: Yale University Press, 1989), 34–57.

6. On Paul's audience for this letter, see Richard N. Longenecker, "The Focus of Romans: The Central Role of 5:1–8:39 in the Argument of the Letter," in S. K. Soderlund and N. T. Wright, eds., *Romans and the People of God*, 49–69, especially 67.

can come to know the invisible God by reason alone, without the aid of supernatural revelation.

Yet, this wisdom actually condemns the Gentiles. Because all human beings are capable of knowing that God exists with "eternal power and deity," the Gentiles are guilty for worshipping things of this world instead of the Creator. "So they are without excuse; for although they knew God they did not honor him as God or give thanks to him, but they became futile in their thinking and their senseless minds darkened" (Rom. 1:21). Their spiritual disorder manifests itself further in bodily disorder. "Therefore God gave them up in the lusts of their hearts to impurity, to the dishonoring of their bodies among themselves, because they exchanged the truth about God for a lie and worshipped and served the creature rather than the Creator, who is blessed for ever! Amen" (Rom. 1:24–25). Human sinfulness eats away at the entire human person: the intellect rejects the truth of the eternal God for gods of this world (including sex, power, and money); the will loves the goods of this world as ends in themselves in ways that cannot be ordered to the true good, God; and the body becomes an instrument of disordered loves and corrupted passions.

Paul boldly makes this charge of sinful disorder concrete. Because the Gentiles worshipped sterile idols rather than worshipping the life-giving God, this disorder corrupted the communion of man and woman as well; Gentiles chose sterile same-sex intercourse over the life-giving communion of man and woman. Paul writes, "Their women exchanged natural relations for unnatural, and the men likewise gave up natural relations with women and were consumed with passion for one another, men committing shameless acts with men and receiving in their own persons the due penalty for their error" (Rom. 1:26–28).[7] Paul makes explicit that the bodily disorder reflects a deeper spiritual disorder. "And since they did not see fit to acknowledge God, God gave them up to a base mind and to improper conduct. They were filled with all manner of wickedness, evil, covetousness, malice. Full of envy, murder, strife, deceit, malignity, they are gossips, slanderers, haters of God, insolent, haughty, boastful, inventors of evil, disobedient to parents, foolish, faithless, heartless, ruthless" (Rom. 1:28–32).

Not only are all human beings capable of knowing that God exists and alone ought to be worshipped, they can also know the truths of the

---

7. On the biblical critique of homosexual acts, a critique that retains its validity today, see Robert A. J. Gagnon's *The Bible and Homosexual Practice: Texts and Hermeneutics* (Nashville: Abingdon, 2001). See also Richard B. Hays, *The Moral Vision of the New Testament: A Contemporary Introduction to New Testament Ethics* (San Francisco: HarperSanFrancisco, 1996), 383f.; John Grabowski, *Sex and Virtue* (Washington, DC: Catholic University of America Press, 2003).

moral law. The Jews have received the revelation of the law of Moses, a clear path for well-doing. Although the Gentiles lack this clarity, they are capable of discerning right action because of the natural law written on their hearts (Rom. 2:14–15). Paul states, "God will render to every man according to his works" (Rom. 2:6). Those who do evil will suffer the wrath of God; those who do good will receive eternal life. Yet, "[t]hough they know God's decree that those who do such things deserve to die, they not only do them but approve those who practice them" (Rom. 1:32). Therefore, despite the power of their Roman civilization, the Gentiles are in fact in desperate need of "the power of God for salvation" (Rom. 1:16) accessible by faith.

Having described the plight of the Gentiles, Paul goes on to describe the plight of the Jews. Both Jews and Gentiles are "under the power of sin" (Rom. 3:9). As Romans 2:13 states, "For it is not the hearers of the law who are righteous before God, but the doers of the law who will be justified." Both the Jews who have the law of Moses and the Gentiles with the natural law must keep the law if they are to be a holy people before God. However, neither were able to do so. Recall the passage from Isaiah: "Therefore justice is far from us, and righteousness does not overtake us; we look for light, and behold, darkness, and for brightness, but we walk in gloom. . . . We all growl like bears, we moan and moan as doves; we look for justice, but there is none; for salvation, but it is far from us. For our transgressions are multiplied before thee, and our sins testify against us; for our transgressions are with us, and we know our iniquities: transgressing, and denying the Lord, and turning away from following our God, speaking oppression and revolt, conceiving and uttering from the heart lying words" (Isa. 59:9–13). Although Paul affirms the unique blessings that the Jews have received (cf. Rom. 3:1–2), he cannot but acknowledge the truth of the prophet Isaiah's condemnation. He exclaims, "What then? Are we Jews any better off? No, not at all; for I have already charged that all men, both Jews and Gentiles, are under the power of sin" (Rom. 3:9). Quoting Psalms 14 and 53, which accord with Isaiah 59, Paul admits that because of idolatry, "None is righteous, no, not one" (Ps. 14:1).[8] All are in slavery to sin and its just punishment, death. The law of Moses given to the Israelites was not able to free them from the bondage of sin and make them a holy people.

How then are Jews and Gentiles to share in the "righteousness of God" and become holy people? Paul explains that "now the righteousness of God has been manifested apart from law, although the law and the prophets bear witness to it" (Rom. 3:21). What is this righteousness

---

8. On Paul's use of the Old Testament in this section of Romans, see Hays, *Echoes of the Scripture in the Letters of Paul*, 46–57.

of God to which the law and prophets witness? It is the salvation that God achieves through Jesus Christ by fulfilling the covenants.[9] Even though human beings are not righteous and fail to keep covenant, God is righteous and brings about the accomplishment of his covenantal promises.

God had promised to bring blessing upon all nations through his covenantal relationship with Israel beginning with Abraham (cf. Gen. 17:1). He had promised an eternal throne to David, and he had promised to dwell perfectly with Israel. Now, as the prophets foretold, God accomplishes these promises, and thus demonstrates his righteous covenant-keeping, in Christ Jesus. Paul explains that God has now sent Christ "to show God's righteousness, because in his divine forbearance he had passed over former sins; it was to prove at the present time that he himself is righteous and that he justifies him who has faith in Jesus" (Rom. 3:25–26). Christ himself is the "righteousness of God" as the true priest-king and true temple. The "righteousness of God," therefore, is recognized by "all who believe" (Rom. 3:22) in Christ. Human beings, Jews and Gentiles, receive the covenantal righteousness of God "through faith in Jesus Christ" (Rom. 3:22).

All self-righteousness is thus excluded; human righteousness comes solely "by his [God's] grace as a gift, through the redemption which is in Christ Jesus, whom God put forward as an expiation by his blood, to be received by faith" (Rom. 3:24–25). The disordered Gentiles and Paul are in the same situation: both depend for healing solely upon the reconciliation won by Christ's cross. As Paul says, "For there is no distinction; since all have sinned and fall short of the glory of God" (Rom. 3:22–23). However, does this mean that Paul and the disordered Gentiles are distinguished solely by the fact that Paul has faith? In other words, could it be that there is no need, or even no possibility, of our giving up our disordered behavior, if only we have faith that God's righteousness will be sufficient for us?

It might seem so. Paul affirms, "No human being will be justified in [God's] sight by works of the law, since through the law comes knowledge of sin" (Rom. 3:20). But notice how this verse compares to Romans 2:13, which said that the doers of the law will be justified. In saying that no one will be justified by "works of the law," a technical term designating the part of the law of Moses not shared in common with the natural

---

9. For interpretation of "the righteousness of God," see Wright, *What Saint Paul Really Said*, ch. 6; idem, "New Exodus, New Inheritance: The Narrative Substructure of Romans 3–8," in Soderlund and Wright, eds., *Romans and the People of God*, 26–35; S. Williams, "The Righteousness of God in Romans," *Journal of Biblical Literature* 99 (1980): 241–290.

law (specifically the ceremonial observances of the law symbolized by circumcision), Paul is not contradicting his earlier claim that it is "the doers of the law who will be justified" (Rom. 2:13). On the contrary, as Paul says, "Do we then overthrow the law by this faith? By no means! On the contrary, we uphold the law" (Rom. 3:31). We uphold the law because by faith in Christ, Christ conforms us to himself by the Holy Spirit so that we are truly able to share in his fulfillment of the moral law. Since Christ is working through us, as Paul remarks, "what becomes of our boasting? It is excluded" (Rom. 3:27). With this in mind we can read correctly Romans 3:28, "For we hold that a man is justified by faith apart from works of the law." The contrast is not between faith and works of moral obedience, but between faith in Jesus Christ and the rituals of the Mosaic law, such as circumcision.

Romans 4 shows that Abraham followed this pattern of justification by faith apart from works of the law, although not apart from works of moral obedience.[10] Paul states that Abraham was justified by the faith he expresses in Genesis 15, "Abraham believed God, and it was reckoned to him as righteousness" (Rom. 4:3; Gen. 15:6). Again, the contrast is not between Abraham's faith and his works of moral obedience, but between his faith and ceremonial observances of the old law.[11] Paul shows the contrast between faith and circumcision explicitly when he asks, "How then was [righteousness] reckoned to him? Was it before or after he was circumcised? It was not after, but before he was circumcised" (Rom. 4:10). Abraham was justified by faith in Genesis 15, but circumcised in Genesis 17. In keeping with the technical sense of works of the law, the point is that circumcision did not justify Abraham. Significantly, this allows Abraham to be the father in faith of both the circumcised Jews and the uncircumcised Gentiles. If both have faith, they can come under the righteousness Abraham received in Genesis 15 before his circumcision.

This is why there is no contradiction between Paul and James on justification. James says that Abraham was justified by works, "when he offered his son Isaac upon the altar" (James 2:21). James continues, "You see that a man is justified by works and not by faith alone" (James 2:24). Clearly here there is no reference to the ceremonial law

10. For further discussion, see Frank Thielman, *The Law and the New Testament: The Question of Continuity* (New York: Crossroad, 1999).

11. Ambrosiaster comments on Romans 4:1, "After showing that no one can be justified before God by the works of the law, Paul goes on to say that Abraham could not merit anything according to the flesh either. In saying *the flesh*, Paul meant circumcision, because Abraham sought nothing on the basis of his circumcision. For he was already justified before he was circumcised," quoted in *Ancient Christian Commentary on Scripture: Romans*, ed. Gerald Bray (Downers Grove, IL: InterVarsity Press, 1998), 109.

of circumcision, but to works of moral obedience. James teaches that Abraham was justified both in Genesis 15 for his faith and then in Genesis 22 for his moral obedience of offering his son Isaac. Paul teaches that Abraham was justified in Genesis 15 for his faith and not in Genesis 17 for his circumcision. In doing so, Paul has not excluded moral works from justification.

Paul's understanding of justification can be depicted as a triangle. The triangle of justification is the new covenant in which God's promise to make his people holy and to dwell with them has been perfected. If one is in the new covenant of holiness, then one is inside the triangle. The three sides of the triangle are the ways to enter and stay in the covenant. As we will continue to see, these three ways are faith in Jesus Christ as Lord and Savior, baptism into his death and Resurrection, and moral obedience under his Lordship. We can distinguish between faith and obedience, but we cannot separate them without doing violence to Paul's theology. Thus the triangle of justification becomes the coin of justification with the two sides being faithful obedience, or "the obedience of faith," and baptism.

Christ and Adam

How then does faith in Jesus Christ justify? "Since all have sinned and fall short of the glory of God, they are justified by his grace as a gift, through the redemption which is in Christ Jesus, whom God put forward as an expiation by his blood, to be received by faith" (Rom. 3:23–25). The ceremonial works of the old law lacked the power to justify because they stemmed from unrighteous hearts and came forth in the blood of animals. The blood of Jesus flowing from his sacred heart (cf. John 7:37–38; 19:34) accomplishes the expiation for sins that the ceremonies of the old law could not accomplish. When the sacrifice of Jesus is accepted in faith, then the believers can be justified before God. Human beings were in a state of sin and therefore could not in any way merit the sacrifice of Jesus on the cross. "God shows his love for us in that while we were yet sinners Christ died for us" (Rom. 5:8). How does Christ's death accomplish man's salvation?

The obedience of Jesus Christ undoes the disobedience of Adam. We saw in Romans 3:23–25 that Paul speaks of Jesus' death as an expiation. Now we see what this expiation entails. The sacrificial offerings of the old law came from unclean hearts and thus could not undo the sin of Adam. Jesus' sacrificial offering of himself comes in an act of perfect loving obedience to the will of the Father. Paul contrasts Adam as the head of the fallen human race with Jesus Christ, the head of the redeemed

200

human race.[12] In an implicit doctrine of original sin, Paul teaches that by the one sin of Adam, sin and death entered the world and spread to all human beings. Yet Adam was a "type" of Jesus Christ whose one act of perfect righteousness will spread righteousness to all who receive it in faith. "For if many died through the one man's trespass, much more have the grace of God and the free gift in the grace of that one man Jesus Christ abounded for many" (Rom. 5:15). The free gift is the grace that restores man as holy before God. "For as by one man's disobedience many were made sinners, so by one man's obedience many will be made righteous" (Rom. 5:19).[13] Just as human beings were "made sinners," now they will be "made righteous," that is, truly righteous.[14]

In our first chapter, we saw how the sin of Adam and Eve destroyed the original justice with which human beings were created. In each of the Old Testament covenants, this lack of righteousness prevented Israel from holding up her side of the covenants. In fact, we have seen the pattern recur with each new covenant or covenant renewal, in that the moment of consummation is the moment of sin. Jesus, Son of God and son of David, ends this pattern through his righteousness and obedience of death on the cross.[15] In him, the king of Israel who establishes justice for his people, Israel is represented before God and personified as a people renewed in holiness. But his holiness extends even to the Gentiles; on the cross, Jesus personifies the new human race made up of Jews and Gentiles and restored in justice.

Baptism and New Creation

After the parallel between Adam and Jesus, Paul shows how Jesus' moral obedience passes on to the moral obedience of Christians. In other words, the free gift of righteousness in Christ is not an excuse for further sin, but the ability for keeping the law.[16] The contrast with Adam

12. See N. T. Wright, "Adam, Israel and the Messiah," in *The Climax of the Covenant: Christ and the Law in Pauline Theology* (Minneapolis: Fortress, 1986), 18–40.

13. For further discussion see Charles B. Cousar, *A Theology of the Cross: The Death of Jesus in the Pauline Letters* (Minneapolis: Fortress, 1990).

14. Cf. Stephen Pfürtner, O.P., *Luther and Aquinas on Salvation*, trans. Edward Quinn, introduction by Jaroslav Pelikan (New York: Sheed and Ward, 1964).

15. For discussion of Jesus' divine sonship in Romans, see Larry W. Hurtado, "Jesus' Divine Sonship in Paul's Epistle to the Romans," in Soderlund and Wright, eds., *Romans and the People of God*, 217–233.

16. See Brendan Byrne, "Living Out the Righteousness of God: The Contribution of Rom 6:1–8:13 to an Understanding of Paul's Ethical Presuppositions," *Catholic Biblical Quarterly* 43 (1981): 557–581.

makes it clear that Jesus Christ is the head of the renewed humanity, but how are people incorporated into Jesus Christ? Or, more specifically, how is the righteous act of Jesus' death communicated to sinners in order that they might share in Jesus' righteousness? Circumcision was the initiation into the old covenant, which lacked the full power to make its members holy. The works of the law thus do not justify. The new covenant established by Christ on the cross has the full power of justification. To become justified thus means to have entered this new covenant, to become a new creation.[17]

Paul shows that this occurs through Christian baptism. He asks, "Do you not know that all of us who have been in Christ Jesus were baptized into his death? We were buried therefore with him by baptism into death, so that as Christ was raised from the dead by the glory of the Father, we too might walk in the newness of life" (Rom. 6:3–4). Two conclusions follow. First, baptism justifies the sinner. It is by baptism that we are incorporated into Christ's death and Resurrection which justifies us. Romans 6 demonstrates that Romans 3:28, "a man is justified by faith and not by works of the law," cannot be said to exclude the sacraments of the new covenant. Baptism is not a work of the old law that does not justify, but a sacrament of the new law that does. Justification thus occurs through the complementary means of faith and baptism. Second, justification includes moral obedience and righteousness. Paul associates our justification by faith through baptism with walking in the "newness of life." Christ's act of obedience undid Adam's act of disobedience. In order to share in Christ's justification, human beings must share in the act that caused their justification. To continue to walk in sin would be a denial of the justification freely offered by Christ and already received in baptism. "Let not sin therefore reign in your mortal bodies, to make you obey their passions. Do not yield your members to sin as instruments of wickedness, but yield yourselves to God as men who have been brought from death to life, and your members to God as instruments of righteousness" (Rom. 6:13).

The body that was used for impurity (cf. Rom. 1:24–25) now becomes an instrument of righteousness and holiness. Surely it is not anything human beings have done on their own that has accomplished such a transformation from wickedness to righteousness. The conviction that human beings in a state of grace can perform acts of righteousness, and thus acts that are meritorious, stems from the conviction that God's

17. See Moyer V. Hubbard, *New Creation in Paul's Letters and Thought* (Cambridge: Cambridge University Press, 2002).

18. See Michael Root, "Aquinas, Merit, and Reformation Theology after the *Joint Declaration on the Doctrine of Justification*," *Modern Theology* 20 (2004): 5–22.

grace is powerful and effective.[18] "For just as you once yielded your members to impurity and to greater and greater iniquity, so now yield your members to righteousness for sanctification" (Rom. 6:19). There is no separation between justification and sanctification since both refer to God's free gift of restoring human beings to holiness. It is true that Isaiah had said, "all our righteous deeds are like a polluted garment" (Isa. 64:6), and this is what our good works are apart from Christ. In Christ, however, our good works are no longer unclean but have become instruments of righteousness and sanctification. Jesus Christ on the cross personifies the holy people of the new covenant. All who enter into the new covenant through faith and baptism must share in the works of righteousness that Jesus initiated.

Divine Filiation

The language of righteousness, justice, and sanctification might leave some readers questioning whether they have in fact been baptized at all. At first glance, Paul seems to indicate that with baptism the battle is over. Sin is destroyed, and the new life of grace dominates. In Christ, Jews and Gentiles have been transferred from the kingdom of sin and death to the kingdom of grace and life. Sin no longer reigns triumphantly. "For the law of the Spirit of life in Christ Jesus has set me free from the law of sin and death" (Rom. 8:2). Nonetheless, while the war may be over, the battle continues.

In what Augustine will later describe as concupiscence, Paul discloses that even after baptism the renewed human creature remains beset by temptations and inclinations contrary to the newness of life. Paul uses the language of spirit and flesh to contrast the inclinations to righteousness and those to wickedness. It is a moral opposition, not an ontological one. He is not praising the soul and despising the body in a Gnostic manner, which would be incompatible with Christianity. As is evident from Jesus' sacrificial death as well as Paul's exhortations to those who have been baptized into his death, the human body can be an instrument of righteousness. "So I find it to be a law that when I want to do right, evil lies close at hand. For I delight in the law of God, in my inmost self, but I see in my members another law at war with the law of my mind and making me captive to the law of sin which dwells in my members" (Rom. 7:21–23). The delight in the law of God shows that the person has been transferred into the new covenant and thus made righteous. Even now that the person is living the new life of the Spirit, the continuing effects of the law of sin show that the process of justification and sanctification is indeed a process still in need of completion.

The full restoration of original justice will bring with it perfect harmony between the intellect, the will, and the passion, and this full harmony awaits our purification through our physical death.[19]

Our return to holiness through Jesus Christ is characterized by an eschatological tension between delay and fulfillment. The term "eschatological" is used to refer to theological views about the end of earthly history and the complete establishment of the kingdom of God. The tension between delay and fulfillment refers to the tendency, on the one hand, for Paul to speak of our waiting for redemption and, on the other hand, for him to say that we have already died and risen with Christ. The struggle for holiness reveals the present reality of our experience of grace as well as of temptation. Our salvation is both already achieved, and not yet. This tension is expressed best through the image of our adoption as children of God: we have already been adopted, but have not yet matured into the fullness of the Son.

The presence of ongoing temptation, however, does not eclipse the reality of the life in the Spirit available to the sons of God. Romans 8 is perhaps the most beautiful exhortation to the glorious gift of divine filiation in the Bible. It begins with a startling claim: through the condemnation of Jesus Christ sin has been condemned in the flesh so that "the just requirement of the law might be fulfilled in us" (Rom. 8:4). The law requires the punishment of sin as well as the observance of its commandments. Since we are now "in Christ" the law has been fulfilled in us under both these requirements.[20] As the Son was perfect in justice and obedience, so those who are "sons in the Son" share in that perfect justice and obedience by the indwelling of his Spirit. Paul is not merely making rhetorical flourishes, but instead revealing the reality of the gift of redemption already given. "You are not in the flesh, you are in the Spirit, if the Spirit of God really dwells in you" (Rom. 8:9). Eternal life begins now.[21]

The reality of our divine filiation means that we will share in the obedience and justice of the Son in our own lives. Jesus manifested perfect justice by giving the total obedience that was due his heavenly Father by freely embracing suffering. The adopted sons of God likewise will become more completely justified through their embrace of suffering.[22]

19. This interpretation of Romans 7 has been heavily debated in recent decades. For an excellent discussion of the debate that argues for our Augustinian reading, see J. I. Packer, "The 'Wretched Man' Revisited: Another Look at Romans 7:14–25," in Soderlund and Wright, eds., Romans and the People of God, 70–81.

20. See Levering, Christ's Fulfillment of Torah and Temple.

21. See Gordon D. Fee, "Christology and Pneumatology in Romans 8:9–11—and Elsewhere: Some Reflections on Paul as a Trinitarian," in his To What End Exegesis? 218–239, esp. 231.

22. See Gorman, Cruciformity: Paul's Narrative Spirituality of the Cross.

The embrace and free acceptance of suffering is the most pure form of obedience to God and thus the fulfillment of justice. Paul brings out this aspect of suffering at the very moment of his highest praises for the reality of divine filiation. "For all who are led by the Spirit of God are sons of God. For you did not receive the spirit of slavery to fall back into fear, but you have received the spirit of sonship. When we cry, 'Abba! Father!' it is the Spirit himself bearing witness with our spirit that we are children of God, and if children, then heirs, heirs of God and fellow heirs with Christ, *provided we suffer with him* in order that we may also be glorified with him" (Rom. 8:14–17, emphasis added).

A reader may have the similar reaction to the invitation given by Jesus that if anyone wishes to be his disciple he must deny himself and take up his cross. The good news of salvation is undeniable, but the free embrace of suffering might cause one to reconsider. It is as if Paul is saying, "God has forgiven your sins and justified you, but the consequences of your sins remain. Through the gift of his Son, suffering and death can now be a means to eternal life. There is a way to come back to God, but the way is difficult." Paul, however, does not leave his reader in the midst of suffering, but focuses the attention on the goal of eternal bliss: "I consider the sufferings of this present time are not worth comparing with the glory that is to be revealed to us" (Rom. 8:18). Through their adoption as sons of God, members of the new covenant participate in the perfect glory of God from all eternity (cf. 2 Peter 1:4). As Paul indicates in his Letter to the Colossians, members of the new covenant also participate in the expiation offered by the Son, Jesus Christ (Col. 1:24).[23] The reward of eternal glory for ourselves and for redeemed humanity triumphs over all sufferings and sorrows.

Paul never considers human beings in the abstract, apart from their relationship to Christ. They are either enslaved to sin, or *in Christ*. When they enter into Christ, everything is transformed. ("For neither circumcision counts for anything, nor uncircumcision, but a new creation" [Gal. 6:15].) Thus in saying that God can bring good out of all things, Paul is not saying that the good and the bad of the universe tend to balance out each other. Instead it refers concretely to Christ. Since God brought the infinite good of redemption out of the infinite evil of the cross, God can bring about our sharing in the goodness of redemption through his bearing of evils. "We know that in everything God works for good with those who love him, who are called according to his purpose" (Rom. 8:28). Paul immediately turns from this statement to the fact that the newly redeemed creature is patterned after Jesus Christ. "For those whom he foreknew he also predestined to be conformed to the image of

23. Cf. N. T. Wright, *Colossians and Philemon* (Grand Rapids: Eerdmans, 1986).

his Son, in order that he might be the first-born among many brethren" (Rom. 8:29).[24] Since our salvation is to be restored in the image of the Son, suffering merely perfects in us the image of the crucified Son. As sons of God adopted out of God's sheer love, we have grounds for great confidence in our eternal salvation, which only our free decision to reject God through sin could negate. Paul concludes triumphantly, "I am sure that neither death, nor life, nor angels, nor principalities, not things present, nor things to come, nor powers, nor heights, nor depth, nor anything else in all creation, will be able to separate us from the love of God in Christ Jesus our Lord" (Rom. 8:38–39).

"And All Israel Will Be Saved"

Romans 1–8 tells the glorious story of how God in Jesus Christ has established a new covenant, the fulfillment of his promises to create a holy people, in which both Jews and Gentiles now share in the righteousness of God through faith and baptism into Jesus Christ. Yet, perceptive readers will have been asking themselves, What about the Jews who have not received Jesus as the Messiah? Paul dedicates Romans 9–11 to answering this question. By means of a grand eschatological narrative, Paul makes clear that God indeed remains faithful to the covenant he has established with the Jewish people through Moses.[25]

Paul shows that the rejection of Jesus by many Jews of Paul's day has served God's purpose by bringing the gospel more quickly to the Gentiles. There is no doubt that Paul, formerly the most zealous of Pharisees, believes that Israel has failed by not recognizing Jesus as the Messiah. "Israel failed to obtain what it sought" (Rom. 11:7). But this is a temporary failure according to the plan of God. "Through their trespass salvation has come to the Gentiles, so as to make Israel jealous" (Rom. 11:11). This is a providential mystery, but Paul makes it very explicit: "a hardening has come upon part of Israel, until the full number of the Gentiles come in, and so all Israel will be saved" (Rom. 11:25–26).

The language of hardening of heart used in Romans 9 and 11 cannot be interpreted to deny human freedom, since this would undermine

24. See Luke Timothy Johnson, *Reading Romans: A Literary and Theological Commentary* (New York: Crossroad, 1997), 132–133.

25. See the excellent study, focusing on Old Testament motifs in Romans 9–11, by J. Ross Wagner, *Heralds of the Good News: Isaiah and Paul in Concert in the Letter to the Romans* (Leiden: Brill, 2002), which is indebted to Hays's *Echoes of Scripture in the Letters of Paul*, 63–83. See also N. T. Wright, "Christ, the Law and the People of God: the Problem of Romans 9–11," in Wright, *The Climax of the Covenant: Christ and the Law in Pauline Theology* (Minneapolis: Fortress, 1992), 231–257.

human responsibility for sin (Romans 1–2) as well as responsibility for faith in Jesus Christ (Romans 3–5). God does not harden the heart of the sinner against the sinner's free will. The hardening refers to God's permissive will expressed in giving sinners the freedom to reject him. The language of hardening their hearts as used for Pharaoh (Exod. 7:3) and Israel shows that human sin does not fall outside of divine providence. The sinner does not succeed in trying to create a world in which God is no longer God. Instead, even the sinner's rebellion exists within the world under God's providence such that God orders those very acts of rebellion to serve his purpose of man's salvation. Pharaoh's rebellion became the precise means by which Moses led Israel out of Egypt. The rejection and condemnation of Jesus Christ on the cross now becomes the precise means by which Jesus leads sinners out of sin. Israel's not accepting Jesus as the Christ has become the means by which God is reconciling to himself all the nations, and eventually Israel itself. After the coming of Christ and the new covenant, the earlier covenants have thus not been revoked. On the contrary, in God's providence the continuing existence of Israel remains ordered, according to Paul, to the fullness of salvation accomplished by the Messiah, Jesus of Nazareth.

Life in the Body of Christ

After displaying the greatness of God's mercy manifested in the new covenant, Paul naturally turns to a more explicit consideration of how members of the new covenant, to be truly holy people, ought to live in this world. Romans 12–15 forms a great *parenesis*, or an extended moral exhortation and guidance for life in Christ. The basis for the moral life, however, is not simply the natural law spoken of in Romans 2.14. The moral life has its grounding in the entrance of the holy people into the holy land, the Body of Christ or the Church, where perfect worship is offered to God. In other words, the moral life is cultic, that is, oriented toward the worship of God.

The moral life in the new covenant is neither the individualistic morality of modernity nor the relativistic, subjectivistic morality of post-modernity. Romans depicts the moral life of the redeemed sons of God. It is a life "in Christ." This means that to understand the moral life of the Christian one must first look to the moral life of Christ.[26] As Paul has already highlighted in the contrast of Adam and Christ, Christ's moral righteousness was expressed through the righteous act of obedience by

26. See Michael B. Thompson, *Clothed with Christ: The Example and Teaching of Jesus in Romans 12:1–15:13* (Sheffield: JSOT, 1991).

207

which he offered himself on the cross. Morality embraced cultic liturgy and vice versa. Christ's sacrificial obedience was the perfect worship of God; the perfect worship of God was Christ's sacrificial obedience. As this was the case for the Son, so it is for his adopted brothers and sisters. Romans 12 begins, "I appeal to you therefore, brethren, by the mercies of God, to present your bodies as a living sacrifice, holy and acceptable to God, which is your spiritual worship" (Rom. 12:1).

Notice the word "therefore": the sacrificial worship of moral living can only happen because of the realities Paul presents in Romans 1–11. Apart from justification by faith in Christ, there could be no offering of human bodies as acceptable worship. As we have seen, however, in Christ bodies can become "instruments of righteousness" (Rom. 6:13). Although Paul does not make this explicit, one can easily recognize the promise given to Israel in Exodus 19:6, "you shall be to me a kingdom of priests and a holy nation." All those in Christ share in the priesthood of Christ since they can offer spiritual worship to God through their bodies. This is the common priesthood shared by all the baptized in distinction from the ministerial priesthood shared only by those who have received the sacrament of holy orders. The attainment of moral purity is not an end in itself, but is directed towards the worship of God almighty. The Son has given the gift of righteousness so that the human creature may enter the eternal Sabbath in which God is forever adored.

Paul grounds his reflection on the specifics of the moral law in Christ by referring to the reality of the Church as the Body of Christ. "For as in one body we have many members, and all the members do not have the same function, so we, though many, are one body in Christ, and individually members one of another" (Rom. 12:4–5). Acts 9 gives deep insight into Paul's doctrine of the Body of Christ. Paul was traveling to Damascus in order to arrest Jewish followers of Jesus. After Paul had fallen to the ground, Jesus said to him, "Saul, Saul, why do you persecute me? . . . I am Jesus, whom you are persecuting" (Acts 9:4–5). Jesus revealed to Paul his profound *identity* with his Church. The followers could be said to be Christ himself. Although the specific truth of the Church as the Body of Christ is not mentioned, one cannot deny that the truth revealed by Jesus to Paul corresponds to the doctrine of the Body of Christ, found even more explicitly in other Pauline letters. The teaching of the Body of Christ not only shows that each Christian is in Christ as a member of his Body, it also shows that all Christians are related to one another with distinct roles and functions. As in a physical body, differences ought not to lead to jealousies and earthly competitions, but should allow the Church to accomplish its diverse goals of what can be summarized by the corporal and spiritual works of mercy (Rom. 12:6–8).

208

Paul instructs the members of the Body of Christ in the paths of holiness. "Let love be genuine; hate what is evil, hold fast to what is good; love one another with brotherly affection; outdo one another in showing honor" (Rom. 12:9–10). "Contribute to the needs of the saints, practice hospitality" (Rom. 12:13). "Bless those who persecute you; bless and do not curse them" (Rom. 12:14). "Do not be overcome by evil, but overcome evil with good" (Rom. 12:21). Further he says they are to be subject to governing authorities and to pay their taxes (Rom. 13:1,7). "He who loves his neighbor has fulfilled the law" (Rom. 13:8). Paul shows from the specific commandments he subsequently lists (Rom. 13:9) that he speaks here of the law in terms of the duties toward other human beings, not those commandments to worship God. As we discussed in the chapter on Moses, the first tablet of the law covers the duties to God and the second tablet covers those duties to other human beings. The first three commandments of the Decalogue can only be fulfilled by loving God. Yet, Paul here speaks of fulfilling the law by loving one's neighbor.

Faith in God, as used by Paul, thus includes love of him. Faith, along with moral obedience toward God by loving one's neighbor, is necessary to fulfill the law and to be filled with justice. Once again we see that when Paul contrasts faith and "works of the law" in Romans 3:28, he is not contrasting faith and the moral law, but faith and the ceremonial observances of the old law. Justification includes obedience to the moral law. More specifically, justification is the source of moral obedience, as well as its completion. It is the same process expressed through the image of our adoption as children of God. When we were not children, there was nothing we could do to earn our adoption. It was God's free love that led Christ to die for us while we were yet sinners (Rom. 5:8). Once adopted, however, we complete our adoption, so to speak, by performing acts of obedience that allow us to mature into the full stature of sons of God (cf. Col. 1:28). God's initiative in justifying us gives us the ability to cooperate with the subsequent process of justification.

Chapters 14 and 15 of Romans focus on the motivation of our actions. The question we ask ourselves should not be merely "Is it the right thing to do?" but "Will it edify?"—that is, "Will it upbuild the Body of Christ of which I am a member solely by the mercy of God?"[27] Dealing specifically with the question of whether Christians can eat food sacrificed to idols, Paul exhorts, "Let us then pursue what makes for peace and for mutual upbuilding" (Rom. 14:19). He then lays down the principle that "it is right not to eat meat or drink wine or do anything that makes your

---

27. On the corporate nature of Pauline ethics, see Hays, *The Moral Vision of the New Testament*, 32–36.

brother stumble" (Rom. 14:21). This attitude puts the needs of others before our own. "Let each of us please his neighbor for his good, to edify him. For Christ did not please himself" (Rom. 15:2–3). The Body of Christ should exhibit harmony between its members as the antitype to the envies of the body of Adam.

The loss of original justice manifested itself in Cain's envy and murder of Abel. Those in the Body of Christ should not become jealous of one another since all possess every spiritual good in Christ. Because spiritual scarcity has been overcome, although material scarcity sadly remains, jealousy and envy should be absent from the Body of Christ. Through the desire to edify one other and to seek to please one another, the harmony is slowly restored. God's reestablishment of a holy people includes the harmony within each person, the harmony between members of the body, the harmony between the person and God, and the harmony between the corporate body and God. These harmonies become one as it is one love with which redeemed persons now love themselves, each other, and God.[28]

Romans 13 possesses the words God used to convert Augustine, "Let us conduct ourselves becomingly as in the day, not in reveling and drunkenness, not in debauchery and licentiousness, not in quarreling and jealousy. But put on the Lord Jesus Christ, and make no provision for the flesh" (Rom. 13:13–14).[29] What Paul wrote at the beginning of Romans remains true at the end, namely that God will judge each person according to his works (Rom. 2:6). Seriously immoral actions earn the sinner eternal death both before and after the gift of grace in Jesus Christ. Salvation consists both in having sins forgiven in Jesus Christ, and in performing loving actions attributable to us because we are now in Christ. Judgment by works remains. The good news is that if we begin with faith in Jesus Christ and share in his death through baptism, then our sins have likewise been put to death and the Spirit of the Resurrection now lives in us. By entering the new covenant, we become the holy people of God prepared to live in his presence for eternity.

The theme of how the new covenant establishes the holy people of God could be continued throughout the canonical Pauline letters. The theme of justification as covenantal righteousness is found in Galatians in much the same way as in Romans. First and 2 Corinthians, 1 and 2 Thessalonians, Philippians, 1 and 2 Timothy, Titus, and Philemon, distinctive as they all are, together highlight the holiness demanded of the Church, a holiness rooted in love overflowing from faith in Christ

28. Cf. Augustine, *De Trinitate*, Book VIII.
29. Augustine, *Confessions*, Book VIII.

(1 Cor. 13; 1 Thess. 4:7; 2 Thess. 2:13; Phil. 1:9–11; 1 Tim. 6:11; 2 Tim. 4:8; Titus 3:7). In Ephesians and Colossians, Paul specifies this general notion of holiness by teaching that the Church, as Christ's Body (holy land), becomes holy through her identification with Christ her head. In this way, the themes of "holy people" and "holy land" extend throughout the Pauline corpus.

9

Hebrews

The Priest-King of the New Covenant

There is a story of the theologian and the physicist who sit next to one another on the plane. At the end of a long conversation, the physicist says to the theologian, "When you get down to it, isn't all religion simply the golden rule, 'Do unto others as you would have them do unto you'?" The theologian quickly replied, "That's like saying that all physics comes down to 'Twinkle, twinkle, little star. . . .'" This anecdote illustrates a profound point: so often we mistakenly reduce religion to the horizontal level of our dealings with one another.[1] Religion, however, is necessarily cultic in the technical sense, that is, oriented to God. The true religion offers the true worship of the true God. The theme of holy land that we have been following in this book refers not to a geographical territory, but to the right cultic relationship with God by which a people can rightly dwell with him in worship.

Hebrews narrates the story of how Christ is leading the people of God into the true holy land. It is clear that the people must become holy before they can enter the temple of true worship. Hebrews thus pays significant attention to the purification of the human conscience and the resulting confidence in our salvation. Nonetheless, Hebrews focuses

---

1. See William C. Placher, *The Domestication of Transcendence: How Modern Thinking about God Went Wrong* (Louisville: Westminster John Knox Press, 1996).

on how Christ brings the new people of God into the true relationship of worship. It tells the story of the new exodus into the new promised land. It is about the new priesthood that Christ establishes as part of the new covenant—a kingly and eternal priesthood that allows man to participate in the true worship of heaven.

The Son of God and the New Exodus

Hebrews begins with the proclamation, "In many and various ways God spoke of old to our fathers by the prophets; but in these last days he has spoken to us by a Son, whom he appointed the heir of all things, through whom also he created the world" (Heb. 1:1–2). That Jesus is the Son of God forms the overall motif for the entire book. The Son of God signifies the eternal Son of the Father as well as the Davidic king who will rule over the nations of the world. The Son referred to in Hebrews 1:1–2 must be transcendent, since he is the one through whom God created the world, including the angels.[2] Yet, the subsequent quotes refer to the Davidic king: "Thou art my Son, today I have begotten thee" (Heb. 1:5, quoting Ps. 2:7); "I will be to him a father, and he shall be to me a son" (Heb. 1:5, quoting 2 Sam. 7:14), and then quote from Psalms 45 and 110, both coronation psalms. Hebrews depicts the fulfillment of the Davidic kingship when the eternal Son was born of the line of David and inherited his throne.[3] It belonged to the Davidic king not only to instill righteousness in the people, but also to establish the people in the land in which God would dwell. By the king's vocation as temple-builder, he brought the holy people into the holy land. Solomon, however, could only build an earthly copy of the eternal temple which God then chose to come down and bless with his glory (1 Kings 8:11). As Son, Jesus enters directly into the reality of the heavenly temple and leads all those in his kingdom to dwell in the glory of heaven.

As we saw in chapter two, the people of God were in bondage in Egypt until they were delivered to the mountain of Sinai at which they could renounce their idolatry and worship the true God. Through Moses and

2. See St. John Chrysostom, *Homilies on the Epistle to the Hebrews: Homilies I and II*, in Nicene and Post-Nicene Fathers, First Series, Vol. 14, *Chrysostom: Homilies on the Gospel of Saint John and the Epistle to the Hebrews* (Peabody, MA: Hendrickson, 1995 [1889]), 363–369. Chrysostom argues that Hebrews 1:1–3 holds the middle path between those early heresies that either confuse the Son with the Father or deny the full divinity of the Son.
3. See Philip Hughes, *A Commentary on the Epistle to the Hebrews* (Grand Rapids: Eerdmans, 1977), 50–72; Frank J. Matera, *New Testament Christology* (Louisville: Westminster John Knox Press, 1999), 187–188.

Aaron God performed great signs and wonders that eventually caused Pharaoh to cast the Israelites out of Egypt (Exod. 3:20). Nonetheless, Pharaoh was mercurial and soon began to hunt down the Israelites so they had to escape through the miracle of the parting of the waters at the Red Sea (Exodus 14). When they came to Sinai, Israel enjoyed a foretaste of the land God promised to Abraham, since God there appeared in the cloud on the mountain. From Sinai through the journeys in the wilderness, Israel enjoyed a further foretaste of the promised land because God began to dwell with Israel in the tabernacle or meeting tent (Exodus 40). Although Israel was not yet in the promised land, they already experienced the true worship of the true God who dwelt with them as with no other nation. The completion of the exodus, however, required the entrance into the land where Israel could rest with God.

Hebrews 2 depicts, therefore, the new exodus of the people of God. The author asks, "how shall we escape if we neglect such a great salvation?" (Heb. 2:3). The language of escape recalls the escape from Egypt, but now the escape is from the punishment due to sin. Signs and wonders before Pharaoh attested the salvation led by Moses and Aaron. The new salvation led by Jesus was also attested by "signs and wonders" by the power of the Holy Spirit (Heb. 2:4). As the first exodus led to the glory first manifested at Mount Sinai, then present in the tabernacle, and finally dwelling in the promised land, so likewise the new exodus leads to glory. As the first exodus included the death of the Egyptians, the new exodus includes the death of sinful humanity. In the death of Jesus, Jesus "taste[s] death for every one" (Heb. 2:9). Because of sin, all humans deserved the just punishment of death. Jesus bears this punishment so that through the exodus of his death and Resurrection he might lead his followers to his glory. "It was fitting that he, for whom and by whom all things exist, in bringing many sons to glory, should make the pioneer of their salvation perfect through suffering" (Heb. 2:10). The Son of God is the pioneer of the new exodus who leads many sons to glory. Yet, how can the Son be made perfect? Is he not already perfect? And why must it be through suffering?

Death has died. One must notice that being made perfect is connected to bringing many sons to glory. Hebrews elsewhere confesses that "Jesus Christ is the same yesterday and today and forever" (Heb. 13:8), and so Jesus cannot have changed from less than God to fully God or from partially sinful to pure of heart. The Greek word translated here as "perfect" also means complete or fulfilled.[4] To be made perfect thus does not imply defect, but only incompletion. That completion, or

---

4. See Paul Ellingworth, *The Epistle to the Hebrews*, The New International Greek Testament Commentary (Grand Rapids: Eerdmans, 1993), 161–163.

perfection, comes in two stages: 1) in Christ's actual death on the cross, in which his human will manifests his full conformity in obedience to the divine will (cf. Heb. 5:7–9 and 10:1–10); and 2) as believers in every generation enter into the salvation that he has won, until all is fulfilled in Christ's second coming in glory.

Hebrews expresses the mystery of our redemption through the language of the defeat of death and the devil. The Son of God took on the flesh and blood of human nature, and thus "for a little while was made lower than the angels" (Heb. 2:9), so "that through death he might destroy him who has the power of death, that is, the devil, and deliver all those who through fear of death were subject to lifelong bondage" (Heb. 2:14–15). Man's punishment for sin has been not only death, but the fear of death. Death here includes all suffering since every suffering is a little death and death is the greatest suffering, the wrenching apart of the created unity of body and soul. By the fear of suffering and death, man has been enslaved to the devil.[5] The pioneer of salvation had to complete his mission to bring many sons to glory through suffering, because the fear of suffering was precisely what barred man from God. Through his Resurrection, Jesus destroyed the power of death. Physical death and suffering remain, but they no longer should inspire paralyzing fear, since they are but the path to the glory of the resurrection of the people of God.

If we reflect upon human experience, we see that although many sins arise from the disordered desire for pleasure, many arise from the fear of the suffering that obedience to God's commands requires. The hallmark of this kind of sin remains apostasy, denying Christ in the face of persecution. This sin also manifests itself in those who flout the Church's teaching on sex and marriage because of the suffering involved in infertility, or in marital chastity, or in not marrying again after divorce. It can lead one to steal from a company or to support unjust wage practices because of the incessant drive for financial security. The way of God involves suffering and precariousness, but it simultaneously conquers suffering by turning suffering into a means to glory. Those who through the fear of suffering break the commandments in fact break themselves, by rejecting the gift of eternal salvation that we receive, in faith, when our lives are configured to the pattern of Christ's sacrificial self-gift.

5. Cf. St. John Chrysostom, *Homilies on the Epistle to the Hebrews: Homily IV*, no. 6 (385): "He here shows that the afflicted, the harassed, the persecuted, those that are deprived of country and of substance and of all other things, spend their lives more sweetly and more freely than they of old time who were in luxury, who suffered no such afflictions, who were in continual prosperity, if indeed these 'all their life-time' were under this fear and were slaves; while the others have been made free and laugh at that which they shudder at."

The New Moses

Jesus' vocation comes to light in the contrast with Moses. Moses was faithful in God's house, and so is Jesus. "Yet Jesus has been counted worthy of as much more glory than Moses as the builder of a house has more honor than the house" (Heb. 3:3). The analogy suggests the image that Jesus is the builder of the house of Moses. Despite Moses' greatness, Moses remains on the side of the people of God. Jesus, in contrast, bridges the gap between God and his people, since he shares flesh and blood with the people of God while also being the one who has created them and called them to be a people. Jesus performs this unique role of standing on both sides of the distinction between Creator and creature through his status as Son. The reality of the Son includes both the eternal Son of God and the earthly son of David. "Now Moses was faithful in all God's house as a servant, to testify to the things that were to be spoken later, but Christ was faithful over God's house as a son" (Heb. 3:5–6). The son contrasts with the servant because the son receives the full authority of the father over the house.[6]

Moses' exodus also includes the tumultuous journey to the promised land. Hebrews 3 quotes Psalm 95, which exhorts Israel not to harden their hearts against God as they had done in the wilderness. The lessons of Israel are still relevant to the new exodus led by Jesus. In other words, the completion of the exodus—the attainment of the true holy land—requires belief and obedience on the part of followers of Christ. The author of Hebrews exhorts the Church, "Take care, brethren, lest there be in any of you an evil, unbelieving heart, leading you to fall away from the living God. . . . For we share in Christ, if only we hold our first confidence to the end" (Heb. 3:12, 14). The sabbath rest of the promised land foreshadowed the sabbath rest of eternal life in Christ.[7] Just as many who were with Moses and entered that covenant did not enter the rest of the promised land, so will many who entered the new covenant in Jesus Christ not enter the rest of eternal life. An earlier moment of belief and obedience will not substitute for ongoing belief and obedience.

6. Matera notes that for the author of Hebrews "the divine sonship of Christ is foundational to Christ's high priesthood" (Matera, New Testament Christology, 189). On Christ's (and, according to rabbinic tradition, Moses') superiority to the angels, see Anderson, The Genesis of Perfection, 36–37.

7. Luke Timothy Johnson, "The Scriptural World of Hebrews," Interpretation 57 (2003): 245–246; cf. the emphasis of St. John Chrysostom, Homilies on the Epistle to the Hebrews: Homily VI (393–397).

The exhortation thus sets before us the great challenge: "Let us therefore strive to enter that rest, that no one fall by the same sort of disobedience" (Heb. 4:11). The gospel always comes with a balance of challenge and peace. The same Jesus who said that anyone who was not willing to carry his cross was not worthy to be his disciple also invited those who were weary and heavy laden to come to him since his yoke is easy and his burden light. Like the Gospels, Hebrews places this great challenge to strive to enter the eternal rest in the context of the source of our striving—namely, Jesus' mercy. Our high priest, Jesus, has been tempted as we are and can sympathize with the sufferings and difficulties of our present life (Heb. 4:15).[8] "Let us then with confidence draw near to the throne of grace, that we may receive mercy and find grace to help in the time of need" (Heb. 4:16). Confidence and striving are not inversely proportionate to each other, as one might imagine. Instead, the greater the level of confidence in attaining heaven, the greater the striving for salvation, since both have their root in faith in Christ and his promises.

Pilgrims on the exodus of the new covenant have grounds for confidence that those with Moses did not have. Moses was a fellow pilgrim, who likewise struggled to enter the promised land and eventually failed to enter it because of his own disobedience. In contrast, the new covenant pilgrimage has already been completed by its pioneer, Jesus Christ. As we will see, since he is the great high priest who has entered into heaven itself the new exodus is already complete in him. Therefore those faithful who remain on the journey have grounds for great confidence because they know that their leader is already home and will bring them to safety. The sacrifice that merits their entrance has already been offered. This is the great message of Hebrews, that through his sacrifice Jesus has led the people of God into the holy land of perfect adoration and worship.[9]

Covenants signify security because of their solemn, indelible character. After the exchange of marriage vows each spouse can rest knowing that the other person is committed for life. Yet, human vows retain the problem that they are made by sinful people who might fail to keep them. The only totally secure covenant would be one made by God. Hebrews reveals that this is exactly what Christians have in the new covenant. This knowledge should give rise to "the full assurance of hope until the end, so that you may not be sluggish, but imitators of those who through

---

8. See Ellingworth, *The Epistle to the Hebrews*, 266–296; also the set of themes developed in Margaret Barker, *The Great High Priest: The Temple Roots of Christian Liturgy* (New York: T. & T. Clark, 2003).

9. See the *Catechism of the Catholic Church*, no. 617.

faith and patience inherit the promises" (Heb. 6:11–12). Here again we see that hope and striving go hand-in-hand.

The precise character of our striving, therefore, is important. The full assurance of hope is not given to those who trust in their own strength to attain heaven. Hope trusts in the oath of the new covenant sworn by Christ on the cross (Heb. 7:20–22, 28). God's covenant with Abraham included God's sworn oath "to show more convincingly to the heirs of the promise the unchangeable character of his purpose" (Heb. 6:17). God's word to Abraham plus his sworn oath are the "two unchangeable things" that should encourage us "to seize the hope set before us" (Heb. 6:18). The oath sworn to Abraham has now been completed by Jesus' own sacrifice and testimony on the cross.

Hope does not trust in itself, but in the anchor of the cross.[10] "We have this as a sure and steadfast anchor of the soul, a hope that enters into the inner shrine behind the curtain, where Jesus has gone as a forerunner on our behalf, having become a high priest for ever after the order of Melchizedek" (Heb. 6:19–20). Hope anchors the soul in the midst of suffering and difficulties because by faith in Jesus Christ we have already entered into the perfect cultic worship of God. As long as we continue in faith, then our death, and our resurrection from the dead, will be the entrance into that perfect worship. The new covenant of the cross secures our hope. This hope frees human beings from the bondage of the devil and fear of physical death since we have assurance of entering into the holy land of God.

Aaron, Melchizedek, and Priest-Kings

Jesus is the high priest of the new exodus. Yet, in which priesthood is Jesus the high priest? In the classic definition of the priesthood still read at every priestly ordination, Hebrews reviews what is common to all priesthood, "For every high priest chosen from among men is appointed to act on behalf of men in relation to God, to offer gifts and sacrifices for sins" (Heb. 5:1). Aaron, who was of the tribe of Levi, was called by God to act as high priest of the covenant with Moses. When Aaron offered sacrifices for the sins of the people, he also had to offer sacrifices for his own sins (Lev. 16:11). The dissimilarity with Jesus is striking. Nonetheless, Jesus was also called by God, just as Aaron was, to be a high priest.

Significantly, however, Hebrews does not cite any texts about Aaron to support the high priesthood of Jesus. Instead, Jesus' calling to the high

10. Cf. *Catechism of the Catholic Church*, no. 1817.

priesthood is supported by quotations from two psalms for the corona-tion of Davidic kings. The first quotation is of Psalm 2:7, "Thou art my son, today I have begotten thee" (Heb. 5:5). What does this psalm that describes the triumph of the Lord and his anointed against the rulers of this world have to do with the priesthood? The clue is found in the next quotation, Psalm 110:4, "Thou art a priest for ever, after the order of Melchizedek."

Like Psalm 2, Psalm 110 concerns the triumph of the Lord and his king over the kings of this world. Yet, unlike Psalm 2, Psalm 110 reveals that the Davidic king was also anointed as a priest, in the order of Melchizedek.[11] As we saw in chapter two, Melchizedek was a priest-king whose name means "king of righteousness." He was identified as king of Salem, the same place that will later be called Jeru-salem (Gen. 14:18). The king of Salem was also the priest of the most high God, and after he received Abraham's tithes Melchizedek offered bread and wine to God. Similarly, after David conquered the city of Jerusalem and made it his new capital (2 Sam. 5:9), David brought the ark of the Lord to Jerusalem, where he sacrificed an ox and a fatling and danced before the Lord while wearing a linen ephod, which was priestly attire (2 Sam. 6:13–14), and distributed bread and raisin-cakes (2 Sam. 6:19). Like Melchizedek, David was a priest-king.

Jesus therefore did not inherit the Levitical priesthood, but the older and greater priesthood of Melchizedek. He was "designated by God a high priest after the order of Melchizedek" (Heb. 5:10). Melchizedek lacked the legal requirements for Levitical priesthood, and thus stands as the pattern of Christ: "Now if perfection had been attainable through the Levitical priesthood (for under it the people received the law), what further need would there have been for another priest to arise after the order of Melchizedek rather than the one named after Aaron?" (Heb. 7:11). Hebrews brings to mind the infancy narratives of Matthew and Luke, as well as the opening of Romans, when it says, "it is evident that our Lord was descended from Judah, and in connection with that tribe Moses said nothing about priests" (Heb. 7:14). In the context of Moses, "priests" here refers to the Levitical priests. Jesus stands as the priest-king of the new covenant.[12]

---

11. For an introduction to the theme of Christ's priesthood in Hebrews, see Matera, *New Testament Christology*, 193–196. On priesthood and kingship as attained by Jesus through his Paschal mystery, according to Hebrews, see Johnson, *The Writings of the New Testament*, 426.

12. See St. John Chrysostom, *Homilies on the Epistle to the Hebrews: Homily XIII* (428); St. Augustine, *City of God*, Book XVI, ch. 22 (680).

Hebrews adds that Melchizedek "is without father or mother or gene-alogy, and has neither beginning of days nor end of life, but resembling the Son of God he continues a priest for ever" (Heb. 7:3). The fact that Melchizedek's priesthood was not limited by years is a type of Jesus' priesthood, which exists eternally because of his Resurrection. Jesus "holds his priesthood permanently, because he continues for ever. Consequently he is able for all time to save those who draw near to God through him, since he always lives to make intercession for them" (Heb. 7:24–25). The adverbs stand out: "for ever," "for all time," and "always." The temporary, earthly aspect of the Levitical priesthood makes it the perfect contrast with the eternal, heavenly character of the priesthood exercised by Jesus Christ.[13] This contrast between the temporary and the eternal informs the interpretation of his sacrifice: "He has no need, like those high priests, to offer sacrifices daily, first for his own sins and then for those of the people; he did this once for all when he offered up himself" (Heb. 7:27). The "once for all" here should be read as once "for ever," "for all time," and for "always," in accord with the passage above. The Levitical priesthood's sacrifices were temporary; Jesus' sacrifice exists eternally. In liturgical terms, this means that the Mass does not sacrifice Jesus again, as has sometimes been suggested, but rather is the means by which the faithful, in the liturgical sacrifice, have recurring temporal participation in Jesus' "once for all" sacrifice.

The Heavenly Temple

If Jesus holds his priesthood eternally, then he must exercise it in heaven. The Levitical priests offered their sacrifices first in the taber-nacle, or tent of meeting, until the time of King Solomon and then later in the temple itself. As we have seen in our third chapter, Moses had built the tabernacle as an earthly copy of the heavenly worship (Exod. 25:40; Heb. 8:5).[14] Moreover, the animal sacrifices offered there only had the power to forgive inadvertent sins, but did not have the power to purify deliberate serious sins—what have come to be called mortal sins. Sin offerings were only for lesser sins, but those who do anything deliberately or "with a high hand" were to be cut off from the people (Num. 15:27–31). For instance, in the old law, there was no sin offering for adultery; a couple thus caught was to be stoned (Lev. 20:10). Hebrews says that the sacrifices of the old law could not "perfect the conscience

13. Compare Ellingworth, *Hebrews*, 393–395.
14. For valuable insight into the temple in Hebrews 8–13, see Beale, *The Temple and the Church's Mission*, 293–312.

of the worshipper" (Heb. 9:9). This includes even the great annual Day of Atonement, or Yom Kippur, on which the high priest offers a bull and a goat for the sins of the people (Leviticus 16). The contrast with the Levitical priesthood serves to sharpen the presentation of the new covenant.

Jesus offers in heaven the sacrifice that regenerates the believers. Jeremiah 31 had prophesied a "new covenant" which would be written on their hearts and include the forgiveness of sins. The new covenant will be "better" than the old covenant insofar as the promises of the old covenant will be fulfilled through the new covenant. In this way, Hebrews is not supercessionist. The old law points to the new and remains fulfilled in the new. Jesus offers his own blood in the true sanctuary. "When Christ appeared as a high priest of the good things that have come, then through the greater and more perfect tent (not made with hands, that is, not of this creation) he entered once for all into the Holy Place, taking with him not the blood of goats and calves but his own blood, thus securing an eternal redemption" (Heb. 9:11–12). The new Day of Atonement has begun. It is, as Zechariah foretold, an everlasting day. Jesus the eternal priest has entered eternally into the eternal temple of heaven in order to bring us an eternal redemption.

How does Christ's death bring about our redemption? Hebrews says that "Christ is the mediator of a new covenant, so that those who are called may receive the promised eternal inheritance, since a death has occurred which redeems them from the transgressions under the first covenant" (Heb. 9:15). What were the transgressions under the first covenant and why was a death required? The old law, like all covenants, includes blessings for keeping the covenant and curses for infidelity. Consider the covenant of marriage. If it is faithfully kept, great joy results. If it is betrayed through brutality, adultery, or neglect, great suffering is inevitable. Deuteronomy 28 lists the blessings or curses that could come upon the people of Israel depending on their fidelity to God's covenant. The curses include suffering, hunger, thirst, exile, and eventual death. Israel was under the curse of exile and death for violating the covenant. Even outside of Israel, all human beings are under the curse of exile and death for the sin of Adam and Eve. Jesus died this death that humanity in general and Israel specifically owed. His death, as the fulfillment of the covenants with Israel, not only redeems Israel from the "covenantal curses" but also is the very ratification of the new covenant. His blood of the new covenant is sprinkled both on the believers and in the heavenly sanctuary (Heb. 9:19–24; Exod. 24:8).

Through Jesus' priestly offering of his own blood in the heavenly tent, he establishes his universal kingdom. As the priest-king in the "line" of David and Melchizedek, his kingship cannot be separated from his priesthood. "When Christ had offered for all time a single sacrifice for sins, he sat down at the right hand of God, then to wait until his enemies should be made a stool for his feet" (Heb. 10:12–13; cf. Ps. 110:1). As the priest-king he instills righteousness in his people since his sacrifice alone can perfect their consciences. Because Jesus exercises his priestly kingship, or kingly priesthood, in heaven itself, he can bring all of his subjects to dwell perfectly with God and thus enter the holy land promised to Abraham. That eternal sanctuary from which Adam and Eve were exiled is restored to man. The whole drama of the Bible thus reaches its climax in this expression from Hebrews 10: "Therefore, brethren, since we have confidence to enter the sanctuary by the blood of Jesus, by the new and living way which he opened for us through the curtain, that is, through his flesh, and since we have a great priest over the house of God, let us draw near with a true heart in full assurance of faith, with our hearts sprinkled clean from an evil conscience and our bodies washed with pure water" (Heb. 10:19–22).[15] We find here a sacramental allusion to efficacious baptism, by which the Christian Church is gathered.[16]

The remainder of Hebrews 10 shows that human beings can reject the perfecting and purifying priestly kingship of Jesus Christ. "If we sin deliberately after receiving the knowledge of the truth, there no longer remains a sacrifice for sins, but a fearful prospect of judgment, and a fury of fire which will consume the adversaries" (Heb. 10:26–27). At first glance this might seem to preclude repentance from post-baptismal sin. By deliberately sinning, we remove ourselves from Jesus' priestly kingship and therefore have cut ourselves off from the sacrifice for sins. Deliberate sin, or what the tradition will later call mortal sin, is the rejection of Christ. As has been the case throughout Hebrews, sin or disobedience is synonymous with unbelief. If we have sinned deliberately, Jesus will appear not as the merciful and faithful high priest, but as the conquering king who subjects us, his adversaries, to his judgment. "It is a fearful thing to fall into the hands of the living God" (Heb. 10:31). If sin is the rejection of Jesus' rule and thus his sacrifice for our sins, then conversion and repentance from sin is the way to come again under his rule. Hebrews 10 does not deny the possibility of such conversion and repentance. For those under Jesus'

15. Chrysostom observes about this verse: "'Having our hearts sprinkled from an evil conscience.' He shows that not faith only, but a virtuous life also is required, and the consciousness to ourselves of nothing evil. Since the holy of holies does not receive 'with full assurance' those who are not thus disposed. . . . They were sprinkled as to the body, we as to the conscience, so that we may even now be sprinkled over with virtue itself" (*Homilies on Hebrews*: Homily XIX, 455).

16. See Hughes, *A Commentary on the Epistle to the Hebrews*, 409–413.

sacrificial kingship of mercy there is not fear, but "the full assurance of faith" (Heb. 10:22) and unwavering hope (Heb. 10:23). The way of conversion and repentance remains open, but only to those who approach Jesus, the embodiment of divine mercy, in faith and obedience.

The concluding chapters of Hebrews are one continuous exhortation to persevere in faithful obedience in order that believers might "do the will of God and receive what is promised" (Heb. 11:36). In light of the drama of redemption depicted under the image of Jesus the priest-king, we see clearly the role of faithful obedience. Accepting the sacrifice of Jesus, and thus his authority, is the only means to the eternal sanctuary. Our faithful obedience on its own could neither purify our consciences nor bring us to dwell in God's own eternal life. Nonetheless, our faithful obedience is the necessary condition for our acceptance of the free gift of salvation in Jesus Christ. There is no other way to be under the rule of his mercy than to believe in him and to live as he commands.

Faith and Promises

The way to the eternal Sabbath rest, perfect holy land, comes through our faithful obedience to Jesus Christ as our merciful priest-king. To complete the course one needs perseverance and endurance. Endurance comes by way of faith, but what is faith? Hebrews 11:1 presents the classic definition, "faith is the assurance of things hoped for, the conviction of things not seen." Faith is forward looking, seeking the end of the eternal rest already achieved by Jesus Christ, but not yet experienced by us in this life. As St. Augustine said in an Easter homily, "As the days of Lent have signified the laborious life in this mortal tribulation, so the days of Easter signify the joy of the future life where we shall reign with the Lord."[17] Although faith in the new covenant centers on Jesus Christ, Hebrews 11 shows the commonality between faith in the old and new covenants.

The new covenant faith builds on and perfects the old covenant faith and even the faith of those outside the covenant. Hebrews 11 adduces the heroic faith of men of old as examples for members of the new covenant to imitate. As an exhortation, the repetitious character of Hebrews 11 serves to move the audience to heroic perseverance in a similar manner, for example, to Martin Luther King Jr.'s "I Have a Dream" speech.[18] Although the new covenant alone has the power to purify the human conscience, human beings in the old covenant and even outside the covenants can still

---

17. St. Augustine, *Sermon 243*.

18. Cf. Michael R. Cosby, *The Rhetorical Composition and Function of Hebrews 11: In Light of Example Lists in Antiquity* (Macon, GA: Mercer University Press, 1988), 85–91.

find acceptance from God (Heb. 11:2). Their salvation comes from Christ even if they lacked explicit faith in him. What then is the character of this saving implicit faith? First it recognizes that God created the world and that God exists in a way distinct from the creation (Heb. 11:3). Second, implicit faith believes that human beings have an obligation to render God obedience and to seek him as their final happiness. The famous verse, Hebrews 11:6, states this succinctly, "For whoever would draw near to God must believe that he exists and that he rewards those who seek him." Saving implicit faith then is not merely the belief that God exists, but chiefly the faith that trusts that God will reward those who seek him.[19]

In order for implicit faith to be saving, those who have it must desire to seek God with all their heart, all their strength, and all their mind. Both people outside both covenants and those in the old covenant possessed this faith that trusted wholeheartedly in God. Abel, Enoch, and Noah, all of whom were before the covenant with Abraham, pleased God and attained righteousness by faith (Heb. 11:4–7). Abraham, Sarah, Moses, Rahab, Gideon, Barak, Samson, Jephthah, David, Samuel and the prophets all exemplify the trusting, forward-looking character of faith. Despite their celebrated faith none of them received what was promised (Heb. 11:13, 39). They all look forward to "a better country, that is, a heavenly one" (Heb. 11:16). The people of the old and new covenants, as well as those outside the covenants, all share in common the desire for the holy land, a land in which they can dwell in perfect abundance in the true worship of God. The celebration of faith in Hebrews 11 is not abstract trust in God, but the specific trust that God will bring those who trust in him to a reality of fulfillment of their deepest desires to dwell with him. All three categories of people desire the holy land, but there is only one holy land. Jesus Christ alone has inaugurated the heavenly kingdom. The desire for the holy land thus always finds fulfillment in Jesus Christ whether faith in him was explicit or implicit. "And all these, though well attested by their faith, did not receive what was promised, since God had foreseen something better for us, that apart from us they should not be made perfect" (Heb. 11:3–40). Those outside the new covenant thus are perfected not apart from, but through, the new covenant of Jesus Christ.

Suffering and Holiness

If those who did not hear explicitly of the saving sacrifice of Jesus Christ possessed such great faith in God, then members of the new cov-

---

19. *Catechism of the Catholic Church*, nos. 846–848.

enant should be able—by faith—to persevere until their physical death or until Christ's final deliverance at the end of time. "Therefore, since we are surrounded by so great a cloud of witnesses, let us also lay aside every weight, and sin which clings so closely, and let us run with perseverance the race that is set before us looking to Jesus the pioneer and perfecter of our faith, who for the joy that was set before him endured the cross, despising the shame, and is seated at the right hand of the throne of God" (Heb. 12:1–2). The faithful men and women constituting the "great cloud of witnesses" in faith had conviction of things unseen. Members of the new covenant, however, can look to Jesus who has endured the cross and risen again. The faith that God exists and rewards those who seek him now has taken concrete, visible form in Jesus.

The reality of Jesus, nonetheless, remains unseen. Members of the new covenant cannot see him exercising forever his eternal priesthood and sitting at the right hand of God ready to rule his enemies. Although the faith has been completed with the new age of Jesus Christ, we still live in the times in between the first and second coming, the continuous Day of the Lord. New covenant faith is bi-directional. Like implicit faith it looks forward to the day when God will bring those possessing it to dwell in the heavenly homeland. Unlike implicit faith it looks backward to the cross and Resurrection of Christ and sees there by faith that all who believe in him will share in his heavenly kingdom. Yet even this picture fails to grasp the reality, since Hebrews makes clear that the sacrifice of Christ is eternal. New covenant faith looks backward and sees the sacrifice of Christ, and looks forward and sees the same. Faith looks at each moment and sees the eternal sacrifice of Christ. This faith transforms each present moment as an unveiling of the true reality of the eternal homeland in God's merciful embrace.

If the true reality of each moment is Jesus Christ's sacrifice, exaltation, and kingdom, then the sufferings of each moment participate in that eternal reality. The goal is the holy land, but to dwell there we must become holy people. Although it might seem otherwise, suffering is not an obstacle to our sabbath rest.[20] Suffering, instead, is the instrument God has chosen to make us holy so that we can enter heaven. Hebrews uses the comparison of earthly fathers who "disciplined us for a short time at their pleasure, but [God] disciplines us for our good, that we may share his holiness" (Heb. 12:10). God's holiness! The mystery of divine filiation, of our becoming children of God, unites the theme of holy land and holy people. As children we participate in God's own nature (cf. 2 Peter 1:4). By sharing in his nature we become filled with the justice

---

20. See St. Augustine, *The Trinity*, trans. Edmund Hill, O.P. (Brooklyn, NY: New City Press, 1991), Book I, ch. 3 (76–81).

of self-giving love. By participating in him we enter into the reality of perfect worship, the superabundant fulfillment of all of our desires.

Hebrews again calls members of the new covenant to finish the race, to strive to enter the promised land of heaven. "Strive for peace with men, and for the holiness without which no one will see the Lord" (Heb. 12:14). The harmony of righteousness includes harmony in oneself, with others, with the whole of creation, and with God. It is the restoration of the original justice of creation. In justice, the gift of divine mercy, the human creature can re-enter the fiery holiness of the divine presence. Because of the eternal character of Christ's sacrifice and kingdom, members of the new covenant already now exist in the divine presence. "But you have come to Mount Zion and to the city of the living God, the heavenly Jerusalem, and to innumerable angels in festal gathering, and to the assembly of the first-born, who are enrolled in heaven, and to a judge who is God of all, and to the spirits of just men made perfect, and to Jesus, the mediator of a new covenant, and to the sprinkled blood that speaks more graciously than the blood of Abel" (Heb. 12:22–24).[21]

Morality and Acceptable Worship

As we saw in Romans, the reality of our present—sacramental and liturgical—connection with heaven requires a holy and upright life.[22] To live immorally is to reject the priestly kingship of Jesus and thus to cut ourselves off from the saving love of God. As Hebrews points out, "our God is a consuming fire" (Heb. 12:29). In the new covenant of Christ, we will experience the holy fire as love since, by the grace of the Holy Spirit who conforms us to Christ, we will possess God's holiness ourselves. Apart from the new covenant of sacrificial mercy, whether we have entered explicitly or implicitly, that holy fire of love will be the fire of our own destruction. God does not change who he is. Rather, he changes us to become configured to the wisdom and self-giving love of his incarnate Son.

21. David Lyle Jeffrey has rightly emphasized the eschatological movement of Hebrews, by way of cautioning against thinking of history as having an inner-historical "end." See David Lyle Jeffrey, "(Pre)Figuration: Masterplot and Meaning in Biblical History," in *"Behind" the Text: History and Biblical Interpretation*, eds. Craig Bartholomew, C. Stephen Evans, Mary Healy, and Murray Rae (Grand Rapids: Zondervan, 2003), 363–390, esp. 377–382.

22. Cf. Virgil Michel, O.S.B., *The Liturgy of the Church: According to the Roman Rite* (New York: Macmillan, 1937), 229–252.

Hebrews 13 describes the life proper to the new covenant. "Let brotherly love continue. Do not neglect to show hospitality to strangers, for thereby some have entertained angels unawares. Remember those in prison, as though in prison with them; and those who are ill-treated, since you are also in the body" (Heb. 13:1–3). The emphasis on the corporal works of mercy parallel those of the last judgment scene in Matthew 25. Then the author turns to the stumbling blocks of sex and money. "Let marriage be held in honor among all, and let the marriage bed be undefiled; for God will judge the immoral and adulterous. Keep your life free from love of money, and be content with what you have; for he has said, 'I will never fail you nor forsake you'" (Heb. 13:4–5). The corporal works of mercy, holy purity, and detachment form the three legs of a tripod. All are necessary for life in the new covenant.

The misguided view that Jesus was more concerned about money than sexual immorality fails to respect the reality of the New Testament. Yet, it is equally true that sexual purity cannot substitute for a greedy heart. In fact, both holy purity and detachment free us from the disordered love of things of this world so we can be free to love God with our whole heart and our neighbor as ourselves. If these three virtues form a tripod, the ground upon which it stands is obedience to the Church, founded upon the apostles and their successors. "Remember your leaders, those who spoke to you the word of God; consider the outcome of their life, and imitate their faith. . . . Obey your leaders and submit to them; for they are keeping watch over your souls, as men who will have to give account" (Heb. 13:7, 17).

The true worship of God includes the cultic and the moral. The last verse of Hebrews 12 before beginning the section of moral instructions of Hebrews 13 exhorts the reader, "let us offer to God acceptable worship, with reverence and awe" (Heb. 12:28). Through the saving sacrifice of Jesus as the high priest, all members of the new covenant become priests sharing in the dignity of the high priest. Hebrews 13:10 says that "we have an altar from which those who serve the tent have no right to eat." Those who serve the tent would be the Levitical priests, and the verse implies that members of the new covenant not only have an altar, but that they eat from the altar. This is suggestive of the practice of the ordained priesthood and liturgical celebration of the Eucharist.

In the context of such sacramental eating, Hebrews describes the offering of the spiritual sacrifices of good works. "Through [Jesus] then let us continually offer up a sacrifice of praise to God, that is, the fruit of lips that acknowledge his name. Do not neglect to do good and to share what you have, for such sacrifices are pleasing to God" (Heb. 13:15–16). Works of mercy are sacrifices to God (cf. Rom. 12); the moral life becomes the form of our eucharistic worship. Or more properly, the

228

Eucharist becomes the form of the moral life.[23] All members of the new covenant are called upon to share in the true worship of the true God by continuously offering to God spiritual sacrifices and then bringing them to their source and summit on the eucharistic altar. Through baptism and the Eucharist, the faithful participate in the eternal sacrifice and worship of Jesus in heaven. We thus share in the perfect sacrifice for sins, becoming in Christ a holy people and attaining the heavenly worship that is holy land.

Although we will now turn to the consummation of the biblical theme of holiness as displayed in the Book of Revelation, the same themes of the new covenantal priesthood could be followed through 1 and 2 Peter and Jude. First Peter proclaims the Church as the temple of the living God in which its members "offer spiritual sacrifices acceptable to God through Jesus Christ" (1 Peter 2:5). As the new "royal priesthood" the people of the new covenant all enter into the holy land in which God dwells through Jesus Christ (1 Peter 2:9). James emphasizes the pursuit of holiness in response to the divine gift of salvation as he evokes the divine wisdom that alone can guide the believers into friendship with God (cf. James 1:5; 4:4). Jude can be seen at the reverse image of the new covenant priesthood insofar as it shows how unbelief and rebellion can enter into the members of the Church, thus preventing them from fully entering God's indwelling presence (Jude 12).

23. See Harmon L. Smith, *Where Two or Three Are Gathered: Liturgy and the Moral Life* (Cleveland: Pilgrim Press, 1995). If the central claim of Hebrews is Jesus' eternal sacrifice and worship, then there must be a concrete way in which the faithful participate in it. We have already spoken of faithful obedience, or obedient faith, as the necessary condition for participating in Jesus' kingdom. Yet, this does not exclude the sacraments of baptism and the Eucharist as the rituals of the new covenant that make such participation possible. Hebrews 6:2 speaks of "ablutions [literally baptisms], the laying on of hands." Tertullian in the second century used the word "enlightenment" to refer to the sacrament of baptism, and Hebrews 10:32 seems to do the same: "recall the former days when, after you were enlightened. . . ." The reference to baptism and the Eucharist seems present also in Hebrews 6:4, "those who have once been enlightened, who have tasted the heavenly gift." Hebrews describes what the practices of enlightenment (baptism) and tasting the heavenly gift at the altar (Eucharist) actually are communicating to the faithful.

10

Revelation

The Lamb as King and Temple

The final book of the Bible depicts the liturgical consummation of history. Regarding the Book of Revelation, Martin Luther is said to have once quipped that a revelation ought to reveal something.[1] Many readers of the book of Revelation have felt similarly mystified by the apocalyptic images and visions, and interpretive theories have multiplied perhaps more than for any other book on the Bible. This chapter does not claim to offer the definitive interpretation on this fascinating and in fact deeply revealing book, but instead will examine the Book of Revelation through the twin themes of holy people and holy land. Revelation, written by John, above all shows how the Lamb of God, Jesus Christ, has led the people of God into the heavenly city of Jerusalem where they can dwell with God and the Lamb in eternal worship. The great mystery is that the Lamb makes us holy and leads us to dwell eternally in and with himself. He is the beginning and the end, the alpha and the omega, of creation and salvation.

1. On Luther's complex engagement with the Book of Revelation, see Craig R. Koester, *Revelation and the End of All Things* (Grand Rapids: Eerdmans, 2001), 10–12. In light of popular misreadings of Revelation, Koester ably introduces readers to the genre of apocalypse. He shows that the goal of joining in the heavenly worship is the guiding theme of Revelation. See also Bruce Metzger's *Breaking the Code: Understanding the Book of Revelation* (Nashville: Abingdon, 1993), which reaches similar conclusions.

As we have seen, at the heart of the old covenant is the promise to make a holy people who can dwell with God in a holy land. In the covenant of Moses, God gave the law to show the people how to live in justice. God also dwelt with the people in the tabernacle in which Israel could offer right sacrifice. Under the covenant with David, the king was to instill justice within the people and also build a temple in which Israel could offer fitting sacrifices to God who now dwelt there. The center of Israel thus was the king and the temple. The king must be just and instill justice. The temple must be the place of right sacrificial worship.

The Book of Revelation unites both themes of king and temple in the person of Jesus Christ. Through the primary identification of Jesus as the Lamb of God, the king and the sacrifice are shown to have become one; holiness and liturgy come together. Jesus is revealed to be both the embodiment of the holy people and the holy land. In other words, the holy people and the holy land have become one in the Lamb of God. Through him, with him, and in him, all the promises to Abraham, Moses, and David are fulfilled: The people of the new covenant have become the righteous dwelling place of God.

Images of Eternal Life in the Trinity

The twin themes of king and temple are already apparent in the opening section of Revelation, the letters to the seven churches. In the preface to the seven letters, it becomes clear that what is to be revealed is eternal life in and with the Trinity through faith and love for the Savior Jesus Christ. The preface reads, "Grace to you and peace from him who is and who was and who is to come, and from the seven spirits who are before his throne, and from Jesus Christ the faithful witness, the firstborn of the dead, and the ruler of kings on earth. To him who loves us and has freed us from our sins by his blood and made us a kingdom, priests to his God and Father, to him be glory and dominion for ever and ever. Amen. Behold, he is coming with the clouds, and every eye will see him, every one who pierced him; and all tribes of the earth will wail on account of him" (Rev. 1:4–7). The Father is "him who is and who was and who is to come," the Holy Spirit is "the seven spirits" (the symbolic number seven indicating fullness and perfection), the Son is Jesus Christ. In the Father, Son, and Holy Spirit, the Church has been made a kingdom of priests, a holy people prepared to receive Christ perfectly at his Second Coming at the end of time.

The letters avoid much of the apocalyptic imagery of the rest of the book. Instead, they focus simply on a powerful exhortation to remain faithful or to repent for corruption.[2] The church in Ephesus is praised for its fidelity and endurance, but rebuked because it has "abandoned the love [it] had at first" (Rev. 2:4). Smyrna, which is suffering poverty and persecution, receives no criticism but merely encouragement. Pergamum is rebuked for tolerating false teachers. Thyatira receives praise for its faith, works, and love, but rebuke for tolerating false teachers, in this case the woman "Jezebel." Sardis is rebuked for appearing alive, but in fact being dead since its works are not acceptable to God. Philadelphia's works and patient endurance merit praise; it is encouraged to hold fast until Jesus comes. Finally, the church in Laodicea, known for its earthly wealth and prosperity, receives a stunning rebuke: "So, because you are lukewarm, and neither cold nor hot, I will spew you out of my mouth" (Rev. 3:16). Taken together, these seven letters constitute a clarion call for fidelity, for brotherly love, for purity of doctrine, and for good works. If these are lost, then the Church's "lamps" or divine light will be put out. But for those who repent or hold fast to the right path, salvation awaits.

The call to fidelity in each of these letters is sealed by an image of eternal life.[3] The images of eternal life come in two forms, those relating to kingship and those relating to the temple. Kingship is present throughout in the language of "to him who conquers, I will give. . . ." More specifically, the one who conquers is promised to participate in Jesus' own kingship. Psalm 2, which is about the Davidic king and is transferred to Jesus throughout the New Testament, now refers to the *followers* of Jesus: "He who conquers and who keeps my works until the end, I will give him power over the nations, and he shall rule them with a rod of iron, as when earthen pots are broken in pieces, even as I myself have received power from my Father" (Rev. 2:26–27; cf. Ps. 2:8–9). Faithful believers will reign with Jesus on his throne: "He who conquers, I will grant him to sit with me on my throne, as I myself conquered and sat down with my Father on his throne" (Rev. 3:21). In each case, the ability to participate in Jesus' kingship depends on holiness. Jesus Christ reigns with the Father in perfect holiness; to attain holiness is to "reign." Jesus' kingship has opened the way for man to become holy and thus reign with him.

The seven letters thus also include references to the holy land in which man will dwell in glorious worship of God. One of two references to paradise in the New Testament is found in these letters: "To him who conquers I will grant to eat of the tree of life, which is in the paradise

2. Cf. G. K. Beale, *The Book of Revelation: A Commentary on the Greek Text*, The New International Greek Testament Commentary (Grand Rapids: Eerdmans, 1998), 223–228.

3. See Murphy, *The Comedy of Revelation*, 213–214.

of God" (Rev. 2:7; cf. Luke 23:43). Eating of the "tree of life" means sharing in the divine life (mediated through Jesus' cross), and in "the paradise of God" those who conquer will eternally receive this life-giving fruit. The letters also make reference to the temple. Addressing the Philadelphians, Jesus says, "He who conquers, I will make him a pillar in the temple of my God; never shall he go out of it, and I will write on him the name of my God, and the name of the city of my God, the new Jerusalem which comes down from heaven, and my own new name" (Rev. 3:12). The threefold name of God the Father, the mystical Body (the new Jerusalem), and Jesus' triumphant name will be written on those who persevere and become the temple. Given the unique holiness of God's name (cf. 1 Sam. 8), the parallel between the three names is startling. The name of God, the name of Jesus, and the name of his city, or the heavenly Church, are all placed on the same level, thereby indicating God's perfect indwelling of his creation. The city is transfigured, as was the human nature of Jesus (cf. Matt. 17), so that it fully participates in the glory and holiness of God. The emphasis on the divine name and divine indwelling recollects the promise in Deuteronomy—taken up in the dedication of Solomon's temple (1 Kings 8)—that God will choose a central sanctuary, in which the proper sacrifice will be offered, and will "make his name dwell there" (Deut. 12:11).

Given the echo of Deuteronomy 12 and the images of the temple, we can conclude that the purpose of becoming a pillar in the temple of God is to offer him perfect worship and adoration. The letters to the seven churches thus do not demand obedience and faithfulness for their own sake, but rather so that the human creature can participate in God's eternal love. Jesus' perfect sanctuary, the new Jerusalem, comes from heaven and is built up of the holy people of God who bear the "name" of God and Christ.

The Temple Liturgy of Heavenly Worship

Revelation 4 and 5 begin with a vision of heavenly worship. "I looked, and lo, in heaven an open door" (Rev. 4:1). The door to heaven is opened. The result is central to Revelation. The opening letters to the seven churches called for repentance and endurance by invoking the perfect heavenly kingdom and temple to come. The vision that follows in Revelation 4 and 5 shows that this heaven is already a reality that the Church participates in through her liturgical and sacramental worship.[4] Indeed, the name of the Book of Revelation comes from the Greek word *apoca-*

4. Cf. *Catechism of the Catholic Church*, nos. 1136–1139.

234

lypsis which means to unveil. The true reality of our current existence is unveiled to be the eternal worship. Once the true kingdom and temple are revealed, they give shape to the endurance and repentance called for in Revelation 2 and 3. Present sufferings, difficulties, and persecutions can be endured more easily since they are unveiled as the fleeting reality of the false "kingdom" of this world that will in time undergo severe judgment. Likewise, by repentance, we enter even now into the heavenly worship.

What is the heavenly worship that is unveiled? Calling to mind the heavenly scenes of Isaiah 6 and Ezekiel 1, Revelation 4 and 5 present God the Father seated on a throne of great splendor and awe, accompanied by the "seven torches of fire, which are the seven spirits of God," namely the Holy Spirit. All creatures of heaven exist in perpetual worship and adoration, because they know the glory of God and share in his inexhaustible love. The twenty-four elders (*presbyteroi*) stand for the hierarchical perfection of the twelve tribes of Israel and the twelve apostles. All humanity will worship God not as isolated individuals, but within the mystical Body of Christ's Church, the people of God. This intercessory role of the Church in heaven is expressed clearly when the elders fall down to worship "with golden bowls full of incense, which are the prayers of the saints [i.e., the faithful on earth]" (Rev. 5:8; cf. 8:3–4).

The heavenly liturgy thus is hierarchical and intercessory. The faithful who pray on earth worship with and through the Church in heaven: The earthly liturgy of the Church participates in the heavenly liturgy.[5] In addition to the elders of the people of God, the "four living creatures" (cf. Ezek. 1:10) represent all of creation, including angelic creation. The elders continuously worship the Lord saying "Worthy art thou, our Lord and God, to receive glory and honor and power, for thou didst create all things, and by thy will they existed and were created" (Rev. 4:11). The four living creatures likewise exist in perpetual adoration, "Holy, holy, holy is the Lord God Almighty, who was and is and is to come" (Rev. 4:8). The worship offered by the four living creatures on behalf of the entire created order highlights the glory of God's nature in itself as the mystery of sheer "to be" not limited in any way. The worship of the elders focuses on God's glory as the Creator. In their worship, which is a sharing in God's glory, the elders as the embodiment of Christ's mystical Body continuously "cast their crowns before the throne" (Rev. 4:10). This self-giving love, in contrast to sinful grasping for divine power, enables the elders truly to "be like God" (Gen. 3:5), since God is love.[6]

5. On the participation, see Metzger, *Breaking the Code*, 47–54.
6. See Koester, *Revelation and the End of All Things*, 73–75.

The Father and the Holy Spirit are present. Where then is the Son? He is about to enter as the victorious head of his mystical Body. Revelation 5:5 says that "Lion of the tribe of Judah, the Root of David, has conquered." The image is of the great Davidic king. Then Revelation 5:6 immediately introduces the figure of "a Lamb standing, as though it had been slain." Jesus is simultaneously identified as the king and the sacrificial Lamb of God, thereby uniting eucharistically the two themes of kingship and temple. Both become one in him.

Is the Lamb going to fall down and worship God or will the Lamb be worshipped? Is he an icon or an idol of the living God? The four living creatures and the twenty-four elders immediately answer the question by falling down before him and worshipping, singing, "Worthy art thou to take the scroll and open its seals, for thou wast slain and by thy blood didst ransom men for God from every tribe and nation, and hast made them a kingdom and priests to our God, and they shall reign on earth" (Rev. 5:9–10). Countless angels and every creature on earth then join in the chorus declaring the Lamb to be worthy of blessing, glory, might, and honor (Rev. 5:12, 13).[7]

The vision of heavenly worship clearly places the crucified Messiah as the object of eternal worship; the Lamb that was slain is the Creator of the world, the Son of God. The creator and redeemer are one![8] The song of praise of the living creatures and elders to the Lamb reveals that through the blood of the Lamb God has made a holy kingdom of priests who will reign on earth. The promise of holy land is fulfilled as well, since the kingdom of priests redeemed by the Lamb also enters into the heavenly worship of God and the Lamb.

The people of God have been made holy through the slain Lamb. Now we see why this vision forms a necessary complement to the exhortations to holiness in the letters to the seven churches. Holiness is not something that human beings could generate on their own. It is a gift borne from the Lamb of God whose blood has ransomed them. Holiness comes through a receptive mode, not a grasping one. When man attempts to *grasp* holiness as his own possession he relives the false desire for wisdom shown in the original sin of Genesis 3. In order for human beings to be restored as a people of justice, they must be reconstituted as creatures who *receive* everything from God as gift and return everything to the one from whom they have received everything.

The gift of holiness thus is the foundation of the priestly vocation of human beings to return everything, in love, to God. It is not merely that

7. For further discussion see Richard Bauckham, *The Theology of the Book of Revelation* (Cambridge: Cambridge University Press, 1993).
8. This theme is emphasized by St. Irenaeus in *Against the Heresies*.

human beings cannot earn their own holiness, but rather that holiness, or original justice, entails that human beings be harmoniously ordered to God by participating in his "gifting" love. The gift aspect of holiness unites the holiness of the people and the holiness of the land. Holiness must be received from God as a gift; insofar as it is received from God it already constitutes a dwelling with God. The people made holy by the Lamb now dwell with God and worship him eternally as priests. Holiness given by God makes us a holy people, and the return gift of everything to God in communion with him makes us dwell in a holy land. The Lamb has enabled humankind to participate in the divine procession of the Holy Spirit as the gift, received and given.[9]

Kingly Authority over History

Revelation continues by exposing the kingly authority of the Lamb. The Lamb unites the new people of God made up of Jews and Gentiles. The 144,000 from the twelve tribes is not a fixed number but the sign of perfection: 12,000 from each of the twelve tribes (Rev. 7:4–8). A countless number of Gentiles are present as well "from every nation" (Rev. 7:9). Showing that the vision of heaven in Revelation 4 and 5 continues and includes specifically the redeemed followers of Jesus, in Revelation 7 the innumerable new people of God are clothed in white robes, made white in the blood of the Lamb (Rev. 7:14). These all cry out, "Salvation belongs to our God who sits upon the throne, and to the Lamb!" (Rev. 7:10). The Lamb shares perfectly in God's kingship.

The subjects of the Lamb's kingdom, baptismally cleansed by the blood of his cross, have finally entered the holy land promised to Abraham and his descendants. They dwell with God, worshipping him in perfect fullness. The Lamb has led them there. Note how the different aspects of holy land are brought together in this extended summary of the Lamb's new people. "They are before the throne of God, and serve him day and night within his temple; and he who sits upon the throne will shelter them with his presence. They shall hunger no more, neither thirst any more; the sun shall not strike them, nor any scorching heat. For the Lamb in the midst of the throne will be their shepherd, and he will guide them to springs of living water; and God will wipe away every tear from their eyes" (Rev. 7:15–17). The Lamb here has become the shepherd. As we have previously noted, in the context of the old covenant this is not merely a pastoral image. Instead, it signifies that the sacrificial Lamb

9. For exploration of this cycle of gift, see St. Thérèse of Lisieux, *The Story of A Soul*, John Clarke, O.C.D., trans. (Washington, DC: ICS Publications, 1996).

237

of God is the Davidic king. As the Lamb of God, Jesus offers himself as a sacrificial victim and thus leads his people to dwell with God in the temple where they can worship him. To put it another way, the Lamb makes us holy and leads us to himself.

Jesus' authority as king manifests itself through his role as judge of history. It is important to realize that his kingly authority as judge is the direct expression of his love: he is judge as the merciful slain Lamb who has died for all. Revelation depicts, in the right hand of God the Father, a scroll that no one is worthy to open (Rev. 5:3). The scroll is human history. No one can open the scroll because no mere human or angel can reverse the cycles of violence that describe history after the Fall. Insofar as creation is on the path of disorder and death, it lacks the meaning that God wills for it. In this state, the scroll of human history cannot be "opened" or made intelligible: its meaning cannot be deciphered. As Macbeth famously cries, "Out, out, brief candle./ Life's but a walking shadow, a poor player/ that struts and frets his hour upon the stage,/ and then is heard no more. It is a tale/ told by an idiot, full of sound and fury,/ signifying nothing."[10]

Yet, as the seer/author of the Book of Revelation is weeping because of this seeming meaninglessness, "one of the elders said to me, 'Weep not; lo, the Lion of the tribe of Judah, the Root of David, has conquered, so that he can open the scroll and its seven seals'" (Rev. 5:5). Jesus' cross and Resurrection reverse the disorder caused by sin. By reordering humankind to God, Jesus gives human history, so broken without him, the meaning that God wills for history from the beginning. Jesus' cross and Resurrection form the key to unlocking the meaning of history. Christ's merciful love stands as the measure of all history, the judge of all history, the power that gives history its true comprehensible pattern. Every free creature is judged by acceptance or rejection of God's love in Christ.

Therefore Christ, the slain Lamb, is the only one worthy to open the seals that otherwise hide God's providential plan, because the slain Lamb reveals and embodies God's providential plan for history. In Christ, the divine judgments are completely revealed. Recall that one of the roles of the Davidic king was to establish peace in the land by conquering the physical enemies of Israel. God did not begin to dwell there in the temple until the king had given the land rest (Deut. 12:10–11; 2 Sam. 7:1). Similarly, throughout the Book of Revelation, the merciful Lamb is seen as executing the divine judgments and thereby establishing the holy land.

Just as Genesis contains two creation accounts, so also Revelation, the story of the new creation, contains two accounts of the new creation:

10. William Shakespeare, *Macbeth*, Act 5, Scene 5.

Revelation 6–11 and Revelation 12–22. These accounts combine to present a profound portrait of the whole of human history under the sign of God's justice and mercy in Christ. In Revelation 6, the first four seals that Christ opens depict the normal condition of history after the Fall. This normal condition is itself God's righteous judgment upon sinners, since sin brings with it its own consequences, suffering, and death. Thus the first four seals release four horseman representing, respectively, foreign conquest, war, plague, and death and disease. The fifth seal, in contrast, indicates the presence of God's holy people, Christ's mystical Body, in the midst of the consequences of sin: "I saw under the altar the souls of those who had been slain for the word of God and for the witness they had borne" (Rev. 6:9). The martyrs cry out for God's justice to be completely established; it is for this justice (for Christ himself) that they have accepted death. The sixth seal depicts the Day of the Lord's victory over sin, the day of judgment, that takes place on the cross and is ongoing until the end of time. Revealing the nature of the judgment, the unrepentant sinners experience Christ's "face," which is pure sacrificial love, as "the wrath of the Lamb" (Rev. 6:16).

Revelation 8 and 9 detail the opening of the seventh and final seal, which completely instantiates God's justice, as befits the fulfillment indicated by the number 7. The revelation of great punishments for those who remain in idolatry—a revelation symbolized by the blowing of seven trumpets that occurs after the opening of the seventh seal—is again directed at repentance, although many will remain steadfast in their hardness of heart: "The rest of mankind, who were not killed by these plagues, did not repent of the works of their hands . . . nor did they repent of their murders or their sorceries or their immorality [the word here is *porneia*, indicating sexual immorality] or their thefts" (Rev. 9:20–21). Beyond the obvious exhortation for the reader to detest and repent from sins, this scene also expresses a deep truth about eternal punishment. It is not as if sinful man would desire to repent and enter heaven upon receiving the punishment of hell. Even the experience of hell would not cause anyone to repent, because hell is precisely the punishment for those who do not wish to repent. In other words, no one is in hell against his or her own will.[11]

In establishing divine justice, the Lamb not only conquers rebellious human individuals but corrupt institutions as well. Revelation 13 describes two great beasts who receive their power from Satan, who is depicted here as the ancient dragon. The first beast with ten horns and seven heads is generally acknowledged to be the pagan city of Rome

---

11. Cf. *Catechism of the Catholic Church*, no. 1033: "This state of definitive self-exclusion from communion with God and the blessed is called 'hell.'"

known for its seven hills and ten rulers.[12] Nonetheless, since throughout its long history Israel had suffered under the violent and brutal regimes of Egypt, Assyria, Babylon, Persia, Greece, and Rome, the first beast can be seen to stand for any corrupt political institutions that abuse their rightful authority to serve their own ends and not the true good of humankind. As history repeatedly shows, human beings idolatrously worship corrupt political power and ignore its injustice. It comes as no surprise to learn that "the whole earth followed the beast with wonder. Men worshiped the dragon, for he had given his authority to the beast, saying, 'Who is like the beast, and who can fight against it?'" (Rev. 12:3–4). The beast, bearing a wound that has healed, has the pretense of imitating the slain Lamb; yet the beast is no meek and humble lamb, but rather appears as a monstrous combination of leopard, bear, and lion. Indeed, the worship of brute power unites all who reject self-sacrificing love: "And authority was given it over every tribe and people and tongue and nation, and all who dwell on earth will worship it, every one whose name has not been written before the foundation of the world in the book of life of the Lamb that was slain" (Rev. 13:7–8). Since those who live by power die by power (Rev. 13:10), the first beast has a mortal wound that gives the appearance of having been healed (Rev. 13:3, 14), but in fact indicates the beast's fate.

The second beast is identified in Revelation 19:20 as the false prophet. The false prophet can be seen to stand for corrupt religious authorities, both pagan and Jewish.[13] Revelation at several points calls the latter "the synagogue of Satan," indicating that some synagogues have become instruments of Satan in persecuting those Jews who accepted Jesus as messiah (Rev. 2:9, 3:9). The second beast therefore appears as a lamb, although it speaks like the dragon (Rev. 13:11). Jesus has been identified as the true Lamb throughout Revelation, and so the second beast that has the appearance of a lamb is a false messiah. The false prophet-messiah, representing the idols of pagan religion and the false messiahs of first-century Israel, deceptively leads the people into idolatrous slavery to power, rather than self-sacrifice: "it deceives those who dwell on the earth, bidding them to make an image for the beast which was wounded by the sword and yet lived; and it was allowed to give breath to the image of the beast so that the image of the beast should even speak, and to cause those who would not worship the image of the beast to be slain" (Rev. 13:14–15).

12. See Koester, *Revelation and the End of All Things*, 128.
13. For the connection with pagan religion, see Metzger, *Breaking the Code*, 75–76. Metzger does not see the connection to the Jewish authorities.

The famous number of the second beast, 666, has been noted to be the sum of the letters in the name of the emperor Nero, when rendered in Hebrew.[14] The reference to 666 together with the call for wisdom also recalls King Solomon, who was known for his wisdom and yet eventually became idolatrous and corrupt, taxing his subjects 666 talents of gold per year (1 Kings 10:14; 11:4, 8). Solomon's kingdom became corrupted by greed, sex, and power. Similarly, the number 666 may depict the idolatrous worship of the creature (the sixth day) over the Creator (the seventh day)—the three sixes indicating a perfect unholy trinity of human self-worship, seven being throughout the Book of Revelation the number symbolizing divine fulfillment. The second beast thus exemplifies an unholy king who worships worldly realities and rejects God's Sabbath justice, a false lamb whose voice is that of Satan—in contrast to the true Davidic king, the messianic Lamb, who is the word of God. The second beast stands for any religious institutions that use their influence to serve power and to persecute the followers of the Lamb.

Behind both beasts—the corrupt religious and political human institutions—stands the ancient serpent or dragon of Satan, the head of the false trinity of power that receives idolatrous worship.[15] The identification of Satan as "that ancient serpent" connects Satan with the original fall of man in Genesis 3. St. Michael the archangel cleared heaven of Satan and his forces, but the latter were allowed to exercise power on earth (cf. Rev. 12:7–9). Revelation reveals that Satan chiefly exercises his power through corrupt human institutions. As the divine plan calls human beings to live together in the kingdom of God, or the city of God, Satan works in the world through the sinfulness of man by instituting false kingdoms and false cities.

The Lamb shows his absolute authority, the authority of divine love, over such false kingdoms by definitively judging the most enduring of human institutions. Revelation 17 and 18 detail "the judgment of the great harlot," the city of "Babylon," who rejects the love by which God desires to "marry" humankind to himself. While Babylon here stands most specifically for the city of Rome (Rev. 17:18), it also represents every other human institution that revels in drunkenness, fornication, and greed, and persecutes the saints of God (Rev. 17:2–6). The lust for wealth is particularly singled out as the cause and root of its destruction (Rev. 18:3, 16–17; cf. 1 Tim. 6:10). In the loose symbolism common to apocalyptic imagery, the city is now the harlot that rides on the first beast. In an anti-eucharistic image, the beast and its followers turn on the harlot and hate her: "they will devour her flesh and burn her up

14. Metzger (*Breaking the Code*, 76) views this as "the most probable candidate."
15. See Metzger, *Breaking the Code*, 77.

with fire" (Rev. 17:16). The kingdom of Satan perversely imitates the kingdom of God. In the kingdom of God, all the followers of the Lamb share in eternal life by eating the flesh of the Lamb. In the kingdom of Satan, the followers simply devour one another in continual hatred and division.[16]

After the great marriage of the Lamb to his bride the Church, the Lamb is identified under the name of "the Word of God" and executes his final judgment on his enemies (Rev. 19:13). "From his mouth issues a sharp sword with which to smite the nations, and he will rule them with a rod of iron" (Rev. 19:15; cf. Ps. 2:9). The beasts and the kings of the earth gather to fight against him (Rev. 19:19). The kings of the earth do not merely represent earthly kings, but include all human beings that participate in the false kingship of Satan. The Lamb conquers the two beasts and throws them into "the lake of fire that burns with brimstone," and all of their followers were slain with the sword of the Word of God (Rev. 19:20–21). Then the Word of God judged Satan and through an angel bound Satan and threw him into the pit (Rev. 20:2–3). Although Satan is depicted as being set free for one more period, his end comes in his final place of torment, the lake of fire (Rev. 20:10).

In addition to judging the beasts and Satan, the Word of God will judge all human beings "by what they had done" (Rev. 20:12–13). Those who have not come under the kingship—of love—of the Lamb and had their sins purified in his blood will likewise enter the fire of hell (Rev. 20:15). Finally, the Word of God destroys death itself. Physical death is undone, and there remains only eternal reward and eternal punishment (Rev. 20:14). By all of these images, Revelation shows clearly that the Lamb inherits, as the Davidic king inherits, the throne of God, a throne of self-giving (eucharistic) love rather than worldly power. By his judgment of love, the Lamb permanently separates the enemies of God, those who have no love, from the holy dwelling place of heaven.

The King and His Temple

As the Davidic king, the Lamb not only conquers the enemies of God and establishes permanent peace, but he also builds the temple of God. In many images, Revelation unveils the truth that the Lamb has indeed already built the holy temple. Even as in time we await the full accomplishment of the new heavens and new earth, we have the consolation of knowing that what Israel has longed for, namely that God would again dwell in her land and end the exile, has already been

16. Cf. Dante, *Divine Comedy*, Vol. 1, *Inferno*.

accomplished by the Lamb in heaven, where God dwells in the blessed and the blessed in God by love.

Revelation 11 and 12 are filled with the imagery of the ark and the temple. It begins with the visionary of Revelation being told to "measure the temple of God and the altar and those who worship there" (Rev. 11:1). The temple he is to measure is none other than the heavenly temple, whose door—Christ—has been eucharistically opened to him (cf. Rev. 3:20; 4:1). The primary meaning of the temple thus no longer is a physical building, but the communion of the saints and angels in the presence of God and the Lamb: the temple is the new people of God, the universal Church.[17]

In the shout of praise at the victory of the new Davidic king, the voices in heaven proclaim, "The kingdom of the world has become the kingdom of our Lord and his Christ [literally, his anointed], and he shall reign for ever and ever" (Rev. 11:15; cf. Ps. 2:2). The reference to "our Lord and his anointed" comes directly from the coronation psalm, Psalm 2. With the Lamb crowned as king, the vision turns to the temple of the king. "Then God's temple in heaven was opened, and the ark of his covenant was seen within his temple" (Rev. 11:19). In the temple is the ark. The ark had been lost since the exile when it was hidden by the prophet Jeremiah (2 Macc. 2). David desired to build the temple after bringing the ark to Jerusalem, and Solomon dedicated the temple after bringing the ark to rest in the temple. Now the Lamb, as the true Davidic king, is revealed to have already brought the true ark into the true heavenly temple.

The image of the ark of the covenant in Revelation 11:19 flows immediately to the image of the woman in Revelation 12:1, who stands in contrast with the harlot Babylon. The woman is the true city of God, the true Israel. The crown of twelve stars shows she is queen of all twelve tribes of Israel and thus is the embodiment of the new Israel, the Bride of Christ. The woman is also the queen mother of the Davidic king. The son whom she bears is "the one who is to rule all the nations with a rod of iron," again quoting Psalm 2 (Rev. 12:5).

The close juxtaposition of the ark of the covenant and the woman is striking. The ark of the old covenant contained the tablets of the Decalogue (the word of God), the staff of Aaron, and a jar of manna. The woman contained within herself the Son of God, the Lamb who is king. The Lamb is revealed to be the true and complete Word of God, to have the authority of Aaron and Moses, and to be the true manna (Rev. 2:17). Mary the mother of Jesus is thus revealed to be the perfect ark of the new covenant. Not only is Mary the mother of the king, she is the mother of all of his followers since they all share, by adoption, in his

17. Cf. Metzger, *Breaking the Code*, 69.

Sonship. Revelation says that "The dragon was angry with the woman, and went off to make war on the rest of her offspring, on those who keep the commandments of God and bear testimony to Jesus" (Rev. 12:17). Revelation 15 returns to a vision of the heavenly temple. God has accomplished his promise to dwell with his people through a final exodus. The song of Moses that signaled the triumph of the first exodus now is mingled with the song of the Lamb (Rev. 15:3).[18] As we have seen above, the new exodus, like the first (which it fulfills), involves plagues of judgment, but this time the plagues are final.

The vision displays that "the temple was filled with smoke from the glory of God and from his power, and no one could enter the temple" (Rev. 15:8). This directly echoes the descent of the glory cloud on Moses' tabernacle and Solomon's temple: "And Moses was not able to enter the tent of meeting, because the cloud abode upon it, and the glory of the Lord filled the tabernacle" (Exod. 40:35). First Kings, referring to Solomon's temple, states, "And when the priests came out of the holy place, a cloud filled the house of the Lord, so that the priests could not stand to minister because of the cloud; for the glory of the Lord filled the house of the Lord" (1 Kings 8:10–11). Revelation reveals that the glory cloud of God's indwelling presence has already filled the everlasting temple. The presence of God with the people in Moses' and Solomon's time was not perfectly fulfilled because the people were sinful and the land, like all things, would pass away. The eternal temple that will never pass away has now been filled eternally with the glory of God through the sacrifice and kingship of the Lamb.

The Marriage of the Lamb

After the great judgment and destruction of the false city of Babylon, the heavenly multitude announces the fulfillment of the true city as accomplished by the eternal marriage of the Lamb and his bride. The opposition of the harlot and the bride shows how evil is a false imitation of the good. The fornication of the city of wickedness with the idolatrous beasts and kings of the world is a corrupt inversion of the consummation of love that takes place between the Lamb and the city of God. The Bride represents the Church as the new community of human beings constituted by faithfulness to the wisdom and love of the Lamb.

The Church has come to the wedding feast clothed in brilliant (baptismal) wedding garments, and "the fine linen is the righteous deeds

18. Cf. G. B. Caird, *A Commentary on the Revelation of St. John the Divine* (New York: Harper & Row, 1966), 196–210.

of the saints" (Rev. 19:8). Holiness has truly come upon man. Sinners and rebels against God have been converted, their sins purified in the blood of the Lamb, and now they perform "righteous deeds" or good works worthy of the Bride of Christ. The revelation of the Bride of Christ adorned with the righteous deeds of the saints demonstrates that the sacrifice of the Lamb has not been ineffective: in Christ human beings can perform acts of righteousness, whereas without Christ this is not possible (cf. Isa. 64:6). The blood of the lamb has turned the polluted garments into fine linen. The righteous deeds truly belong to the members of the Church; the Church's holiness, however, is not her own achievement, but the gift of Christ.[19] As the Davidic king, the Lamb has finally fulfilled the divine promise of instilling justice in humankind and making them a holy people.

The entire story of the Bible is the story of creation and the new creation. Creation includes God's ongoing bestowal of being to this world and his ordering of all things in the world to their proper ends. Creation was made "very good," but sin broke this goodness and humankind could not reach the end of fellowship with God for which we were created. While the covenants before Christ lacked the full power to renew creation, Isaiah prophesied that a time would come when God would restore creation: "For behold, I create a new heavens and a new earth; and the former things shall not be remembered or come into mind" (Isa. 65:17). The promise of a new heaven and a new earth indicates something even greater than a return to Eden. The whole of creation will be remade with the gift of eternity inscribed upon it so that creation will no longer be dispersed over space and time but will participate in the fullness of existence that is God himself.[20]

This new creation has happened in Jesus Christ. The followers of Christ on earth, who are still being conformed to the image of the sacrificial Lamb, do not yet experience that fullness of being they will have in the new creation. Revelation thus unveils to those *in via*, on the way, that the perfection of creation already exists in heaven and they have only to persevere in God's love in order to attain it. "Then I saw a new heaven and a new earth; for the first heaven and the first earth had passed away,

19. Cf. Wilfrid J. Harrington, O.P., *Understanding the Apocalypse* (Washington, DC: Corpus Books, 1969), 222–226.
20. Citing Nachmanides, the great thirteenth-century commentator on the Torah, Gary Anderson describes the Jewish understanding of this reality: "Not surprisingly, the entrance into the Holy Land is imagined as a return to the glories of Eden. But not simply Eden as at creation, but an Eden *deepened* through the revelation of and obedience to God's Torah. A simple equation—last things equals first things—cannot and should not be drawn. Last things assume and *go beyond* first things. The end recasts the beginning, not the reverse." (Anderson, *The Genesis of Perfection*, 179)

and the sea was no more" (Rev. 21:1). Creation must be re-created as the true holy land it was meant to be. We see clearly here that the concept of holy land is not first and foremost geographical, but rather is liturgical. It refers to the reality that all creation is indwelt fully by God.

The new Jerusalem, the city of David, symbolizes the true holy people or holy kingdom established by the true Davidic king. "And I saw the holy city, new Jerusalem, coming down out of heaven from God, prepared as a bride adorned for her husband; and I heard a great voice from the throne saying, 'Behold, the dwelling of God is with men. He will dwell with them, and they shall be his people, and God himself will be with them'" (Rev. 21:3). The holy people are the perfect holy land indwelt by God. Human beings were meant for communion with God, and God has already established this perfect communion. The image of the city of Jerusalem combined with the image of Bride provides a glimpse of what the new heavens and the new earth are like. The new Jerusalem, a holy kingdom, is the holy land perfectly filled with the divine presence.

The people have become the Bride of the Lamb through God's all-powerful love. An angel called to the visionary, "'Come, I will show you the Bride, the wife of the Lamb.' And in the Spirit he carried me away to a great, high mountain, and showed me the holy city Jerusalem, coming down out of heaven from God, having the glory of God" (Rev. 21:9–11). The Bride is the city of Jerusalem. The holy people are the holy land where God has chosen to make his name dwell. The ultimate unity and holiness of the heavenly city contrasts with its anti-type, the archetypal city of fallen man, Babel, as well as with the city of the earthly Jerusalem.[21] The city of man has received final re-creation in the city of the Lamb. The pride and fear of Babel give way to the wisdom and love of the heavenly Jerusalem.

The new Jerusalem needs no temple because the kingdom has become the temple. The Lamb is both king and temple: "And I saw no temple in the city, for its temple is the Lord God the Almighty and the Lamb" (Rev. 21:22). Again we see the full unity of the holy people and holy land. The role of the king was to instill justice in the people so they could enter the temple where God dwelt. Jesus Christ is both the king who has made his people righteous and the temple in which they dwell with God. "And the city has no need of sun or moon to shine upon it, for the glory of God is its light, and its lamp is the Lamb" (Rev. 21:23).

---

21. Cf. M. Robert Mulholland Jr., *Revelation: Holy Living in an Unholy World* (Grand Rapids: Zondervan, 1990), 46–53. For the judgment of the earthly Jerusalem see Matthew 24, Mark 13, and Luke 21. For a discussion of the social character of salvation, see Henri de Lubac, S.J., *Catholicism: Christ and the Common Destiny of Man* (San Francisco: Ignatius Press, 1988).

As the true and eternal holy people and holy land, the Lamb has caused his followers to share in his new creation.

The new creation, however, respects the full freedom of man to reject the gift of holiness. Even in the vision of the new Jerusalem, the one who sat upon the throne depicts the two paths that lie open to each human being: "He who conquers shall have this heritage, and I will be his God and he shall be my son. But as for the cowardly, the faithless, the polluted, as for murderers, fornicators, sorcerers, idolaters, and all liars, their lot shall be in the lake that burns with fire and brimstone" (Rev. 21:7–8). This is the choice between death and life set before Israel by Moses in Deuteronomy 30.

Indeed, human beings possess only two ultimate destinies, one of which is less a destiny than a frustration and loss of the real destiny. We can become eternally adopted children of God sharing by his mercy in inexhaustible wisdom and love, or eternally sinners frustrated by our lack of love. Becoming God's adopted children brings together both aspects of holiness because it includes our justice before God, as well as God's presence in us. In contrast, the lake of fire represents the unholy people dwelling in an unholy land. Sinners cannot dwell in God's presence, since their sin is itself the rejection of God's ordering of creation in preference for their own false order.

Revelation thus places the true reality of the new creation before us so that by God's mercy, we can choose to repent and to persevere in a love governed by God's wisdom, in order to enjoy the heritage of the city of the Lamb. In fact, our desire for the glory of heaven is the means that God uses to draw us to himself. We desire happiness, and true happiness is none other than the fulfillment of our deepest longings through eternal contemplation and self-giving love.[22] By giving ourselves to God in love, we become the persons God intends us to be, and receive the fulfillment he desires for us.

Revelation depicts the perfection of creation and its complete abundance by means of the image of *water* flowing from the new city. As we saw in John, the image of water flowing from the temple was prophesied in Ezekiel 47, where the water flowing from the temple turned the stagnant waters into fresh waters, thus allowing all things in the water to come back to life. This baptismal water symbolizes the new creation by the Holy Spirit. "Then he showed me the water of life, bright as crystal, flowing from the throne of God and of the Lamb, through the middle of the street of the city; also, on either side of the river, the tree of life with its twelve kinds of fruit, yielding its fruit each month; and the leaves of

---

22. See C. S. Lewis, "The Weight of Glory," in his collection *The Weight of Glory and Other Addresses* (New York: Macmillan, 1980 [1949]), 3–19.

the tree were for the healing of the nations" (Rev. 22:1-2). The water of life is linked to the tree of life, which is the fulfillment of Israel's twelve tribes by the fruits of the true tree, Christ's cross. The image of the tree of life that stood in the midst of the Garden of Eden can now be fully understood. Redeemed and re-created by the Lamb of God, and watered now with the water of his own divine Spirit, creation has finally become the means by which man loves his Creator. Through the sacrifice of the Lamb, creation is no longer an idol, but again an icon of God.[23]

The Book of Revelation is ultimately strange not because of its flashing fires and beastly battles, but because it reveals a perfected and completed creation which we do not yet experience. Human beings cannot conceive of the goodness that God has prepared for those who love him (cf. 1 Cor. 2:7-9). How can one think of a reality no longer dispersed over time and space? How does one put into words the reality of complete abundance when the human experience is one of scarcity and loss? How does one show that the complete perfection of all human desires leads to an ever-greater bliss, when our earthly experience of desires and joys is that they are short-lived?

In short, the strangeness of Revelation is precisely that it depicts a consummation of holiness. The reality of sinfulness and temptation, combined with acute suffering and horrible violence, make the reality of holiness strange to us. Revelation unveils that this true reality of holiness already exists. We already participate in the heavenly marriage and liturgy on earth through our faithfulness and prayers expressed in the earthly liturgy of the sacraments (cf. Rev. 5:8). The liturgical view of heaven discloses the sacramental view of our present life. These material elements and rituals have, through Christ's merciful love, the sacramental power to connect the faithful in this valley of tears to the glories of the heavenly Jerusalem by uniting us in and with the crucified and risen Lord.

23. See also the essays in John Polkinghorne and Michael Welker, eds., *The End of the World and the Ends of God: Science and Theology on Eschatology* (Harrisburg, PA: Trinity Press International, 2000).

Conclusion

Transformation and Holiness

St. Bonaventure taught that one must become "a man of desires" in order to make the journey to God. In a similar vein, C. S. Lewis said that the problem with man was not that his desires were too strong, but that they were half-hearted. He compared the sinner to the child happy to play in the mud because he has not experienced the delight of vacation at the shore. Again, sin has made man desire too little. The salvation wrought by Jesus Christ renews our desires so they become strong enough to lead us into the new heavens and new earth. The overall story of the Bible reveals that God offers the greatest transformation possible: our desires will again be strong enough to love God above all things and thus share in God's own eternal beatitude.

"I came that they may have life, and have it abundantly" (John 10:10)

The psalms frequently speak of the great desire for God. "Thou hast put more joy in my heart than they have when their grain and wine abound" (Ps. 4:7). "Take delight in the Lord, and he will give you the desire of your heart" (Ps. 37:4). The simple cry, "Save me, O God!" (Ps. 69:1), manifests the holy desire for the preservation of one's own life. What is this but the desire for happiness? The frequent proclamations of blessedness or happiness show that the psalms unlock the clear path to happiness. "Blessed is the man who fears the Lord, who

249

greatly delights in his commandments!" (Ps. 112:1). Blessedness and delight come to the person who obeys God. Again, "Blessed is the man who walks not in the counsel of the wicked, . . . but his delight is in the law of the Lord, and on his law he meditates day and night" (Ps. 1:1–2). The psalms thus invite man to seek his happiness in God alone. "Plead my cause and redeem me; give me life according to thy promise! Salvation is far from the wicked, for they do not seek thy statutes" (Ps. 119:154–155).

As with the psalms, so also the whole of the Bible responds to man's desire for life, for salvation.[1] The good news is the message of salvation. In Jesus Christ, God has granted what man most deeply desires—God's salvation, God's life, God's happiness.

This objective fulfillment is revealed to be holiness. The drama of sin and salvation is lived out in our desires—in other words, as St. Augustine expounded in his great *City of God*, by what we love. The great battle is between the false love of self (*amor sui*) and the true love of God (*amor Dei*). From Genesis to Revelation, the effect of sin is shown to be the rule of a false happiness that sees everything ordered to one's own subjective pleasure.[2] The fruit of the tree was "good for food, and a delight to the eyes, and was to be desired to make one wise," but it was also the rupture of man's covenant with God (Gen. 3:6). Idolatry, greed, and sexual immorality all imitate this pattern of placing what subjectively satisfies over what objectively fulfills. As the theme of this book has shown again and again, the Bible depicts this reality in terms of an unholy people living in an unholy land. Human beings have lost the gift of original justice and therefore desire the things of this world in such a way that they have closed themselves off from the presence of God.

Salvation restores human beings to their true fulfillment. The proclamation of God's mercy and his gift of holiness means that his people

1. In summarizing her *The Comedy of Revelation*, Francesca Aran Murphy remarks,

As we made our way through the Bible we found human beings seeking the good. In the Pentateuch, the good informs the 'master image' of the promised land. . . . The Pentateuchal good is earthy and elusive, oscillating beyond possession. It is not only the object of a human quest but also, even before Abraham set out in search of it, the subject of a divine promise. In the Deuteronomistic history, the good is pictured in the person of the king. . . . During the intertestamental period the promised land is imaginatively relocated into heaven. The New Testament somersaults across this logic. The Good is supernatural, and also concrete and personal: it is the body of Christ. (Murphy, *The Comedy of Revelation*, 307)

2. On this topic, see the essay by Michael Waldstein, "Dietrich von Hildebrand and St. Thomas Aquinas on Goodness and Happiness," *Nova et Vetera* 1 (2003): 403–464.

can again become holy people dwelling in a holy land.[3] This is true happiness, an objective state of the fulfillment of all of one's desires. False happiness sees everything ordered to my subjective pleasure. True happiness recognizes that my fulfillment as a creature made in the image and likeness of God lies in loving everything ordered to the goodness of its Creator. This leads to the objective fulfillment of all one's desires in accord with and even beyond one's nature in the image of God. Loving God for his own sake in charity—and not for my subjective pleasure—fulfills our nature.

Thus, the right ordering of desire is holiness. In other words, holiness means to love God above all things and to love one's neighbor as oneself (Matt. 22:37–40). This is the restoration of a holy people and a holy land. Human beings again rightly love God more than ourselves (holy people) and thus find, by God's grace, that we can dwell in his presence (holy land). As Augustine puts it, the "house of David," when fulfilled in Christ, is "the house of God because it is God's temple, built not of stones, but of human beings, for the people to dwell there for ever with their God and in their God, and for God to dwell there with his people and in his people."[4]

By loving God more than ourselves and becoming holy people we become able to dwell with God in the holy land. The paradox is that in the very loving of God more than ourselves, human beings discover the fulfillment of our very selves. Jesus reveals this dynamic throughout his preaching, "For whoever would save his life will lose it, and whoever loses his life for my sake will find it. For what will it profit a man, if he gains the whole world and forfeits his life?" (Matt. 16:25–26). As we saw in the psalms, it is not the desire for profit or fulfillment that is condemned. What is condemned is the desire to find fulfillment in the world that will never truly satisfy. Psalm 16 expresses the truth that our desire for the fulfillment of ourselves is attained only in God: "Thou dost show me the path of life, in thy presence there is fullness of joy, in thy right hand are pleasures for evermore" (Ps. 16:11).

The one who seeks God for God's own sake will ultimately know pleasures greater than sinful man can imagine. Sinners will eventually lose their ability even to be subjectively satisfied and will experience eternal frustration. The saint will love God and all things toward God and thereby, in a fullness beyond our imagining, will experience eternal joy and happiness.

3. On God as a God of *mercy*, see John Paul II's encyclical *Dives in Misericordia* (1980), in J. Michael Miller, C.S.B., ed., *The Encyclicals of John Paul II* (Huntington, IN: Our Sunday Visitor, 2001).
4. St. Augustine, *City of God*, Book XVII, ch. 12 (742).

Love and the History of the Church

Through the covenants with Israel as fulfilled in the new covenant of Jesus Christ, God has invited human beings to share in his eternal beatitude as his adopted children. This gift of divine filiation is not only in heaven, but begins on this earth through the community of the Church. Divine filiation is ultimately about the human heart being re-created by the Holy Spirit so that, in Christ, it can again love God the Father (holy people) and receive God the Father's love (holy land). As the one who lived this unity of holiness and love, this dynamic of loving the Father and receiving his love, Jesus Christ the eternal Son invites all human beings to enter into his Body and thus participate as other sons in this communion with the Father in the Holy Spirit.

The history of the Church forms the extended presence of Christ among us. Because Christ embodies the fulfillment of holy people and holy land, so also his Body, the Church, continues to embody this fulfillment as a locus of true union with God in righteousness and true worship. Although the Church's members often fall short, the Holy Spirit enables the Church to proclaim and administer, as the new holy temple, the truth and holiness of Christ.

The earliest history of the Church is recounted in the book of Acts. Acts is known for not having a definite conclusion. In fact, it ends in the middle of the story. This is because the story of the Church does not end but continues until our present day. Acts presents the new Church as the community sharing in God's holiness. This sharing above all consists in the ongoing transformation from sinfulness to righteousness, from dwelling without God to dwelling with God. Transformation comes as a gift, but not all will receive it. With the gift of the Holy Spirit at Pentecost, the apostles began to preach the good news of the Resurrection of Jesus Christ. Many received this good news with joy and entered the community of the Church, first Jews and then later Gentiles (Acts 2, 10–15).

Nonetheless, many, including members of the Church, refused the transformation called for by Jesus through his apostles. In Acts 5, Ananias and Sapphira lied to Peter and the apostles by pretending to have sold everything and given it to the Church while actually having maintained much of their independent wealth. They sought to be in the Church without living out the radical demands of life in Christ that they had professed. God judges Ananias and Sapphira as a warning to all members of the Church about the eternal death that awaits us if we, despite our public profession of faith, lack sincere faith and true desire for holiness.

The call for authentic transformation meets with resistance in the Church and in the world.[5] A pastor once defined holiness for his congregation as "the willingness to stand apart for Jesus." This summarizes well the truth that the transformation in Christ offered through participation in his Body will continue to be resisted and those who seek transformation must ask for the gift of courage. Jesus has already won the war, however, so difficulties should not sway his followers from seeking him. Jesus said, "In the world you may have tribulation; but be of good cheer, I have overcome the world" (John 16:33).

The good cheer of Jesus' victory is not a disembodied reality; rather, the fruits of his Incarnation remain with us through the visible structure of the Church. In the book of Acts, participation in the victory of Jesus requires participation in the sacraments, obedience to the teachings of the apostles, repentance, and conversion of life. The early community "devoted themselves to the apostles' teaching and fellowship, to the breaking of the bread and the prayers" (Acts 2:42). The "breaking of the bread and the prayers" is the liturgical celebration of the Eucharist. The apostles speak for God in the world. The greatest change in the new covenant—the inclusion of the Gentiles in God's covenant apart from the Mosaic law—was not accomplished during Jesus' ministry, but under the authority of the apostles. At the council of Jerusalem in which they made this decision, they responded to God's calling to have placed them as his mouthpiece on earth: "For it has seemed good to the Holy Spirit and to us. . . ." (Acts 15:28). When Ananias and Sapphira lied to Peter, he said to them, "You have not lied to men but to God" (Acts 5:4). When Peter and the apostles tell the Jewish authorities, "We must obey God rather than men," they are not criticizing organized religion, but rather showing that they have replaced the Jewish authorities of their day as God's ordained authority.[6]

Yet, it must be emphasized that the visible structure of the authority of the apostles and the sacraments is not an end in itself, but serves the true transformation in love. Although Christ has already brought about the fulfillment of holy people and holy land, we are not yet fully what he intends us to be. Even in the community of the redeemed, human beings may often not experience subjectively the joy of salvation. We may feel like an unholy people in an unholy land. Thus all creation, including the Church, is still "groaning," as St. Paul says (Rom 8:22), for the consummation of all things in the state of glory. The perfect peace in God that is promised us cannot be fully realized on earth. Augustine

---

5. For further insight, see R. R. Reno, *In the Ruins of the Church: Sustaining Faith in an Age of Diminished Christianity* (Grand Rapids: Brazos Press, 2002).
6. Johnson, *The Writings of the New Testament*, 225–228.

remarks that "[a]nyone who hopes for so great a blessing in this world and on this earth has the wisdom of a fool."[7] Nonetheless, in the objective character of the Church's teachings and sacramental worship, we find the communion with Christ in holiness that truly is a foretaste of glory, despite the suffering and sin that mark this present life. As St. Paul teaches in 1 Timothy, "the church of the living God [is] the pillar and bulwark of the truth" (1 Tim. 3:15).

St. Athanasius reminds us that in order to read correctly the writings of sacred scripture, one must imitate the lives of the saints who wrote them.[8] There can be no true understanding of God's plan of holiness apart from the ongoing conversion and transformation of the student who places himself at the feet of Christ his teacher. Holiness may sound abstract or arcane, when in fact it is the very opposite. We all experience both within ourselves and in the world a painful lack of holiness—the hatred, paralyzing fear, violence, oppression, greed, and lust that cause so much suffering and bitter grief in this world. Each of us experiences the frailty and contingency of the world, the busy rush of time, the burden of the past, and the tenuous character of the future. Each of us desires to be caught up into a permanent love, a communion that will fulfill us and not leave us empty, bored, and desolate, a permanent fruition of all that is good. As spiritual creatures who seek relationships that last, and who experience the desire and call to be more than everlasting dust, we seek a "happiness" that is found only in union with God.

Here on earth we are indeed "on pilgrimage."[9] In his amazing mercy, God wills to make us holy in his incarnate Son, Jesus Christ. God not only knows our true "name" and loves us, he also welcomes us into an eternal, mystical sharing in the glory of his own "name," his divine identity, as sons and daughters in the Son. Our true country is with God, dwelling eternally in his inexhaustibly glorious mystery. This is "holy land" or perfect peace: God dwelling in and with humankind. Yet, for us to dwell with God in his peace, we must be "holy people" abiding by the law of love in obedience to God who is love, since sin destroys communion.

As Augustine emphasizes, salvation is a social reality: "This peace the Heavenly City possesses in faith while on its pilgrimage, and it lives a life of righteousness, based on this faith, having the attainment of that peace in view in every good action it performs in relation to God, and in relation to neighbor, since the life of a city is inevitably a social

---

7. Augustine, *City of God*, Book XVII, ch. 13 (743).
8. Athanasius, *On the Incarnation*, trans. by a Religious of C.S.M.V. (Crestwood, NY: St. Vladimir's Orthodox Theological Seminary, 1993), 96.
9. Augustine, *City of God*, Book XIX, ch. 17 (878).

life."[10] The contemplation in faith of the divine Love impels us, by God's grace, to acts of love.[11] God alone can make us holy, fit to dwell in and with him in an unfathomable communion whose riches will never be exhausted. The salvation revealed in the Bible is none other than the path by which God makes us holy and enables us to dwell in perfect union with him.

The demands of holiness for complete transformation would lead us to despair if we trusted in ourselves for our salvation. Only because our salvation is already complete in Jesus Christ and made present to us through the Church can we experience the joy and confidence of the new covenant. "May the God of peace himself sanctify you wholly; and may your spirit and soul and body be kept sound and blameless at the coming of our Lord Jesus Christ. He who calls you is faithful, and he will do it" (1 Thess. 5:23–24).

"He who testifies to these things says, 'Surely I am coming soon.' Amen. Come, Lord Jesus!" (Rev. 22:20).

---

10. Ibid., Book XIX, ch. 17 (878–879). The unity that exists between ethics and worship of the true God belongs at the heart of early Christian "public ethics," as Markus Bockmuehl has shown in his *Jewish Law in Gentile Churches: Halakhah and the Beginning of Christian Public Ethics* (Edinburgh: T. & T. Clark, 2000).

11. Ibid., Book XIX, ch. 19 (880).

Index

Aaron, 72, 75, 76, 77, 219–20
Abel, 38, 42, 210
abiding, 185
Abiram, 76–77
abortion, 35, 144n14
Abraham, 20, 51–54, 198–99
Abrahamic covenant, 9, 41, 46–51,
    56, 59, 64, 96, 158
Absalom, 100
Acts, 252, 253
Adam, disobedience, 200–201, 202
Adam and Eve, 9, 29–32, 42, 47
    disobedience, 200–201, 202
    as holy people, 32
    pride, 45, 50, 60, 118, 158
    rebellion, 33–37
    sin, 201, 222
Adonijah, 100
adoption, 158, 204
adultery, 72
Ahab, 102
Ahaz, 103
Ahijah, 102
Ai, 87–88
Alexander the Great, 105
allegorical sense, 22
already/not yet, 12n5, 204
altar, 228
Amalekites, 76, 94
Ambrosiaster, 199n11

Amnon, 100
Amorites, 86
Amos, 132, 133
anagogical sense, 22
Ananias and Sapphira, 252, 253
Ancient of Days, 132
Anderson, Gary, 10n1, 33n17,
    163n52, 245n20
Andrew of St. Victor, 118n9
angel of the Lord, 163
angels, 235
animals, 27, 30
Antiochus Epiphanes, 105
apocalypse, 231n1
Apollinarian heresy, 170
apostasy, 216
apostles, 235
    authority, 149–50, 190, 253
Aristotle, 81, 168
Arius, 168
ark, 44–45
ark of the covenant, 59, 71, 73, 74,
    82, 83, 84, 92, 96, 98, 243
Asherah, 104
Ashtaroth, 92
Assyria, 240
Assyrians, 103
Athanasius, 168, 186n45, 254

Augustine, 11n4, 12–16, 18, 20, 21,
34n19, 135, 146, 149, 193, 203,
210, 224, 250, 251, 253–54
autonomy, 33n18, 140

Baal, 89, 102, 103, 104
Babel, 45–46, 87, 246
Babylon, 104, 105, 240, 241, 243, 244
Balthasar, Hans Urs von, 18n23
baptism, 164, 175–78, 180, 182, 188,
190, 200, 223, 229n23, 247
and new creation, 201–3
Barth, Karl, 17n19
Bathsheba, 100, 144
Bauckham, Richard, 21n35, 33n18
beasts, 240–42
beatitude, 28n9, 249, 252
beatitudes, 145–46
beauty, 27, 43
Benjaminite, 94
Bernard of Clairvaux, 32n16
Bible
Catholic reading, 22
central points, 16
as history, 16–18
interpretation, 12n5
theological reading, 15–19
biblical studies, 16n19
biblical theology, 19
blasphemy, 69
blessedness, 183, 249–50
blessing, 27, 45, 46, 55, 56, 59, 78,
79, 90–91, 222
through Abraham, 47–48, 198
blood of the covenant, 66, 70, 159
Bockmuehl, Markus, 255n10
body, 36, 202, 208
Body of Christ, 186, 187, 190, 194,
207, 208–11, 235
Bonaventure, 249
bread of life, 179
Bride of Christ, 245
burning bush, 61–62, 63, 84
burnt offerings, 69, 96

Cain, 37–38, 41–42, 43, 45, 50, 210
Caird, G. B., 19n29

Caleb, 76
Cana, marriage at, 173
Canaanites, 76
"canon within the canon," 14
catechesis, 12, 16
Catechism of the Catholic Church, 17,
30n12, 135, 152
chaos, 43–46
charity, 14, 15, 22
cherubim, 128
children of God, 189
Christian mysticism, 55n18
Christology, and ecclesiology, 187
Chrysostom, John, 216n5, 223n15
church, 185–87
apostolic structure, 150
as Body of Christ, 183, 186, 187,
190–91, 208–11
infallibility, 186
interpretation of Bible, 16–19
church history, 252
circumcision, 51, 67, 83, 84, 85, 194,
199–200, 202
City of God, 11n4, 244
City of Man, 11n4
civil rights, 144
civil war, in Israel, 91, 95, 100
cloud, 73, 83, 98, 169, 244
concupiscence, 203
confession, 190
conquest, 84–88
conversion, 165, 223–24, 253
corruption, 127
Council of Nicea, 168
covenant renewal, 88–89, 100
covenants, 9, 19, 139, 169, 194, 198
focus of biblical narrative, 88
and hope, 90
narrowness and broadness, 59, 96
and obedience, 195
and reconciliation, 83
and sacrifice, 53–54
and security, 218
and trust, 48–49
creatio ex nihilo, 26
creation, 23–32, 167, 170, 245, 248
creatureliness, 25

cross, 178, 188–89, 205, 238, 248
crucifixion, 162–63
culture, 42
curse, 35, 78, 79, 90–91, 134, 135, 222
Cyrus, King, 105

Daniel, 131–32
darkness, 66
David, 94–96, 144, 151
Davidic covenant, 9, 20–21, 83, 96–98, 101, 104, 158
Davidic king, 122, 128, 130, 148, 151, 161–62, 182, 214, 233, 236, 238
Davis, Ellen F., 12n5
Day of Atonement, 75–76, 82, 222
Day of the Lord, 112, 123, 132–35, 138, 140, 155–56, 160, 161, 163, 226, 239
days of creation, 26, 85, 140
death, 31, 36, 44, 52, 66, 86n5, 164, 215–16, 222, 242
deliberate sin, 223
demons, 148, 149
Deogratias, 12, 13, 15
descendents, 41, 59
desires, 30, 249–51
destruction, 44–45, 52
Deuteronomy, 75, 77–78, 105
devil, 33, 38–39
diaspora, 137
Dinah, 55
disciples, 164
disharmony, 39, 73, 88, 102, 168–69
disobedience, 223
disorder, 38, 46, 50, 52–53, 61, 88, 141, 161, 196
divine filiation, 189–90, 204–6
divine kingship, 93, 141
divorce, 35, 216
Dome of the Rock, 152
domination, 35, 37, 38
Dostoevsky, Fyodor, 33n18

Ecclesiastes, 107
Eden, 9, 20, 25, 29, 31–32, 36, 47, 58, 140, 248
Egypt, 56, 59–60, 64–67, 72, 101, 240

Eichrodt, Walther, 19n29
election, of the Jews, 195
Eli, 92
Elijah, 102–3, 134, 142, 154
Elisha, 103, 142, 178
Emmanuel, 141
emotions, 30
endurance, 224
Enlightenment, 19
Enoch, 42
Esau, 54–55
eschatology, 113n3, 204, 206, 227n21
eternal, and temporary, 221
eternal life, 176, 178, 204–5, 233, 242
eternal punishment, 239, 242
ethics, 76
Eucharist, 159–61, 164, 178–80, 182, 185, 188, 190, 228–29
evangelization, 164
seed, of Eve, 39
exile, 10, 21, 78, 102, 103–5, 111, 169–70, 222
end of, 128–30, 133, 147–48
in own land, 137–38
exodus, 62, 64–68, 84, 127, 142, 158, 177, 214–15, 217
see also new exodus
expiation, 200
Ezekiel, 125–31, 169, 176, 181–82, 188
Ezra, 105

faith, 51, 83
as forward–looking, 224–25
and obedience, 200, 217
vs. pride, 49
and works, 184, 199
fall, 30n12, 33–37, 58
false gods, 64, 103–4
false messiah, 240
false prophets, 240
fear, 189
Feast of Tabernacles, 176–77
Fisher, John, 116n6
flesh, 170, 174, 179–80, 182
flood, 44, 87, 96
food. See living bread

foot washing, 184
forbidden fruit, 50
forgiveness of sins, 148–49, 153n34,
    159–60, 175, 190, 222
four horsemen, 239
Fowl, Stephen, 15
freedom, 25, 33n18, 206–7, 247
Frei, Hans, 18
friendship, with God, 74, 184–85
fruitfulness, 35–36
fulfillment interpretation of Old Tes-
    tament, 74n25

Garden of Gethsemane, 160
genealogy, 139–40
Gentiles, 156, 195–97, 206
Gideon, 90
God
    dwelling, 32, 76, 169
    glory, 74, 83, 134, 168, 171, 186–87
    goodness, 42
    holiness, 10, 68–69, 115, 227
    indwelling, 107, 183–87, 191, 244
    justice, 127
    love, 24, 32, 112
    mercy, 53, 112, 127, 158, 165
    name, 62–64
    promises, 88, 111–12, 116, 131
    rest, 28, 32, 69, 71–72, 140
    as spirit, 15
    wisdom, 24, 26–27, 32, 109
    wrath, 90, 119
golden calf, 72–73, 89, 102
Goliath, 94
good shepherd, 180–82
good works, 228
Gospels, 139, 165
grace, 193, 201, 203
gratitude, 50
Great Commission, 164
greed, 250
Greek culture, 105, 240

Ham, 45
Hannah, 92
happiness, 28n9, 114, 146, 183, 185,
    247, 249–51

hardness, of heart, 66, 206–7
harlot, 176, 241, 243, 244
harmony, 31, 34, 37, 43, 146, 210,
    227
Harrison, Carol, 34n19
Hauerwas, Stanley, 16
Hays, Richard B., 12n5
healing, 148, 150
heart, 131, 177
heavenly worship, 234–36
hell, 37, 242
Herod, 141
Hezekiah, 104
Hilary of Poitiers, 182n36
historical criticism, 16–19
historicism, 10n2
history, 238
holiness, 10, 11, 15, 20–21, 22, 24–25,
    28, 43, 51, 52, 61, 77, 88, 148,
    163, 195, 200, 202–3, 250
    in Body of Christ, 209
    consummation of, 248
    as gift, 236–37
    and justice, 144, 161
    and kingship, 99
    and law, 58, 69
    and love, 252
    and suffering, 226–27
    and transformation, 252–55
holy land, 9, 10, 19, 20, 45, 58–59, 90
    Eden as, 31–32, 36
    Jesus as embodiment of, 15
    promised land as, 85
    in Revelation, 233–34
    and temple, 99
holy nation, 68, 69, 82
holy people, 9, 10, 19, 20, 58, 90
    Adam and Eve as, 32
    Jesus as head of, 15
    and new covenant, 210
Holy Spirit, 135, 171–72, 175, 177–
    78, 184, 190, 227, 235
    and the church, 185–86
    as dove, 143n10
    indwelling, 204
homosexuality, 196
hope, 105, 112n1, 218–19

Hosea, 132, 176
House, Paul R., 19n29
humility, 37, 77, 118, 161–62

"I am," 63–64, 83, 98
Ice, Laura, 20
idolatry, 24, 37, 60–64, 69, 72–73, 87,
    89, 101, 124, 125, 127, 169, 197,
    239, 250
idols, 86n5, 196
image of God, 28, 38, 39, 45, 46, 69,
    174
image of the Son, 206
immorality, 37, 227, 239
implicit faith, 225, 226
"in Christ," 204, 205
incarnation, 15, 74n25, 168, 170–71,
    253
infertility, 216
injustice, 34, 37, 38, 42, 43, 45
intercession, 65, 74, 120
intermarriage, 101
Irenaeus, 17n19
Isaac, 53–54
Isaiah, 104, 117–24
Ishbosheth, 95
Ishmael, 52
Israel
    as bride, 114
    failure of, 206
    pride of, 169
    punishment of, 87
    purification of, 134
    restoration of, 118
    salvation of, 206–7
    as virgin, 125

Jacob, 54–55, 59, 83, 172–73
James, on justification, 199
Japheth, 45
Jeffrey, David Lyle, 227n21
Jehoash, 103
Jehoiada, 103
Jephthah, 91
Jeremiah, 125, 141
Jericho, 87
Jeroboam, 102

Jerusalem, 48, 95, 98, 220
    see also new Jerusalem
Jesus
    authority, 164
    baptism, 142–43, 145
    blood, 200
    as Davidic King, 139–42, 143, 145,
        151, 152–53, 182, 232
    death, 164, 187–89, 215, 222, 238
    enthronement, 162, 164
    fulfillment of Old Testament, 10,
        14, 31, 139–40, 154, 225
    glory, 154, 173, 186–87
    as high priest, 208, 214, 218, 219–
        23, 228
    humility, 37n22, 161–62
    as image of God, 170
    inaugurated kingdom, 135
    mercy, 14, 218
    as new Adam, 156n40
    as new Moses, 217–18
    obedience, 200–201, 202, 207–8
    passion, 161–64, 189
    resurrection, 154, 163, 164, 171,
        186, 189, 215, 216, 221, 238
    righteousness, 112, 201
    sacrifice, 156, 188, 200, 221–22,
        226
    sonship, 189
    suffering, 118n9, 162, 218
    as temple, 156, 159, 167, 173–74,
        180
    temptations, 144
    transfiguration, 153–54
Jews, 197
Jezebel, 102
Joab, 95, 100
Job, 106–7
Joel, 132–33
John, 139, 165, 167–191
John Paul II, Pope, 33n18
John the Baptist, 142, 171
Jonathan, 95
Jordan River, 84, 142
Joseph, 55–56
Joseph (husband of Mary), 141
Joshua, 73, 76, 84, 87, 89, 142

Josiah, 104
Judah (son of Jacob), 55, 56
Judah (tribe), 95
Judaism, 195
Judas Maccabeus, 148
Judges, 90–91
judgment, 132–35, 139, 157n43, 163, 223, 239, 242
justice, 9–10, 37, 50, 51, 52, 53, 77, 82, 97, 101, 107, 112, 144, 161, 194
    of creation, 227
    and holiness, 161
    and suffering, 205
justification, 149, 193, 194, 199–200
    and baptism, 202
    as covenantal righteousness, 210
    and obedience, 203, 209

kabod, 169
keys of the kingdom, 152–53
king, kingship, 9–10, 20–21, 78, 79, 81–82, 83, 93, 97, 122, 141
    corruption of, 100–102
    and holiness, 99, 101
    and justice, 114, 115
    as mediator, 114, 130
    in Revelation, 232, 233
King, Martin Luther, Jr., 224
kingdom of God, 145–46, 149–50, 153, 158, 163–64, 174, 225, 235, 242, 243, 246
kingdom of priests, 68, 69, 82
kingdom of Satan, 242
kingdoms, 157–58
Koester, Craig R., 231n1
Korah, 76–77

labor, 36
Ladd, George Eldon, 19n29
ladder, 55, 83, 172
lake of fire, 247
Lamb of God, 171, 231, 232, 236, 237–40, 248
land, 41, 59
    curse upon, 35–36, 37
Last Supper, 160, 161, 183, 185

law, 9–10, 20, 57, 68–72, 86, 96, 101, 115, 154, 198–99, 203
    and holiness, 99, 147
Levenson, Jon D., 20n32, 53n15, 54n16, 60n5, 118n9, 181n34
Levi, 76
Levitical priesthood, 220–22, 228
Leviticus, 75–76, 77
Lewis, C. S., 249
lifting up, 175
light, 66
literal sense, 22
literalism, 86–87n5
liturgical offering, 48–49, 51
liturgy, 69, 71, 75
living bread, 178–80
living water, 130, 134, 176–78, 179, 188
Lot, 53
love, 14–15, 112, 161, 185
    for God, 124, 125, 146, 209, 236, 247, 250, 251
    and holiness, 252
    for neighbor, 151, 209–10
    of self, 250
Luke-Acts, 165
Luther, Martin, 231

Macbeth, 238
Maccabees, 105, 111, 148, 169
Malachi, 132, 134–35
male-female relationship, 35
Manasseh, 104
manna, 67–68, 76, 179
Mark, 165
marriage, 132, 216, 222, 228
    of the Lamb, 242, 244–45
martyrs, 239
Mary Magdalene, 189
Mary (mother of Jesus), 141, 188, 243–44
Matera, Frank J., 217n6
Matthew, 139–65
meaninglessness, 238
mediation, 65, 66
mediator, 55, 69, 73–74, 90, 120, 130
Melchizedek, 48, 96, 114, 220–21
mercy, 158, 228

Messiah, 138, 172
metaphors, 32n15, 86n5
Michael, St., 241
Milton, John, 23–24, 33n17
miracles, 148, 178–79
Miriam, 76
misogyny, 35
Moberly, R. W. L., 64n13
modernity, 33n18, 207
monarchy. See king, kingship
money, 228
moral life, 207–8
    see also holiness
moral sense, 22
mortal sin, 223
Mosaic covenant, 9, 20, 59, 64, 69,
    73, 74n25, 78–79, 82, 89, 96,
    128, 158, 159
Moses, 58, 60, 83, 154, 217, 218
    as mediator, 65, 69, 71, 73, 75
Mount Carmel, 102
Mount of Olives, 155, 160
Mount Sinai, 60–61, 62, 68, 70, 74,
    83, 85–86, 103, 158
Mount Zion, 54n16, 105
Murphy, Francesca Aran, 18n26,
    79n34, 250n1

Nachmanides, 245n20
Nadab and Abihu, 75
nakedness, 39, 45
Nathan, 97
nations, 51, 83, 96, 121, 134, 198
natural law, 197, 198–99, 207
natural theology, 195–97
nature, 31
Nero, 241
new covenant, 105, 112–13, 122, 124,
    138, 141, 154, 159–60, 164, 173,
    194, 200, 210
    in Hebrews, 219, 220, 222, 224–25,
    226, 228
new creation, 11, 21, 45, 71, 72, 74,
    84–85, 119, 124, 134, 140, 163,
    179, 189
    and baptism, 201–3
    in Revelation, 238–39, 245–47

new exodus, 124, 142, 214, 215, 217,
    244
new Jerusalem, 124, 234, 246, 247,
    248
new life, 203
new temple, 124, 128–30, 138, 156
New Testament, hidden in Old Testa-
    ment, 135
Nicodemus, 174–75
Noah, 42, 44–45, 52
Noahic covenant, 9, 44–45, 46, 59,
    120, 126
northern kingdom, 102, 104, 129
Numbers, 75, 76–77

obedience, 101, 164, 183, 202, 205,
    224
obedience of faith, 194–95, 200,
    229n23
old covenant, 224–25
Old Testament, Christian reading of,
    74n25, 135
oppressors, 43
order, 30–31, 43–44
original sin, 61, 66, 189, 193, 201

pagan religion, 240
parables, 157–58
parenesis, 207
passions, 30
passover, 66–67, 70, 83, 159, 173
Passover lamb, 66, 128, 188
Paul, 193–211
peace, 31, 43, 71, 149, 253
peace offerings, 69, 96
penitential psalms, 116n6
perfection, 85, 215–16, 225
persecution, 235
perseverance, 224, 226
Persia, 105, 240
Peter, 151–53, 160, 190–91
Pharaoh, 59–60, 65–67, 207, 215
Pharisees, 151
Philistines, 92, 94, 95, 100
pilgrimage, 218, 254
plagues, 64–67, 127
pornography, 35

postmodernity, 33n18, 207
power, 31, 33, 34, 38, 240–42
prayer, 113
pride, 9, 24, 25, 37, 39, 42–43, 45–46,
    49, 51, 72, 94, 102, 112, 140–41,
    161
priests, priesthood, 96, 73–74, 75, 82,
    96, 214, 219–21, 228
promised land, 10n1, 62, 68, 76, 78,
    82, 84–85, 215
prophets, 10, 21, 102, 117, 142, 154
Proverbs, 106, 108–9
providence, 10–11n2, 29, 109, 207
psalms, 113–17, 249–50
purity, 68, 183

Qoheleth, 107
quails, 76

rainbow, 9, 44, 46, 47, 96, 126
Ratzinger, Joseph, 153n34
reconciliation, 82–83, 90, 97, 121,
    134, 175
redeemer, 120–22
Rehoboam, 102
remnant, 118n9
repentance, 116n6, 223–24, 235, 239,
    247
repentence, 253
rest, 28, 85, 148, 155, 218
    see also Sabbath rest
restoration, 105
righteousness, 108–9, 147, 158, 194,
    202–3
righteousness of God, 195, 197, 198
rock, 152
Roman Empire, 105, 147–48, 240,
    241
Romans, 193–210
royal steward, 152–53

Sabbath rest, 69, 71, 148, 208, 217–
    18, 224, 226
sacraments, 32n15, 75, 253
sacrifice, 49, 53–54, 69, 71, 82, 134,
    155–56, 158, 221
sacrificial lamb, 66, 70, 188

sacrificial meal, 70–71, 73
sacrificial offering, 49–50, 68, 73, 75,
    76
saints, 254
Salem, 220
salvation, 250
    of Israel, 206–7
    in Psalms, 116
    as social, 194, 254
Samaritan woman, 175–76
Samaritans, 103
Samson, 90
Samuel, 91–93
sanctification, 203
Sarah, 47, 52
Sarna, Nahum M., 62n9, 63n12
Satan, 23–24, 149, 239, 240
Saul, 93–95, 151
Sawyer, John F. A., 117n8
Schleiermacher, Friedrich, 17n19
Schneider, Tammi J., 91n10
scroll, 238
seals, 239
Seitz, Christopher R., 11n2
self-righteousness, 198
selfishness, 50, 51
Senior, Donald, 140n5
separation, 11n4
Sermon on the Mount, 145–47
serpent, 33, 38–39
Servant, 117–24, 143
Seth, 42
seven, 85, 140, 232, 241
sexual immorality, 53, 216, 228, 239,
    250
shame, 29–30, 31, 189
Shechem, 88–89
Shem, 45, 46
shepherds, 130–31
    see also good shepherd
signs and wonders, 215
sin, 29, 44, 45, 46, 52, 75, 82, 196,
    197, 215, 223
    completeness of, 86–87
    destruction of, 113
    enslaved to, 205
    judgment of, 133

sin offerings, 221
sinners, 148–49
Sirach, 109
six, 85, 241
slavery, 61, 62, 65, 67, 72, 101, 181, 197
Smith, Harmon L., 229n23
Sodom and Gomorrah, 52–53, 87, 91
sojourning, 112n1
Solomon, 93, 98–99, 100–101, 144, 145, 155
son of David, 217
son of God, 97, 143, 145–46, 153, 158, 214, 217
son of man, 20, 151n29, 153, 157, 174, 175, 181
Song of Songs, 107–8
soul, 29, 36
southern kingdom, 102, 129
space, 26
spiritual enemies, 148–49
spiritual sense, 22
Stalin, 43
"still small voice," 103
striving, 107, 218–19, 227
Stuhlmacher, Peter, 19n29
suffering, 39, 107, 164, 204–6, 215–16, 219, 222, 235, 248
  and holiness, 226–27
suffering servant. See Servant
"synagogue of Satan," 240
syncretism, 103
Synoptic Gospels, 165
systematic theology, 16n19, 19n29

tabernacle, 27, 57, 71, 74, 82, 83, 98, 169
Tamar, 100
tax collectors, 148
temple, 21, 27, 29, 79, 81–82, 83, 97, 98–99, 169–70, 171, 176, 214
  cleansing of, 155–56, 173
  creation as, 29
  destruction of, 156
  heavenly, 221
  as micro–cosmos, 157n41
  rebuilding of, 111, 129, 169

in Revelation, 232, 234, 242–44
  see also new temple
  temporary, and eternal, 221
temptation, 203–4
ten commandments, 69, 74, 82, 209
Terrien, Samuel, 19n29
Tetragrammaton, 63n12
thanksgiving, 116
theology, and biblical interpretation, 16n19
Thomas Aquinas, 15n17, 149, 177n24
thorns and thistles, 35, 37
time, 26
transformation, 252–55
transgressions, 197
tree of knowledge of good and evil, 30–31
tree of life, 30, 36–37, 233–34, 248
Trinity, 172n14, 187
trust, 48, 94
Twain, Mark, 25
twelve tribes, 89, 149, 235

union with God, 132
Uriah, 100
Uzzah, 96

valley of dry bones, 128
vanity, 107
vine and branches, 184–85
vinegar, 188–89
violence, 24, 31, 34, 37, 38, 39, 43–45, 61, 73, 77, 102, 162
Vos, Geerhardus, 19n29

Walsh, Jerome T., 103n27
Wansbrough, Henry, 19
warfare, in Old Testament, 86n5
water, 174–75, 176–78, 247–48
Watson, Francis, 16n19
Weinfeld, Moshe, 181n34
Wells, Jo Bailey, 11n4
Wenham, Gordon J., 91n9
wickedness, 56, 126–27, 202, 203, 244
wilderness, 65, 67, 142, 144, 217
wisdom, 34, 46, 100–101, 106–9, 177, 179, 241

Wisdom of Solomon, 108–9
Witherington, Ben, III, 20
Word, 167–68, 174, 182
work, 36
works of the law, 198, 199, 200, 209
works-righteousness, 195
worldly kingship, 141
worship, 42, 47, 48, 51, 54, 62, 65,
    69, 75, 78, 98, 155–56, 207–8
  corruption in, 127
  cultic and moral, 228
  in Hebrews, 213–14

Wright, Christopher J. H., 20n32
Wright, N. T., 10n1, 21n34, 142n9,
    195n3

YHVH, 63n12

Zechariah, 123, 132, 133–34, 155,
    156, 177
Zion, 95, 111, 114, 125, 138
Zipporah, 64

Made in the USA
Lexington, KY
17 August 2011